Catholic Education: Distinctive *and* Inclusive

D1556335

371.0712 SuL

BOOK NO: 1847519

1847519

Catholic Education: Distinctive *and* Inclusive

by

John Sullivan

St Mary's College, University of Surrey,
Twickenham, United Kingdom

UNIVERSITY OF WALES COLLEGE NEWPORT
LIBRARY AND INFORMATION SERVICES CAERLEON

KLUWER ACADEMIC PUBLISHERS

DORDRECHT / BOSTON / LONDON

A C.I.P. Catalogue record for this book is available from the Library of Congress.

ISBN 1-4020-0060-X

Published by Kluwer Academic Publishers,
P.O. Box 17, 3300 AA Dordrecht, The Netherlands.

Sold and distributed in North, Central and South America
by Kluwer Academic Publishers,
101 Philip Drive, Norwell, MA 02061, U.S.A.

In all other countries, sold and distributed
by Kluwer Academic Publishers,
P.O. Box 322, 3300 AH Dordrecht, The Netherlands.

Printed on acid-free paper

All Rights Reserved
© 2001 Kluwer Academic Publishers
No part of the material protected by this copyright notice may be reproduced or
utilized in any form or by any means, electronic or mechanical,
including photocopying, recording, or by any information storage and
retrieval system, without written permission from the copyright owner.

Printed in the Netherlands

TABLE OF CONTENTS

ACKNOWLEDGEMENTS

I want to thank first some of my teachers in academic life, then my students and finally my colleagues and family. Without the very different kinds of help offered by all these people, it is unlikely that this book would ever have come to fruition. The origins of this work and the influences that have been brought to bear upon it extend far beyond the actual period of my life when it was written.

Dr John Watt, one of my History teachers at Hull University in the late 1960s, without his ever realising it, exerted an enduring influence on me. Through him I had my first close encounter with dedicated, painstaking scholarship. He also instigated my long-term interest in researching the implications of religious ideas for institutional life and for the wider community. Then John O'Neill, a Divinity lecturer at Christ's College, Liverpool, threw me in at the deep end of theology in a way that was exhilarating, liberating and confidence-building. A few years later Dr Patrick Sherry guided me through my first research degree (MLitt) at Lancaster University, teaching me in the process some of his own disciplined approach to study and to the craft of writing. The late Dom Illtyd Trethowan of Downside Abbey was, throughout the 1980s, an important and highly valued intellectual mentor for me. He fostered my scholarly aspirations, encouraged me to pursue my interest in Blondel and sharpened my capacity to read critically my own writing. I was always in some awe of him, despite his humility and kindness. Though initially disappointed when getting my drafts back from him full of corrections and suggestions, I derived great benefit both from his close attention to the plausibility and coherence of an argument and also from his sensibilities about clarity, economy and elegance.

The people who most directly and significantly influenced the progress of this book and to whom I am most indebted for its appearance are Dr Paddy Walsh and Professor Denis Lawton (London University Institute of Education) and Dr Terry McLaughlin (University of Cambridge). Paddy and Denis were doctoral supervisors who provided constant encouragement at the same time as they challenged me to clarify the nature, scope and implications of the study. I have been enormously enriched by the breadth of their expertise, the shrewdness of their comments and the kindness of their approach. Terry volunteered generous, detailed, constructive and pertinent advice. He provided a model of how to combine clarity and penetrative depth in critical analysis. With the help of all these guides, I hope I have managed to keep to a minimum the defects, oversights, imbalances that they could envisage might threaten this book. I continue to strive to move a little nearer the standards set by these scholars it has been my privilege to know.

I have always found that the work of being a teacher, first with teenagers, and in more recent years with other experienced teachers as students in my classes, has been a great benefit in writing. One learns so much from one's students – from their insights and experience of life, from their questions and perplexities, from their achievements and difficulties, and from their challenges and encouragement. Many students who have shared in the development of the MA programme in Catholic School Leadership at St Mary's College, Twickenham have read, commented on, explored and tested out some of the key concepts in this book. I believe that the ideas I attempt to articulate here relate more clearly to the practice of Catholic education because of the scrutiny given them by my students.

A particular and more personal debt of gratitude is owed to former and current colleagues at St Mary's. Sr Mary Jo Martin RSHM, whose energy and enthusiasm for, as well as realism about, the task of Catholic education offered lively and intelligent engagement with and commentary on some of the issues grappled with here. Jim Madden, whose lengthy experience of leadership in Catholic education, combined with a disarming yet warm and self-effacing, humility, gentleness and spiritual depth, more than adequately equipped him to help me with so much wisdom about what is enduring and important. Both of these wonderful colleagues encouraged me to persevere in the face of various obstacles, assuring me that I had something worthwhile to say. Sr Frances Orchard IBVM, Dr Rosie Penny and Liz Coombs have also helped me in important though different ways, in coping with pressures, in affirming the call to write and in making the work ready for publication.

I have emphasised at certain points in this book the importance of interconnectedness in learning and the mutual influence of the religious and non-religious dimensions both within a Catholic approach to education and more broadly throughout our lives. Given this emphasis, it is not surprising that I feel impelled to acknowledge that I have learned a great deal about the mysterious dialectic between distinctiveness and inclusivity, outside as well as inside the library, the study and the classroom. Family life has not only sustained me; it has taught me much about how important it is to balance space-making with boundary-setting; it has also provided a powerful model of how communion and diversity can not only co-exist, but better than that, can reciprocally enrich each other. My deepest thanks for their love and loyalty, their sacrifices and support, go to my first teachers, my parents, and to the people who continue to teach me most about what really matters, my wife Jean and our four children, David, Mark, Kathryn and Paul.

INTRODUCTION

As Western societies became increasingly secularised, many people have attempted to draw upon Christian principles for conduct while dispensing with the narratives, scriptures, doctrines and devotional practices that have traditionally been associated with such ethics. These sets of stories, beliefs and disciplines are sometimes viewed as 'baggage'; they are considered by many to be burdensome, out-of-date, unsubstantiated, unnecessary and therefore merely optional. Surely, it might be thought, one does not need the institutional and communal trappings of religious faith in order to display a concern for truth, honesty in communication, integrity in all dealings, consideration for others, tolerance of their shortcomings, care for the environment or a responsible exercise of freedom.

The attempt to promote a broadly Christian morality without being encumbered by its attendant metaphysics and mysticism, however, turns out to be a much more complex and frustrating process than at first seemed likely. No sooner are 'limbs', that look like being useful 'tools' for the moral life, torn from the 'body' to which they really belong, than the life-force ebbs out of them. Concepts, qualities and virtues that take much of their meaning and significance, their character and shape, their 'tone' and 'colour', from being integrated into a particular and comprehensive religious way of life, become distorted, shallow and endlessly plastic. In this process they appear to lack consistency, purchase on our lives and any capacity to direct and guide our actions. The failure to attend to the overall 'architecture' of the Christian life, in an effort to accommodate a public who believe less and less in the edifice as a whole, has led to the opening up and selling off of 'rooms' that lack ceilings, or walls, or floors. In picking and choosing, from the debris of a discarded religious lifestyle, merely those behavioural 'bricks' or traits that seem attractive, many people soon find that they have constructed habitats that are unserviceable, ramshackle and inhospitable.

In marked contrast to this narrow and minimising focus on principles for conduct that have become separated from their originating worldview, a more 'full-blooded' approach to Christian discipleship requires us to attend to the communal setting and personal lifestyle that underpin a set of beliefs and a code of practice. To be a follower of Jesus the Christ, in any age, entails a pattern of behaviour, a code of conduct, a form of morality; but this is a *response* to one's prior reception of the gospel of God's unconditional love. We do not earn our way into God's favour by living rightly. Only through endless conversions, with the help of grace and by availing ourselves of the power of the Holy Spirit do we open ourselves in an expectant and active receptivity to God. Such behavioural discipleship is also part of the way one appropriates the resources of the living tradition of the church. The church mediates the gospel message and embodies its teaching in a community where the mixture of human and divine is so entangled that it is impossible to be sure where the dividing lines are between the two dimensions. In discipleship we find that relationship, affiliation, and belonging are as integral to commitment as are belief or behaviour. Our affections and will are to be engaged. This demands of us that, over a lengthy period of time, we dwell within the group dynamics of significant others, that we share in a family of faith, with all the burdens and blessings of community life.

To the extent that this is true, Christian education will necessarily go beyond instruction; for inculcating a set of beliefs and doctrines, though necessary, is insufficient. It will also have to transcend mere training. Christian upbringing is not simply about ensuring that we become habituated into a particular collection of activities, such as reading scripture, saying prayers or performing charitable deeds, though it does require each of these elements as part of its 'repertoire'. Christian education, understood in a full sense, that is, education carried out with the development of Christian persons so that they are able to share in God's life as its goal, requires formation.

Religious formation has four essential dimensions. First, it draws upon a conceptual 'tool-kit', that is, a way of thinking. Integral to that way of thinking, for example, is a belief in the transcendence and immanence of God, plus a conviction that Jesus the Christ is simultaneously our best picture of and mode of access to God, as well as our best insight into what humanity can become, with the help of God's grace. Second, it requires a particular pattern or way of behaving. Cruelty, lying and selfishness, for example, are to be ruled out, while loving care for others, honesty and self-denial are to be aspired to. Third, it inducts adherents into ways of worshipping, both individually and collectively. Participation in the Eucharist and prayerful reading of scripture are typical examples, together with the capacity to express praise, thanksgiving, contrition and petition. The liturgy is potentially the church's most significant educational activity, but what it offers cannot be appreciated and appropriated if there is reliance solely on induction into and familiarity with a way of worship. In human terms, and for optimal educational efficacy, the liturgy depends upon the ways of thinking and behaving as much as it relies on the ways of praying of the people assembled. Of course, one can neither predict nor restrict the operation of divine power in the salvific fruitfulness of any particular liturgical celebration. The liturgy relies, too, however, on the character and quality of the way of belonging of a particular people. In order that such belonging has formative quality, constitutive of effective community life, members of a congregation need to spend time together, and over a long duration. They need opportunities to share their gifts and their needs, their joys and their sorrows, offering each other mutual support and jointly contributing to projects of service beyond the confines of their own limited community. They need to develop bonds of trust and a quality of relationships so that they matter to each other.

I have suggested that those who wish to separate out certain aspects of conduct and particular virtues from the multi-dimensional religious traditions, communities and practices from which they take their nature, function and efficacy run the risk of performing a kind of vivisection. I have also argued that discipleship, and therefore formation and Christian education, should be seen in a holistic way, rather than as one-dimensional. If we hope to share in God's life and to prepare others to accept this life, then the context in which learning takes place is crucial. The context for learning deeply affects how the object of study is apprehended and received. Who we find ourselves learning with makes a significant difference to the quality of the educational experience. The life-style in which we are already embedded radically changes what we can comprehend. It is because the Catholic Church recognises this that she strives, wherever possible, to promote education in a Catholic environment. In many countries this means that there are Catholic schools, separate from others in important ways and offering, to varying degrees, a distinctive approach to education. Behind the provision of separate Catholic schools is not just the desire to communicate a set of religious beliefs that would not otherwise receive privileged attention, beliefs that are thought necessary for salvation. A strongly motivating factor that underpins the Church's efforts to maintain separate religious schooling is the keen sense that the environment in which learning takes place constitutes an atmosphere that can make all the difference to the outcome one wants. It can facilitate and enhance the formation of Christian persons. The atmosphere in school can also, however, inhibit and perhaps even destroy such a goal. This atmosphere will be made up of several elements: its cultural capital, its pattern of practices, its network of relationships, its emotional tone and its configuration of explicit and tacit assumptions, will all have a part to play. As theologian Delwin Brown says, 'inhabitants of a tradition enter its stories, enact its rituals, play its roles, explore its visions, try its arguments, feel its sensibilities.'[1]

The provision of separate schools based on a Catholic worldview, however, faces opposition and misunderstanding, both from within the church and from those who are external to its membership. First, key aspects of that worldview are deeply controversial. Disputes arise about how to interpret tradition, how to express doctrine, how to order worship, how apply moral teaching, how to build the ecclesial community, how to exercise authority within it, how to communicate with outsiders and how to assess relative priorities within all these areas. The task of establishing schools based on a distinctive worldview is not straightforward if that distinctiveness is open to question and if its parameters are unclear.

Second, at any one time, at least some aspects of the church's teaching and practice are in a state of flux; there is disruption and discontinuity as well as stability and continuity. A tradition and its canons tend to lay down what should be preserved. They also provide resources with the capacity to authorise creative responses to new demands.[2] The church exists in history; its boundaries shift in response to changing circumstances, emerging opportunities and new threats. Outside influences affect the internal balance at any particular moment.[3] Any social organisation maintains its cultural identity by adjusting to the changing practices of others as well as by the unfolding of its own internal logic. The church shares in that process. The task of establishing separate schools based on a distinctive worldview cannot be settled or secured except temporarily and provisionally, since that distinctiveness derives partly from responses to circumstances, factors and developments that are outside the church's control and that are themselves undergoing constant change.

Third, to commit oneself too readily to any particular form of distinctiveness is to run the risk of idolatry. In such cases, human achievement is misread as the work of the divine, the signpost is treated as if it were the destination, provisional signs of promise are falsely taken as indicators of permanence and possession. True discipleship requires us to be open to a God who still speaks, one who is leading us, through the Holy Spirit, into a greater fullness of truth, and a God who transcends the church. This process of being led further into truth is unfinished. By turning inwards too soon, defending what we already have, we also run the risk of slipping into complacency, as if we believe we have all that is necessary and have nothing further to learn. Such a stance would lead to isolation, thereby contributing both to our own impoverishment and to a failure to communicate the gospel as effectively as possible.

Fourth, the desire to provide separate schools that have a mandate to offer religious formation in a holistic manner can lead to the temptation to over-emphasise distinctiveness in various ways that are damaging. One can exaggerate distinctiveness both by ignoring how much has been borrowed from others who are outside one's community or tradition and also by downplaying how much is still shared with them. This is to distort reality. One can undermine the constructive potential of distinctiveness by over-protecting and isolating it. This leads to a failure to engage in dialogue and so to an abdication of responsibility for the educational welfare of others. One can promote distinctiveness so strongly in the pluralist marketplace of educational services that such promotion slips into appearing not so much a positive advocacy of a set of ideals, but more a negative critique of the stances of others. This can be divisive. One can construct the distinctiveness in such a way that schools based on it become elitist. High hurdles are set on entry, thereby ruling out many who students and teachers who could otherwise have benefited from membership. Expectations are so demanding that students and staff who fall short of these requirements experience defeat and despair. This type of emphasis could make faith-based schools vulnerable to the accusation that they are exclusive. It will be apparent that there is a paradox here. A gospel that focuses on the unending forgiveness and love of God for all, that invites saints and sinners alike to share in that love and life, and one that is inherently and inescapably inclusive, surely cannot be the basis for a form of education that is exclusive. This paradox is at the heart of what follows.

Notes

[1] Delwin Brown, *Boundaries of Our Habitations*, New York, State University of New York Press, 1994, p.86.

[2] On tradition's creativity as well as its continuity, see Brown, op. cit., pp. 3, 45, 144.

[3] Kathryn Tanner, *Theories of Culture*, Minneapolis, Fortress, Press, 1997, pp.36, 111.

CHAPTER 1

TWO POLARITIES: AN INTERPRETATIVE KEY

In this chapter, first I describe two polarities at work within Catholicism and indicate their relevance to an understanding of the enterprise of Catholic education. I then suggest that a critical appreciation of the relationship between these two polarities has a significance for Catholics that extends beyond schooling. In this second section I also show how those outside the Catholic community, concerned with promoting liberal democracy in a pluralist society, might apply some of the conceptual categories and lines of approach adopted here to their own enquiries. Third, some of the new challenges facing Catholic schools are then summarised. This is followed by an attempt to show both loss and gain in the responses made by Catholic educators to changes in their environment. Fifth, consideration is given to the accusation that Catholic schools are insufficiently distinctive or counter-cultural. The need for a fresh articulation of the rationale for Catholic education is highlighted in section six and this is followed by a brief indication of the kind of balance that will be striven for throughout the rest of the book. The final section of the chapter is meant to serve as an advance organiser for readers, orienting them to the main angles of approach and the types of sources they can expect to encounter should they proceed further.

1.1   Two polarities

Conservatives in any religion often exaggerate the 'solidity' or fixed nature of their tradition, apparently being oblivious to the fact that it is in a state of flux, constantly open to development and subject to the vicissitudes of history. They are tempted to misread the tentative, provisional 'signposts' set up by a particular community as a result of the hard lessons of experience, falsely taking them as signs of arrival rather than as guides for the journey. They want to rest in the religious 'house' that has already been constructed by their predecessors and they are keen to preserve its décor and maintain the 'furniture' accumulated over the centuries. Tempted to have excessive confidence in the 'capital' invested by their forebears, they fear the risk that new speculation in the 'marketplace' of ideas might incur. They feel a deep sense of attachment and loyalty to their inheritance and wish to protect it from those who seem, only too casually, desirous of dismantling it. While they might be delighted to welcome newcomers into the faith community, this process is expected to take place on the terms of those already enjoying 'possession'. They do not expect to learn from 'outsiders'. In acknowledging the experience of God that is mediated within the faith community, they assume that the divine is contained therein and so fail to attend to God's work beyond its borders.

'Fidelity', 'continuity', 'obedience' and 'tradition' are words with a positive resonance for conservatives, while 'creativity', 'innovation', 'liberal' and 'progressive' immediately signal threats and invite suspicion. Authority offers security and discipline keeps us on the right track in attending to a word that God has already spoken. Distinctiveness is sharply defined and strongly defended. Much less effort is expended on trying to be inclusive. As a result, to some observers, the claim to be religiously distinctive can resemble a willingness to be exclusive.

Those who are progressives in religion are alert to the signs of the times and quick to acknowledge the potential value in new ideas. They underestimate the part played by memory in the life of a community and they show impatience with those who seek to filter new proposals through the lens of past criteria. Earlier 'gold' standards, for example, in matters of doctrine, morality or worship, far from being held in awe, are regarded with some scepticism. Such progressives believe that they 'travel light', and being unburdened by the shackles of the past, they are ready to be responsive to the needs of the present. They do not want to be confined by the architecture of their predecessors; nor do they think it necessary to consult traditional wisdom when seeking to reconstruct the religious community. While feeling confident about the future, they fail to take adequately into account the role inexorably played by history, both in the lives of individuals and in that of the community. Although careful to avoid institutional idolatry internally, as they face outwards they can be naïve in their prematurely positive assessment of contemporary culture.

'Fidelity', 'continuity', 'obedience' and 'tradition' are words that, for progressives, have associations of a fearful caution and they serve to obscure an excessive desire to maintain control. 'Creativity', 'innovation', 'liberal' and 'progressive' indicate a positive 'reading' of the world as infused with the presence of God's grace and a willingness to step forward bravely in a spirit of freedom and authenticity. Distinctiveness tends to be blurred and under-emphasised in the interests of openness. As a result, to the ears of some hearers, the claim to be religiously inclusive can sound like a readiness to accommodate that slides into an abandonment of tradition and assimilation into secular culture.

Although I believe that these bold assertions apply to many different religious groups, I can only speak for the one with which I am familiar, that is Christianity in the Roman Catholic tradition. I shall seek to substantiate, later on in this work, and in the specific context of a study of Catholic education in England and Wales, the central claim that an understanding of the relationship between distinctiveness and inclusiveness offers a useful interpretative key to the nature of Catholicism. To be more precise, I intend to explore the bearing of this claim on the theory and practice of Catholic education. Before doing that, however, I suggest (1.2., below) the wider significance, beyond that highlighted in my own enquiry, of a sophisticated appreciation of the ultimate compatibility of the two apparently contrasting emphases described above. In order to assist me in the development of a coherent argument about how these differing emphases relate to one another, I intend to treat distinctiveness and inclusiveness as polarities that operate in tension, both of which are required for a form of Catholicism (and Catholic education) that has integrity.

Neither conservatives nor progressives, as I have so crudely caricatured them, do justice to these polarities. As a result, both 'parties' tend to contribute to an unnecessary and damaging polarisation within the church. In this polarisation there is a temptation to assume too readily both that the virtues are displayed by the 'side' with which one sympathises and also that the defects are mostly owned by those from whom we feel distant. It will already be clear from my sketchy comments above that I believe both conservatives and progressives are partly right and partly wrong, and this in regard to both what they are for and what they neglect. Much, though not all, of what they defend should be taken more seriously; much, though not all, of what they neglect should be given a great deal more weight. I believe it is essential for the health, authenticity and fruitfulness of Catholic education that *both* polarities are given the utmost respect in future discussions. This will entail that the polarities are constantly held in a creative tension.

1.2   Wider significance of understanding the polarities

That this issue might be a matter of deep concern to Catholics in general and for Catholic educators in particular is to be expected. A study of the relationship between distinctiveness and inclusiveness casts light on the enterprise of Catholic education for all age groups and in every kind of setting. It also offers assistance in the resolution of some of the sharply controversial debates that keep recurring over religious education in Catholic schools.[1] These often revolve around the respective weight to be given to the heritage of the past and the culture of the present. As a crossroads between theology and pedagogy, religious education is an arena that is simultaneously privileged, in terms of the importance ascribed to it by the faith community, and subject to extreme pressure because of polarisation within that community.[2] Jim Gallagher describes two different notions of faith that are operative behind this polarisation. There is an 'understanding of faith given at baptism, sustained by authority, threatened by inquiry, undermined by doubt, characterised by clarity, productive of certainty.' This is to be contrasted with an understanding of faith as 'a free and personal act, fostered by community, growing through ceaseless inquiry, seeming to need the tension of doubt for its development, walking in uncertainty, open to infinity.'[3] It is often difficult for religious educators who rely on one of these approaches to embrace the perspective of those who rely on the other.

Religious educators who build on the foundational principles analysed in this book should display a capacity to discern both the universality and the particularity of Christianity. They will maintain a balance between witness and listening. They will be confident and comprehensive in their presentation, but neither defensive nor hectoring. Far from relying on fear as a motive for engagement in learning and hoping for conformity as its goal, they will create hospitable spaces for a critical appreciation and a creative appropriation of the living tradition of Catholicism by students. They will acknowledge the plurality of theological *loci*, or sources, rather than work only from the catechism, syllabus or textbook. They will be respectful of the insights, not only of the devout and committed, but also of the doubtful, those who deviate from the norms laid down as well as of those who are marginalised either in society or the church. In short, they will offer a view of faith that is both distinctive and inclusive.

For the role of Catholics more generally in society, the tools developed in the following chapters furnish potentially useful guidance in pastoral and policy decisions in many different areas. These include questions such as the following. What stance is to be adopted in relation to the state? What kinds of partnerships can be established with other groups in matters of social ministry? How can a balance be struck between a prophetic and a pastoral emphasis in moral matters? A prophetic approach emphasises the counter-cultural challenge and the transcendent call to perfection from God in traditional religious teaching, while a pastoral approach starts with people where they are, accepting God's immanence and unending forgiveness in their complex and messy circumstances?

This study also provides some conceptual resources with which to address two other (closely related) topics currently under discussion in the universal church, topics that are not usually considered in the literature on Catholic education. The first of these is the need for and nature of *formation*, a term that deliberately implies a process that penetrates deeper into the psyche than training, the imparting of information or what often passes for education in mainstream schooling. Formation is described in a recent Roman document as an integral process, one that seeks a correlation between life and truth, between theology and the human sciences, between communicating a tradition and the hopes and values of young people.[4] Formation is usually associated with preparation for religious life in some particular religious order of men or women. It implies discipline, depth and long-term commitment. It is often carried out over a lengthy period and it takes place away from the world and its distractions. Programmes of formation attend to specific teachings and practices and their bearing on the spiritual life. They also give much emphasis to the benefits and responsibilities of belonging to a particular (religious) community. My exploration of the connections between distinctiveness and inclusiveness should prompt those charged with formation to ensure they maintain an appropriate balance. On the one hand they will, rightly, emphasise the particularity of the tradition into which people are being inducted. On the other hand, they should provide sufficient space for the flourishing of individuals who possess a diversity of needs, strengths and weaknesses. In the past, formation sometimes aimed for a degree of conformity from new members of a religious community that stripped them of their individuality. Such an approach gave inadequate attention to the essential polarity of inclusiveness.

The second issue under debate in contemporary Catholicism that might benefit from my analysis of the two polarities, distinctiveness and inclusiveness, is the role of particular *charisms* in the Church. To identify a charism, whether of an individual or of a group, is to draw attention to a special gift or talent, one that can be deployed for the greater good of the church and the whole people of God. The notion of charism is linked to the notion of vocation: different people (and groups) have different parts to play in the drama of salvation.

In a sense we can claim that there is a general and a special dimension to being a Christian. We have a common need for salvation and we are offered a common Saviour. The Word is to be addressed to all, without fear or favour. The church should be open to all, whatever their station in life. Through baptism there is a common priesthood of all believers, who should attempt to be the eyes, ears and hands of Christ in the world of their time. This is the general aspect of being a Christian. Each person enjoys particular gifts and talents; each person also struggles with particular shortcomings. In responding to the universal call of God as they face particular historical, cultural and economic circumstances, each Christian also has a special, perhaps even unique, vocation. There is no one right way to live out one's Christian faith, just as there is not merely one instrument to be played in an orchestra. This is what I mean by the special aspect of being a believer. Part of the distinctiveness of Catholicism is shared by all adherents of that faith, while within that distinctiveness there is scope for some legitimate diversity in expressing this in the actual circumstances in which we find ourselves.

Throughout its history the church has encouraged people with similar 'specialisms' to join together in particular movements, organisations or religious orders. Since the Second Vatican Council (1962-65) there has been, in many parts of the Catholic Church, a radical re-appraisal of the role of such religious groups and their distinctive charisms. In emphasising the universal aspects of the faith, for example, the vocation of all believers, there has been some loss of confidence within the church as to how to articulate and how to put into institutional practice the charisms of particular religious orders. Alongside a marked decline in numbers, it has been deliberate policy in many parts of the world for religious orders to hand over responsibility for activities previously run by them to lay people. Religious as well as lay people acknowledge that this process has often taken place without adequate arrangements for transition or continuity. As a result, some of the special aspects, or charisms, that were part of the distinctiveness of Catholicism have been neglected, downgraded or even lost. The 'orchestra' now plays without benefit of some interesting 'instruments'. In such cases, too narrow an interpretation of distinctiveness has been operative.

Why, however, should people *outside* Catholicism consider that my examination of the relationship between these polarities might repay their effort to 'listen in' to a controversy that is internal to one particular faith community? A simple and relatively superficial answer might be that the Catholic Church has been, and still is, the largest body of religious believers in the world. It has millions of adherents and is represented in every country. In many parts of the world that Church is a major presence in society and exerts a significant and enduring influence. A failure to understand such a body and the controversies that cause anxieties in its members could be a dangerous omission. It would leave unexplained huge gaps in the mapping of the cultural landscape in most countries. This might be considered a major handicap to the development of policies that seek to respond adequately to social pluralism.

A more limited, but also more cogent answer might be put thus. The argument that I shall lay out in this book opens up a debate within Catholicism about how distinctiveness and inclusiveness are to be interpreted – and how the understanding arrived at can be related to education. Alongside my interrogation of these two polarities I attempt a re-articulation of the rationale for Catholic education, a rationale that addresses societies that are pluralist, liberal and democratic.[5] Of course, other faith communities have similar tasks to perform; they must find ways to support a constructive engagement with the social and political cultures to which they belong. And they will feel the same pressures to do this in such a way as to preserve what they believe to be their enduring values and to advance what they believe are their distinctive insights into human flourishing.[6] A parallel debate is being conducted in many countries about the key principles of liberal democracy.

In the face of increasingly assertive minority groups, liberal democracy seems to require a regenerated theoretical underpinning. Just as Catholics might argue about the respective weight to be given either to distinctiveness or to inclusiveness in religious matters, so liberal democrats are now re-examining the respective weight to be given to substantive and procedural principles, to 'thinner' and thicker' interpretations of liberalism.[7] How neutral can liberals afford to be when dealing with individuals and groups who do not share their liberalism? Do some forms of liberalism so emphasise individual freedom that they prevent the development of the qualities and habits necessary for the construction and sustenance of a community permeated by liberal principles and values? What kinds of 'bias' or support for liberalism are legitimate in publicly provided institutions and in social life more generally? [8]   In the educational context, how 'strong' must be the promotion of liberalism, if it is to survive, without overriding the rights of those with other perspectives on life? [9] What kinds of allegiance to liberalism are appropriately to be worked for and what are the limits to pluralism that must therefore be accepted as a necessary price? What kinds of regulations must be made by a liberal state in relation to the rights of children, parents and minority groups?[10]

This debate within liberalism echoes in some respects the arguments that I shall explore in relation to Catholic education. How can particularity and identity be protected and advanced? How can corrosive intrusions be guarded against? Is it possible to extend genuine openness in a way that is consistent with maintaining integrity? In a pluralist society, it is as important for those outside a faith community as for those who are insiders to consider the relationship between the demands of citizenship and the requirements of religious commitment. The necessity for this is not contradicted by the fact that the terms in which they do this and the weighting they attribute to the principles invoked will necessarily be different. Religious and secular moral considerations need to be brought together in public debate in a religiously plural world.[11]

Although it is not my purpose to defend this claim, I believe that my examination of the competing claims of distinctiveness and inclusiveness in Catholic education does offer conceptual resources that can contribute to debates *outside* Catholicism, about the necessary conditions for sustaining liberal democracy in secular schools. Catholics and secular liberals alike have to cope with 'otherness' and difference, within and beyond their own communities. Those with religious convictions should not expect to find these emasculated, undermined or refused admittance in *any* kind of school. There can be exclusive forms of liberal humanism just as there can be exclusive expressions of religion. But there can be no return to any form of theocracy, either in society or in school. My hope is that, by exposing the lines of argument about distinctiveness and inclusiveness within Catholic education to a wider audience, I succeed at the same time in drawing to the public attention 'goods of persons and communities not otherwise made prominent in public discourse'.[12] I do not expect those who are outside my own faith community to accept my presuppositions, my interpretation of the essential 'ingredients' of a Catholic world-view, or the arguments presented here. However, I would be disappointed to encounter the criticism that my delineation in this book of the polarities, distinctiveness and inclusiveness, and the creative tension between them, cannot be fruitfully applied to discussions elsewhere about the relationship, especially in education, between liberalism and pluralism.

1.3 New challenges for Catholic schools

Can one be both Catholic and catholic in the sphere of education? Is the attempt to offer a distinctive approach to education, one that meets the special requirements of a particular religious community, compatible with openness to the needs and perspectives of those outside the tradition and of society in general? Is it possible to provide a form of education that manages at the same time to avoid being either secular or sectarian? These closely related questions seem to underlie many of the debates about Catholic education that are currently taking place all over the world. They have a bearing on decisions and practice regarding the purpose, nature, and role of Catholic schools in many different countries.

For example, Catholic schools are important institutions in post-Apartheid South Africa, where reconciliation and social reconstruction are major priorities. In India and Pakistan, where Christians comprise a tiny minority in nations that are keen both to assert their independence from a Western colonial past and to maintain credibility with vociferously resurgent Hindu and Muslim communities, the stance taken by Catholic schools can be a crucial element in social harmony. In the 'tiger economy' of Ireland there have been massive cultural challenges to a previously supremely dominant Catholicism. The institutional Church there faces disintegration in numbers and structures and devastating erosion of authority in many areas. The creativity and success with which Catholic schools manage to balance distinctiveness with inclusiveness will offer test-cases for the Church's viability and future in that country. In Northern Ireland denominational schooling has sometimes been accused of being a major factor contributing to damaging divisions among the community.   Should a policy of separate schooling be sustained in such circumstances?[13]

In many European countries, despite the long history and major influence of different forms of Christianity on educational provision, the Church faces probing questions about what are the appropriate expectations to have today about faith-based schooling. For these societies are marked by secularisation in the social, institutional and personal dimensions of life. They have seen a serious decline in Christian affiliation and practice. According to Johannes Van der Ven, the church population is 'greying,' with a very marked drop in the numbers of young people attending.[14] Many parishes are being closed or amalgamated. The church is well on the way to becoming a volunteer church; it must rely less and less on official hierarchical bureaucracy and is slowly responding to a massive reduction in clergy. More than a third of Catholic parishes in Europe are without priests.[15] Most European countries have experienced in recent decades an increasing inflow of people from faiths other than Christianity. Radically different attitudes to authority and to institutional intrusion into private life are revealed in the responses made by many people. There is a growing realisation that private religiosity differs in subtle but important ways from church religiosity.[16]   Consumerism, rapid change, increased choice, resistance to delayed gratification and a shift in attention away from the past and onto the present cumulatively lead to a neglect of the collective memory, and therefore of the roots of identity, security and continuity.[17] To these changes one can add some significant modifications in attitudes regarding self, knowledge and values brought about as a result of an exponential increase in engagement with new technology.

1.4   Systemic change: loss and gain

The internal dynamics of any organisation or system cannot help but change in the face of modifications in its external circumstances.   Self-definition, internal priorities and stances, both 'offensive' and 'defensive', with regard to the outside world, are all reconfigured when former debating partners (whether allies or opponents) disappear and when new threats (and opportunities) present themselves. All kinds of changes in public policy can impinge upon a Catholic school. These could relate either to aspects of the curriculum (for example, sex education, citizenship, the use of information and communications technology) or even with regard to the framework for and underlying philosophy of the whole curriculum. Alternative policy decisions that could significantly alter the ground-rules for Catholic schools include those governing funding arrangements, for these could influence pupil enrolment, the range of resources available for learning and the levels of remuneration for staff. Accreditation, inspection and quality assurance measures affect programmes of learning. Local, regional or national decisions sometimes seek to prescribe the terms of reference for and the constituencies to be included in school governance, the nature of opportunities for staff development, and to lay down rules for performance management. At such times it could be asked of a school if it 'is being led by the changes in its environment or by the plans it has made for itself?'[18] The religious effectiveness of a church school is bound up with the kind of interaction it facilitates between its institutional life, the faith experience of individuals and the culture of the society that surrounds it.

For over a hundred years before the period of the Second Vatican Council (1962-65) the Catholic Church displayed an inward-looking and self-protective stance vis-à-vis the world. Distinctiveness was interpreted in a separationist mentality, with clearly marked borders that allowed no ambiguity as to whether one was inside or outside the Church. Ideologically, a 'closed' system was in operation, one that was receptive to only a limited number of external influences. Catholics were encouraged to protect their faith from contamination by keeping to a minimum, as far as was possible, their contact with those 'beyond the fold.' Whereas formerly Catholic schools 'tended to isolate themselves against outside influences,' now they deliberately open themselves up to a wide range of influences, seeking 'close connections with families and the local community.'[19] Such a move is part of a more general trend within Catholicism. Despite occasional (and ineffective) attempts to restore the status quo ante, the institutional church relies less often than hitherto on the discipline of a compulsory, universalising conformity; instead a more positive 'reading' of the world has been adopted. A hallmark of the contemporary Catholic Church, by comparison with half a century ago, has been a more inclusive approach to the diversity of experience and perspectives enjoyed by its members as well as by the communities it seeks to serve.

This progress has not been achieved without some accompanying loss. Part of the cost has been a blurring of the cognitive parameters of faith. Catholic schools in many parts of the world offered students a common language with which to enter the faith community anywhere, an 'armoury' with which to face down the modern world, one that was equipped with a precise set of formulae to be remembered. There was a high degree of clarity about orthodoxy, rather than a confusing range of interpretations from which to choose. When the 'currency' of dogma is unquestioned, when the 'gold standard' of authority is unassailable (as far as insiders are concerned), when the agenda for discussion is carefully controlled, when uncomfortable questions are prevented from surfacing and when unprivileged voices cannot receive a hearing – in these circumstances the web of beliefs and the set of practices that are integral to Catholicism are experienced *as a totality*. Here, all elements mutually reinforce one another; each piece of the 'jigsaw' is a necessary part of the picture; each 'brick' in the building bears part of the 'load.' Take one aspect away and the whole edifice of faith becomes lop-sided and is in danger of collapsing.

Order and obedience, consistency and universality, serve to surround the faithful in a supernatural cocoon, protecting them from the snares of the devil, in the multifarious forms of false egalitarianism, misleading democracy, overweening rationalism, proud individualism, selfish materialism, or dangerous freedom of thought.   Educational   experience   within   the   Church   deliberately   and comprehensively embraced many features simultaneously.   The 'curriculum' of Catholic schools included doctrines to believe, devotions to edify the spirit and discipline to tame the will. All of these were punctuated and blessed by sacraments to bring home to us the presence of the sacred, to feed us on our journey and to deepen the process of conversion that attunes us to God's will. One was expected to dwell in this 'fortress' and accept without reservation its culture and curriculum *as a totality*. The comprehensiveness, coherence and compulsory nature of the 'package' that was Catholicism was part of its attraction for some. These features certainly contributed to its self-confidence as well as to its institutional strength and organisational energy in the face of adversity and opposition.

It is not surprising that the Church felt justified in this stance when confronted by fierce anti-clericalism in some countries, periodical outbursts of anti-Catholicism in others, followed by other, contending attempts to establish totalitarian societies in fascist Italy, Nazi Germany and communist Russia and China. A willingness on the part of the hierarchy to accede to demands for change internally within the Church in the 1960s came about not only because of the compelling (and cumulative) nature of the logic of arguments that had been germinating, particularly in France and Germany, from the 1930s onwards. Nor was it a result of the strategic wisdom or political 'clout' of reformers. It happened, in part at least, because of the apparent collapse of competing totalitarian systems. Once the external environment changes, whether for the better or for the worse, the elements internal to a system that has been built up partly in response to that environment carry a different significance for those who belong to it. At times of major cultural change there are bound to be some adaptations, in discipline, in self-understanding or in emphasis, by a body of religious believers. The consequences, however, of such adaptations are rarely, if ever, clear in advance of experiment.

One of the unintended side-effects of the reconfiguration of Catholicism that took place after Vatican II was, I believe, an over-emphasis in Catholic education on the distinction between belief and believing. Hervieu-Léger argues that 'the process of believing (as compared with any specific belief) includes not only particular convictions, but also the practices, languages, gestures and habits in which these beliefs are inscribed. Such believing is belief in actions, belief lived out.'[20] Once the intimate connection between belief and believing is misunderstood, separate 'items' in the Catholic vocabulary become distorted and the cognitive aspects of faith are divorced from appropriate cultural surroundings and from communal 'plausibility structures.' It is partly because they understood so well the 'integral' nature of Catholicism, the coinherence (and mutual corrections) of its institutional, devotional and intellectual dimensions, that I turn (in chapters four and seven, below) to the work of Friedrich von Hügel (1852 – 1925) and Maurice Blondel

(1861 – 1949) as debating partners in my re-articulation of the nature of Catholic education. Each of these two writers displayed, although to different degrees and in different ways, a concern to hold together both the distinctiveness and the inclusiveness which I shall argue are essential, and inter-related, elements within Catholicism and therefore which should feature as constitutive dimensions in Catholic schools.

I have already referred to the shift away from the notion of Catholicism as a totality, related this to the breakdown of other totalitarian systems and suggested an unfortunate side-effect of developments that generally I perceive in a positive light as echoing more closely the teaching of the Gospel. Here I wish to acknowledge another unfortunate side-effect of a different aspect of the move away from distorted forms of Catholic 'integralism.'

Hervieu-Léger points to two types of integralism, neither of which, in my view, are in harmony with the Gospel. She says[21] that

> Tensions arise, for a religious group, between [a] an integralism *ad extra*, which is concerned with conformity to tradition in spreading or communicating it, and [b] an integralism *ad intra*, which aims for conformity to tradition in deepening its hold on believers.

The first type of integralism seeks some kind of control over the world, an opportunity to direct it. The second type requires some degree of separation from the world. These represent two different expressions of a 'totalising propensity' within religions, that is, the temptation to keep control over people, either, in the first case, at the collective level, or, in the second case, at the individual level.

However, these two distorted forms of integralism have been abandoned in favour of first, offering a presence of service in the world, and, second, facilitating individual responsibility and an encouragement to claim the full fruits of baptism as part of the priesthood of believers. This means that Catholic educators now face a new challenge. One might describe this challenge as a call to witness to strength through vulnerability rather than through victory or conquest. The challenge is that of combining two apparently conflicting features. First, can Catholic educators maintain a strong enough presence and presentation of religion to give adequate witness to its nature, scope and claims? Second, can they, at the same time, remain sensitive, vulnerable and open to the needs and insights of pupils and colleagues; can they avoid allowing the school's 'promotion' of religion to slip into forms of dominance or control that become intrusive, threatening or restrictive? Once again, in seeking to address this practical dilemma, one that faces teachers in Catholic schools everywhere, I believe that no progress is possible without drawing upon the conceptual resources provided by a deeper understanding of the relationship between distinctiveness and inclusiveness in Catholic education.

1.5   Conformist or counter-cultural?

In many countries, such as Australia, the USA and the UK, the very success of
Catholic schools in meeting secular criteria for acceptance, accreditation, or funding
has led to them being increasingly attractive to parents from outside the Catholic
community.   However, while some have applauded the increasing openness,
inclusiveness and social concern displayed by Catholic schools, others have felt that
there have been major losses with regard to distinctiveness, clarity of mission and
faith-formation.   According to this view, compliance with contemporary cultural
norms has taken precedence over fidelity to tradition and school has slipped from
being an instrument for spreading the Gospel into functioning as a tool of a secular
society.[22] Three recent commentators on the situation facing Catholic schools today
pose the challenging question: 'How well versed are those who lead, teach and work
in Catholic schools in Church and Catholic school history, the documents and
scripture?'[23]

In each of these three countries similar criticisms might be levelled against
Catholic institutions of higher education. While they demonstrably contribute to the
common good, do they address sufficiently the expectations of their founding faith
communities in offering something truly distinctive, perhaps even counter-cultural?
Robert McLaughlin, a philosopher based in New York, offers a pessimistic reading
of Catholic Higher Education in the USA.   He laments what he calls its self-
destructive policies, complains about the disconnection between academic and
religious life and argues for a much more explicit influence of religion in
classrooms.[24]

In a recent Australian overview of the ideology governing Catholic education,
Denis McLaughlin quotes Michael Warren thus:

> The best schools raise serious questions about the culture, critique it, and put it into
> perspective. ... Of its very nature, education... should offer some critical distance
> from which to view the culture. Catholic education should do this in a special manner,
> since it is based on Jesus' extensive set of principles, that turns popular wisdom in its
> head.[25]

But, the question can justifiably be posed: do Catholic schools equip their pupils
to critique the prevailing culture of society? Or do they simply prepare them to
belong to this society and to be ready to perform the same kind of roles as
everybody else?   Should there be something different about the capacities and
commitments of those who graduate from Catholic schools, as compared with the
qualities and preoccupations of those from other forms of education? We also find
in McLaughlin's literature survey the comment, relating to the Australian context,
that:

> All the talk about the 'school community' and 'holistic education' cannot hide the fact
> that less admirable qualities of society's values have become absorbed by the schools in
> the process. If a transformative shift had occurred, the difference between the state and
> the Catholic school system would be striking. [26]

This view might well prompt an investigation as to the extent to which the values of Catholic schools have been permeated by norms and expectations that come from elsewhere and that are incompatible with their foundational principles. Among such 'foreign' norms we might find certain attitudes that sit uneasily when placed alongside the Church's official guidelines for her schools (see chapter four, below). Differences of view could arise over claims to knowledge and the understanding of the purpose(s) of education. Tensions could emerge through clashing expectations for the kinds of relationships to be established within schools between adults and children and between schools and families and the wider community. The role of the state, scope for religious freedom, allowance for diversity – all can be the focus of lively controversy in debates about Catholic education.

McLaughlin quotes another commentator thus:

> The most striking thing to a visitor from Mars about the schools of New South Wales would be their sameness: same structures, same courses, same daily routines, same examinations. And Catholic schools, except for their religious orientation, are no exception.[27]

If this statement were applied to the UK, many teachers and parents would feel that the comment was justifiable. A leading English exponent of Catholic education nearly a decade ago bemoaned the failure of Catholic schools to live out their founding principles in a way that demonstrated their radical difference.

> The weakness of the Catholic school system has often been its inability to establish a confident internal polity that eschews that element of divisiveness inherent in the attempt to develop the practices operating in secular schools: aggressive competition, the premium placed upon worldly success, the use of selfish rewards... the need for outward conformity in social attitudes.[28]

Again, this accusation of undue conformity to norms common to society, rather than adherence to a more radical vision, deserves careful consideration by all Catholic schools, regardless of the country where they are located. The qualities that are striven for in schools that claim to reflect the Gospel should embrace interdependence and mutual support, endless forgiveness, self-sacrifice, an openness to the will of God and a willingness to offer prophetic witness in the world.[29] The Vatican Council's *Declaration on Christian Education* (1965, par 9) reminds believers of the radical demands of any form of education based on the Gospel and issues a strong challenge to Catholic schools everywhere: 'The Church should offer its educational service first to the poor or those deprived of family help or those who are far from the faith.'

In a recent survey[30] Chester Gillis asks 'What constitutes a "Catholic" institution – is it history and heritage, simple nomenclature, episcopal approbation, or self-description?' The question about identity constantly recurs in discussions about Catholic education. If Catholic affiliation or willingness to abide by Catholic 'house-rules' and priorities takes precedence over all other considerations, for some Catholic schools and colleges certain kinds of problems can be anticipated. These might include difficulties about academic freedom, institutional autonomy, student enrolment, staff selection (and promotion) and about the standing of the institution in quality ratings when these are carried out solely according to secular criteria. Gillis points out that, with government assistance, (for example, funds for research or grants for students) comes government regulation and certain legal obligations (for example, relating to equal opportunities).[31] Inevitably, once a school (or a whole school system) seeks to benefit from external support, it lays itself open to pressure to comply with external norms. However, if it can draw upon a rationale for itself that facilitates a creative fidelity in relation to tradition, it will be in a better position to adapt to external expectations.

1.6   Towards a new rationale

A full discussion of a Catholic institution's sense of identity must take into account the parameters of ecclesial – and more precisely, episcopal, - oversight and the complex relationships that obtain in any particular country between the church and state and between a school and its local, regional or national political community. For the purposes of this study, and in order to keep the work within manageable limits, I omit an examination of the kinds of oversight – and of the issues arising – that might be exercised in respect of Catholic schools and colleges. This would require a degree of detailed contextualisation that exceeds my present capacity and one that is not necessary for the principal questions at stake here.

Instead, by exploring in some depth how being distinctive relates to being inclusive in Catholic educational philosophy, I hope to articulate the key elements that should feature in *any* form of education that claims the label 'Catholic', in whatever context this takes place. I shall indicate in the chapters that follow those changes within the living tradition of Catholicism which lead to the need for the development of a new rationale for Catholic education. Reference will also be made to changes external to the church that impinge upon the endeavour to provide Catholic education while contributing constructively to the societies in which it is situated.   'Articulacy maintains the plausibility of a culture's values.' It can legitimately be hoped that 'remedying the lack of articulacy about our values will serve a regenerative purpose.'[32]

This ideological regeneration is made necessary in part because of the intensification of what Padraig Hogan has called 'the intrusion of political purposes into schooling'. This has happened in many countries to such a degree that 'the capacity of the churches to insulate their schools from unwelcome influences has declined dramatically.'[33] Hogan suggests that the widespread success (in the field of education) of the market ideology that became evident in many countries throughout the 1980s and 1990s was made easier where

> a more substantive vision had lost its influence or had somehow become mute amid a throng of competing outlooks. Not so much the actual loss of belief in an educational vision, as a self-defeating reticence to *articulate* the belief. Reticence, the failure to articulate afresh a vision of moral purpose in response to new challenges, contributes to a waning of belief itself.[34]

I believe that such a regenerative articulation can be carried out without being marred by either the kind of triumphalism about one's own tradition that is blind to its real shortcomings or by feeling the need to offer a negative story about other traditions. At the same time I believe that the enhanced confidence and clarity that are provided by such a project can jointly prompt genuine openness to and appreciation of those outside the 'family' of one's own faith. Such a project can also equip religious adherents to engage responsibly and collaboratively with 'outsiders', in service of the common good, without surrendering anything essential to their own tradition.[35]

1.7   Getting the balance right

There is no guarantee that re-articulation of the main principles of Catholic education will, on its own, lead to the outcome for which I hope. There is a real polarity at work; justice has to be done to both poles in the re-articulation that this work promises. Does the effort to be inclusive necessarily undermine loyalty to the distinctiveness of Catholicism? Does the desire to protect the distinctiveness of Catholicism lead inevitably to a premature closure of certain options for inclusiveness? The Canadian philosopher Charles Taylor, in a recent essay, speaks of two related senses of the word 'Catholic': universality and wholeness, or, more precisely still, 'universality through wholeness.'[36] He argues that the oneness of Catholicism requires both a sense of identity and of complementarity, or, as I have put it, a dual emphasis on both distinctiveness and inclusiveness. 'Our great historical temptation has been to forget the complementarity, to go straight for the sameness.' When this happens 'unity is bought at the price of suppressing something of the diversity in the humanity God created.' In this situation 'unity of the part masquerad[es] as the whole.' Such 'universality without wholeness' is not true Catholicism.[37]

However, a policy of openness that is not accompanied by discernment and a concern for fidelity to tradition is also a perilous path for the Church. William Shea, an American philosopher and theologian, in responding to the Taylor essay just quoted, asks if Catholics 'can participate fully in this culture without drowning in it intellectually and spiritually,' when 'its life forms and practices undercut the forms and practices of historical Catholicism?'[38] Without such discernment and caution, the abandonment of an exclusive Catholicism merely opens the door to other forms of exclusiveness and tribalism, ones that allow no room for religious presuppositions. In this case Christian educators find themselves forced, in the professional arena at least, to suppress their spiritual convictions and having to obscure their openness to the transcendent by referring only to arguments that can be accepted on non-religious grounds. Shea asks: 'How can [we] welcome all and thereby risk intellectual chaos and moral vacuity, on the one hand, and on the other uphold a sacramental and communitarian Catholic viewpoint and thereby risk suspicions of ideological control on research and teaching?'[39] Although his question is asked in the context of the (American) Catholic university, I believe its force has much wider application for Catholic educators. They must attend simultaneously to the 'strictures of modernity and the exigencies of faith,' being 'faithful to and critical of both Church and culture, letting go of neither and finding a way to live in and with both.'[40]

Difficulties in getting the balance right between distinctiveness and inclusiveness and a temptation to err more on the side of religious 'protectionism' are understandable where a faith community feels threatened, insecure or subject to persecution. Even in the case of the world's largest religious community, the Roman Catholic Church, however, there are obstacles to its policies, limits to its appeal and resistance to its claims. This is despite the fact that it enjoys a reputation for being historically venerable, geographically widespread, institutionally powerful, intellectually impressive and spiritually fertile. The right to educate according to the teachings of the Church is not readily accorded, even in areas where Catholicism is strongly represented. Debates internal to the faith community about the rationale for Catholic schools often function as a focus for debates about the future of the Church itself. Controversy about the religious curriculum, for example, is often heated since it arouses deeply conflicting interpretations of the nature of Catholicism and of its central beliefs. A whole shift of perspective within the Catholic Church has occurred since the beginning of the 1960s, from a position where there was, universally, an experience of religion dominated by authority, to one where, in the circumstances of many people's lives, there is a reliance on the authority of experience. Such a shift has both advantages and disadvantages for Catholic education. One can reasonably surmise that it facilitates a new emphasis on openness and inclusiveness within the Church. At the same time, one must acknowledge that such a shift also makes more difficult the features once so marked in Catholic education: clarity, consistency, continuity and distinctiveness.

Questions about identity focus on *who we are, where we have come from, what do we stand for* and *why we are here*. Questions about inclusiveness focus our attention on *who we are for*, and *how should we operate*? Although questions about identity clarify our distinctiveness and tend to look primarily inwards, they cannot be addressed without attention to what we are distinct from and the surrounding environments and cultures with which we have to engage. The confidence, clarity and seriousness of outlook that accompany a renewed appreciation of distinctiveness should galvanise a religious community to turn its attention outwards, in order to share the 'goods' it believes it has to offer, indeed feels it has an imperative duty to communicate effectively to others.

In parallel, questions about inclusiveness clarify the kinds of openness that should be displayed by a religious community if its message is to be heard and if the world is to be served. They also challenge that community however, to work hard at ensuring that such openness does not become careless about the state of the 'home' that we invite people to enter. Without attending to – and creatively maintaining and protecting – what is distinctive in our tradition, we merely invite people into an open space that is neither hospitable nor nourishing.

The stance of the Catholic educational community towards insiders or outsiders that I will be arguing for in this book is one that attempts to avoid two extremes. The way forward entails neither an inflexible, one-way transmission, a 'take-it-or-leave-it' attitude, on the one hand, nor should there be a reluctance to give witness or offer a counter-cultural teaching. Watering down the tradition in order to make it acceptable serves nobody well. A willingness to be humble, open, receptive and vulnerable does not require of a community self-deprecation to a degree that is suicidal. Nor does a desire to convey a tradition faithfully, to appreciate it critically, or to appropriate it creatively, necessarily lead to any lack of respect for those who stand outside of it. If we wish to be heard, we have to listen; but if we wish to engage in dialogue, we also must be willing to speak. It is only possible to be open-ended from a 'position'. Such a position cannot be founded on the shifting sands of 'relevance'. Looking out at the positions of others is assisted by standing on solid ground securely, rather than tottering on the brink of a personal (or communal) precipice.

The relationship between distinctiveness and inclusiveness in Catholic education resembles in some respects the polarity between solidarity and subsidiarity in the political arena. Solidarity without subsidiarity leads to totalitarianism; it can be suffocating, imprisoning and narrowing. Subsidiarity without solidarity leads to isolationism; it contributes to fragmentation, is impoverishing and also ends up in narrowness of outlook. When solidarity and subsidiarity are held in creative tension they balance, correct and enrich each other. So too in Catholic education, distinctiveness and inclusiveness are correlative terms with a reciprocal relationship: each is implicated in the other, with both polarities reinforcing and qualifying their correlates. Essential to the distinctiveness are the features of universality, openness and inclusiveness; yet the resources and willingness to maintain openness depend and draw upon the 'capital' of something distinctively enduring and 'solid'. Is it possible for Catholic education to maintain its particularity without becoming parochial? Can it avoid being a mirror of secular education without slipping into sectarianism? This is a concern primarily addressed to the Catholic community itself.

At the same time, however, debates external to the faith community about the role and rights of Catholic schools (and other forms of faith-based education) prompt fundamental questions about the nature of society. How does one protect the state from undue influence by religious bodies? How does one ensure even-handedness in addressing the needs of various minority groups? What degree of central support must there be for the cultural values that underpin any particular society? What kinds of trade-offs are necessary in promoting simultaneously social cohesion and high academic standards while securing the allegiance (including votes and taxes) of groups whose worldviews differ significantly from that of the majority of citizens? I contend that, if these kinds of questions within society in general are to be grappled with in any satisfactory manner, as part of defending and advancing the common good, their investigation will be enriched by an understanding of the issues I explore in this book. Debates within the Catholic educational community about the appropriate balance to be struck between distinctiveness and inclusiveness should be of interest to the wider community. They are also relevant to other faith communities who seek to situate themselves in society in a way that does justice to their own tradition and that encourages a constructive engagement in contemporary culture.

1.8   Angles of approach

From my opening remarks it should be apparent that this study investigates the implications of two, apparently conflicting, emphases within Catholicism for the educational arrangements of that particular faith community. In order to establish the foundations for, scope of and limitations on each of these two emphases – which I have called polarities – it is necessary to draw upon key aspects of the theological 'treasury' or tradition of Catholic Christianity. To assist me in demonstrating how central religious ideas relate to educational policy for a particular faith community, I bring together Christian (and more specifically Catholic) theology, philosophical analysis and educational theory and practice with regard to the *raison d'être* of Catholic schools.

At the same time, and to a much lesser degree, this book serves two purposes in addition to seeking to resolve a problematical issue in the rationale for Catholic education. First, it challenges Catholics to bring aspects other than education from their ecclesial and institutional life into harmony with both of the polarities described.   Second, it contributes to debates within the wider educational and political community about how to promote the common good in a pluralist society while drawing upon the resources and respecting the traditions of particular groups.

Chapter Two brings into sharper focus the two polarities within Catholic education, distinctiveness and inclusiveness. An ambivalence about the respective weight to be attributed to each of these polarities is highlighted and the different kinds of imbalance and distortion that follow from such ambivalence are indicated. In this chapter I suggest that the need to address the central question at stake here, whether or not Catholic education can justifiably claim to both distinctive *and* inclusive, is made more urgent by the operation of a world-wide phenomenon that I call the managerial imperative. Then, in order to clarify the gap in current literature that I am seeking to address, I situate my line of argument in relation to two important studies, one from the UK and one from the USA, claiming that each neglects (a different) one of the polarities.

Although the question under investigation here is of concern to Catholic educators all over the world, it is impossible within the bounds of one book to take into account the vastly different contexts in which they seek to implement universal principles. Chapter Three sets the wider question in the particular context of Catholic education in England and Wales. Despite the specificity of this context, with social, political and educational arrangements that are not duplicated everywhere, I believe that many of the features described, for example, factors for change, theological developments and the need for clarity about distinctiveness, are relevant wherever the endeavour of Catholic education is attempted. Readers from other countries will obviously bring to their interpretation of this chapter their knowledge of a range of different circumstances that surround Catholic schools, but they should recognise most of the issues explored here as having application elsewhere.

An extended commentary on key Roman documents about Catholic education is provided in Chapter Four. These authoritative guidance documents are intended to lay the foundations upon which any particular Catholic school – and school system – is built. Many Catholic educators seem unaware of the official 'story' that is meant to underpin the operation of their schools. How then, can they even begin to reflect it in their practice? Their own attempt, with all its particular difficulties and achievements, to live out the Gospel in the Catholic school context rarely informs the drawing up of official policy for such schools. This disconnection, between what I call (in Chapter Nine) 'promulgation' and 'reception', is itself an illustration of an imbalance between the polarities of distinctiveness and inclusiveness in Catholic education. As a step in my argument, this chapter seeks to clarify the constituent elements of the 'story' or theory that provides a conceptual framework for Catholic education. In order to bring out the essential interconnectedness of these key elements I use the example of a Catholic thinker, Friedrich von Hügel (1852 – 1925), whose work has rarely been related to education.

Chapter Five examines the worldview that underpins the guidance documents analysed in the previous chapter. By drawing attention especially to the role of religion in education and to a Catholic understanding of the human person, I bring into focus important aspects of the distinctive perspectives held by Catholic educators, perspectives that challenge – and, in turn, are challenged by – secular forms of education. The desire for separate schooling relies upon the distinctive worldview outlined in this chapter.

Having clarified the nature and importance of distinctiveness within Catholic education, I then turn my attention in Chapter Six to the other polarity, that of inclusiveness. The normative status of inclusiveness is explored, both from theological and from pedagogical perspectives. Possible constraints on inclusiveness are considered. This leads into some indications of what might be *excluded* within Catholic education.

Chapter Seven aims to retrieve the notion of 'living tradition' within Catholicism and to apply such a notion to the harmonious resolution of the apparent incompatibility between distinctiveness and inclusiveness. My argument is heavily dependent on an articulation of the thought of a figure whose work is almost totally unfamiliar to Catholic educators, one who made a major contribution to the reconstruction of Catholicism that took place during the twentieth century. This is Maurice Blondel (1861 – 1949). Because neither of the two principal writers whose thought I draw upon as vital intellectual resources for regenerating a rationale for Catholic education are well known to those working in that academic and professional field, let me here briefly introduce them.

It is perhaps no accident that there is a close connection between the two writers who have helped me, first, to cast light on how key elements in the philosophy of Catholic education might be held together (von Hügel) and, second, to retrieve the notion of living tradition (Blondel). Despite their very different temperaments and the significantly different contexts in which they worked, the two men were full of mutual admiration. Blondel was a professional philosopher in a strongly anti-clerical and sceptical secular university atmosphere, in a still predominantly Catholic France wracked by serious crisis in church-state relations. Von Hügel, on the other hand, wrote as an amateur autodidact freed from academic institutional ties, in the more liberal atmosphere of still securely Anglican England, where Catholics were in a tiny minority. They had much in common. The American historian Marvin O'Connell[41] suggests that:

> Both were extremely devout laymen of independent means, both tireless workers in their chosen fields of research, both alert to contemporary developments in history and science, and both dedicated to bringing traditional Catholic thought into line with the insights provided by modern scholarship. Both were unabashed elitists, who found it hard to function effectively outside a small circle of intimates. They even shared a finicky concern for their physical health that sometimes bordered on hypochondria.

Both suffered from their nervous disposition and also from the handicap of deafness, in the case of von Hügel, and of blindness, as he got older, in the case of Blondel. In their writings both were to leave behind a major legacy which those who came after them could draw upon. Yet each of them failed in his own lifetime to convince the primary target group whom he had set out to influence, in Blondel's case the secular university sector and in von Hügel's case, his fellow Catholics.

For a short period of time, during the first decade of the twentieth century, in the context of the modernist crisis that shook the Catholic church, each stimulated the other to articulate his thought more precisely and clearly. To this extent each was indebted to the other. The major influence, however, was undoubtedly Blondel, whose work had already made a big impression on von Hügel before he had published anything of significance.

Both writers enjoyed a renaissance of wider interest as the shadows cast by modernist crisis were gradually dispersed. Von Hügel's work was very much more appreciated and praised by Christians who came from outside his own denomination than from those within it (although he had his admirers and adherents there too). Blondel's work was taken up and discussed, both positively and negatively, much more by Catholic theologians, who were not his principal intended audience, than by secular philosophers, whom he had hoped to engage.

Despite the continuing stream of commentaries on and critical editions of Blondel's work which are published in Europe, scarcely any interest has been shown in him in either Britain or Australia, or in other English-speaking parts of the world, and relatively little in the USA. Almost all of his work remains untranslated from French. There is no major summary, presentation or analysis of the full range of Blondel's philosophical and religious thought available in English. Much of his voluminous output has long been unavailable even in French, although that is beginning to be rectified with the gradual publication of a critical edition of his work.[42] Even for native French speakers/readers, many find Blondel inaccessible because of the complexity of his arguments, the difficulty of his language and the frequently tortuous nature of his style. The position is further complicated by the fact that Blondel often wrote his more controversial (religious) works under a pseudonym, employing at different times eight such pseudonyms! Despite this obscurity, Blondel exerted considerable influence on the development of a Catholic understanding of tradition. This is not so strange an assertion when we acknowledge that almost none of the important architects of the church's re-thinking at the Second Vatican Council (with the exception of the longer-term influence of Newman) were English; they were either French or German. I indicate the extent of Blondel's influence in Chapter Seven (in the opening paragraph of section 7.3.).

In Chapter Eight I take into account some of the criticisms that have been levelled against separate Catholic schooling. Even if they were to satisfy their own faith community that justice can be done in school to the implications of a Catholic worldview and to the two polarities being examined here, some might argue that, on secular grounds, the cost is too high, that other social priorities are neglected. However, I contend that, far from being inward-looking and failing to concern themselves with the responsibilities of citizenship, Catholic schools both should, according to the logic of their own rationale and in practice do, contribute to the common good. The chapter presents a multi-strand defence of this claim that Catholic schools have a positive role to play in a pluralist society.

In the final chapter I summarise the main outcomes of the study, draw together different 'threads' of the argument and suggest how one might move beyond this work, either by further investigation or by more faithful and more creative application of the principles described here. Such creative fidelity would, of course, express and rely upon *both* the polarities under scrutiny in this book. It would be both distinctive *and* inclusive.

Notes for Chapter 1

1 In England and Wales, the launch of any major religious education programme for Catholic schools always seems surrounded by controversy and bitter accusations of either excessive accommodation and 'sellout' to contemporary culture or of a disregard for the real experience and the diverse needs of students.

² For sophisticated and balanced French and Belgian discussions on the relationship between a faith tradition and contemporary culture in the teaching of religion, see André Fossion, *La Cathéchèse dans le champ de la communication*, Paris, Cerf, 1990; Xavier Thevenot & Jean Joncheray, *Pour une éthique de la pratique éducative*, Paris, Desclee, 1991; Camille Focant (ed), *L'Enseignement de la religion au carrefour de la théologie et de la pédagogie*, Louvain-la-Neuve, 1994; Bernadette Wiame, *Pour une inculturation de l'enseignement religieux*, Brussels, Lumen Vitae, 1997. See also *International Journal of Education and Religion*, vol. 1 (1), 2000, which explores many of the challenges that multiculturalism and pluralism present for religiously affiliated schools and for religious education. Contributors to this issue come from the USA, The Netherlands, Germany, and the UK.

³ Jim Gallagher, *Soil for the Seed,* Great Wakering, McCrimmons, 2001, p.85.

4 Congregation for Institutes of Consecrated Life and for Societies of Apostolic Life, *Inter-Institute Collaboration for Formation*, Boston, Pauline Books, 1999, p.17.

5 For impressive attempts to relate Catholic Christianity to religious pluralism, see Michael Barnes, *Religions in Conversation*, London, SPCK, 1989; Jacques Dupuis, *Toward a Christian Theology of Religious Pluralism*, New York, Orbis, Books, 1999; and Joseph O'Leary, *Religious Pluralism and Christian Truth*, Edinburgh, Edinburgh University Press, 1996. On the relationship between Catholicism and liberalism, see R. Bruce Douglass and David Hollenbach (eds), *Catholicism and Liberalism*, Cambridge, Cambridge University Press, 1994; Kenneth Grasso, Gerard Bradley and Robert Hunt (eds), *Catholicism, Liberalism, & Communitarianism*, Lanham, Maryland, Rowman & Littlefield, 1995; Gene Burns, *The Frontiers of Catholicism*, Berkeley, University of California Press, 1992. From a different (Reformed) Christian tradition, see Richard Mouw and Sander Griffioen, *Pluralisms & Horizons*, Grand Rapids, Michigan, Eerdmans, 1993. See also Pierre Manent (translated by Marc LePain), *The City of Man*, Princeton University Press, 1998.

6 For an example of the first, see Fatima Mernissi, *Islam and Democracy*, London, Virago Press, 1993; for an example of the second, see Michael Rosenak, *Roads to the Palace*, (Jewish texts and teaching), Oxford, Berghahn, 1999.

7 See Michael Sandel, *Democracy's Discontent;* and Amy Gutmann and Dennis Thompson, *Democracy and disagreement*, (both Cambridge, Massachusetts, Harvard University Press, 1996.)

8 On these and related questions, see Robert Bellah (et al, eds), Habits of the Heart, London, Hutchinson, 1988; Bellah (et al, eds) *The Good Society*, New York, Vintage Books, 1991; E. F. Paul, F. Miller and J. Paul (eds), *The Communitarian Challenge to Liberalism*, Cambridge, Cambridge University Press, 1996.

9 Louis Porcher & Martine Abdallah-Pretceille, *Éthique de la diversité et éducation*, 1998 ; Henri Pena-Ruiz, *Dieu et Marianne: Philosophie de la laicité*, 1999; both Paris, Presses Universitaires de France.

10 On these issues, see Eamonn Callan, Creating Citizens, 1997; Meira Levinson, *The demands of liberal education*, 1999, both Oxford, Oxford University Press; James Dwyer, *Religious Schools V. Children's Rights*, Cornell University Press, 1998; James Fraser, *Between Church and State: Religion and Public Education in America*, New York, Macmillan Press, 1999.

11 Robert Audi, *Religious Commitment and Secular Reason*, Cambridge, Cambridge University Press, 2000, provides an important investigation into these issues. Signe Sandsmark, *Is World View Neutral Education Possible and Desirable?*, Paternoster Press, 2000 offers a Christian response (from a Lutheran perspective) to liberal arguments. On contemporary Church-State relationships in the domain of public service organisations, including faith-based schools in the USA, Germany and the Netherlands, see Charles Glenn, *The Ambiguous Embrace*, Princeton University Press, 2000. On reconciling universal and particular perspectives, see Thomas Green, *Walls: Education in*

Communities of Text and Liturgy, University of Notre Dame Press, 2002. Also on the role of religion in public education see Martin Marty, *Education, Religion and the Common Good*, San Francisco, Jossey-Bass, 2000; Stephen Webb, *Taking Religion To School*, Grand Rapids, Brazos, Press, 2000; Russell, McCutcheon, *Critics Not Caretakers*, New York, State University of New York Press, 2001.

12 Brian Stiltner, *Religion and the Common Good*, Lanham, Maryland, Rowman & Littlefield, 1999, p.11.

13 See Michael McGrath, *The Price of Faith: The Catholic Church and Catholic Schools in Northern Ireland*, Dublin, Irish Academic Press, 1999; Denis Carroll (ed), *Religion in Ireland: Past Present & Future*, Dublin, Columba Press, 1999.

14 Johannes Van der Ven, *Education for Reflective Ministry*, Louvain, Peeters, 1998, pp.26-7, 35.

15 Ibid., p.35.

16 Ibid., pp.12, 37.

17 On the importance of collective memory for religious communities, see Danièle Hervieu-Léger, *La Religion Pour Mémoire*, Paris, Cerf, 1993.

18 Herman Lombaerts, *The Management and Leadership of Christian Schools*, translated by Terry Collins, Groot Bijgaarden [Belgium], Vlaams Lassallianns Perspectief, 1998, p.14.

19 Ibid., pp.80-81.

20 Hervieu-Léger, op. cit., p.105.

21 Ibid., p.172.

22 On the need for Catholic schools to offer an alternative to predominant cultural norms, see Thomas Giardino in *Catholic School Leadership*, edited by Thomas Hunt, Thomas Oldenski and Theodore Wallace, London, Falmer Press, 2000, p.28. James Heft in the same collection (p.212), says: 'ultimately, the leaders of Catholic schools, colleges and universities should never desire that their graduates simply "fit into" society but rather that they should help transform it.'

23 Thomas Hunt, Thomas Oldenski and Theodore Wallace, ibid., p.2.

24 Robert McLaughlin, in *The Common Things*, edited by Daniel McInerny, American Maritain Association, The Catholic University of America, 1999, pp.102-117, especially pp.107, 109, 115. For debates about Catholic Higher Education, see, in addition to McInerny, John Paul II, *Ex Corde Ecclesiae*, 1990; Philip Gleason, *Contending With Modernity*, New York, Oxford University Press, 1995; Michael Buckley, *The Promise and Project of the Catholic University*, Washington DC, Georgetown University Press, 1999; Christopher Janosik, 'Catholic Identity in Catholic Higher Education,' *Catholic Education*, 3 (1), September 1999; William Shea, *Trying Times*, Atlanta, Scholars Press, 1999 and Alice Gallin, *Negotiating Identity*, University of Notre Dame Press, 2000; John Wilcox and Irene King (eds), Enhancing Religious Identity, Washington DC, Georgetown University Press, 2000.

25 Denis McLaughlin, *The Catholic School: Paradoxes and Challenges*, Strathfield, NSW, St Pauls Publications, 2000, p.36. For an assessment of past achievement and tasks ahead for Catholic schools in Australia, see John McMahon, Helga Neidhart & Judith Chapman (eds), *Leading the Catholic School*, Richmond, Victoria, Spectum Publications, 1997 and Ross Keane & Dan Riley (eds), *Quality Catholic Schools*, Archdiocese of Brisbane, 1997.

26 Denis McLaughlin, [quoting Murphy], op.cit., p.37.

27 Ibid., pp.69-70.

28 V. A. McClelland, as quoted by McLaughlin, op. cit., p.70.

29 For assessments of recent difficulties and progress and of choices to be made and priorities to be addressed in US Catholic schools, see James Youniss and John Convey, *Catholic Schools at the Crossroads*, New York, Teachers College Press, 1999; Youniss, Convey and McLellan (eds), *The Catholic Character of Catholic Schools*, University of Notre Dame Press, 2000; Thomas Hunt, Thomas Oldenski and Theodore Wallace (eds), *Catholic School Leadership*, London, Falmer Press, 2000.

30 Chester Gillis, *Roman Catholicism in America*, New York, Columbia University Press, 1999, p.261.

31 Ibid., p.264.

32 Alexandra Klaushofer, quoting Charles Taylor in 'Faith Beyond Nihilism: The Retrieval of Theism in Milbank and Taylor', *The Heythrop Journal*, vol. 40, no. 2, April 1999, p.142.

33 Padraig Hogan, 'Europe and the World of Learning: Orthodoxy and Aspiration in the Wake of Modernity', *Journal of Philosophy of Education*, 32, (3), 1998, p.362.

34 Ibid., p.367.

35 The need for such a re-articulation of the rationale for Catholic education is highlighted by William Losito in Hunt (2000, p.59). "There is no community of Catholic intellectuals pursuing a coherent agenda of inquiry to serve as a significant resource for educational leaders who are grappling with the formulation of a sacred vision for education in a secular, pluralistic society." Losito also laments (p.60) the failure to engage in a sustained dialogue about the content of the guidance documents on education that have been issued by Rome in the thirty-five years since closure of the Second Vatican Council.   An important exception to this lack of engagement is Gini Shimabukuro.   See Shimabukuro, *A Call to Reflection: A Teacher's Guide to Catholic Identity for the 21st Century*, Washington, DC, The National Catholic Educational Association, 1998.

36 Charles Taylor, in *A Catholic Modernity?* edited by James Heft, New York, Oxford University Press, 1999, p.14.

37 Ibid.

38 Shea, ibid., pp.43-44.

39 Ibid., p.55.

40 Ibid., p.57.

41 Marvin O'Connell, *Critics on Trial: An Introduction to the Catholic Modernist Crisis*, Washington, D.C., Catholic University of America Press, 1994, pp.155-6.

42 By Presses Universitaires de France, Paris, from 1995 onwards.   The first two of nine projected volumes have appeared so far.

CHAPTER 2

DISTINCTIVENESS AND INCLUSIVENESS:
INCOMPATIBILITY OR CREATIVE TENSION?

In bringing into a sharper focus the two polarities sketched out in Chapter One, I shall concentrate on Catholic schooling in the public sector. This means that I omit treatment of those contexts other than schooling which also provide opportunities for educating Catholics in their faith. Among these might be included sermons, liturgy, missions, catechesis, sodalities, sacramental participation, religious literature, pilgrimages, scripture study and other forms of adult and higher education. The crucial roles of the family and the parish in Catholic education are not addressed. I concentrate my attention on 'ordered learning' in formal educational settings, rather than the Catholic community's total range of processes for education and formation in faith, without assuming that my area of focus is either the most important or the most effective element within those processes. Such ordered learning is central to, but smaller in scope than, the faith community's total formative process.

More particularly still, in focusing on Catholic schooling I do not explore whether the Church should have alternative strategies for carrying out its educational mission nor whether current structures are the most appropriate ones for this purpose. The study *is* intended to be normative for Catholic education, but not in either of these ways, nor in terms of particular details of content; instead its prescriptiveness relates to the principles which should govern, guide and permeate Catholic schooling as a whole.

Among these principles an insufficiently acknowledged ambivalence is identified, one which is of major significance for the practice of Catholic education in the school context. In addressing this ambivalence in the following chapters, I draw upon historical studies of Catholic schooling in England and Wales, engage with recent philosophical analysis of educational issues and concepts which are relevant to the main question being posed here and examine the theoretical 'story' of Catholic education in the light of its potential internal contradictions, its practical implications and in the face of some criticisms which have been levelled against it. My aim is to articulate the tension between two particular, apparently contrasting, imperatives within Catholic education and then to suggest a way to reduce, if not entirely to resolve, the tension between them.

As part of this process, I also refer to theological developments within Catholicism and that for two reasons: first, because they constitute one of the factors influencing the changing context in which Catholic education is set and second, because they cast light on the foundational principles which govern Catholic education. It is beyond my scope to seek to *justify* these theological elements; my task is rather to establish the *bearing* they have on Catholic education. I do not seek to be comprehensive in my treatment of Catholic theology. Instead I restrict myself to those elements that are relevant to the framing, and, I hope, at least to the partial resolution, of the central issue at stake in this book - the relationship between distinctiveness and inclusiveness in Catholic education.

Catholic schools, funded jointly by the church and the state, represent approximately 10% of the total number of maintained schools in England and Wales. [1] Despite their current healthy attendance figures, popularity with parents and record of securing a very high incidence of positive inspection reports,[2] I believe that Catholic schools may well be weakened, both in the effective implementation of their mission and in their self-advocacy, by a failure to acknowledge and to resolve an internal ambivalence in their philosophy and purposes. This leads to confusion about the goals of Catholic schools and to lack of clarity when dealing with criticisms of them. Such confusion and incapacity to respond adequately to criticism, either from within or from beyond the church, applies, I believe, to varying degrees, in most countries where Catholic schools have been established.

The worldview underpinning Catholic education in any country and the key concepts that mark out its central features are drawn from a Catholic community that is universal, as well as from local interpretations which operate at both national and diocesan levels. Therefore I draw upon relevant authoritative Catholic educational literature, both from Rome, intended to guide the universal church, as well as material from the Conference of Catholic Bishops in England and Wales, applying central guidance to one particular national context. Unless I indicate to the contrary, I shall refer most frequently to this English and Welsh context.

In this chapter four steps are taken. First, two imperatives in Catholic education, to be distinctive and to be inclusive, are brought into focus and the problematical nature of their relationship is indicated. Second, a feature of the educational scene external to Catholicism is described and it is suggested that this feature both highlights and compounds the unresolved tension between distinctiveness and inclusiveness within Catholic schools. This feature I call 'managerialism'. As part of my critique of managerialism, I emphasise the central importance for education of some overarching 'story', which gives it a sense of direction and guiding values. Third, in building on the Catholic 'story,' I signal my employment, later on in this book, of the notion of 'living tradition' as a possible way of resolving the tension between distinctiveness and inclusiveness. Fourth, two contrasting responses to the current condition of Catholic education are considered in order to clarify further the parameters of the problem being addressed and the stand-point being adopted here. Each response, in different ways, highlights the need for greater clarity about both distinctiveness and inclusiveness and a better understanding of how these two imperatives are interconnected.

2.1   Two imperatives

What is the central problem to be addressed here? It arises from two apparently conflicting imperatives within Catholicism. On the one hand, the mission of the Church is to transmit something distinctive, a divinely sanctioned message for life (and eternal life). This imperative has overtones of the prophetic stance, of transcendence, of teaching with authority, of conveying truth in its comprehensiveness and without compromise. It suggests the notions of boundaries to be protected and of 'wine' to be preserved. The value of the 'currency' of Catholic doctrine is to be guarded by vigilant oversight of all 'issues' or pronouncements on behalf of the Church. This is to ensure that justice is done to the message to be conveyed. The purity and efficacy of the 'medicine' of salvation available through the Church needs to be relied upon by whoever avails themselves of it. Strong border controls and customs stations are to be maintained to prevent contamination from alien ideas which might be corrosive of truth and to assess carefully 'foreign imports' for their likely 'impact' on the 'economy' of the faith and the lives of the faithful.

On the other hand, an equally important imperative for Catholicism is to be fully inclusive, to be open to all types of people and to all sources of truth. The gospel to be offered is not only to be addressed *to* all people, which might simply require an unwavering and consistent effort to proclaim the message. It is also - and this is crucial for my argument - *for* all people and must take into account their differing situations and experiences, their insights and perplexities, their challenges and needs, their hopes and fears. [3] The salvific power of the message to be conveyed depends not only on its authoritative source, its accurate and comprehensive transmission, and due respect for its distinctive nature. It also relies on its capacity to embrace the concerns, to meet the needs and to address the perspectives of all God's people, in a way that is open to and inclusive of the diversity of their circumstances and cultures.

This second imperative implies or emphasises pastoral care, immanence, learning by listening, receptivity and accommodation, flexibility in the face of historical and cultural change and of vulnerability.[4] It seeks to avoid a fearful isolation from others and to encourage a full-hearted collaboration with them wherever possible and an involvement in the world rather than a retreat from it. This aspect of Catholicism acknowledges its own shortcomings, mistakes and sinfulness, its pilgrim status of still being 'on the way' and therefore its incompleteness, and, in parallel with this, it seeks to be attentive to the workings of the Holy Spirit beyond its 'borders'. As a result, it embraces liturgical variety, welcomes cultural pluralism, seeks harmony between different perspectives, recognises the spiritual truths and values inherent in other Christians and in other religions and encourages free and constructive dialogue with people of other persuasions. If these goods are to be secured, then defenders of distinctiveness and guardians of orthodoxy must allow easy access to and for 'outsiders' and should seek neither to inhibit the exchange of ideas and experiences, nor to obstruct joint endeavours between Catholics and others.

These two imperatives do not sit easily together. The differing ways they coexist and interpenetrate one another and are expressed in the precepts and policies of Catholic educators have great significance for Catholics and for others in society. The degree of success with which they are held in balance will influence the acceptability of Catholic schools in a plural, mainly non-religious society. This balance is not easy to maintain. At times one imperative may appear to dominate Catholic educational thinking and practice, to the detriment of the other.

Where distinctiveness is emphasised, the integrity of faith is at stake. Catholic schools must endeavour to pass on the fullness of the faith. An undue willingness to be inclusive in the sense of accommodating the perspectives and priorities of those who cannot accept the message in its entirety might lead to a distortion of truth and a fateful damaging of the salvation prospects of those pupils who have been included but misled. Where inclusiveness is stressed, the welcoming nature of faith is at issue. In Catholic schools the particular (and diverse) academic, social, spiritual and other needs of pupils are to be addressed, regardless of their relationship to Catholicism. If too strong a priority is given to defending the distinctiveness of Catholicism, (and following from this, the distinctiveness of Catholic education,) there is a danger of exhibiting undesirable features, such as exclusiveness, rigidity, closed mindedness, intolerance, excessive confidence that truth is already fully possessed, and therefore of displaying an unwillingness to learn from others.

The two imperatives should be seen as complementary rather than in contradiction to one another. Instead of considering inclusiveness as something to be set against distinctiveness within Catholic education, one might claim that two kinds of distinctiveness are to be (simultaneously) of concern. The first is the distinctiveness of the Catholic tradition, which is to be maintained and communicated. The second is the distinctiveness (in the sense of the uniqueness and incommunicability) of each person (pupils, their families and staff) who comes into contact with Catholic schools. This second aspect of distinctiveness, being sensitive to the particularity of each person and being willing to welcome them and learn from them, should receive a high priority in Catholic education, not only because of respect for human dignity, but also because, in terms of their own theology, Catholics acknowledge God's presence *in* their pupils.[5] This way of considering the two imperatives only relocates the problematical nature of their relationship; it does not dissolve it. I shall therefore continue to refer to the polarity in the terms 'distinctive' and 'inclusive'.

Furthermore, from the point of view of the teaching act, communication and receptivity, like distinctiveness and inclusiveness, are correlative terms: one implies the other. We can distinguish, logically, if not chronologically, two phases in this correlation. First, as a teacher, my communication requires not only clarity about something distinctive and particular on my part, but also a receptivity from others, an openness on the part of my pupils. This is one aspect of their correlation. But, second, if my communication is to be effective, I must be receptive to their situation and perceptions and I must attend to their communication with me. In the context of Catholic education, no awareness of distinctiveness is possible without awareness of difference, and no possibility of inclusiveness remains without there being a distinct body (of people and truth) to which one can belong and by which one can be included.

Although the problematic nature of the relationship between distinctiveness and inclusiveness arises internally, from within Catholicism, issues external to that faith exert considerable influence on the unstable tension between these imperatives. These issues provide part of the context for this work. They challenge Catholic education with a new and particularly sharp voice. But they also reveal in an interesting way that there are resources for education from within the Catholic 'story' that may be relevant to others.

2.2   The managerial imperative

In what follows I describe a problem that I believe is widespread in education and then suggest that it has particular relevance to my attempt here to resolve the tensions within Catholic education already indicated. In my work as an educational management consultant I have come to recognise more and more keenly the defects of 'managerialism' and the dangers posed for schools by too ready an adoption of the managerial imperative. What are these defects? Much of the managerial literature aimed at improving educational practice seems to display a universalism which is blind to cultural differences, curriculum specialisms, the climate of particular communities and the role of traditions as foundations for identity and our outlook on the world.[6] Such standardisation diminishes education, rather than enhances it. Atomistic objectives and competencies are described without reference to the perspectives and passions of the people involved.[7] A false sense of certainty and the dangerous illusion of control is hinted at as the desired outcomes if the relevant competencies are developed. In reality, there are so many variables involved in education that, no matter how confident a teacher is in employing a range of techniques, she can never claim predictive powers with regard to their effects with any particular group of pupils. This would not allow for a free response on their part. The ambiguity, complexity, particularity, creativity, unpredictability, open-endedness and essentially personal dimensions of educational practice can soon be lost sight of when too strong an emphasis is laid on 'managing' education.[8] In the industrial model of school, alongside line management and total quality control,

> budgets are kept and scrutinised by accountants, press officers try to ensure a positive public image, and performance indicators are put in place to monitor output variables. Above all, there is concern that the product, that is the student, should be delivered effectively and efficiently in accordance with the requirements of the various customers, for example, employers, government, further and higher education.[9]

This is not to reject the important part that sound management can play in education.

Pupils and teachers can benefit enormously from effective management and they suffer greatly in its absence. Many of the skills outlined in educational management literature, if sensitively employed with intelligent attention to context and to purpose, do enhance the quality of learning and assist in harnessing the talents of each for the good of all. But too great a readiness to map out performance indicators, programmes of study, attainment targets, development plans, and the scaffolding of competencies required at various stages throughout the teaching profession[10] can lead to specifications which are too elaborate, leave too little to chance, reduce the possibility of appropriate reciprocity and interaction between teachers and learners and slip too easily into conceiving of education as a technique requiring merely one-way transmission. [11] The outcomes of educational exchanges are essentially unpredictable and unamenable to control, even at the same time as teachers intend them to be purposeful, orderly and carefully structured.[12]

One of the features of the managerial movement within education is an emphasis on accountability, which requires continuous monitoring and regular evaluation. These practices are likely to become much attenuated if they are part of a managerialism which is insufficiently informed by a carefully thought through educational philosophy and ethic, (which includes, for example, a view of the human person, society, well-being, education and relationships). Lacking such a foundation, the practice of monitoring can very easily slip into increased surveillance for increased compliance and evaluation can be reduced to counting what is easily measurable. The attempt to increase control through the practices (and associated external agencies) of monitoring and evaluation is likely to induce fear and resistance on the part of both teachers and students.

Furthermore I think that educators who accept too readily the managerial approach seek to reach certainty about those short - and medium -term outcomes which are amenable to objective measurement. This is to seek certainty at the wrong 'end' of education, for reasons I have given already. It would be better, I believe, to look for certainty at the beginning of our endeavours, to aim for greater clarity about our purposes in education and those beliefs and values which frame the whole process for us.

Two caveats are necessary here. First, I accept that workable 'visions' for education only emerge in the light of a considerable degree of trial and error. I become clearer about what I am trying to do as a result of both successful and unsuccessful practice, in dealing with difficulties and in the midst of encountering misunderstanding and opposition. My emphasis on clarity about purpose rather than outcomes is then more a matter of the degree of priority to be accorded to principles and aims. These are by their nature rather general and elusive. It can be too readily assumed that they are both understood and accepted, leading too swiftly to a concentration on apparently more concrete and measurable behavioural outcomes as indicators of progress. Judgements about pupil achievement, teacher performance, the quality of a course, the effectiveness of a policy or the value added by a school cannot be reached without a proper weighing of the aims and purposes of the people involved, and with regard to these aims and purposes, their grounding, worth and coherence.

Second, I accept that teachers should seek an objective view of the effectiveness of their efforts, the curriculum and the school as a whole, insofar as this is possible. However, monitoring and evaluation, like other 'tools' of management, should serve, rather than obscure, a larger vision and purpose which is at the heart of the educational endeavour.

From my own observations I would claim that Catholic schools probably suffer as much as other schools from these defects of managerialism. Furthermore, I believe that the potential for managerialism to damage education is strengthened in a context, like that of a church school, which gives high priority to a mission statement and which heavily underlines the legitimacy of authority (divine, scriptural, ecclesial). [13] In such a context it is often too readily presumed, and with insufficient warrant, that certain ideals are shared and a particular code of behaviour accepted. [14] After a Headteacher has been appointed by school governors, there can be a temptation to confuse the general mandate to lead with his or her personal vision of Catholic education for this particular school. Sometimes the comment that 'this is a Catholic school' precludes debate and gives the impression that the essence of Catholicism is uncontested by Catholics themselves and that the application of Catholic beliefs to the practice of education is straightforward.

In his analysis of 'mission' in organisations generally, Pattison considers its connotations of higher purposes, of obedience to superiors, of urgency, and of implementation being both inexorable and costly. While the notion has galvanising power, it is also open to defective interpretations.

> Mission may appear to justify narrowness, imperialism, conquest, and changing others and the world rather than living alongside them. The implicit radical, invasive, sectarian, dualistic overtones of this concept may energise outreach at the expense of seeing people outside the organisation as 'objects' to be saved.[15]

If employed in this way, the concept is liable to support a drive for distinctiveness which, in failing to attend to the particular circumstances and needs of individuals, is insufficiently inclusive. Catholic schools, which by their nature are more liable than many to the use of the language of 'mission', need to guard against these dangers.

For a variety of reasons, which are explored later, many teachers who work in Catholic schools do not have a clear view of Catholicism. As a result they lack any distinctive vision of Catholic education. This makes some aspects of school evaluation especially perplexing or even burdensome for them, at the same time as it makes more complex the task of Catholic school management and leadership. All teachers are subject to scrutiny and pressure through appraisal, inspection and league tables based on pupil performance. [16] In Catholic schools they are also inspected by diocesan-approved officers who report on the quality of the school as a Catholic community. This inspection assesses the degree to which the school mission is being implemented, as shown by religious teaching, worship, permeation of Catholicism through the curriculum and school life and community relations. Furthermore, there are additional expectations as regards their own example as teachers. In these circumstances it is not surprising that some teachers in Catholic schools perceive the recent emphasis on monitoring, evaluation and school review as a form of increased surveillance for increased compliance.

Yet, when they are set in a larger context of long-term goals, pervading values and well-founded principles, some of the strategies employed in school management can be freed from the manipulative functions to which they are prone. Neil Postman recently advocated a return to the 'metaphysical' rather than the 'engineering' aspects of education, that is answers to the question 'why?' have priority over 'how?'[17] Postman argues that education flourishes best when it is sustained by an overarching narrative, a story that "tells of origins and envisions a future, a story that constructs ideals, prescribes rules of conduct, provides a source of authority, and, above all, gives a sense of continuity and purpose."[18] This kind of narrative must have "sufficient credibility, complexity and symbolic power" to enable those who rely on it to organize their lives around it.[19] Such a story will "give point to our labours, exalt our history, elucidate the present, and give direction to our future."[20]

Postman reiterates my concern that education under the sway of managerialism is in danger of seeking to *control* the process of learning, but with no worthy end in view. If schools are to be important sites for education, what goes on there must engage our attention, arouse our interest, capture our energies and direct our efforts. For this to occur, education must serve non-trivial ends and offer a god or gods who call us to give ourselves fully to a larger, worthy purpose. In this process our lives will not be confined or diminished but liberated and enhanced. Those who start the educational journey with ends in mind, can also demonstrate flexibility about routes and allow for detours, backtracking, starting again and changing direction.

Postman's primary aim is not to justify or to demonstrate the coherence of a particular narrative but to emphasise that any enduring educational endeavour needs to draw upon a comprehensive and powerfully illuminating and motivating 'story'.[21] This 'story' will be 'foundational'. That is, it will provide key concepts, goals, metaphors and values for the conduct of education. However, it is not to be held uncritically, nor is it unrevisable. Indeed the best of stories will have the capacity to cope with criticism, revision and constant adaptation to changing circumstances. Neither the basis nor the plausibility of Postman's thesis rest upon religious assumptions. He proposes several stories or myths as frameworks for education (for example, democracy, America, multiculturalism and spaceship earth). Many of them are held much more lightly than are the key narratives of any particular religion. By comparison with these, Postman's myths make fewer demands and they are more vulnerable to modification and even jettisoning, if they no longer serve their purpose. His proposals are intended to prompt us to relate education to our greatest purposes and priorities in life.

Such a desire is of course not new. Indeed it is a traditional view of both education in particular and of society in general that there is need of "some higher spiritual principle of co-ordination to overcome the conflicts between power and morality, between reason and appetite, between technology and humanity and between self-interest and the common good."[22] But it is a view that has been considered outmoded for some time in mainstream educational thinking. This is due to it being seen as connected too closely with discredited religious world-views, which no longer command allegiance, and also because education is seen as having internal aims, rather than as serving extrinsic purposes. In an increasingly plural and secular society it is not surprising that discussion of education policy becomes detached from particular narratives which might hold the allegiance of only a minority of citizens and appeals more and more to general procedural (rather than to substantive) principles. With the failure of the Enlightenment project to deliver all that was expected of it in terms of rationality, autonomy and well-being, and with a re-appraisal of the limits of individualism, the need for community, the foundations of reason and shortcomings of materialism, this traditional view of the centrality of narrative is once again considered worthy of serious attention.[23] While I acknowledge that the diverse forms of post-modern critique which follow the supposed failure of the Enlightenment project call into question the possibility of such narratives, for the purposes of this argument I assume that such critiques can be met.[24]

The term 'narrative' here is being used in a special sense. The focus is less on the chronological ordering of events which make up a 'story' and more on the ordering of lives which can follow from adopting the 'story' as a guide for life. A story can structure our priorities, elicit our energies, sustain our efforts in the face of difficulties and encourage us to co-operate with others who share its vision of embodied ideals. In this sense the story is normative. It tells us how things *should* be, rather than how they *have* been. Even when the story appears to be based on the past, for example, a divine revelation or a salvific event, its significance for those who adhere to it is its promise for the future.[25] This kind of story is meant to provide us with a vision towards which we can strive.

One of the characteristics of leadership, as distinguished from management, is the presence of such vision and the capacity to inspire others to engage with it. If the possessors of a vision seek to prescribe too closely the details of the route to be taken, rather than to inspire others to make the journey towards the ends held up before them, they slip into managerialism. In seeking such a level of control, they betray a lack of trust in others and in the intrinsic attractiveness of the goal.

2.3   *Resolving the tension through living tradition*

I have made two main points so far. First, Catholic education needs to resolve the in-built tension between the claims to distinctiveness and inclusiveness. Perhaps this is a task that faces each generation, for with any fresh interpretation of her distinctive identity, the church needs a corresponding re-evaluation of what inclusiveness entails. In arriving at this sense of distinctive identity the church has to review, not only her own constituent 'elements' and principles, but also how these differ from and relate to alternative perspectives on offer 'from outside' her own ranks. Therefore, an understanding of inclusiveness is inevitably affected by any modified sense of distinctiveness.[26]

Second, the tension between distinctiveness and inclusiveness is highlighted and compounded by developments outside Catholic education, within what I have called the managerial imperative. In describing this imperative I have noted both negative and positive features. One should be aware of the danger of seeking excessive control, which squeezes the life from teaching and learning. At the same time, there is a need for the provision of visionary leadership set in the context of some overarching 'story' or rationale for education.

Managerialism challenges Catholic educators in four ways. First it tempts them to import into schools priorities (for example, concern for their market position and success in narrowly prescribed league tables) and modes of working (for example, enforced compliance and alignment within the school as an organization and 'zero tolerance' of failure) which sit uneasily with, even when they do not directly contradict, key features of Catholic education. Second, by pressurising school leaders to establish ever-increasing levels of control over key aspects of teaching and learning, it further underlines the dangers of a one-sided emphasis on distinctiveness within the context of Catholic education. Without an adequate emphasis on inclusiveness, new control mechanisms in the service of an authoritative, universal and unavoidable mission can become overbearing and pay too little attention to local realities and needs. Third, the lack that I have indicated within managerialism, of an adequate 'story' with which to frame and give purpose to schooling, should prompt Catholic educators to re-present their own account of the nature and purpose of education as an important resource for rectifying the shortcomings of managerialism. Fourth, it might be claimed more generally that managerialism, as a development which faces all schools, brings out more sharply an already existing tension in Catholic education and that an acknowledgement of its defects has implications for how this tension might be addressed.

The way I seek to resolve this tension, both as it arises from within Catholic education and as it is expressed in the context of the managerial imperative, is through a retrieval of the notion of living tradition. Much more will said about this in chapter seven. Here I merely sketch out a simplified overview of the relevance of living tradition to the issues already raised.

Liberal education gives a very high priority to the promotion of autonomy and to freeing students from the constraints of ignorance, prejudice and superstition.[27] It seeks to maximise the exercise of liberty by promoting sufficient levels of rationality among the population to enable them to choose their own projects in life. At the same time it seeks to minimise the possibility of any interference (for example, by parents, traditions or authority figures) in the individual's identification and pursuit of the good. A defect of liberal education is that it has neglected the role of tradition in the formation of both personal identity and of the community, so that its teaching of concepts, skills and attitudes is insufficiently embedded in a tradition and inadequately illuminated by a comprehensively developed 'story'. If education is set in the context of a tradition and a 'story' then schools are enabled to function as 'constitutive' communities.[28] The upshot of Postman's argument, outlined above, is that schools need to find an appropriate comprehensive narrative which can direct their work. But a defect in emphasising tradition *per se* is that it can become backward-looking, closed, authoritarian, demanding conformity and cramping creativity. Traditionalists can be so assured of possessing the truth that their communication becomes one-way, concentrating on transmission and neglecting reception.[29] In this way active learning is discouraged and the tradition is no longer living.

A focus on 'living' tradition draws on the strengths of tradition but avoids its limitations by being open to new questions and perspectives, attentive to the needs, insights and potential contributions of people within and beyond the church. To focus on 'living' tradition allows for a two-way transformation in communication: it brings tradition to bear on us so that we hear its challenge to change in the light of its ideals; it also allows the tradition to be transformed by our questions, insights and experiences. A retrieval of living tradition should leave room for both critical solidarity and critical openness. Critical solidarity *with* tradition fosters a sense of belonging, commitment and distinctiveness. Critical openness *from* tradition facilitates openness and inclusiveness. Critical openness can also be reflexively directed back *at* tradition.

But how open can a tradition, such as Catholicism, afford to be, without losing essential features? John Courtney Murray, who might arguably be considered a principal architect of the modern Roman Catholic church's positive response to western democracy,[30] asked a similar question about the 'open society' in 1960:

> how open can it afford to be, and still remain a society; how many barbarians can it tolerate, and still remain civil; how many "idiots" can it include (in the classical Greek sense of the "private person" who does not share in the public thought of the City), and still have a public life; how many idioms, alien to one another, can it admit and still allow the possibility of civil conversation?[31]

Clearly there is within Catholicism a distinctive tradition (vis-a-vis other Christian denominations) which includes canon law, liturgy, spirituality, ecclesiology, doctrine, morality and sacramentality. History, continuity and authority are emphasised. There also coexist within Catholicism elements of diversity with regard to spirituality, ecclesial organization, inculturation and teaching about the Holy Spirit leading us more fully into truth and breaking through our human barriers and categories. However, flexibility, accommodation and reinterpretation run the risk of dissolving distinctiveness and identity. How far can the 'external protections' and permissions provided by a liberal society be applied internally (within the church generally and within church schools in particular) without serious loss?[32] As Eamonn Callan points out,

> parents who feel alienated on religious grounds from the public culture of their society may view with something akin to terror the possibility that their children will come to identify with that culture, because in so doing they could no longer share a way of life with their children that is for them a precondition of intimacy....The influences they seek to shield their children from are influences they shun themselves as a threat to the only life worth living.[33]

Equally important, how far (within Catholic education) may internal restrictions (for example, relating to pupil admissions, staff appointments and promotion, curriculum content, or constraints on criticism, debate or behaviour) be imposed in the interests of maintaining a way of life in its integrity without contradicting the very ethos being espoused?

The key question being addressed here is: can Catholic education combine distinctiveness with inclusiveness? And, if it can, what qualifications on this combination might be required to ensure, on the one hand, that its distinctiveness does not harden into exclusiveness or an overbearing prescriptiveness, and, on the other hand, that its inclusiveness and openness do not slip into emptiness or dissolution?[34]

Furthermore, I believe that this key question is being asked at a transitional period in the church's self-understanding. Internal rethinking and external pressures, taken together, prompt the church to review several features of its life. These include its understanding and exercise of authority, the need for dialogue with 'outsiders', the dangers of excessive control and the conditions for 'reception' of truth and for internalisation of values. They also include the relationship between faith and culture, and the application of moral teaching to its own institutions as well as the relevance of Catholic social teaching for society at large. One might claim that what I have called a transitional moment in the church's self-understanding is equivalent in importance to MacIntyre's notion of an 'epistemological crisis'.[35] In a recent collection of essays on the contemporary Catholic school Paul Hypher brings out something of this transitional moment. "Catholic schools founded with one set of objectives are now being required to adapt to newer objectives relating to openness, dialogue, mission, other faiths, option for the poor, racism and religious freedom, while at the same time remaining true to their original purpose."[36] In the re-thinking required by this transitional moment, it is possible that certain aspects of the Catholic tradition can be shown to have relevance beyond that specific faith community. Among these features might be a coherent worldview, strongly articulated moral values, a compelling and realistic vision of integral human development and a powerful sense of community, together with ways of balancing its benefits and burdens.

In order to address the needs arising from this transitional moment, I will attempt to provide (in chapters four and five) an account of the Roman Catholic 'story' in relation to education. This will serve as some form of equivalent to Postman's plea for a metanarrative governing education, specifically here for Catholic schools. This metanarrative cannot, without loss of continuity with tradition, be entirely or even substantially new. But by keeping in mind the tension between distinctiveness and inclusiveness, I hope to *re-present* the tradition in such a way as to reduce the ambivalence I referred to in section 2.1.

Then I will unpack some of the implications of this metanarrative for those who work in Catholic schools (in chapters six and seven) and for society as a whole (in chapter eight). In doing so I hope to show some progress in addressing what McLaughlin has identified as "the lack of a coherent modern statement of a Catholic philosophy of education which deprives the Catholic educational community of important resources with which to confront questions of distinctiveness."[37] During the process of developing my central argument about the ultimate coherence of the two polarities constantly at work in Catholic education, I hope to illustrate one particular moment in the developing relationship between a substantive faith community (Roman Catholicism) and liberalism. The steps in the argument, together with some of the key concepts employed, can also serve to highlight some aspects of the thinking required for the ongoing task of inculturation faced by that community.

2.4.1. *Entering the conversation : between Arthur and Bryk*
The nature, purpose and standpoint of my argument can be clarified further by relating it to two contrasting responses to the condition of Catholic education. These responses are to be found in two substantial recent studies. The first of these is *The Ebbing Tide* by James Arthur.[38] The book focuses on major issues of policy and practice for Roman Catholic education in England and Wales in the period 1960-90. Arthur provides a very clear and helpful historical background to these issues, which include concerns about curriculum, pupil admissions, staffing and control. The context in which Catholic education developed in this country and the goals it has pursued both before and since the Second Vatican Council (1962-65) are set forth in a balanced and well-argued manner. He gives a detailed outline of government education policies and a lively and penetrating, if somewhat jaundiced, analysis of the response of the Catholic bishops. Rather more controversially, he posits various models of Catholic schooling, which serve to demonstrate to his satisfaction the stages along which Catholic education has been eroded, even betrayed, albeit unintentionally and unwittingly. In the terms of my argument, Arthur's case might be that distinctiveness has been sacrificed in the interests of (a false understanding of) inclusiveness.

Arthur's main points can be summarised as follows. The Catholic bishops have concentrated their energies more on quantitative than qualitative issues regarding Catholic education, that is on the provision of sufficient places rather than on maintaining distinctiveness. (p.2) An inadequate response to government education policies on their part has meant that "it is difficult to implement the 'official' principles of Catholic education." (p.2.)[39] The overlap and distinction in structures (diocesan, religious orders, national) for Catholic education [40] "do not easily lend themselves to long-term decision-making." (p.161.) As a result, the "Catholic voice in education is neither united nor coherent." (p.167.) In the vacuum left by the overall failure of the bishops to address adequately issues of curriculum, admissions, staffing and control, many Catholic schools "have pursued a line of development which is not in harmony with their founding principles" and they have "lost sight of the Christian principles which support the ideals of Catholic education." (p.225.) Alongside the weakening in practice of Catholic education, there has been a "conspicuous lack of reflection on the goals which underpin the Catholic school system. Educational philosophy, psychology, management, curriculum theory and policy studies have all developed in the mainstream of educational research, to the neglect of the Catholic dimension in education." (p.247.)

A major implication of Arthur's thesis is that, in the integration of faith and culture, which is at the heart of Catholic education, faith has been subordinated to the priorities of a secular culture. This weakening of the Catholic dimension is shown, for example, by inadequate attention to mission statements, by a patchy and unconvincing use of professional development days to address issues of ethos and by a failure to permeate the curriculum with Catholic principles.[41] I believe that this part of Arthur's thesis is accurate, although it would be unjust to accuse all Catholic schools of these shortcomings; many have struggled heroically on one or more of these areas. It is certainly fair to claim that many staff (including many of those who are personally committed to Catholicism) find it very difficult to articulate either a general rationale for Catholic education or any non-superficial presentation of how Catholic principles should inform policies and practices in schools. I explore some of the reasons for this situation in chapter three.

There are four further comments to be made on the argument of *The Ebbing Tide*. First, the criticism of the bishops for their inadequate defence of the qualitative aspects of Catholic education is over-stated. It is true that the structures in place for developing Catholic education policy are somewhat dispersed, thereby hindering concerted effort. But the diversity can also be seen as strength, if it allows for experimentation on a smaller scale than an all-or-nothing basis among Catholic schools. Too zealous an approach by the bishops to enforce an official line might have been interpreted by teachers as heavy-handed and as displaying both that concern with control outlined earlier as a defect of the managerialist imperative and an accompanying lack of trust.

The reluctance of the bishops to speak out on educational policy issues in the authoritative way desired by Arthur may be due more to a desire to encourage their flock than to any lack of concern on their part for the health of Catholic education. This flock has undergone rapid assimilation into the mainstream of English society. After a period of marked dependence on clerical authority, English Catholics were invited to accept the kind of lay responsibility called for in the documents of the Second Vatican Council. Arthur's criticism of the bishops would be less strong now, given that they and their representative agencies have, in the last few years, issued many guidance documents for Catholic education.[42] Furthermore, within these recent documents, it seems to me that a fine balance has been established between general principle and practical implications, between ideals and reality. The tone set is clear and firm without falling into paternalism or hectoring.

My second response to Arthur's book is simply to record my impression that its vantage point seems somewhat removed from the burdensome and complex realities of office, where compromise is often required if the best that is possible in less than ideal circumstances is to be achieved. Those who adopt the moral high ground and carp at the shortcomings of others may maintain a certain kind of uncontaminated purity, but at the expense of removing themselves from the field of battle and so rendering their remedies inaccessible. It is not clear whether Arthur would have preferred that the Bishops had adhered to an uncompromising line, even at the cost of massive closure of Catholic schools. If such a strong approach had been adopted, the defence of the distinctiveness of Catholic education could have been upheld more consistently but perhaps at the cost of displaying exclusiveness - a religious elitism - that is alien to Catholicism.

My third comment is that Arthur appears, at least on the basis of *The Ebbing Tide*, to confuse faith with *the* faith and church with *the* church. By this I mean that he treats the external, objective, institutional and hierarchical dimensions of the church as if they include without remainder and must totally dominate the internal, subjective, personal and community dimensions. In practice the relations between these different dimensions are fluid, complex, difficult to pin down and reciprocally interacting. As a result of his approach, Arthur seems uncomfortable with pluralism and desirous of greater uniformity.[43]

My final comment is to accept as valid many of the principal themes which permeate Arthur's argument. There *are* resources within Catholicism for a comprehensive and distinctive vision for education. These resources are *not* well enough known by Catholic teachers. In several respects the Catholic 'story' *will* challenge both government policy and present practices within Catholic schools. Catholic educators *should* hold religion and education together and avoid any separation between them. Arthur is correct in arguing that approaches to education are both logically and morally bound to be affected by "the Church's understanding of our nature, truth, sin, grace, revelation and our supernatural end". (p.81.) But when he goes on (p.83.) to assert that "the articulation of the essential, timeless, non-negotiable aspects of Catholic education as compared with the circumstantial, contemporary and adaptable aspects have been neglected by the Catholic community", my acceptance is qualified by two concerns. First, he seems to yearn for a classical rather than a historical approach to culture,[44] and, second, he misconceives the complex relationship between culture and faith, assuming too readily that culture is always to be informed and corrected by faith in a one-way movement.[45]

A contrasting response to the condition of Catholic education is illustrated in *Catholic Schools and the Common Good*.[46] This is an authoritative examination of the workings of Catholic high schools in the United States of America. It is very relevant to secondary schooling on this side of the Atlantic and, indeed, to other parts of the world where there is an attempt to provide education based on religious principles. The book draws on a very substantial sample of evidence: from independent schools[47] and those run by dioceses or parishes; from single sex and co-educational schools; from large, medium and small-sized institutions; from those which have a long history and those which are fairly recent; from those which are all-white, those which are almost all minority and those which are thoroughly integrated racially; from schools which are stable financially and those which are struggling in this respect; from those which are selective academically, socially or religiously and those which are completely non-selective.

Its findings should be of interest to but also perplexing to a number of different groups. First, these findings encourage those who advocate the continuing need for church schools in an increasingly secularised society.   Second, they are not, however, completely convincing to those who suspect (perhaps Arthur is an example) that Catholic schools have sold out to secularism, for the distinguishing features of Catholic schools are certainly not described in this work in terms which are recognisable as quintessentially Catholic.[48] Third, these findings challenge those who propose the abandonment of such schools and a move toward a fully integrated, single public educational system.   Fourth, they are confusing to those who argue for greater choice and diversity among schools. For while on the one hand they seem to bear out the value of an alternative to a monolithic, single state school system, at the same time they present a powerful critique of many of the values espoused by the choice lobby (in many countries) and promoted through initiatives of the last Conservative government in the United Kingdom.[49]

The authors describe a cultural change over the last thirty years with regard to the nature, composition and ethos of Catholic schools in the USA. Where they were culturally isolated, doctrinaire and racially segregated,[50] now there is a significantly increased number of ethnic minority and non-Catholic students, increased representation and responsibility for lay staff, a warm and welcoming atmosphere.[51] The typical Catholic school (in the USA) is more internally diverse with regard to race and income than the typical public school. Charges of elitism and exclusivism are outdated and unwarranted.   Catholic teachers are now better trained and educated, more likely to have had teaching experience in the public sector and to be more in touch with the rest of contemporary culture.[52] They are far more likely to be lay staff, for the predominance of members of religious orders has ceased, due to massive defections from the priesthood and the various congregations, to new types of deployment among many of those who remain and to a huge reduction in those entering 'religious' vocations. Bryk and his colleagues show that in 1967 there were 94,000 religious staff in Catholic schools, a figure that had fallen to 20,000 by 1990.[53] It has also to be acknowledged that religious orders *led* the change of priority in their ministry to the poor and to the inner city and, in the process, to welcome non Roman Catholic pupils into their schools. It remains to be seen whether or not the Catholic community will maintain the option for the poor within the inner city schools as the numbers of religious declines further.

Key features of such schools include an emphasis on a relatively constrained, academically focused curriculum for all students, "a pervasive sense, shared by teachers and students, of the school as a caring environment,...and an inspirational ideology that directs institutional action toward social justice in an ecumenical and multicultural world."[54] A range of evidence and argument is presented that suggests that this academic emphasis, sense of community and strong value system do contribute to the effectiveness of Catholic schools. Such schools tend to be smaller than their counterparts in the public system, more frequently single sex and offer a wider range of extra-curriculum experiences. They also expect teachers to extend their role beyond instruction, so they accept a morally educative role and a part in community-building that is developmental personally, socially and spiritually for students.[55] Disruptive behaviour is less frequent, teacher-student tensions are much reduced, levels of engagement with study are higher, (although choices among courses are fewer), the character of instruction is more traditional, (this in terms of format, setting, use of materials and pedagogy), and teacher satisfaction seems higher, despite lower salary levels.[56]

Detailed statistics about both teacher and student outcomes are provided which tell very favourably for Catholic schools. These cover such aspects as high staff morale and effectiveness, low absenteeism and high student interest in work, together with low disruption, truancy and drop-out rates. [57]   The authors also confirm Coleman's finding [58] that "students' personal and academic background plays a more substantial role in the public sector in determining subsequent academic experiences" [59] and that Catholic schools promote "higher levels of achievement, especially for disadvantaged students."[60]

Among the main differences claimed for Catholic schools we find an explicit, deliberate and confident interest in character formation, rather than leaving students to make up their own minds about moral choices, and an emphasis on spiritual leadership among principals.[61] This finding may appear attractive to those who have defended recent conservative government policies. However, it is clear that the underlying vision operative in Catholic schools, as described by Bryk and his colleagues, is seriously at variance with much contemporary rhetoric about market metaphors and morality. For example, "radical individualism and the sense of purpose organised around competition and the pursuit of individual economic rewards" are not promoted in the schools he describes.[62] The kinds of instrumental levers that are advocated in public educational policy, such as school improvement plans and accountability systems [63] - in England we might add to these appraisal and inspection – rely on a narrow and incomplete understanding of human nature and motivation. Too many public schools display a lack of moral authority, whereas in Catholic schools there is a strong commitment to the dignity of each person and a shared responsibility for advancing a just and caring society. A strong sense of community is built up in the life of a school when it draws from such images as the person of Christ, the notion of the Kingdom of God and the resurrection destiny to which all are called. Cumulatively, these images provide a vision that is powerful, integrative, deepening and evocative, in a way that an overemphasis on test scores, performance standards and professional accountability can never be.[64]

I emphasise the wealth of evidence on which the book is built, especially its range, for several reasons. First, it brings out the great diversity that exists behind the simple phrase 'Catholic school'. These institutions are not monolithic. Second, the descriptions of the different circumstances of the schools bring out the importance of context as a factor both in their effectiveness and in the particularity of their expression of Catholicism. Third, despite the wide range of different contexts in which Catholic schools operate, one of the striking features of Bryk's interpretation is that what these schools have in common is far more important than the differences between them. Fourth, Bryk has a different intention and audience from Arthur, one that leads him to give a very different emphasis to the evidence about Catholic schools. Arthur's book seeks to provoke the Catholic community to bring its schools more into line with Catholic principles. Bryk's work is addressed to the wider academy and educational policy-makers, in order to prompt them to consider the relevance and possible transferability of key features of Catholic schools to the public sector. Arthur, in addressing the Catholic community, relies on evidence and perspectives that are accepted as valid and relevant by that community. Bryk's work relies much more heavily on social science and empirical evidence, particularly statistical evidence, than does Arthur, whose work exhibits both a longer historical perspective and a more personal interpretation.

The Ebbing Tide is passionate, angry, committed and relies for its persuasiveness on readers already sharing the author's presuppositions regarding the integrity and value of Catholicism. It challenges Catholics to reaffirm the distinctiveness of their schools. By contrast, *Catholic Schools and the Common Good* is more detached, more tentative in its interpretations, rests on no explicit commitment to religious faith and merely presses readers (and policy-makers) to be open to the possibility that some features of Catholic schools might profitably be replicated in the public sector. It also follows logically from Bryk's argument that the constitutional ban on funding for Catholic schools might be reconsidered.

2.4.2. *Taking up position: proximity and distance*

How, then, do I place my argument in relation to those outlined in these two major studies by Arthur and Bryk? With regard to Arthur, there are four points to be made here. First, I wish to associate myself with his analysis that recent British government education policies have been built upon a philosophy of life and set of values that are seriously at odds with a Catholic worldview. Second, I wish to disassociate myself from his suggestion that Catholic principles relating to education have been 'betrayed', either by bishops or by teachers in Catholic schools. Although if his case rests on a weak sense of 'betrayal', meaning an insufficiently deliberate, energetic and sustained campaign to defend essential features of Catholic education, his accusation is, I believe, partly true, while remaining too harsh a judgement to be accepted without careful qualification.

Third, I fully accept two implications of his argument. First, the Catholic 'story' about education needs to be freshly articulated in the context of our society and in the light of the re-appraisal of Catholic theology which has taken place since the Second Vatican Council. Second, much needs to be done to ensure that teachers in Catholic schools are familiar with, enthused by, committed to and capable of living out this 'story' through their professional work and personal example.

Fourth, in contributing to a fresh articulation of a Catholic philosophy of education my approach differs in several ways from Arthur's. I am less anxious than he is about plurality within Catholicism while feeling at the same time less confident than he appears to be that the Catholic 'story' is unproblematical. I also believe that my employment of the notion of 'living tradition' offers a more inclusive conception of church than that which pervades *The Ebbing Tide*, where the objective and institutional pole tends to subsume the subjective and personal pole rather than relate to it in a more reciprocal manner.

In relation to Bryk there are four further points to be made here. First, there are important differences between the context in which Catholic schools operate in the USA and that in the United Kingdom.[65] As examples of differences in context I would mention funding arrangements, the respective strengths of religious orders, and, in parallel with this, the degree to which lay leadership has been assumed in schools.[66] In addition there is the greater degree to which Catholic schools in England and Wales are subject to state regulation,[67] the extent to which society is secularised, the nature and impact of government policies and the respective positions of church and state in the two countries. These differences should make us cautious in seeking too close a correlation in the functioning of Catholic schools. This is not to deny their common features. There are differences too in what the respective common schools are like, for example, with regard to curriculum, standards, acceptable levels of behaviour, governance and accountability. These differences between the two systems make comparisons difficult between Catholic schools in the USA and the UK regarding either quality of education or commitment to mission.

Second, Bryk's work demonstrates, among other things, some of those defects of managerialism as well as the need for visionary leadership I mentioned earlier. The authors claim at the end of their study: "the problems of contemporary schooling are broader than the ineffective use of instrumental authority. At base is an absence of moral authority."[68] The application of a 'public theology' in school, functioning as an 'inspirational ideology' matches Postman's call for a 'metaphysical' rather than an 'engineering' approach to education, with which I aligned my own position.[69]

Third, Bryk's work provides evidence in support of the case that Catholic schools do contribute to the common good. I develop this case at some length (in chapter eight) in response to my consideration of a range of objections to the maintenance of state-supported separate Catholic schools in a plural society.

However, fourth, the depiction by Bryk *et al.* of the 'public theology' or the 'inspirational ideology' of Catholic schools, (terms which they use interchangeably,) is, in my judgement, inadequate. It does not serve as a foundation for Postman's overarching narrative, nor for that fresh articulation of a Catholic philosophy of education that Arthur indicated as necessary and to which I hope to contribute here. This inadequacy is due partly to the question the authors were seeking to answer: 'what makes Catholic schools particularly effective, in secular terms?' In itself, this is a perfectly valid question to ask. But in order to achieve a deeper penetration of the 'public theology' of Catholic schools a different question must also be asked: 'what makes them particularly effective as *Catholic* schools?'

One cannot complain that the theological elements included by Bryk (et al) are inaccurate or misleadingly stated. For Bryk does satisfactorily bring out (pp.35-41.) the shift from a neo-scholastic form of Catholic theology to one which he calls 'social Catholicism', hinting at some of the associated shifts in nuance over rationality, freedom, authority, spirituality, sense of community and relationship between church and world.[70] Furthermore, his emphasis on dignity, responsibility, social justice and persons-in-community and the role of 'symbolic images' (p.303.), such as Christ, the Kingdom of God and our Resurrection destiny, does reflect pervasive elements within modern Catholicism.

However, the scope of his analysis precludes any in-depth treatment of the underlying 'architecture', coherence, richness and diversity of Catholic theology and how this relates to Catholic education. This would have to include Christology, ecclesiology, anthropology and the application of a sacramental perspective to curriculum issues. The sinful human condition, the call to conversion, the path to redemption, the need for salvation and the relationship between nature and grace are among the elements that are not brought out sufficiently. Treatment of these would have provided a context for greater appreciation of the centrality of Christ, the kingdom he preached and his invitation to new life.

The authors do succeed in representing an 'inspirational ideology' for Catholic education, but not, I contend, a 'public theology'. One way of distinguishing between the two is to view an 'inspirational ideology' as a loosely connected set of slogans which (a) function as summaries of key themes within a belief system, (b) attract and focus the energies of those they are directed towards and (c) serve the interests of the sponsoring body (in this case, the church). By comparison, theology is, at its simplest, a reflection on our knowledge and experience of God. In more academic terms, theology is a systematic reflection on the faith experience of the church or believing community. It will interrogate the nature, meaning, foundations, coherence and implications of a religious tradition's truth claims, worship and lifestyle. I assume that the modifier 'public' merely indicates an effort to spell out the bearing of the theology on an area of public life, such as politics, work, or education. While an 'inspirational ideology' may not necessarily conflict with a 'public theology', it operates at a shallower level, does not depend on a *habitus* or disposition of personal belief and does not require the same critical underpinning. It tends to 'look out from', to adopt, or to borrow elements from a belief system, rather than to 'look back' *at* them in reflection or to inhabit them in any depth, with conviction, as a totality and with a sense of ownership.

In Bryk's treatment of Catholic schools the elements of the 'ideology' are incomplete, with too little justice being done to the traditional 'story', they are presented uncritically and they are insufficiently related to one another. While the potential of Catholic education to be inclusive in its practice is demonstrated, such inclusiveness is not sufficiently related to Catholic principles. In turn this is because issues of distinctiveness are not adequately treated. I maintain that neither of the two terms - distinctiveness and inclusiveness - can be properly understood without a highly developed appreciation of the other. This is the task I have addressed here.

Notes for Chapter 2

[1]According to *Education in Catholic Schools and Colleges: Principles, Practices and Concerns*, A Statement from the Catholic Bishops of England and Wales, Catholic Education Service, (Manchester, Gabriel Communications, 1996, p.2), there are 2000 primary and 450 secondary schools, with 746,000 pupils and 35,000 teachers, plus a further 190 primary and secondary schools in the independent sector. In addition, there are 17 Catholic sixth form colleges, catering specifically for the 16-19 age range and 5 Catholic Colleges of Higher Education. Two Catholic primary and eight secondary schools are part of an ecumenical educational endeavour, although one of these, St Augustine's in Oxford, seems likely to revert to a single denominational status. Grant aid for maintained Catholic primary and secondary schools has risen since 1944, from 50%, to 75% in 1959, 80% in 1967, to 85% in 1975.

[2]A summary of the evidence (from 1993-1996) about standards of achievement, quality of education and religious ethos in Catholic schools is provided in *Learning from OFSTED and Diocesan Inspections*, Catholic Education Service, London, 1996.

[3] On attending to the soil (of our lives) as well as to the seed, and on fidelity to people's situations, as well as to the Word of God, see Jim Gallagher, *Seed for the Soil*, Great Wakering, McCrimmons, 2001, pp.72, 74.

[4]A biblical warrant for accommodating ourselves to all people so as to help them to have a share in the blessings of the gospel is suggested by 1 Corinthians 9.19-23.

[5]The notion of humans being made in God's image is considered in 5.7., below.

[6]For an example of such management literature, see Brent Davies and John West-Burnham (eds), *Reengineering and Total Quality in Schools*, London, Pitman, 1997. For the deficiencies of the metaphor of engineering as applied to education see Neil Postman, *The End of Education*, New York, Vintage Books, 1996. For criticisms of managerialism in education see Stephen Ball, S.Gewirtz and R Bowe, *Markets, Choice and Equity in Education*, Buckingham, Open University Press, 1995; David Bridges and Terence McLaughlin (eds), *Education and the Market Place*, London, Falmer Press, 1994; Jenny Ozga, 'Deskilling and Professions: Professionalism, Deprofessionalisation and the new managerialism', in *Managing Teachers as Professionals*, edited by Hugh Busher and Rene Saran, London, Kogan Page, 1995; and Gerald Grace, *School Leadership*, London, Falmer Press, 1995.

[7]Ronald Barnett provides a sustained critique of recent reliance on competencies in higher education in *The Limits of Competence*, Buckingham, Open University Press, 1994. His criticisms are relevant to the wider field of educational management. A notable exception in educational management literature to the omission of treatment of the personhood and emotions of leaders and teachers is David Loader, *The Inner Principal*, London, Falmer Press, 1997. Loader shows that a new sensitivity to self, a new awareness of others and a better understanding of the educational task are intimately connected with one another.

[8]For a different set of criticisms of what she calls 'Jurassic Management', see Helen Gunter, *Rethinking Education*, London, Cassell, 1997.

[9]Jasper Ungoed-Thomas, 'Vision, Values and Virtues', in Halstead and Taylor, *op. cit.*, p.144.

[10]As laid down in 1996 by the Teacher Training Agency for newly qualified teachers, for subject leaders, for those preparing for headship and for experienced headteachers.

[11]A useful discussion by Joseph Dunne in *Back to the Rough Ground*, (Notre Dame, University of Notre Dame Press, 1993) casts light on the difference between *techne* and *phronesis*, and the application of this to an understanding of teaching.

[12]Margret Buchman and Robert Floden, (eds) *Detachment and Concern: Conversations in the Philosophy of Teaching and Teacher Education*, London, Cassell, 1993, (pp.211-216) bring out several dimensions of uncertainty in teaching, for example, those relating to assessments of student learning, to the effects of their teaching, as well as uncertainties about content and the scope of teachers' authority.

[13]Stephen Pattison, in *The Faith of the Managers*, (London, Cassell, 1997, p.2.) highlights the religious

tone and imagery used in much management language. He refers to management as "a set of ideas, rituals, practices and words...that provide a total world view and way of life that binds existence and organisations together and shapes people, purposes and actions in a fundamental way." *cf. ibid.*, p.39.

[14]Pattison refers to the tendency, in organisations under the sway of managerialism, to require an "unthinking acceptance of 'official' reality as determined from above." *Ibid.*, p.54.

[15]*Ibid.*, p.71.

[16]Pattison compares the function of appraisal (or individual performance review) with that of confession in mediaeval Catholicism. "It is a means of engendering conformity and control in the individual." He goes on to claim that "appraisal is, in some ways, the most personally immediate sign and sacrament of the modern managed organisation." *Ibid.*, pp.196-197.

[17]Neil Postman, *op. cit.*, p.3.

[18]*Ibid.*, pp.5-6.

[19]*Ibid.*, p.6.

[20]*Ibid.*, p.7.

[21]"The idea of public education depends absolutely on the existence of shared narratives *and* the exclusion of narratives that lead to alienation and divisiveness." Postman, *op. cit.*, p.17.

[22]Christopher Dawson, (originally writing in 1961), quoted by V.A.McClelland in *Christian Education in a Pluralist Society*, London, Routledge, 1988, p.28.

[23]Alasdair MacIntyre has been a leading figure in restoring narrative to academic respectability. See especially his *After Virtue* (1981) and *Whose Justice? Which Rationality?* (1988), both London, Duckworth.

[24]For penetrating analyses and judicious assessments of the significance of postmodernism for either religious or educational theory and practice, see Michael Paul Gallagher *Clashing Symbols*, London, Darton, Longman & Todd, 1997, chapter 8 and also his chapter 'The New Agenda of Unbelief and Faith' in *Religion and Culture in Dialogue*, edited by Dermot Lane, Dublin, The Columba Press, 1993.

[25]In the case of the Christian 'narrative', its normative status depends upon claims about *historical* truths and it also partially depends on the proclamation of truths about how things *are*.

[26]Within a holistic perspective, a system's unity is not to be found in how constituting elements fit together, but rather in *how the system distinguishes itself from its environment*." (Emphasis in original.) Allan Beavis & A. Ross Thomas, 'Metaphor as Storehouses of Expectation', *Educational Management & Administration*, vol. 24, no. 1, pp.93-106, 1996, at p.95.

[27]For an analysis and critique of liberal education, see Ruth Jonathan, 'Liberal Philosophy of Education: a paradigm under strain', *Journal of Philosophy of Education*, vol. 29, no. 1, 1995 and the same author's *Illusory Freedoms: Liberalism, Education and the Market*, Oxford, Blackwell, 1997.

[28]See 8.4.3 (below) for an explanation of this term and an argument that separate Catholic schools, as constitutive communities, can be defended on the grounds that they contribute to the common good.

[29]For the importance of the notion of 'reception' within Catholicism, see Frederick Bliss, *Understanding Reception*, Marquette University Press, 1993 and Daniel Finucane, *Sensus Fidelium: The Uses of a Concept in the Post-Vatican II Era*, San Francisco, International Scholars Press, 1996.

[30]See chapter eight for further treatment of Murray's main contributions to Catholic thinking and its relevance to Catholic education.

[31]Murray, quoted by Robert Cuervo in *John Courtney Murray and the American Civil Conversation*, edited by Robert Hunt and Kenneth Grasso, Grand Rapids, Michigan, William Eerdmans Publishing Company, 1992, p.87.

[32]Will Kymlica, *Multicultural Citizenship*, Oxford, Clarendon Press, 1995, p.204. "External protections are intended to ensure that people are able to maintain their way of life *if they so choose*, and are not prevented from doing so by the decisions of people outside the community."

[33]Eamonn Callan, 'The Great Sphere: Education against Servility', *Journal of Philosophy of Education*, vol. 31, no. 2, 1997, pp. 223, 226.

[34]Patrick Hannon asks if 'openness' is the enemy of 'faithfulness', 'dialogue' at odds with 'prophecy'? in *Church State Morality & Law*, Dublin, Gill & Macmillan, 1992, p.128.

[35]Alasdair MacIntyre, *Whose Justice? Which Rationality?*, pp.361-2. An epistemological crisis occurs

when the range of unsolved problems and unresolved issues within a tradition prove so untractable that they lead to sterility, incoherence and a breakdown of certitude.

[36]Paul Hypher in *The Contemporary Catholic School*, edited by T. McLaughlin, J. O'Keefe & B. O'Keeffe, London, Falmer Press, 1996, p.230.

[37]Terence McLaughlin (1996), *op. cit.*, p.139.

[38]James Arthur, *The Ebbing Tide: Policy and Principles of Catholic Education*, Leominster, Gracewing, 1995.

[39]"The bishops have failed to establish any solid base from which to criticise government education programmes." *ibid.*, p.68.

[40]I say more about these in chapter three.

[41]*Ibid.*, p.186.

[42]For example, *Evaluating the Distinctive Nature of the Catholic School*, (revised edition, 1999), London, Catholic Education Service, (CES); *Spiritual and Moral Development*, CES, 1995; *The Common Good and Catholic Social Teaching*, 1996, *Religious Education: Curriculum Directory for Catholic Schools*, 1996, *A Struggle for Excellence*, 1997, *The Common Good in Education*, 1997, and *Catholic Schools & Other Faiths*, 1997, *Foundations for Excellence*, 1999, all from the Catholic Bishops' Conference of England and Wales.

[43]Arthur's comment that "there are in fact many differing interpretations of Catholic education current" seems to me to be a lament as much as a statement of fact. (*op. cit.*, p.81.)

[44]For this distinction see Bernard Lonergan, *Method in Theology*, London, Darton, Longman and Todd, 1972, pp. xi, 124, 301, 326, 363.

[45]For nuanced treatments of the relation between faith and culture see Michael Paul Gallagher, *Clashing Symbols*, London, Darton, Longman and Todd, 1997; Dermot Lane (ed) *Religion and Culture in Dialogue*, Dublin, Columba Press, 1993; Eoin Cassidy (ed) *Faith and Culture in the Irish Context*, Dublin, Veritas, 1996; and Michael Himes and Stephen Pope (eds) *Finding God in All Things*, New York, The Crossroad Publishing Company, 1996.

[46]Anthony Bryk, Valerie Lee & Peter Holland, *Catholic Schools and the Common Good*, Harvard University Press, 1993.

[47]All US Catholic schools are private in the sense that they receive no grant aid from the state.

[48]See p. 45, below.

[49]Cf. the British government White Paper, *Choice and Diversity*, London, 1992.

[50]Bryk (et al), *op. cit.*, p.15.

[51]*Ibid.*, p.10.

[52]*Ibid.*, pp.72-3.

[53]*Ibid.*, p.34.

[54]*Ibid.*, p.11.

[55]*Ibid.*, pp.77-8.

[56]*Ibid.*, pp.93, 97, 124, 136, 220. Chester Gillis (in *Roman Catholicism in America*, New York, Columbia University Press, 1999, p.203) says that the lower salaries enjoyed by teachers in Catholic schools are counter-balanced by the fact that 'discipline is easier to maintain, parents are interested and involved, the children are more easily motivated, and religiously based values are held in common. He quotes (Gillis, p.201) a teacher: 'the satisfaction exceeds the compensation.'

[57] Gillis also refers to the lower costs per student, massively lower drop-out rate and much better results enjoyed by Catholic schools. However, he also points out that the achievement of good academic results is not their raison d'etre. 'They were created to educate young Catholics in the faith and to pass the tradition on to the next generation' (Gillis, pp.208-9).

[58]J.S. Coleman (1982), *High School Achievement: Public, Catholic and Private Schools Compared* and (1987) *Public and private High Schools*, both New York, Basic Books.

[59]Bryk, op. cit., p.256.

[60]*Ibid.*, pp.256, 266.

[61]Students in these schools also have less choice about curriculum tracks and vocational options.

[62]*Ibid.*, p.11.

[63]*Ibid.*, p.318.

[64]*Ibid.*, p.303.

---

[65]See chapter three for further detail on the UK context of Catholic education. For the US context, see Thomas Hunt (ed), *Catholic School Leadership*, London, Falmer Press, 2000 and James Youniss (et al, eds), *The Catholic Character of Catholic Schools*, University of Notre Dame Press, 2000.

[66]The transfer from religious to lay leadership in Catholic schools seems to have occurred earlier and more rapidly in the UK.

[67]Bryk's claim (p.308.) that "the external regulatory shell is substantially thinner for Catholic school principals" would have to be modified to read 'marginally thinner' to apply accurately to England and Wales.

[68]*Ibid.*, p.326. In their search for the key organisational elements that produce the desired outcomes observed in Catholic high schools they focus on the 'public theology' at work in these schools and they call for "more serious dialogue between the instrumental and the evocative realms." (*ibid.*)

[69]See note 6.

[70]This must be qualified by Bryk's emphasis on the continuing influence of neo-scholasticism.

CHAPTER 3

CATHOLIC EDUCATION
IN ENGLAND AND WALES

In this chapter I set my study of the relationship between distinctiveness and inclusiveness in Catholic education in the particular national context of England and Wales. First, I describe a Catholic school system that is both diversified and decentralised. Second, I comment on important changes in the composition of Catholic schools and in the position of Christianity in general and of Catholicism in particular. When combined with the effects of government legislation these changes present new challenges and opportunities to Catholic educators who now need to re-examine the rationale for Catholic schools and the foundational principles that should underpin and permeate all their work. Third, I summarise theological developments within Catholicism that are relevant to re-thinking about Catholic education. Fourth, I indicate factors which have a bearing upon the lack of clarity about the distinctive nature of Catholic education currently shown by many of those involved in Catholic schools and suggest why there is a need for greater clarity. Fifth, I make a preliminary analysis of types of distinctiveness. Sixth, I offer a personal summary of a Catholic view of education in anticipation of the more extended examination carried out in chapters four and five. Finally, I analyse those general characteristics of Catholicism which provide a foundation for the distinctive components in Catholic education which are explored in the next chapter.

3.1.   National context

Ever since the restoration of the hierarchy in 1850, the Catholic Church in England and Wales has always given a high priority to its schools. To such an extent has this been so that, where a choice had to be made between building a church or a school, the preferred option was to be the establishment of schools.[1] For many years the Catholic community saw its schools as instrumental in the preservation of their identity. Given their memories of persecution and discrimination, their experience as a minority group who remained suspect in the eyes of many, the crushing poverty suffered by many of their members living at the margins of society and the heavy burdens of paying for separate schools,[2] it is little wonder that the Catholic community jealously defended the distinctive character of its schools. Their independence from state interference was to be guarded with unceasing vigilance, while Catholics themselves would be compelled by church law to send their children to such schools.[3]

Such distinctiveness necessarily entailed a degree of exclusiveness, in the sense that the Catholic community envisaged for its schools a role in protecting children from contamination either by Protestantism or by secular ideologies. The focus was 'domestic' or inward-looking rather than seeking to serve the wider community, in so far as Catholic schools were primarily intended to educate the children of fellow Catholics. A fortress mentality for the institutional church prevailed both at the international as well as the national and local levels. Where Catholics were a minority group, as in England and Wales, this fortress mentality could lead to a ghetto situation where barriers to the outside world served also as protection from threat and as an assurance of safety for souls.

In the period between the restoration of the hierarchy and the 1944 Education Act, an Act which provided a solid basis for the continuation and extension of the 'dual system', the Catholic Church in England and Wales saw itself very much as a junior daughter within the wider Catholic world. She sought to be faithful in all things to Rome, accepted obedience as a cardinal virtue and strove to do justice to the ultramontane spirit in all matters, ranging from clergy-laity relations, styles of theology and spiritual and moral discipline.[4] Bishops in this country saw the damaging effects of a cultural struggle in Germany, of anti-clericalism in France, of the condemnation of attempts to adapt the church in America and the crushing of modernism generally in the early years of this century. Tight discipline was maintained, wherever possible, at all levels in the English and Welsh Catholic church. Indifferentism would be guarded against, obedience would be insisted upon, experimentation ruled out and uniformity enforced. All this was part of a wider counter-cultural stance adopted by the Catholic Church, one that was to be significantly modified by the Second Vatican Council (1962-65).[5]

Despite the fact that Catholic schools have been considered crucial for the preservation of the identity and life of a highly disciplined and authoritarian church, it is perhaps surprising that both before and after the 1944 Education Act a feature of the Catholic school system in England and Wales has been the patchiness of its provision. Official church policy for education has been that all Catholic pupils should be taught by Catholic teachers in Catholic schools. The pressure on parents to send their children to church schools was 'on pain of sin'.[6] However, a significant number of Catholic pupils never attended Catholic schools. Provision has never matched the overall need for places.[7] This is mainly due to the enormous burden imposed by the increasing costs of building new schools and the uneven capacity of different Catholic communities and dioceses to meet these financial demands.

It is also partly a reflection of decentralisation in the decision-making bodies of Catholic schooling. At present there are twenty-two dioceses in England and Wales. According to Canon Law, each bishop has jurisdiction over the Catholic schools in his diocese. On some issues the bishops deliberate together and release joint statements about education (and other matters).[8] But over many issues there appears to be no co-ordination of episcopal decision, action or oversight regarding Catholic schools. To complicate this picture further, one must take into account the roles of several other bodies.

The Catholic Education Service acts on behalf of the Bishops' Conference in the provision of general guidance about Catholic education and in negotiations with government (and, where appropriate, opposition parties) over the implications of current or proposed policies for Catholic schools. Each diocese has a Schools Commission, with clergy and lay representation, whose full or part-time officers advise on and, in partnership with schools, implement the education policy of their own particular diocese. This task is often shared with the diocesan Religious Education Centre (sometimes called Christian Education Centre).[9]

Also to be taken into account, there are many different religious orders, both of men and women, involved in Catholic education. Some of these run their own schools and therefore are trustees in law for the property and its governance.[10] The position is made even more complex by the fact that some of the religious orders responsible for Catholic schools in England and Wales are based overseas.[11]

Each particular Catholic school, whether independent or maintained, has its own governing body, which has some members appointed by the diocesan or order trustees, some elected by the parents and, in the case of maintained schools, some nominated by local political parties. The rights and responsibilities of governors are enshrined in law. However, where perceptions and priorities about Catholic education differ and where jurisdiction appears to be either unclear or overlapping, there can be serious tensions between parents, governors, trustees and diocese.[12] These might, for example, be about decisions relating to building programmes, closure, amalgamation, staff appointments, admission of pupils or proposals to change the nature of the school. Differences in perceptions and priorities can lead to conflict between parents, Headteacher, governors and local parishioners over staff performance, pupil discipline, and the degree to which the Catholic ethos should be maintained.

Diversification in the structures of the United Kingdom system of education increased after legislation (in the late 1980s and the early 1990s) removed sixth form and further education colleges from local authority control and introduced City Technology Colleges, Grant Maintained and other types of school.[13] Catholic schools have been affected by these developments, which compound the complex situation described above. The 17 Catholic sixth form colleges have been subject to a very different regime of funding, control and inspection since 1992, one which makes the promotion of their Catholic ethos harder to maintain than when their status was the same as voluntary aided schools. One Catholic sixth form college (De La Salle, in Salford) closed after an unsatisfactory (Further Education Funding Council) inspection report. Another (St Philip's, in Birmingham) was closed after protracted and painful internal debate about its Catholic nature and its multi-faith student intake. This particular episode proved extremely controversial among the wider Catholic community because the development of the arguments represented a clash between apparently incompatible models for Catholic education. It might be argued that the college's closure represented a victory for an exclusivist, closed, elitist, unquestioning, inward-looking and defensive form of Catholicism.   An alternative view might be that the trustees finally woke up to, and took a courageous, if unpopular, stand against, the effects of a creeping secularisation and a corrosive liberalism within Catholic education itself.[14]

Following increased pressure from government to diversify provision, to increase parental choice, and, in aid of that choice, to clarify the value basis and particular nature of their 'product' or 'service', schools have been encouraged to emphasise their differences from one another. A complaint made against the predominant comprehensive school system was that it emphasised the similarities between schools, leading to a bland uniformity, reducing parental choice and giving too much power to professional providers rather than to the 'consumers'.

As a response, most Catholic schools, at least since the late 1980s, have drawn up their own particular mission statement, or summary of fundamental principles, emphasising their *raison d'être* and indicating the ideals which they hope to embody through their curriculum and ethos. These mission statements are guided partly by the charism and tradition of a particular religious order (where that applies). They will also be influenced by the prevailing Catholic philosophy of education, which will be mediated through national guidelines and by diocesan and other authorities and advisers. This philosophy will meet with varying degrees of understanding and support from teachers in Catholic schools.[15] They also reflect the particular circumstances, perspectives and priorities of the people who draw them up. Flexibility in response to pastoral realities has not always been a marked feature of Catholicism.   Recent encouragement from Rome of a pastoral approach in education, one that is sensitive to the diversity of situations and cultures encountered by teachers, sounds very different from an earlier emphasis on uniformity.[16] O'Keeffe (1992) refers to the current variety in provision as a 'patchwork quilt', one where a multiplicity of models of Catholic schools can be discerned.[17]

Diversified expressions of Catholicism, in schools as elsewhere, are inevitable, given certain social changes. Catholics are increasingly assimilated rather than living as a group set apart. There has been a new emphasis on acknowledging plurality in society. Within the church there is now less stress on the need for uniformity. Taken together, these changes allow more scope for the process of inculturation, or adapting the communication of the Gospel to diverse local circumstances and cultural conditions.

This diversification has not yet been mapped provisionally, let alone adequately. It is not my aim here to remedy this situation. Instead, my focus is on those aspects of that philosophy of education that I believe Catholic schools should jointly subscribe to if they are to act in harmony with the church's teaching. This focus on their commonality in no way rules out scope for legitimate differences in their interpretation of how to express this philosophy in their particular circumstances, although it does restrict it. Limitations of space prevent me from exploring here issues arising from posing the interesting questions: 'what, if anything, makes a particular (Catholic) school unique?' and 'what, if anything, makes it Catholic in a special way?' Anneke de Wolff points out that, in British, American and European discussions about the identity of Christian schools, of whatever denomination, such identity has been treated as a group phenomenon.   Much more emphasis has been given to how they (jointly) differ from non-Christian schools as compared with how they differ among themselves. She also observes that the changeability or dynamic nature of the identity of Christian schools is neglected in studies of Christian schools because concern about their identity, being closely linked with concern about the continuity of the tradition, is seen in static terms.[18]

3.2.   Factors for change

Many factors have contributed to important changes in the context in which Catholic education now takes place.   These include the changing nature of the staff and student composition within Catholic schools, the position of Christianity in general and Catholicism in particular in society, government legislation and developments in theology. These factors will be briefly addressed in turn.

Catholic schools now have fewer staff from religious orders. Between the mid 1960s and the late 1980s the number of teachers from religious orders fell by three-quarters in the case of men and by nine-tenths in the case of women.[19]   There has been a substantial increase in lay leadership, so that where most Catholic schools were at the beginning of the 1960s led by priests or religious, within less than two decades scarcely any remained in this position.[20]   The percentage of staff who are not Catholic has increased to about 12% in primary and over 40% in secondary schools. More than 10% of pupils in Catholic primary schools and more than 16% of pupils in maintained Catholic secondary schools come from non-Catholic families. This change in composition presents new challenges to - and requires a fresh understanding of - distinctiveness within Catholic education. In particular, it prompts further consideration of how to relate the mission of such schools to staff and pupils who are not Catholics and how to include such people properly within the school community.

I leave on one side here the whole issue of how the 'religious' staff played a particularly powerful role in embodying the 'Catholic identity' of a school. They had a vocation that was made explicit, one that was marked by particular charisms and spiritual traditions. Their lifestyle was celibate, they wore distinct clothing and resided in a separate community. A lengthy period of personal formation prepared them to integrate faith and teaching. Many enjoyed international connections and a highly developed sense of belonging to the universal church. Not surprisingly, in many countries, including in Britain, the USA and in Australia, they contributed significantly to the development of the Catholic school system and they offered a counter-cultural, even a *contra mundum* stance. However, in the light of changes in Catholic understanding of the church since Vatican II, it is a little more problematic to assume that the presence of religious can give schools their Catholic identity, even if they were available in sufficient numbers. A major task still faces Catholic schools in building on their legacy and adapting past forms of spiritual formation to current circumstances.

Christianity, and in particular the Anglican Church, still has a privileged position within English society. It is linked with parliament and with public conceptions of morality. Its influence shows in the pattern of public holidays. There is still widespread support for denominational schools, Religious Education and collective worship.[21] Many people who normally exhibit only a remote connection with church membership associate rites of passage and state occasions with religious ceremonies. Bishops' comments on social issues are widely reported. In political life no party major wants to antagonise the churches if this can be avoided. The churches then, continue to exert a significant social influence within England and Wales.

Despite this, the position of the churches is neither clear nor secure. The presence of large numbers of adherents of faiths other than Christianity, many of whom come from races and cultures outside the United Kingdom, ensures that the term 'religious' should not be associated too readily with 'Christian'. It puts new demands upon the expression of neighbourliness in the context of a multi-racial society and requires of Christians a new openness to truth and goodness in previously neglected sources. The influx into English society of large numbers of Christians from a variety of cultures has two effects. First, it prompts a rethinking about what is essential to Christianity as compared with what might be termed 'cultural baggage', that is, accidental accretions which can be shed without serious religious loss. Second, it gives renewed emphasis to the need for openness to expressions of Christianity which are less familiar but no less valid than those which are native to this country and its culture. It also calls into question an exclusive understanding of Christianity, so that it might be asked, does God speak, work and save through other religions?

Alongside this, a steady reduction in church attendance among Christians of all the main denominations, which seems to have accelerated since the early 1960s, has been one feature of the reduced grip of a Christian world-view on the ethos of the nation.[22] There has been increasing secularisation of social institutions and practices. There is a heightened awareness of the precariousness of all claims to possess the truth, whether about religion, morals, politics, society, or education. Exponential changes in patterns of material consumption and increased levels of marital breakdown illustrate features of society that have had an influence on educational practice in all schools. Catholic schools have not been exempt from such influences.[23]

The 'dissolution of boundaries of a distinctive Catholic subculture' as a side-effect of accumulated social change and ecclesial practice is especially relevant for my exploration of the tension between distinctiveness and inclusiveness in Catholic education.[24] As explicit external threats to Catholicism have diminished, and as Catholics have become more accepted into national culture, it appears that more subtle and insidious challenges have arisen. These challenges emerge both as the unforeseen price of social assimilation and as the result of a (still unfinished) thinking through and living out of a major internal reinterpretation of the nature of Catholicism. The church's understanding of the dialectic between distinctiveness and inclusiveness at any particular time is modified both by the conceptual categories available (including the intellectual adversaries encountered) and also by the challenges to Gospel-based living presented by changing social contexts.

When a distinctive approach to a religiously based form of education (one that takes place in separate schools) is linked to an exclusive approach to church membership, there are fewer demands for a sophisticated defence of distinctiveness. This is because there is less dialogue with those (outside the church) who hold different views. This lack of a felt need for a sophisticated defence of distinctiveness is perpetuated if the church displays an authoritarian enforcement of uniformity and strong demands for obedience in doctrinal, moral and spiritual matters, and where there is little accommodation to local cultures or to individual circumstances. It is almost as if the presence of high walls surrounding the church - keeping people in as well as ruling others out - obviates the need for the construction of the wide bridges which become necessary if there is to be encounter and intercourse on any significant scale between 'insiders' and 'outsiders'. As soon as dialogue becomes widespread - due to the combination of an increased openness to the world on the part of Catholics and a reduction of suspicion against Catholics on the part of society - then a different approach to distinctiveness is required. The current emphasis on a greater degree of inclusiveness within Catholicism generally, one which allows for some plurality as a necessary by-product of inculturation, leads to the need for a fresh understanding and a re-appropriation of distinctiveness in the particular context of education.

By moving away from a 'ghetto' mentality and entering into a (reciprocated) greater openness with people of other persuasions, Catholics have found themselves lacking an appropriate 'plausibility structure'.[25] Can they be accepted and included in society without being 'swallowed', without loss of what is essential to and distinctive in their identity? And if they seek to be inclusive in turn, within their own schools, how is this to be managed in a way that is compatible with the claim to offer a distinctive 'reading' or interpretation of life and, following from this, a distinctive approach to education? Maintaining this distinctiveness will impose some limits on the extent of inclusiveness.[26] Furthermore, if they are sensitive to the dissolution of boundaries of their own subculture, Catholic educators will be concerned that their own efforts - to include the increasing numbers of pupils (and staff) who come from other faiths or with no religious affiliation - should avoid any dominating attempt at assimilation.

The delicate task of self-preservation, balanced by maintaining openness to others of a different persuasion, has, of course, confronted other faith communities in the past and it continues to test them. The Islamic community, which is currently asking for the same rights for separate schools as those enjoyed by, for example, Catholics and Anglicans, might find the wrestling of the Catholic community with these issues of interest and relevance as they weigh up the implications, in terms of costs, responsibilities and relationships, of state-supported separate Muslim schools.

The avoidance of dominance or assimilation is necessarily in some tension with the claim of any religion to possess the truth. This is as true for Catholic Christianity as for Islam.

I have referred to changes in the composition of Catholic schools and also in the position of the churches in society. I have already suggested that a by-product of government legislation has been the fresh impetus it has given to the task of articulating the distinctive nature of Catholic education. For the purposes of my argument, two aspects to this fresh impetus will be picked out, one negative, in the form of a sharp challenge, the other positive, in the form of an opportunity. When taken together these two aspects have caused the Catholic community to re-emphasise that the difference between state-sponsored and church-sponsored education goes well beyond simply a particular diet of religious instruction and more attention to collective worship.

First, there is the spur provided by features (or at least the consequences) of government policy which the bishops (and others concerned for the health of Catholic education) perceive as being unconducive to its flourishing. The encouragement of increased competition between schools, which was intended to act as a lever for raising standards and widening choice, has been seen by some Catholics (as well as by many others) as having effects which are detrimental to sound education, damaging to pastoral care and undermining of community spirit.[27] Moral dilemmas arise for schools about the tactics they might employ for survival in a competitive atmosphere. For example, will they be tempted to give less attention to (or even to be less ready to admit) those pupils who appear to contribute least to the schools' reputation in examination league tables?[28] Will they be so ready to collaborate with other schools when they are encouraged to view educational provision as a competitive market?

> Competition brings the temptation to play the system to the advantage of one institution...It tends to undermine the integrity of the school as a moral society...[so that it] cease[s] to take the broader view and to feel concern for the whole service...Competition poisons the wells of community[29]

Second, there is the opportunity provided by arrangements for school inspection.[30] Catholic diocesan authorities and many Heads of Catholic schools have tended to welcome the requirement on teachers in all schools to promote spiritual and moral development and to be subject to inspection on this. This is despite the fact that their understanding of spirituality, morality and development differs in important respects from that of the government and despite the generally anti-OFSTED feeling among many teachers.[31] They have also welcomed the opportunity for Catholic schools to have a separate and parallel inspection which focuses directly on the provision of religious education, collective worship and the religious ethos of the school - all in the context of the specifically denominational aims and values.[32] This arrangement is an encouragement for those who espouse the importance and role of such schools in our society. The fact that all maintained church schools are subject, on a regular basis, to this form of inspection, the outcome of which is published immediately afterwards, injects an element of urgency into the deliberations of teachers about the denominational nature of their school and their work within it.

For many years prior to the present arrangement, religious inspections of Catholic schools were carried out in a patchy way, with little evidence of regularity, consistency or rigour. Reports were not published. Criteria for such inspections were unclear. No training for this kind of inspection was provided. Rarely were teachers other than Religious Education staff observed in action. Now the criteria for inspection, both OFSTED and also religious inspection, have been made available at a level of detail and documentation hitherto never experienced. Some obscurity remains about the criteria for spiritual and moral development in county schools, but the Catholic community has responded to the new situation by seeking (through its Board of Religious Inspectors and Advisers) much greater levels of rigour and consistency in religious inspections. The Catholic Education Service and the dioceses have drawn up (sometimes very substantial) guidelines for the content and conduct of these inspections. I believe that there is a degree of transparency, rigour, professionalism and practicality about such documentation that goes well beyond previous guidelines for identifying the distinctiveness of Catholic schools. Openness about such criteria has been commended and appreciated, even if the resulting paperwork is often felt to be excessive.

A religious inspection under current arrangements takes place every four years and is a major event in the life of the school, for the ensuing report will almost definitely affect public perceptions of the school, and therefore its pupil intake (and thereby staff job security). Preparation for inspection, dialogue with inspectors during the process and communication with parents and governors about the outcomes, combine to stimulate considerable discussion about the distinctive nature of church schools and the implementation of their mission.

There is the danger, however, that, by focusing too closely on how we might recognise the quality of Catholic education in the context of an inspection, an interpretation of Catholic education might be distorted. Giving a proper emphasis to evaluation is well overdue, but an evaluation-led approach to clarifying the special character of Catholic education is not enough by itself. An inadequate philosophical underpinning of the enterprise of Catholic education opens the way to sloppy thinking, to ambiguous expression, to unclear boundaries, to uncertainties at the level of policy, to the danger of internal incoherence and to capitulation either to secular take-overs or to theological imperialism. Such a lack tempts people to fudge 'hard' cases. For example, with regard to the composition of pupil admissions, what percentage can come from non-Catholic families without detriment to the Catholic character of a school? As for staff appointments and promotions, are non-Catholic teachers to be considered second-class citizens in terms of the ideal to be aimed for? Furthermore, should all senior posts be held by Catholics? What are the criteria for establishing who is a Catholic - and who applies these criteria? Other controversial issues to be addressed might relate to appropriate lifestyle for teachers (if they are considered as models for pupils), school behaviour policies (which are congruent with the school's mission), grounds for advocating pupil exclusions and criteria for making decisions over school budgets and priorities.

3.3. Theological developments

Changes in the self-understanding of Catholic educators have also been brought about through theological development. For almost a hundred years after the 1870 Forster Act set out to ensure the provision of universal elementary education in England and Wales a feature of Catholicism which helped to preserve the distinctiveness of that faith, nationally and internationally, was the predominance of neo-Thomist theology.[33]   This ensured a certain commonality of theological language between the universal and the local church; it fostered a particular form of apologetics in the defence of the faith; and it preserved a form of intellectual discipline that was shared by clergy of all ages. It also focused attention on some intellectual concerns, to the neglect of others, being particularly exercised to demonstrate the rationality of faith, the dangers of the Enlightenment and liberal thinking and the incursions of a secular state. In defending an ecclesiology that treated the church primarily as an institution, neo-Thomist theologians paid insufficient attention to the relevance for faith of personal experience and they also failed to consider the implications of historical understanding.[34]

This stance was to be significantly altered both during and in the aftermath of the Second Vatican Council.[35] The modern world had been rejected and liberalism had been seen as threatening ecclesial truth-claims by its indifference, disguised as tolerance. This negative stance was reversed.[36] The Council gave respectability and prominence in Catholic thinking to notions of collegiality, pluralism and diversity, the social apostolate and a more inclusive attitude within the Church.[37]   Its deliberations prompted a rethinking of key concepts that have a bearing on education: truth, knowledge, salvation, humanity, conversion and revelation. Important council documents were issued which re-expressed the mind of the Church with regard to its own nature and constitution, to revelation, ecumenism, the role of the laity, missions, non-Christians and religious freedom. Cumulatively these added up to a significant modification in self-understanding and in the stance to be adopted toward the world. One major shift in emphasis was to encourage a more positive attitude toward the world and a greater willingness to encourage involvement with others outside the church in human struggles for justice and peace, as opposed to a stance that had been more withdrawn, isolated and tending to avoid contamination.[38]

In rapid succession Catholic theologians entered into serious dialogue with a host of thinkers from other intellectual traditions, movements and disciplines and in the process their understanding and expression of Catholicism was transformed.[39] By comparison with the earlier neo-Thomist emphasis, post Vatican II theology often displays a noticeably different style and tone. It seems less confident and certain. It relies less on logic. It is more sensitive to outside perspectives. It takes into account diversity and plurality. It is less imperialist. It adopts a historical rather than a classical mentality. It gives greater weight to co-operation and dialogue with those who are outside the Catholic community and it brings out more clearly the social implications of gospel teaching.[40]

This has led to changing expectations of the laity in the life of the church and also, to some degree, a recognition that the experience, perspectives and contributions of women have been neglected by theologians and church authorities. Religious education in Catholic schools in the years after the Council reflected some of these changes. Its central focus was not so obviously doctrinal. Its tone was less dogmatic and authoritarian.   It adopted more frequently a multi-dimensional approach to the study of religion. It sought more explicitly to take into account the experience and viewpoints of pupils. It was more open to criticism and questioning; it was more open to and positive about non-Catholics.

3.4.   The need for clarity about distinctiveness

These theological developments, when taken together, add up to a major reinterpretation of the nature of Catholicism.   This inevitably has important implications for Catholic education.   I am not suggesting that the majority of Catholic teachers have assimilated this rethinking in any depth. On the contrary, for reasons that are beyond the scope of this study to demonstrate, I believe that many Catholic teachers exhibit serious gaps in their theological understanding. These gaps are due to several factors: changes in the pattern of family and parish life, confusions in Catholic education in the period after the Council, (arising from an inadequate understanding of these theological developments) and the pressures of accommodating themselves to secular requirements for professional accreditation.

The main lines of theological development should, however, be taken into account if a serious case is to be made for the continuation of the policy of separate Catholic schools. An understanding of the nature and purpose of Catholic education is intimately connected with an understanding of the church's mission.   Any development in the church's self-understanding, along the lines I have indicated above, is bound to influence how this mission is formulated. Therefore, without an understanding of these theological developments, any attempt to re-articulate the distinctive nature of Catholic education for our times is necessarily flawed. I will seek to substantiate this claim by demonstrating later (in this chapter and in chapter four) the relationship between the key principles governing Catholic education and the Catholic theology and view of human nature which underlies these principles.

In many Catholic schools one of the five annual non-teaching days, which all teachers in maintained schools are contractually obliged to work, is allocated to consideration of some aspect of Catholic ethos. When account is taken of the guidance material provided by the Catholic Education Service[41] and the dioceses and the new opportunities for extended reflection on leadership and management within Catholic schools provided by Catholic Higher Education colleges,[42] it is possible to claim that there is an unprecedented level of discussion as to the distinctive nature of Catholic schools.[43] While such discussion is to be welcomed, one must be careful to distinguish the frequency with which a topic is referred to and the depth of insight achieved. The availability of relevant, clear and accessible support material, while again to be welcomed, does not guarantee its serious take-up or any prolonged engagement with it.

I would also contend that the recent substantial increase in the amount of support materials provided for Catholic teachers cannot sufficiently address the need to articulate afresh a Catholic philosophy of education, one which takes into account the challenges presented by changes in society, education and the church. The documents produced to support Catholic schools in their task are intended to be practical rather than philosophical in nature and purpose. Their primary aim is to provide guidance for governors and senior staff in schools and for diocesan officers and others who have a role to play in implementing the Catholic community's educational policy and priorities. Such documents draw upon theological sources, scriptural passages, the teachings of church councils and popes and the lengthy tradition of church provision for education.

Despite the practical purpose of the documents, however, the teaching contained within them is often articulated in abstract principles and with a universality of scope that needs to be related to particular contexts and translated into more practical terms. The authoritative *Catechism of the Catholic Church,* [44] in clarifying its purpose, says: "This catechism ... is meant to encourage and assist in the writing of new local catechisms, which take into account various situations and cultures, while carefully preserving the unity of faith and fidelity to Catholic doctrine." First it refers (p.11) to "the adaptation of doctrinal presentations and catechetical methods required by differences of culture, age, spiritual maturity, and social and ecclesial condition among all those to whom it is addressed." Then it goes on to remind readers (from an earlier Roman Catechism) that "teachers must not imagine that a single kind of soul has been entrusted to them, and that consequently it is lawful to teach and form equally all the faithful in true piety with one and the same method!"[45] The quotation provides evidence of a move away from the assumption that preserving distinctiveness in Catholicism necessarily entails the imposition of uniformity. It suggests that distinctiveness is compatible with, perhaps even that it requires, a degree of flexibility in meeting diverse needs and a measure of adaptability in expressing faith. Such a significant shift of emphasis is echoed in another document intended to serve as guidance for the universal church, the *General Directory for Catechesis,* issued in 1997. Once again, there is strong affirmation for the belief that commitment to the message entrusted to the church and commitment the real diversity that makes up humanity go together. Fidelity to tradition and adaptability in presentation of the faith are compatible.[46]

While such universal principles are necessary, nevertheless, on the admission of those who have drawn them up, they are insufficient. The next chapter will seek to identify and to analyse the key concepts for Catholic educators, to relate these to one another and to subject them to scrutiny in a way that mediates between universal principles and particular practices.

Guidance materials for practitioners produced in this country are not able at present to draw upon any lengthy or sustained *local* tradition of philosophical reflection on education which is rooted in a Catholic perspective yet open to and in constant dialogue with other philosophical outlooks. Despite a rich tradition of thinkers who have contributed to the articulation of a Catholic philosophy of education, for example, among others, Augustine, Aquinas, Newman, Chesterton, Maritain and Lonergan, none of these writers directly addressed the enterprise of Catholic education as currently situated, particularly in the school context. Of these, the first two lived long before the age of mass education; only Newman and Chesterton were English (although Lonergan studied for a time in this country) and neither of these could be considered either philosophers or educators in a professional sense; in the case of the Frenchman, Maritain, and the Canadian, Lonergan, their attention, when they wrote about education, was focused on Europe and North America in the 1940s and 1950s; these constituted very different social, political, intellectual and educational environments from that of late twentieth century England and Wales.

John Henry Newman's most developed thinking on education was set in and aimed at a university context, although some of what he wrote elsewhere has continuing relevance for my attempt to develop a Catholic perspective on education.[47]   I summarise Newman's thinking on Christian education and demonstrate its relevance to my argument in 5.2. Jacques Maritain devoted a series of lectures to the topic of education from a philosophical perspective, and two chapters to a presentation of a Thomist view on education.[48] Maritain's contribution to a Catholic philosophy of education for today will be explored in 5.6. Bernard Lonergan gave a course of lectures at a summer school in 1959 that specifically addressed topics in philosophy of education.[49]   But he seems to have made little effort at this point to become familiar with educational contexts and issues outside his own experience as a seminary professor. These lectures are more valuable to those interested in the development of Lonergan's thought than to those interested in philosophy of education. It is in various and disparate passages from his later works, which were not addressing educational issues at all, that one can find material which illuminates thinking on education, particularly his notion of conversion.[50] Chesterton wrote no sustained work on education, although some brief remarks of his do provide a helpful insight into the very heart of a distinctively Catholic perspective.[51]

Of all these writers Maritain contributed most to our topic, but even in his case much of what he wrote remains far removed from the kind of philosophy of education debate which has been conducted in this country since the Second World War. In the context of a liberal, increasingly pluralist, democratic society, with ever reducing social and moral consensus, we have become accustomed to employing 'thin', procedural principles and values in public educational advocacy and to leaving aside 'thicker' and more substantive principles and values for use as a private option. I believe that in the current context described above, with its elements of both challenge and opportunity for Catholic schools, there will be a welcome for a renewed emphasis on a more rigorously philosophical Catholic approach to education.[52]

Without such an approach, the credibility of the church's witness in professional educational circles might be undermined by restricting discussion to the repetition of pious statements, which operate only at the level of rhetoric but which neither describe nor influence reality. Discussion internal to Catholic schools about their distinctiveness might lead to demoralisation of staff who note that platitudes are uttered and perfection aspired to but that clarity about attainable goals is in short supply. Ecumenical co-operation might be put in jeopardy if the similarities and differences between the Christian churches in their approaches to and perspectives on education are not recognised, appreciated or taken into account.[53]

In this context, without a sound appreciation of the foundations of (each relevant party's respective) distinctiveness, superficial dialogue runs the risk of fixing attention on the lowest common denominator. Dialogue between Christians and people of other faiths could be severely weakened if Catholic teachers are not equipped to bring a distinctive contribution to that dialogue. In this respect uncertainty and lack of clarity are as disabling and open to misinterpretation as closed-mindedness. Both a discerning confrontation and an appropriate co-operation with secular approaches to education are rendered extremely difficult and unlikely without serious philosophical engagement on the part of (at least some representatives from) the Catholic community. Greater clarity about their own educational philosophy among Catholics should enable them to contribute constructively to the debate about education within the wider community.

It should not be assumed in advance that the outcome of a greater clarity about a Catholic approach to education will necessarily be welcomed on all sides within Catholic schools. One of the advantages of a blurring of boundaries and a proliferation of interpretations of Catholic education is the easing of social intercourse and relationships, among staff and with pupils, stemming from the avoidance of confrontation over value clashes.[54] Another is the fudging of difficult issues referred to earlier in this chapter. As John Haldane says, "it is likely that a defensible account (of Catholic education) will be as challenging as it may be reassuring."[55] The perception of an element of "strangeness" within - and therefore possibly a sense of alienation from - Catholicism may be felt more strongly once there has been progress in elucidating its distinctive perspective on education. Any vision with the capacity to inspire and guide practice in a comprehensive way is likely at the same time to be powerful enough to render some people uncomfortable. This might well include, although for different reasons in each case, pupils, parents, teachers, parishioners and politicians, as well as clergy and their bishops.

3.5. Types of distinctiveness

As a preliminary step towards getting a sharper focus on the key concepts within Catholic education, let me clarify what will not be explored here. I shall not be dealing with Catholic theology as a whole. Nor will I concentrate on those aspects that are sometimes picked out as distinctive of Catholicism within the wider family of Christianity. Among these one might include, for example, the role of the papacy, veneration for Mary, belief about purgatory, or the theories about real presence of Christ in the Eucharist.[56] Nor will I attend to specific moral teachings, devotions and disciplines, relating, for example, to contraception, clerical celibacy, or the sacramental practice of confession.

These aspects may well mark out ways in which Catholic religious life differs from other forms of religious life. However, what is distinctive to a tradition and what is essential to it are not necessarily identical: elements within a tradition can be essential without being distinctive; they can also be distinctive without being essential. There are two senses of distinctiveness being referred to here. The first is concerned to stress the specific nature and source of a belief or a practice: it clearly belongs integrally to and plays a special role in a particular tradition. The second refers to the uniqueness of a belief or practice, being concerned to stress that it belongs exclusively to that tradition, that it is not shared with others. I am more concerned here with the first of these two senses of distinctive.

I contend that the aspects of Catholicism listed above do not serve as foundational, constitutive and organising principles for Catholic education in the same way as those elements that I focus on later in this chapter. Furthermore, to focus on those features that separate Catholics from others is to seek distinctiveness by exclusion, by emphasising what others do not believe or do not practise. In contrast, I argue that the essential principles underlying a Catholic philosophy of education constitute a mode of distinctiveness with the power to be inclusive.[57]

My analysis of the distinctiveness of Catholic education does not therefore entail picking out elements that are not shared by other Christian traditions.[58] Much that Catholics hold as of central importance in education is accepted by others. It will be suggested that the distinctiveness of Catholic schools rests not so much upon special building blocks, each of which is peculiar to Catholicism, as upon a particular configuration of characteristics, which mesh and interlock with one another. I believe that the same assertion could defensibly be made for other forms of faith-based education. All attempts to educate in any systematic way imply a view of human nature, a reading of the world and a perspective on what is of central importance and true worth within - and possibly beyond - it. Perhaps a helpful analogy is to hear these elements as notes in a symphony rather than as bricks in a building.[59] The analogy highlights the fact that the ultimate constituents of a symphony are both the notes and their relations. In a piece of music sounds are not heard in isolation from one another; rather we 'co-hear' them in the auditory atmosphere of their mutual interrelationships and reciprocal resonance. What must be identified are those beliefs and concepts which are architectonic and integrative, which unify what might otherwise be disparate elements, those which provide direction, order and purpose for Catholic education, those which give to teachers a sense of its point and its importance.

Something of what I am striving for is conveyed by the term 'economy', as used by Newman.[60] Newman's treatment of the term 'economy' embraces several meanings. These include the shape, balance and interconnectedness of doctrine, the inadequacy of religious language to its object, and the cautious (and pedagogically prudent) unveiling of truth to believers, so that they can cope with it according to their intellectual capacity and moral maturity. To reflect on the 'economy' of Catholic theology or to enquire about the 'economy' of Catholic educational principles is to look for a pattern of relationships and exchanges in an interconnecting set of ideas which displays wholeness and balance. Originally referring to the organisation of a household, 'economy,' in the sense employed by Newman, implies something that cannot be exactly specified or laid out for inspection by an autonomous rationality. Within the 'economy' there lie precious truths or 'treasures' which can reflect God's presence. In order to benefit from this treasure, we are expected, in communion with the Church, to live by these truths, rather than to dissect them in a detached, objective and individualistic manner. Any knowledge we have remains at the tacit level and it resists attempts to make it too explicit. Our understanding at any particular moment is bound to be imperfect, yielding only a shadow rather than the substance of God's reality.

Despite this caveat, I think it will be helpful here to offer a preliminary (and exceedingly economic!) outline of a Catholic approach to education. The purpose of this personal summary is merely to orient the reader to my provision of a more detailed analysis of Catholic self-understanding and a review of the major documents and key principles that govern Catholic education. It is also intended to anticipate the more extended outline (offered in chapter five) of the worldview on which the Catholic approach to education is based. It does not purport to be an authoritative representation of the Catholic tradition.

3.6.   A personal summary of a Catholic view of education

If asked to summarise, from a perspective informed by faith, his or her approach to education, a Catholic might reply in the following way. God's authority as our creator and redeemer, as our source and our final goal, is to be recognised. Jesus the Christ revealed to us true humanity and divinity, embodied a pattern for worthwhile living and offers us a personal relationship which is salvific. God's Holy Spirit is constantly available to us all in every circumstance of life as presence and power. We are called to enter into union with Christ, through accepting the presence of the Spirit, through prayer, conversion of lifestyle from one currently ruled by sin into one modelled for us by Jesus in the Gospel.

All truth comes ultimately to us from God, whatever its mode of mediation. Part of coming to appreciate creation is to learn to see the interconnectedness of all reality. This entails developing a holistic, rather than a partial or fragmented outlook. We do not attain this outlook in isolation but in the context of experiencing life in community. Education is to be carried out within a harmonious relationship with the living tradition of the Church. That body is founded to carry on Christ's mission and to convey his word. Teaching the faith is to be carried out in partnership with parents, who are our first and most important educators. True education acknowledges an objective moral law that we disobey only at the cost of personal diminishment and social (and ecological) destruction. Education should be recognised as an invitation to continuous conversion into a more Christ-like personality, to personal holiness and to social transformation. This will entail development of the whole person. All dimensions are to be addressed. These include the physical, intellectual, social, aesthetic, emotional, vocational, moral and spiritual aspects of our being. By learning, growth, development and sacrifice (literally, 'making holy' the substance of our lives) we shall be ready to enjoy eternal life with God and in communion with others.

3.7. Key features of Catholicism

This outline suggests significant differences of emphasis from secular and liberal approaches to education; it does not identify what is distinctive about a specifically Catholic as opposed to a more generally Christian approach.[61] Richard McBrien argues that it is the prominence given to the Petrine ministry of the papacy as an integral institutional element in the church's self-understanding of itself, which most clearly distinguishes that church from all Christian churches.[62] Catholic doctrinal and disciplinary traditions relating to the nature of the church appear to be the locus of the principal differences between Catholics and other Christians. Using the analogy of the flag of the United States of America, McBrien explains the difference between characteristics that are distinctive in content from those that are distinctive in their configuration. The US flag is tri-coloured, a feature shared with the flags of many other countries. These colours are red, white and blue, a feature also shared by the flags of many other countries. It contains stars, a feature similarly displayed on flags from several countries. McBrien points out that "what is *distinctive* about the United States' flag is not any of its several *characteristics* but the precise *configuration* of those characteristics. So, too, with the Catholic Church in relation to all of the other churches and traditions within the Body of Christ."[63] I do not claim that this reference to 'configuration' adequately establishes the distinctiveness of Catholicism. That requires a more elaborate specification of the characteristics integral to this faith. McBrien's emphasis does, however, serve to remind us that particular elements should not simply be seen in isolation from one another. It is necessary to understand the way they interlock, modify and reinforce each other. The precise configuration will also be affected by both historical and cultural changes. That is, the articulation of the distinctiveness of Catholicism at any particular time and place cannot help but be influenced by the conceptual categories, questions, assumptions and perspectives of those who are addressed.

A key feature in Catholic self-understanding is the universality of the Church, a quality contrasted with sectarian and reductionist tendencies. This suggests a high degree of openness to all truth (as coming from God) and a comprehensive (as compared with a partial or not fully rounded) embrace of all aspects of Christian experience. McBrien brings this out by stressing the *both/and* nature of Catholicism (as compared with an either/or approach): "graced nature, reason illumined by faith, law inspired by the Gospel, tradition within Scripture, faith issuing in works, authority in the service of freedom, unity in diversity."[64] It is the combination of elements, rather than an emphasis on one pole being opposed to the other in each polarity that characterises Catholicism. It is part of the very nature of the Church that it is pluralist, ecumenical, open to new life and to new discernment of truth. This is because the Holy Spirit continues to call all its members into the fullness of truth, a state that is a task and an aspiration rather than a possession or an achievement. It is also part of the very nature of the Church to be concerned with the preservation of identity, stability and tradition, and the teaching of an authoritative revelation already received. These two aspects of the Church mutually qualify and complete each other.

McBrien stresses three particular principles within Catholicism, which, taken together, he claims, bring us to the very heart of that faith. These are sacramentality, mediation and communion.   The sacramental perspective looks out for God everywhere since all reality is saved; it sees the divine in the human, the infinite in the finite, the spiritual in the material, the transcendent in the immanent and the eternal in the historical. God is to be found in all things: other people, communities, movements, events, places, the world at large, the whole cosmos.   From this perspective the visible, the tangible, the finite, the historical are all actual or potential carriers of the divine presence.[65]

Closely connected to acceptance of sacramentality is the notion of mediation. Here the claim is that "created realities not only contain, reflect or embody the presence of God, they make that presence spiritually effective for those who avail themselves of the sacred realities.   Our encounter with God is a mediated experience".[66]   By spiritual effectiveness McBrien means that we find ourselves changed in a positive way through each of our encounters; through them we are healed, transformed and renewed.[67]

The emphasis on communion reminds us that we are radically social beings, that we meet God through the mediation of a community of faith, not in isolation from one another, despite what some mystics might claim, and no matter how deep is our personal relationship with God.[68]   Individualism and excessive claims for autonomy are seen as antagonistic to this notion of communion and community.[69]

All three principles are open to distortion and abuse. Sacramentality can slide into idolatry, mediation into magic and communion into authoritarianism.[70] Avery Dulles, in his study *The Catholicity of the Church*, also points out the dangerous extremes to which Catholicism has sometimes been liable and from which it needs correction. Among these errors he includes triumphalism, clericalism, juridicism, papalism, dogmatism and ritualism.[71] Triumphalism displays an arrogance about the superiority of the Catholic church over all others and proclaims its inevitable triumph over all adversity and opposition. Clericalism exaggerates the differences between the ministerial priesthood and the priesthood of all believers and divides the church into first-class citizens, the clergy and second-class citizens, the laity. Juridicism exalts the place of law within the church, reduces morality to obedience and obscures both the gratuity of the Gospel (which comes to us as a gift and cannot be earned) and the freedom it offers. In similar fashion, papalism, dogmatism and ritualism exaggerate respectively the importance and role of the Pope, of the exact and uniform expression of doctrine and of precise rules for liturgy, each of which has a legitimate place in the overall 'economy' of the church.

Behind many of these errors or distortions there lies what we might call the shadow side of the positive insights of Catholicism. If God's presence to us through creation is emphasised too strongly, so that God appears close, available, intimate and immanent, perhaps God's transcendence and the distinction between God and creation is insufficiently emphasised, thereby allowing the finite and the imperfect to be attributed divine status.[72] We live between the inauguration of God's kingdom, already begun at Calvary, and its final consummation at the Parousia or end of time, between the 'already' and the 'not-yet.' Although we can be assured of God's presence in our lives and confident that God's kingdom, with its grace and its offer of forgiveness and healing, has already broken into our world, we should not prematurely act as though this kingdom is fully established, nor should we assume that we have, through the Church, already arrived at our heavenly destination, so that further conversion and change, personal, institutional and social, is no longer necessary. We must always be ready to be led further into truth and to be open to new aspects of God's teaching. This means that we should avoid canonising either the past or the present and that we should not equate continuity with immutability.[73]

Part of this openness to the future within the Catholic tradition relates to the consciousness of death as a gateway to eternal life. It has been said that "the quintessential left by a Catholic education is a lasting consciousness of the fact and meaning of death."[74] The statement is not meant to induce a morbid approach to life. We discover what lasts and what offers true life in the process of learning to die to self in countless small ways and as we are freed from a grasping possessiveness with regard to the good things we experience. There is little evidence that Catholic schools in recent years have given much emphasis to preparing pupils for death. Perhaps this partly stems from a reaction that has taken place since Vatican II against a previous world-denying and somewhat puritanical style of Catholicism. However,

> Vatican II did not simply try to *balance* our concern for this world and our concern for the world to come;....the hope of heaven should *animate and purify* our attempts to cherish humanity. ...We view our present life wrongly if, in the light of Heaven, we treat it as of no value at all; or if we cling frantically to pleasures that are only meant to be transitory; or if we suppose that this life is our only life, a journey into nothingness and not into light.[75]

One of the ways to understand better that a 'healthy awareness of death' is not a contradiction in terms and that self-denial and affirmation of the world go together, even require one another, is through a deeper exploration of human nature in the light of the Incarnation. This will show that a growth in our understanding of the relationship between the human and the divine has repercussions elsewhere in our thinking. I explore connections between an understanding of human and divine nature (in the light of belief in the Incarnation) in 4.5, below. First, however, I intend to analyse and comment on the Church's teaching on education from Vatican II onwards. This teaching has a more conciliatory tone towards the world and dissolves any notion of a schism between the natural and the supernatural.[76]

In this chapter I have provided a particular context for my theoretical examination of the relationship between distinctiveness and inclusiveness in Catholic education. Some of the factors influencing change and re-thinking about Catholic education relate specifically to the context of England and Wales, while others emerge from theological developments at an international level. Catholic schools in this country face challenges and opportunities stemming from the specific historical, social, political and educational situation here, but they also draw many of their foundational principles from the world-wide church. In the following chapter I analyse the major authoritative resources provided by the church for Catholic schools as they reflect on their rationale, priorities and guiding principles.

Notes for Chapter 3

[1] James Arthur (*The Ebbing Tide*, Leominster, Gracewing, 1995, p.15) quotes a resolution of bishops from the Westminster Province in 1852 as evidence that this preference was formal policy. For two recent studies that offer detailed historical background to the provision of Catholic education in England and Wales in the period 1850 – 2000, see V. A. McClelland and Michael Hodgetts (eds), *From Without the Flaminian Gate*, London, Darton, Longman & Todd, 1999 and Mary Eaton, Jane Longmore and Arthur Naylor (eds), *Commitment to Diversity: Catholics and Diversity in a Changing World*, London, Cassell, 2000.

[2] By 1996 the Catholic community was paying about £20 million annually in support of its denominational schools. See Catholic Education Service, *Education in Catholic Schools and Colleges: Principles, Practices and Concerns*, (Manchester, Gabriel Communications, 1996), p.2. Although these costs are still very high, it must be borne in mind first, that a much higher level of government grant is now available than was the case in the nineteenth century and during the first half of the twentieth century and, second, that the Catholic community is, as a whole, much less burdened by poverty than it was a century ago.

[3] In the rulings of Canon Law earlier this century canon 1374 said that Catholic children must not attend non-Catholic schools. Canon 2319 laid down an automatic excommunication for parents who knowingly and willingly arrange for their children to be educated in a non-Catholic religion...and also for those who marry with a pact...for the non-Catholic education of their children. See Michael Gaine, 'Roman Catholic Educational Policy', in *Religious Education: Drift or Decision?*, edited by Philip Jebb, London, Darton, Longman & Todd, 1968, p.138.

[4] In an essay, 'Transformations in English Catholicism: Evidence of Secularization?' (which appears in *Religion and Modernization*, edited by Steve Bruce, Oxford, Clarendon Press, 1992) Michael Hornsby-Smith observes (p.131.) that "up to the 1950s Catholics differentiated relatively little between creedal beliefs, non-creedal beliefs such as papal infallibility, teachings on moral issues (especially those dealing with personal sexuality, such as contraception), and disciplinary rules (such as the mass attendance obligation, the prohibition of intercommunion or the frequency of confession)."

[5] See section 3.3 for a summary of developments within Catholicism brought about by this Council.

[6] See note 3.

[7] McLaughlin, O'Keeffe and O'Keefe point out that "by the end of the mid 1960s only 60% of Catholic children had access to a Catholic school." *The Contemporary Catholic School,* (hereafter, *CCS*) London, Falmer Press, 1996, p.6.

[8] I refer to some of these statements below.

[9] The respective remit of these bodies is not always clear to the schools they are meant to support. Differences in emphasis and poor communication between them are not unknown in some dioceses.

[10] For example, there are schools owned and run by the (male) Jesuits and Benedictines and the Notre Dame and the Ursuline Sisters. Some schools owned by religious orders are in the independent sector and others in the maintained sector. Some members of religious orders also work in (either independent or maintained) Catholic schools, which are not owned by their order. The position is made even more complex by the fact that some of the religious orders responsible for Catholic schools in England and Wales are based overseas. Gerald Grace refers to the contribution of religious orders to Catholic education as a form of 'strategic subsidy'. See his chapter 'The Future of the Catholic School: An English Perspective' in *From Ideal to Action*, edited by Matthew Feheney, Veritas, Dublin, 1998, pp.193, 245-6. The Catholic community would benefit from further research into the substantial contribution of different religious orders to education.

[11] I have known situations where locally elected governors have been overruled in school policy decisions by trustees from another country. Just as foundation governors who do not comply with their bishop's requirements in upholding Catholic education can be replaced, so also can representatives of trustees who fail to implement the policy of their 'mother' body.

[12] See James Arthur (1995), *op. cit.*, p.153 on increased tension between the parental and episcopal poles of authority.

[13] 128 (out of 2450) Catholic schools opted for Grant Maintained Status, in some cases with the blessing

of their diocese, in some cases in defiance of it.

[14]See especially two articles in *The Tablet*: 'The Battle for St Philip's', (10th October, 1992), pp.1261-2, by Michael Walsh and 'Shades of the Ghetto', (7th November, 1992), pp.1396-7, by Gerry Hughes; and also Vince Murray's chapter 'Other Faiths in Catholic Schools' in *CCS*.

[15]See chapter four for a detailed analysis of the key constituents of this Catholic educational philosophy.

[16]See *General Directory for Catechesis*, issued from Rome by the Congregation for the Clergy, London, Catholic Truth Society, 1997, pp. 212, 246, 276.

[17]Bernadette O'Keeffe, 'Catholic Education in an Open Society: the English Challenge' in *The Catholic School and the European Context*, edited by V. A. McClelland, Hull University, Aspects of Education, Number 46, p.43, 1992.

[18]Anneke de Wolff, 'The Identity of Christian Schools', unpublished paper presented at the Philosophy of Education Society of Great Britain Conference, Oxford, 1997, pp.1-2.

[19]Hornsby-Smith, *op. cit.*, p.136. says there were "202 secular clergy in Catholic schools in 1964; in 1988 there were 26.

[20]Bernadette O'Keeffe, 'Catholic Schools in an Open Society: the English Challenge', in *The Catholic School and the European Context*, (edited by V. A. McClelland, Aspects of Education, No.46, Hull University, 1992, p.41): "At the beginning of the 1960s, most Catholic schools still had priests or Religious as headteachers. By the end of the 1970s almost all day schools had lay headteachers."

[21] For surveys of church-state relationships with regard to education in England and Wales, see Priscilla Chadwick, *Shifting Alliances*, London, Cassell, 1997 as well as *From Without the Flaminian Gate*, op. cit. and *Commitment to Diversity*, op. cit. (See note 1, above).

[22]Grace Davie, *Religion in Britain Since 1945: Believing Without Belonging*, Oxford, Blackwell, 1994. Catholics have also been affected by this trend, although less dramatically. See the studies by Michael Hornsby-Smith, (1987), *Roman Catholics in England: Studies in Social Structure since the Second World War*, (1991) *Roman Catholic beliefs in England: Customary Catholicism and Transformation of Religious Authority*, both Cambridge University Press. In his essay 'Transformations in English Catholicism: Evidence of Secularization?', (*loc. cit.*, pp.137-8) Hornsby-Smith refers to the decline in Mass attendance, the virtual disappearance of benediction, the reduction in the number of priests and the decline in the frequency of confession. However, he also notes areas of growth, as well as decline, in the development and expression of English Catholicism, for example, with regard to lay participation, group prayer, scripture reading, ecumenism and social action for justice and peace. (pp. 122, 123, 137, 138.) He has brought his analysis further up-to-date in *Catholics in Britain*, (edited by Hornsby-Smith, London, Cassell, 1999), and in his essay, 'The changing social and religious context of Catholic schooling in England and Wales', in *Commitment to Diversity* (See note 1).

[23]For two major studies which explore the effects of changes in the wider society on the self-understanding of late twentieth century English Catholicism, see Anthony Archer, *The Two Catholic Churches*, London, SCM, 1986 and Desmond Ryan, *The Catholic Parish*, London, Sheed & Ward, 1996.

[24]Hornsby-Smith (1992), *loc. cit.*, p.128.

[25]For an analysis and employment of the notion of 'plausibility structures' which legitimate and provide support for a worldview or way of thinking, see the works of Peter Berger: *The Sacred Canopy*, New York, Doubleday, 1969; *A Rumour of Angels*, (1970) and *The Social Construction of Reality*, (1971) both London, Penguin; *The Homeless Mind*, (with Brigitte Berger and Hansfried Kellner), London, Penguin, 1974; *The Heretical Imperative*, London, Collins, 1980.

[26]See chapter six for an examination of the limits of inclusiveness in Catholic schools.

[27]See, for example, the comment by O'Keeffe and O'Keefe (in *CCS*, p.306): "The competitive climate in which Catholic schools function places self-interest, competition, success and the power of personal choice high on the agenda."

[28]According to Nicholas Pyke, "schools no longer have time to concentrate on the vulnerable." ('Young minds in trouble', *The Tablet*, 15th February, 1997, p.211)

[29]John Prangley, 'Examination factories', *The Tablet*, 15th February, 1997, p.208.

[30]The introduction in 1993 of a new national system of inspection has forced all schools to review their progress towards providing high quality teaching, high standards of pupil achievement, effective

opportunities for spiritual, moral, social and cultural development and value for money in the use of resources. After the disbanding of Her Majesty's Inspectorate, inspections are now carried out under the aegis of the Office for Standards in Education (OFSTED).

[31]The following comment brings out a key difference: "Although both the National Curriculum Council and OFSTED make it clear that spiritual and moral development do not necessarily depend on religious belief, in the Catholic synthesis of the human and the divine they must." *Spiritual and Moral Development Across the Curriculum*, London, Catholic Education Service, 1995, p.3. See chapter five for an analysis of a Catholic perspective on human nature and development.

[32]This form of inspection, called a Section 23 (formerly Section 13) inspection, is also available for Anglican and Jewish schools. Of course such communities, along with the Catholic community, have always had the right to inspect their own schools. Now state funding, albeit at a very low level, is available for these religious inspections, with the minimum of strings attached. Control over the content and conduct of these inspections remains with the respective religious communities.

[33]From being one style of theology competing for attention alongside several others within Catholicism, neo-Thomism, which is an adaptation of the thought of (the thirteenth century philosopher and theologian) Thomas Aquinas, was elevated into pole position, made normative for all clerical intellectual formation and fervently advocated as an eternally essential foundation and the sole valid medium for the expression of Catholicism by Pope Leo XIII, for example in his (1879) encyclical *Aeterni Patris*. An authoritative analyst of the nature, influence and changing fortunes of neo-Thomism is Gerald McCool. See his two studies, *Catholic Theology in the Nineteenth Century: The Quest for a Unitary Method*, New York, Seabury Press, 1977; and *From Unity to Pluralism*, New York, Fordham University Press, 1992. For a recent study on the Thomistic tradition in education, see *Earthen Vessels*, by James Arthur, Hugh Walters and Simon Gaine, Leominster, Gracewing, 1999.

[34]As was demonstrated in the ferociously negative Roman response (the decree *Lamentabili Sane Exitu*, the encyclical *Pascendi Dominici Gregis* (both 1907), increased censorship, the anti-modernist oath and the vigilance committees) to the challenges posed in the early years of this century by 'modernist' thinkers such as the French biblical and historical scholar Alfred Loisy (1857-1940) and the Anglo-Irish theologian and spiritual director George Tyrrell (1861-1909).

[35]Two books which examine at length the nature and depths of (as well as some of the unresolved ambiguities brought about by) the shift in stance adopted at Vatican II, especially in the relationship between Catholicism and liberalism, are Gene Burns, *The Frontiers of Catholicism*, Berkeley and Los Angeles, University of California Press, 1992, chapters two and three; and R. Bruce Douglass and David Hollenbach (eds), *Catholicism and Liberalism*, Cambridge University Press, 1994, chapter three.

[36]Dermot Lane summarises the shift in stance as one that displayed: "the ecclesial recognition of other Churches, respect for the value of non-Christian religions, the affirmation of the principle of religious freedom, the acknowledgement of the importance of human rights and social justice, the endorsement of a 'new humanism', and a real concern for the salvation of the world." (*Religion and Culture in Dialogue*, edited by D. Lane, Dublin, Columba Press, 1993, p.16.)

[37]For instance, it moved away from considering the church as being simply coextensive with the Catholic Church, or as identical with the Body of Christ, or even more narrowly, as something to be equated with the hierarchy. Richard McBrien, 'Before and After Vatican II', *Priests and People*, August-September 1996, pp.297-302, at pp.297-298.

[38]In tracing the changes brought about by Vatican II, Richard McBrien observes: "Preconciliar Catholicism tended to limit the essential, or constitutive, mission of the Church to preaching, teaching catechesis, and worship (understood as the whole sacramental life). Ecclesial engagement with the wider world through ministries of justice and peace, for example, was regarded as only antecedent or preparatory to the essential mission of the Church. A sharp distinction, therefore, was maintained between the sacred and the secular orders." ('Before and After Vatican II', *Priests and People*, August-September, 1996, p.299).

[39]Debate ensued with existentialists, Marxists and feminists. The categories and perspectives of sociology and psychology were welcomed for the light they cast on the genesis and development of religious ideas and the functioning of religious bodies. New understandings of 'wholeness' and

spirituality were gleaned from secular sources and from other religious traditions.

[40]A typical example of the renewed emphasis on the gospel mandate for education for justice is the comment by the Jesuit Michael Campbell-Johnson: "the needs of the poor take priority over the wants of the rich; the freedom of the weak takes priority over the liberty of the powerful; the participation of the marginalised groups takes priority over the preservation of an order which excludes them." ('Education for Justice', *The Tablet*, 23rd May 1992, p.641) The implications of this emphasis on education for justice for schools in the inner city are brought out succinctly by Bernadette O'Keeffe in 'Beacons of hope', *The Tablet*, 24th May 1997, pp.667-8. This article summarises and indicates the significance of *A Struggle for Excellence: Catholic Secondary Schools in Urban Poverty Areas*, Bishops' Conference of England and Wales, 1997.

[41]See chapter two, note 41.

[42]For example, in 1997 a MA degree in Catholic School Leadership, the first of its kind in Britain, was launched at St Mary's College, Twickenham. This course aims to equip students to exercise leadership roles and responsibilities in Catholic education; to promote a deeper understanding of Catholic principles relating to education; to facilitate a critical engagement with representative literature and research on school leadership and management; and to develop an appreciation of how Catholic principles can be integrated into and expressed through a range of leadership and management tasks.

[43]Some of the religious orders (for example the Sacred Heart Sisters and the Society of Jesus) have also reflected on the relevance of their particular charism in the context of late twentieth century education. For an example of such rethinking, see *Foundations*, compiled by Carl Meirose, SJ, for the Jesuit Secondary Education Association, Washington, DC, 1994.

[44] London, Geoffrey Chapman, 1994, p.6.

[45] Ibid., p.11.

[46] Congregation for the Clergy, *General Directory for Catechesis*, London, Catholic Truth Society, 1997, pp.132, 246, 279.

[47]See *The Idea of a University*, London, Longmans and Green, 1912.

[48]See *Education at the Crossroads* (Yale University Press, 1943), 'On some typical aspects of Christian education', pp.173-198 of *The Christian Idea of Education*, ed by Edmund Fuller (Yale University Press, 1957) and 'Thomist Views on Education', pp.57-90 of *Modern Philosophies and Education*, ed by Nelson Henry, (University of Chicago Press, 1955). Alain Mougniotte has collected, edited and provided a commentary on the whole range of Maritain's educational writing in *Maritain et L'éducation*, Paris, Éditions Don Bosco, 1997. A very accessible introduction to Maritain on education is offered by Hugh Walters in *Earthen Vessels* (see note 35, above). See my comments on Maritain in chapter five, section six, below.

[49]See Collected Works of Bernard Lonergan, volume 10: *Topics in Education*, edited by Robert Doran and Frederick Crowe (Toronto, University of Toronto Press, 1993).

[50]For the relation between conversion and objectivity in knowledge, see my two articles in *Theology*, 'Subjectivity and Religious Understanding', November 1982, pp.410-417, and 'Lonergan, Conversion and Objectivity', September 1983, pp.345-353.

[51]G. K. Chesterton, 'A New Case for Catholic Schools', in *The Common Man*, London, Sheed and Ward, 1950.

[52]For signs of a renewed interest in a Catholic philosophy of education, see the jointly written article by David Carr, John Haldane, Terence McLaughlin and Richard Pring, 'Return to the Crossroads: Maritain Fifty Years On', *British Journal of Educational Studies*, vol XXXXIII, no. 2, June 1995, pp.162-178.

[53]On the ecumenical imperative in Christian education in general and for particular case studies of ecumenical experiments in education, see Priscilla Chadwick, *Schools of Reconciliation*, London, Cassell, 1994.

[54]McLaughlin, T. H., 'Values, Coherence and the School', in *Cambridge Journal of Education*, vol.24, no. 3, 1994, p.459.

[55]John Haldane, 'Philosophy and Catholic Education', *The Sower*, April 1995, p.31.

[56]I do not deny the enduring centrality of the Eucharist to Catholicism, but I would claim that particular theories about 'what happens' in the sacrament, such as transubstantiation, are not crucial to the

'economy' of Catholicism and they are not relevant to the argument I develop in this book.

[57] In chapter six I show how and in what respects inclusiveness is entailed by a Catholic approach to education.

[58] Cf the different views of (a) Milman and (b) Newman in the nineteenth century: (a) "These things are in heathenism, therefore they are not Christian" (b) "These things are in Christianity, therefore they are not heathen." Quoted in Dulles, Avery, *The Catholicity of the Church*, Oxford, Clarendon Press, 1985, p.61.

[59] I owe this analogy to Paul Hager, (who quotes it from Bertrand Russell) in 'Relational Realism and Professional Performance', unpublished paper for Philosophy of Education Society of Great Britain Conference, Oxford, 1996, pp.164-5.

[60] For an analysis of Newman's various uses of the term 'economy'. see Ian Ker, *John Henry Newman*, Oxford, Oxford University Press, 1990, pp.49-52, 705, and the same writer's *Newman and the Fullness of Christianity*, Edinburgh, T & T Clark, 1993, p.11.

[61] I say more about liberal education and some its elements which are in tension with Catholic principles, in chapters five and six.

[62] McBrien, Richard, *Catholicism*, vol. II (Geoffrey Chapman, London, 1980, p. 1171.

[63] McBrien, *op. cit.* pp.1172-3.

[64] McBrien *op. cit.* p. 1174.

[65] *op.cit.* p.1180. cf. McBrien (1994) 3rd edition, pp.9-10. cf. Dominic Milroy, 'What Makes a Catholic School Catholic?', *Priests and People*, August, 1996, p.339.

[66] McBrien, (1994), p.11.

[67] McBrien (1980), p.1183.

[68] McBrien (1980), p.1181. and (1994), p.12.

[69] McBrien (1980), p.1181.

[70] McBrien (1994), p.11.

[71] Dulles, *Catholicity of the Church*, p.159.

[72] Dulles, *Catholicity*, p.6.

[73] Dulles, *ibid.*, pp.98-9.

[74] H. O. Evennett, quoted in *Signposts and Homecomings*, edited by David Konstant, Slough, St Paul Publications, 1981, p.118.

[75] Richard Conrad, *The Catholic Faith*, London, Geoffrey Chapman, 1994, pp.63-4.

[76] Mary Boys, *Educating in Faith : Maps and Visions*, San Francisco, Harper & Row, 1989, p.89.

CHAPTER 4

DISTINCTIVE COMPONENTS IN
CATHOLIC EDUCATION

The central issue of this book is the coherence of the claim that Catholic education is both distinctive and inclusive. Are these two features of Catholic education, distinctiveness and inclusiveness, compatible, and, if so, how is their relationship to be understood? Does the claim to offer a distinctive philosophy of education, one which is seen as requiring, in the context of this country, the provision of separate, denominational schools, necessarily entail a degree of exclusiveness on the part of the Catholic Church? How does the claim that 'to be Catholic is to be inclusive' relate to the claim to be distinctive?

Before any of these questions can be satisfactorily answered, it is necessary to clarify the nature of and foundation for the claim that Catholic education is distinctive. Only when this has been done will it be possible to consider the kinds of exclusiveness and inclusiveness which necessarily follow from (or are debarred by) a Catholic philosophy of education. The main task of this chapter is to clarify the key components of the claim to distinctiveness. In the following chapter I delineate the distinctive worldview which underpins the educational principles described here. Taken together, in focusing on the components, foundations and implications of the claim to distinctiveness in a Catholic philosophy of education, these two chapters will indicate further the problematical nature of the relationship between distinctiveness and inclusiveness, before I suggest a way forward in chapters six, seven and eight.

First, I provide here a summary and analysis of the principal Roman documents that contain the Church's official teaching about Catholic schools. Second, I bring out the interconnectedness and coherence of the various themes and principles which together constitute a distinctively Catholic educational philosophy. Third, in order to demonstrate how some of the themes emerging from the documents can be held together without contradiction, in a creative tension, and in such a way that they mutually support and illuminate one another, I draw on the thought of a writer whose work has been almost completely neglected in the literature on Catholic education, Friedrich von Hügel (1852-1925). Von Hügel deserves careful study as part of this thesis because he demonstrated in his life and writings that the Catholic attempt to combine distinctiveness and inclusiveness is possible.

4.1.1   Declaration on Christian education

I have already mentioned (in 3.3) the shift of emphasis brought about by the rethinking carried out at the Second Vatican Council (1962-65). As a result of this shift of emphasis it is possible to discern a more positive attempt in church teaching to promote the fullest development of the human person and to integrate Christian education more closely into the whole pattern of life. God reaches out to us in all dimensions of our existence, not merely inwardly in our spiritual lives or via the workings of conscience. In the *Declaration on Christian Education (Gravissimum Educationis)* we read that

> education should pave the way to brotherly association with other peoples, so that genuine unity and peace on earth may be promoted. For a true education aims at the formation of the human person with respect to his ultimate goal, and simultaneously with respect to the good of those societies of which he is a member.[1]

Preparing people to enjoy life with God does not in any way entail inviting them to turn away from this world, its needs and their responsibilities. Although they are to be illumined by faith, Catholic schools must also "have the same cultural aims as all other schools and be opened to the contemporary world."[2]

In addition to this positive stance towards the world, four further points can be picked out from this Declaration as having relevance to mapping the key concepts within a Catholic view of education. First, the special importance granted to parents as the primary educators of their children is underlined.[3] Second, the kind of community atmosphere to be created and maintained at school, one that is "enlivened by the gospel spirit of freedom and charity," is stressed. Third, attention is given to the importance of striving to relate all of human culture to the news of salvation.[4] Finally, the autonomy of the various branches of knowledge is affirmed. These are to be taught "according to their own proper principles and methods and with due freedom of scientific investigation."[5]

It can be seen that, taken on its own, *Gravissimum Educationis* does not constitute substantial building blocks for a Catholic philosophy of education. This was recognised within the document itself: "these principles will have to be developed at greater length by a special post-conciliar Commission and applied by episcopal conferences to varying situations."[6] The third and fourth principles mentioned above, namely that which concerns the relationship between faith and culture and that which defends the autonomy of the various disciplines, are particularly important for this study. They recur in later Roman documents and I will comment further on them in due course. The second principle, with its emphasis on freedom and charity, provides guidance on the ethos, 'atmosphere' or 'climate' which is necessary if education is to avoid being domineering and if it is to be open to the particular perspectives and needs of students.

In fact, that further development of principles hinted at the start of *Gravissimum Educationis* was delayed for some time after the Council closed in 1965. It may well be claimed that the progress of Catholic education after the mid nineteen-sixties was influenced less by the Council's direct teaching on education than indirectly by piecemeal and partial assimilation of other Council teachings. A more responsible role for the laity within the church was encouraged. This would show itself in various ways. Greater participation within the liturgy and more familiarity with the scriptures would provide a sound starting point. From this Catholics should be stimulated to search for God's revelation in their own experience, rather than merely in sacred writings or in the past. They should be more open to fellow-Christians and to people of other faiths. As a result of these changes in attitude, it could be expected that they would show greater readiness to contribute to the transformation of the world. The Church shared in society's general advocacy of the need for freedom from coercion, with more allowance made for personal choice. This itself is a far cry from some of the pronouncements of nineteenth century popes such as Gregory XVI and Pius IX, who both rejected in their encyclicals freedom of conscience and the idea of tolerance.[7]

4.1.2. The Catholic school

It was not until 1977, twelve years after the Council closed, that a major document relating to education was issued from Rome. This was *The Catholic School*. It was to be followed by *Catechesi Tradendae* (1979), *Lay Catholics in Schools: Witnesses to Faith* (1982), and *The Religious Dimension of Education in a Catholic School* (1988). A decade later, two further significant Roman documents relevant to Catholic education were issued. The first of these was the *General Directory for Catechesis* (1997). The second, in 1998, was *The Catholic School on the Threshold of the Third Millennium*.

In *The Catholic School* we find an acknowledgement of the existence of objections to Catholic education, including a general rejection of church institutions, accusations of proselytism, of outdatedness, class distinction, poor educational results and difficulties over staffing and finance.[8] None of these objections is given more than a cursory mention. This is a pity. First, they are grave allegations and merit a serious response. Second, there is some evidence from this country as well as from the USA and from Australia that children in Catholic schools generally receive a sound education, one that equips them well by comparison with the educational outcomes secured by secular schools.[9] Rather than face accusations of shortcomings in Catholic schools, the Sacred Congregation goes on to reiterate the need for Catholic schools to bear institutional witness for the Church and its values, especially in the face of certain damaging or debilitating influences in society. These include relativism, materialism, pragmatism, depersonalisation and a mass production mentality and cultural pluralism.[10]

Five positive principles or themes emerge, some taking up points from *Gravissimum Educationis*, others providing fresh nuances. The first of these principles is indicated in a phrase which has become more and more influential - or at least repeated - in the literature on church schools, the 'integral formation of the whole person'.[11] As yet this expression is still being treated in a fairly undeveloped way, without further description and without an attempt at analysis. It will be taken up again in both the next two sources, each time being given a little more 'thickness' in treatment.

The second principle is that Christ should be the foundation of the whole educational enterprise in a Catholic school.[12] An understanding of Christ will offer new meaning to life and will show how human values find their fulfilment and unity.[13] This centrality of Christ, although it is not unpacked or explained in this way, might nevertheless with justification be taken to imply three things. First, his teaching should be fully and faithfully conveyed, in order that children receive the *information* necessary for salvation, enabling them to hear and respond to the Gospel. Second, a personal relationship with Christ is aspired to. This relationship is advocated as an ideal for pupils to strive towards and it is encouraged as worthy of both communal and individual effort. It should be embodied in and witnessed to by the teachers, to ensure that children receive an appropriate *formation*. Third, the principal decisions and policies of the school are referred to both the teaching and the person of Christ in the context of personal prayer, corporate worship and joint reflection; this would ensure that Christ would truly serve as a reference point or *touchstone* within the school.

The remaining three principles will be treated briefly here since they will crop up again when we survey the next two documents. At first sight it might appear that there is some tension between the third principle and the fourth and fifth ones (which should be taken together as mutually supportive). The third principle states that, with regard to a Catholic school, "its task is fundamentally a synthesis of culture and faith, and a synthesis of faith and life: the first is reached by integrating all the different aspects of human knowledge through the subjects taught, in the light of the Gospel; the second in the growth of the virtues characteristic of the Christian."[14] This is a compressed or dense statement; neither its meaning nor its implications are immediately apparent.

The relationship to be established between faith and culture presupposes a positive reading of and response to creation, stemming from the deeper appreciation of the implications of belief in the Incarnation which was shown both during and after Vatican II. Cultures vary enormously in their composition and they may, to varying degrees, contain features which do not harmonise easily with Christian beliefs, for example, in their attitudes or practices regarding the body, nature, gender, the environment, the individual, or people of other races. Therefore further guidance will be needed, both to facilitate accurate discernment of what is peripheral and what is central to a culture, and to give insight into what is compatible with and what is hostile to Christian faith. Cultural analysis in the light of Christian faith should reveal what should be shunned as essentially dangerous. It should also confirm what can be warmly embraced as positive and beneficial and what can be safely engaged with in an attempt to convert it from being merely neutral or perhaps only a minimal support for faith in its present state into a more secure ally.

Even on the most optimistic estimate of pupils' maturity and motivation, this analysis is beginning to sound like a task that is well beyond the capacities of most of them, and, indeed, of most of their teachers. The whole topic of inculturation has become an extremely important one in the modern church, as attempts are made to relate the many different African, Asian and Latin American cultures to the Gospel in a move away from European cultural dominance.[15]   The issue is complex, controversial, taxes the minds of the most sophisticated thinkers and is certainly still an area of church development that is unlikely to be resolved in the near future.[16] Schools will contribute to the discussion. They will provide a test-bed or arena for experimentation. How might this occur? One way is by appropriating the notion of living tradition within the academic and community life of the school. Another way is by extending the notion of differentiation to the realm of religious education and worship. If these two strategies are combined, pupils can be helped to develop their own response to and expression of the religious tradition, rather than be expected to conform to it unthinkingly or to assimilate it uncritically. This process will also have to take into account the diverse levels of familiarity with and commitment to the Catholic tradition prevalent among pupils (as well their parents and the staff).[17]   But schools will also need much more guidance than is currently available.[18]

An outcome of a better understanding of the respective rights and values of faith and culture and their interrelationship might well be the emergence of a much more rigorous and radical critique of our own culture than we have witnessed so far. It would be ironic if, after praising the values represented by church schools, and lauding the success enjoyed by them, politicians were to find that, as they more truly discovered their own identity, such schools entered into a more confrontational mode with prevailing political values.

The fourth and fifth principles that we can identify in *The Catholic School* concern the autonomy of the various subjects taught and the development of the critical faculties of pupils. "Individual subjects must be taught according to their own particular methods. It would be wrong to consider (them) as mere adjuncts to faith or as a useful means of teaching apologetics."[19] The value in the subjects lies not only in the different types of knowledge they yield, the skills they demand of us, and the attitudes they foster, but also in their methodology. This means that the church cannot tell physicists how to do physics, historians how to practise history, artists how to work through their chosen medium, and so on. There cannot be a Catholic science, mathematics, music, sociology or physical education curriculum, in the sense that such subjects are studied differently from the way they would be studied in secular schools. There must not be any theological imperialism or undue pressure on the natural autonomy of the disciplines that would distort them.[20]

These subjects can be treated in such a way that they raise larger questions than the disciplines themselves directly address. I am not referring here to the selection of subject matter of specific interest to Catholics as exemplary material for study, for example in literature, music, art, history and so on. Would such selection consider those artefacts which are produced by Catholics or those which, whether produced by Catholics or not, addressed matters considered of great moment by Catholics? To move down this route would create difficulties for some areas of the curriculum and it would distort the nature of the different disciplines in a way clearly condemned by the Sacred Congregation. As John Haldane says, "a Catholic approach to history is not to be confused with an approach to Catholic history."[21] Both are legitimate activities within Catholic schools.   But the first is more important than the second.   The autonomy of the discipline makes it possible, but not obligatory, for us to invite students to examine history in a perspective that is *sub specie aeternitatis* and as "the working out of a particular providential plan."[22] It needs to be made clear to students that it is not historical methodology that suggests such a reading of history, for questions about purposes wider than those of the actors involved do not automatically arise. It is from a religious world-view that further questions arise about the material yielded by the discipline of history.[23] The same could be said for science.[24]

This means that there are two extremes to be avoided. One would be to present the various subjects of the curriculum in such a way that they all illustrate and serve a particular world-view, its perspectives and values, in this case, Catholicism. In itself, this is a valid and possible way of interpreting the disciplines, through the eyes of faith. However, if this is the *only* role played by the curriculum areas, there is the danger of ignoring the autonomy of individual curriculum subjects and also of indoctrinating students. I have already noted that the first of these is condemned in the document under review. The same is true of the second danger. The fifth principle refers to

> the systematic formation of the pupils' critical faculties to bring them to a measure of self-control and the ability to choose freely....They must be taught to subject (what is offered by the organs of social communication) to a critical and personal analysis, take what is good, and integrate it into their Christian human culture.[25]

However, within church documents, including the ones under review, there seems to be little recognition that the development of critical faculties is just as likely and just as legitimately to be directed at the Catholic faith and its intellectual and institutional expressions as at anything else.

The second extreme to be avoided is to distinguish too absolutely a secular from a religious curriculum and to rule out in advance the raising of religious questions and moral issues in the teaching of the various curriculum areas. To respect the autonomy of the disciplines does not entail that one cannot legitimately ask questions or suggest perspectives. What we bring to a subject can make a difference to what we find in it.   This is not distortion, so long as we respect the methodological criteria properly to be employed in that area of study.

It is also possible to emphasise the autonomy of the disciplines in such a way that their mutual interrelationships are ignored. It would be wrong to treat each one in isolation from the others to such a degree that we lose sight of the fact that they are depicting only an aspect of a larger reality.   To leave pupils with a compartmentalised view of knowledge will not help them to develop critical faculties, concepts and attitudes that are transferable. It will not equip them to develop a synthesis between culture and faith. Just as God's grace can work in all of us to complete and transform our nature, rather than to diminish or erase it, so too all areas of knowledge can be penetrated by a religious perspective without loss of their particular nature. A better appreciation of this viewpoint depends upon a deeper analysis of a Catholic perspective on human nature and an exploration of the relationship between humanity and divinity. This will be taken up in the next chapter.

Several implications follow from the teaching of *The Catholic School*. First, in various curriculum areas, examples of the impact of faith should be considered in a church school, for example, in art, drama, music, literature and history. Second, challenges to faith (and to the ensuing lifestyle entailed by it) should be confronted as they arise from the evidence and perspectives yielded by different school studies, for example, in geography, science, technology and social studies. Third, from a faith perspective, each subject should be seen *sub specie aeternitatis* and therefore viewed as having a derived, rather than an absolute, autonomy. Given that each curriculum area is, in scriptural terms, a 'principality', pupils should be assisted in developing a capacity to critique its presuppositions and methodology, and thereby alerted, not only to its insights, but also to its bias and incompleteness. In this way pupils can learn to resist reductionist claims which might be made by those who adopt uncritically the perspectives and the categories deriving from the various disciplines. The capacity of teachers to combine successfully the three principles of integration of faith and culture, autonomy of the disciplines and development of the critical faculties of pupils will depend, in part at least, on their display of those inclusive pedagogical virtues which I outline in chapter six.

I conclude this section with two comments. Any attempt to distinguish *sharply* a secular from a religious curriculum is not in harmony with a Catholic perspective on education. Yet clearly it has to be admitted that there is some tension - but not contradiction - between the threefold imperative advocated in *The Catholic School:* to develop a synthesis between culture and faith, to respect the autonomy of the disciplines and to cultivate freedom of choice and critical faculties among pupils.

4.1.3. Catechesi Tradendae

Strictly speaking, this papal encyclical is not about Catholic schools, but about catechesis. Catechesis is the deliberate and ongoing process of deepening the faith of believers and putting them, not only in touch with, but also in communion with Jesus Christ.[26] In a sense the document relativises the importance of schools in this task by making it clear that the principal form of catechesis is that of adults and by its insistence that the pre-eminent place for it is the parish.[27] However, there are also several pointers here for how Catholic education, wherever it takes place, should be directed and for some of its characteristic features. I pick out five points from the encyclical for particular consideration.

First, the encyclical is unequivocal about the central importance of religious education in a Catholic school. The distinctive importance given to this subject should be reflected in the quality of its provision. "The special character of the Catholic school, the underlying reason for it, the reason why parents should prefer it, is precisely the quality of the religious instruction integrated into the education of the pupils."[28] Catholic schools should consider the practical implications for the allocation of time, resources and status to this crucial aspect of the curriculum. They should take any necessary steps that are required to ensure high quality provision. The wider Catholic community must endeavour to provide appropriate pre-service education and training, followed by continuing professional development opportunities.

Second, the activity of catechesis should strengthen both the internal life of the church, as a community of believers, and also its external activity as missionary, that is, as bringing the message of the Gospel to the diverse situations and structures in which people find themselves.[29] This suggests that Catholic education should be concerned, internally, for the spiritual welfare of Catholics and externally, for the common good. There is a close connection between these two, such that proper attention to the one correlates to an adequate consideration of the other.

Third, catechesis is a multi-dimensional activity that is bound up with the whole of the church's life. It cannot be restricted to the imparting of doctrinal truths in isolation from a study of the gospels, the experience of Christian living and church membership, sacramental celebration, engagement with apologetics, apostolic activity and missionary witness.[30] This suggests a comprehensiveness of approach and a co-ordination of methods and messages which can perhaps only be adequately developed in an atmosphere which allows education to be conducted along faith-based lines and in the light of assumptions governed by a religious worldview. Here a mutual exclusiveness marks both secular and faith-based approaches to education. In a secular context, there is no mandate to treat religion as the privileged bearer of truth or as having any right to be embedded in the public life of the school. In a religious context, not to allow this is to emasculate religion by denying its claims, character and scope for operation.

The message for Catholic educators here is twofold. First, they should see their vocation as part of the missionary work of the Church. To act in isolation from and without reference to the wider Church, even in the process of living out 'Gospel values,' would be profoundly un-Catholic. This emphasis on belonging goes much further than mere mutual protection, of 'looking after one's own'; for the benefits of ecclesial participation are not yielded without suffering the accompanying burdens of mutual responsibility, correction and accommodation, of chafing and friction.[31] Second, they should endeavour to adopt the multi-dimensional approach to education in faith, as indicated in the encyclical, so that there is a permeation of the Christian message throughout the curriculum and in all aspects of community life in the school.

This last point is related to a fourth theme of *Catechesi Tradendae*, that of the need for a 'balanced renewal'.[32] Without the comprehensiveness of the organic and systematic approach mentioned in the previous paragraph, the various elements can become distorted in our understanding and cannot play their particular part. The encyclical looks for a balance between fidelity to traditional content and openness to innovation in methodology, recognising that excess in either of these is possible: "routine leads to stagnation, lethargy and eventual paralysis. Improvisation begets confusion...and the fracturing of unity."[33] In a context of balanced renewal, where adequate time is given to doctrine, celebration and commitment,[34] a proper place will be found for the ecumenical dimension of Christian teaching and also for conveying the Church's social teaching.[35]

Fifth, a theme of major importance for my argument is briefly touched upon at several points in *Catechesi Tradendae*. This is the need for the catechist, and, by implication, the educator, to be attentive to the developmental stage, interests, language and values of learners and sensitive to their diverse cultural backgrounds.[36] This inclusive form of pedagogy is advocated, not from any prudent or clever attempt to 'win' the attention of learners or to manipulate their affections, but rather as a necessary expression of respect for human dignity. It is based a belief in the sacredness of each person and of acceptance that the Holy Spirit works beyond, as well as within the bounds of the visible church. The language of inclusiveness and inculturation in the context of education is not highly developed in this encyclical. Despite this, there is sufficient emphasis on these themes to justify my claim that they should be considered central features of any Catholic school and essential elements in the distinctiveness claimed for such schools.

4.1.4. Lay Catholics

The Sacred Congregation for Catholic Education issued *Lay Catholics in Schools: Witnesses to Faith* in 1982. This reiterates two themes we have already covered and then goes on to develop in some detail a new requirement or key ingredient for Catholic schools. The notion of integral human formation, one which responds to all the needs of the human person, and which leads to the fullest development of all that is human in us, again receives strong affirmation.[37] The synthesis of culture and faith is also once again highlighted as a major aim.[38] Where this document moves further than those touched upon already is with regard to the need to nurture the vocation and spirituality of the teacher.[39]

One reason for this is to provide pupils with models of people who have internalised a synthesis of culture, faith and life and who operate with a sense of vocation. If pupils can experience such teachers this increases the possibility that in due course they too will develop such a synthesis and a similar sense of vocation. At least they will have witnessed these things for themselves. The document *Lay Catholics* lays fresh emphasis on nurturing the spirituality and vocation of teachers because of the increasingly important role played by lay people within the church in general and in Catholic schools in particular. Since Vatican II there has been heightened awareness of the lay apostolate. *Lay Catholics* recognises the huge personal demands made upon teachers acknowledges that they cannot impart what they do not possess in themselves.

I have already noted earlier that Catholic schools are now staffed by far fewer clergy and professed 'religious' brothers and sisters and with far more lay people than used to be the case, and that few of these lay teachers have received a comprehensive Catholic higher education themselves. Many are neither theologically literate nor have they benefited from any deliberate spiritual formation. It is a special concern of *Lay Catholics* that teachers in a Catholic school should participate in its liturgical and sacramental life, that they should have a mature spiritual personality, and that their religious formation should be of the same high level as their general, cultural and professional formation.[40]   If teachers are not oriented towards personal sanctification and do not possess a clear sense of their apostolic mission, if their own development is imbalanced or lacking key ingredients, then the school will wander further and further away from its objectives. Such concern is reminiscent of Newman's emphasis on the role of personal influence in assisting us to find the truth.

> Persons influence us, voices melt us, looks subdue us, deeds inflame us.[41] ... We shall find it difficult to estimate the moral power which a single individual, trained to practise what he teaches, may acquire in his own circle, in the course of years.[42]

4.1.5. The religious dimension

Six years after *Lay Catholics*, another, more substantial, set of guidelines for reflection and renewal was published by the Congregation for Catholic Education, entitled *The Religious Dimension of Education in a Catholic School*. Once again we find extensive treatment of three themes that are now familiar. Firstly, respect for the autonomy of different academic disciplines and the methodology proper to them is stressed. These disciplines "are not to be seen merely as subservient to faith."[43]

Secondly, the synthesis of faith and culture is underlined. This is now brought out with a slightly different emphasis, one that reminds us less of the benefits to culture of close alignment with faith and more of the inadequacy of faith if it is not enriched and given body by culture. "Faith which does not become culture is faith which is not received fully, not assimilated entirely, not lived faithfully."[44] On the other hand, this relationship is not to be purely one-sided, in the sense that the openness is from only faith to culture. There is an expectation that the various subjects - science, technology, history and art are mentioned in particular - will not ignore the religious dimension; indeed religious values and a religious motivation are to be cultivated in all subject areas.[45]

Thirdly, integral human formation as a goal is reinforced, this time filled out in two ways: by reference to a Christian 'reading' or analysis of the person and then also by a stress on the call to perfection which must be part of the systematic presentation of faith. In summary form, the human person "is created in the 'image and likeness' of God; elevated to the dignity of a child of God; unfaithful to God in original sin, but redeemed by Christ; a temple of the Holy Spirit; a member of the Church; destined to eternal life."[46] The personal example of teachers will be crucial in modelling what integral human formation and development will look like. Teachers will need to display affection, tact, understanding, serenity of spirit, a balanced judgement, patience in listening to others and prudence in the way they respond.[47]

So far I have picked out from this document the emphases on academic autonomy, the mutually enriching relationship between faith and culture and the full development of each student - and what these require of teachers. The climate in which all this has to be worked at is one permeated by the Gospel spirit of freedom and love.[48] There is a danger that the distinctiveness of Catholic schools will be defended on the grounds simply that they provide a caring ethos. But this is a quality that is both aspired to and successfully achieved in many types of school. The shift in attention from doctrinal orthodoxy and moral correctness in teaching to the wider experience of pupils of the whole curriculum, both explicit and hidden, has, however, clarified what is implied by offering a consistent and humane approach to education in a Catholic context.[49] This shift is more a matter of degree than a radical re-orientation, since both doctrinal orthodoxy and moral correctness still play a significant role in a Catholic philosophy of education, as I seek to demonstrate in chapter five.

4.1.6. Catechesis and Catholic schools in the third millennium

At the end of 1997 the *General Directory for Catechesis* (*GDC*) was issued by the Congregation for the Clergy.[50]   Although its remit goes well beyond formal educational settings, important guidance for Catholic schools is included. This was followed in 1998 by a much smaller and more specific document, *The Catholic School on the Threshold of the Third Millennium*, issued by the Congregation for Catholic Education.[51] Both of these documents substantially reiterate themes that I have already highlighted in previous church teaching on education. In terms of my investigation into the compatibility between the polarities of distinctiveness and inclusiveness within Catholic education, both these documents have interesting contributions to make.   Without lacking confidence in tradition or in the core message of the church, both display a high degree of openness to the different circumstances of those to whom the Gospel is to be conveyed and to their diverse needs. Both emphasise the inclusive nature of Catholicism and they stress the need for sensitivity and flexibility on the part of educators.

It is important to know the culture of students and to assess the extent of its penetration into their lives (*GDC*, p.212.). In their dealings with students, teachers require knowledge of psychology, they should reflect the pedagogy of Jesus and draw upon an inclusive understanding of factors that affect catechesis (*GDC*, pp.249, 156, 141-2.) A pervasive theme in the *GDC* is that a standardised, undifferentiated, one-way transmission fails to do justice to the requirements of an inclusive pedagogy.

The Directory favours (GDC, p.165.) a combination of kerygmatic and existential approaches to communicating faith. The former is 'descending': it stresses the objectivity, authority and distinctiveness of the 'message'. The latter is 'ascending'; it enquires into and builds on the experience and perceptions of students. While great emphasis is given to the central role of the *Catechism of the Catholic Church* as a crucial reference point and also to the importance of ensuring an accurate, comprehensive, balanced and systematic presentation of the faith, the integrity of this communication must be matched by a readiness to adapt (*GDC*, pp.130-132; 119-20.)

There are two additional themes in the *GDC* that deserve mention here. One of these has particular relevance for a re-articulation of the rationale for Catholic schools. This is the priority given to interdisciplinary dialogue (*GDC*, p.74.), a process that has a firm bearing on the theme of interconnectedness, explored further in 4.2. (below). The other has interesting implications for the style of management in schools that should be exercised if my overall argument about the connections between distinctiveness and inclusiveness is cogent. Although I cannot go into this here, the encouragement given (*GDC*, p.252.) to catechists and teachers to develop their own style suggests a personal and creative role that would be seriously impaired if some forms of managerialism or over-dominant leadership were at work.[52]

The Catholic School on the Eve of the Third Millennium (*TTM*) reaffirms the central role of Catholic schools as part of the church's mission. It connects the vitality of the heritage to be passed on with its 'capacity for prudent innovation'. It stresses the need to 'go toward men and women *wherever they are*, in order to reach them, and also that a distinguishing feature of Catholic schools should be that they are 'for all' (*TTM*, pp.6, 10). A high profile is given within this brief document to the promotion of the human person. All subjects should collaborate in the formation of mature personalities (*TTM*, pp.11, 15). Among the qualities that are required for this to be effective is a 'genuine reciprocity' (*TTM*, p.19). It is implied in the document that, without the mutual respect and interchange of views that reciprocity expresses and facilitates, the full development of the persons cannot be promoted, and therefore there cannot be a fruitful synthesis of life, faith and culture.

4.1.7. Prioritising themes

In reviewing key features of Catholic education, as outlined in the relevant Roman documents from Vatican II onwards, it has become clear that three themes have emerged as of central importance. These are the integral development of the human person, the autonomy of the various branches of knowledge and the synthesis of faith and culture. It is not easy to see how these three can be held together, since they emphasise different priorities: the first emphasising the individual, the second focusing on the academic subjects of study while the third underlines the importance of religion in the conduct and interpretation of life. It has also become clear that these three are supposed to be integrally bound up with one another. In one way or another each of these themes is affected by a Catholic interpretation of the relationship between nature and grace and between humanity and divinity. This relationship will be explored in the following chapter. At this point however, I would contend that a better understanding of these three themes is the most fruitful way to get at the heart of a Catholic concept of education in the school context. Even from among these three, I believe it is possible to single out one theme as having overriding priority, as being the most central way of all to get to grips with what is meant by Catholic education, namely the integral formation or development of the whole person. It would, however, be unwise to treat this main theme in isolation, because special light can be cast on it by a deeper appreciation of the other two themes - the autonomy of the branches of knowledge and the synthesis between faith and culture.

I leave on one side at this point several other important features that are considered equally important for Catholic education in the documents I have analysed. These include, first, an understanding of the person of Christ and his call to perfection, a theme that I tackle in chapter five. Second, there is the need for building a school community that is based on the Gospel spirit of freedom and love, a theme I explore in the context of analysing inclusiveness in chapter six. Third, another priority is the desire of the church to give to the world a positive institutional witness to the importance of education, a theme I develop further in chapter eight. I believe that a deeper exploration of what might be meant by integral development of the human person promises to shed most light on the particular question being wrestled with here, which is: what is the relationship between distinctiveness and inclusiveness in Catholic education?[53]

4.2.   Interconnectedness

At different times some of the emphases within Catholic education inevitably alter. This might be because different theological schools of thought and styles of expression rise to prominence or fall into disfavour within the church itself. It might arise in response to external challenges from differing types of opposing philosophies as these are brought to bear upon both theorists and policy makers. Another prompt for such differing emphases might be new questions or concerns which emerge in the course of a society's or a culture's development. The church's educational philosophy will be articulated differently if the prevailing style of her theological or philosophical thinking is being expressed in terms borrowing heavily from, for example, Thomism (whether traditional or transcendental) or process theology, or existentialism, or liberation theology. Catholic claims to offer a distinctive education will stress different aspects of the church's message depending upon whether threats to this are perceived as coming from, for example, communism, nationalism, naturalism, hedonism, scientism, modernism or relativism. Defenders of Catholic education will revise their advocacy as they respond to newly emerging concerns and questions raised about, for example, industrialisation, secularism, pluralism, feminism, racism, ecology, medical ethics and issues arising from sophisticated and powerful computerised information systems.

Of course, I am not denying the strong element of continuity within Catholic education. Most of what had been argued for in earlier statements of the church's educational philosophy remains. Religion is the core of the curriculum. Christ is the model for human life. The church is the medium of living tradition that cannot be bypassed. The spiritual dimension of life must receive due attention. Morality is to be seen in objective terms. Mortality should be kept in view. All areas of knowledge are to be interrelated.

It is this last aspect, the interconnectedness, that I wish to underline here, for three reasons. First, the particular form of a belief system's interconnectedness will have implications for the kinds of education that it seeks to foster. Second, it is belief in the *essential* interconnectedness of the various elements of Catholic education that leads to a desire on the part of the Catholic community to establish and maintain separate schooling, rather than to provide *additional* teaching of those elements which have not been covered in mainstream schooling. One might claim, in the light of the previous analysis of Catholic principles, that neither the explicitly religious nor the apparently secular can be properly appreciated if taught in isolation from the other. Third, without an emphasis on interconnectedness, some of the key elements within Catholic education that have been highlighted could be distorted.

According to an authoritative document issued on behalf of the Catholic Bishops of England and Wales, "Catholic education is distinctive not by being exclusive (for it gives to all human activities their due emphasis), but by bringing into all such activities a special perspective which is derived from communion with Christ."[54] I take this to mean three things. First, Christ is to be of paramount importance in the life of a Christian. Second, through relationship with Christ a believer will find that all things will 'make sense', but only in the light of a continuing process of conversions in our thinking and lifestyle. Third, in the context of Catholic education it is appropriate to consider the relevance of the teaching and example of Christ for all aspects of knowledge and action. At the heart of Christian faith is the belief that "in Christ all things hold together" (Colossians 1:17) and that therefore a Christian should "take every thought captive for Christ" (2 Corinthians 10:5). Relationship with Christ requires radical conversion in our thinking and lifestyle, without which we cannot appreciate the salvation he offers. "The unspiritual man does not receive the gifts of the Spirit of God, for they are folly to him, and he is not able to understand them". (1 Corinthians 2:14).

It is sometimes hard for outsiders to appreciate that, in the context of Catholic education, this special perspective means more than simply a feature to be added to what would otherwise be a standard educational programme, for example, more time for specific religious teaching, or more frequent occasions of collective worship. All the various elements within education, as the bishops' report indicates, are affected by its focal point, its leading principle, its special perspective: "curriculum, syllabus, discipline, systems of reward and punishment, worship, relationships, community, catechesis."[55] Chesterton recognised that, according to its own logic, Catholic theology would be all-pervasive in a school following a Catholic conception of education; such theology could not be taught for only part of the time, in separate packages labelled religious education, and then hidden away or left on one side. As he said,

> every education teaches a philosophy; if not by dogma then by suggestion, by implication, by atmosphere. Every part of that education has a connection with every other part. If it does not all combine to convey some general view of life, it is not education at all.[56]

This is as true for the Catholic as for any other approach to education. Therefore not only will religious teaching be distinctive in Catholic education, but many other aspects of school life are expected to reflect Catholic principles or priorities, for example, sex education, teacher appraisal, pupil assessment, parental rights and

relationships with the local community. If the programme offered to pupils should
be consistent, there should still be room for individual creative interpretation and
response on their part. This means that teachers should take care not to impose an
integrating framework which is so strong that it inhibits pupil initiative.

There is also an interconnectedness between what is frequently understood to be
the enduring four dimensions within Catholic education: its interpretation of its
central message, the kind of community it seeks to be, the nature of service to be
fostered and the worship to be offered. Each one of these four requires the
assistance of the others; each one will have repercussions on the others. What
Chesterton in his essay on Catholic education called atmosphere or environment is
sometimes spoken of as "permeation". Such permeation should include both the
explicit and the hidden curriculum. It also embraces extra-curricular activities, the
school's social arrangements for staff and students and the methods used to evaluate
progress towards carrying out the school's mission.

This notion of permeation flows from the central importance given to religion
within a Catholic school and from the belief that "religion affects and is affected by
every element in the formation of a person."[57] I will show (in 4.3.2) how von Hügel
insisted that the religious dimension of life attains its greatest richness only when all
other aspects of human life are equally well developed.[58] Any omission, imbalance
or exaggeration in one area of study will have repercussions elsewhere and will
certainly undermine religious maturity and well-being.

> Thus personal relations and family life, physical health and nutrition, the study of the
> humanities, the rigorous pursuit of the sciences, engagement in politics, construction of
> the social order, involvement in commerce and the production of goods, all are of the
> greatest concern to Catholic Christianity, because all are aspects of the whole person
> and in their interplay, sometimes harmonious, sometimes contentious, full humanity
> emerges.[59]

The advocacy of permeation is at the same time a refusal to accept any rigid or
permanent compartmentalising of school life, for example, into secular and religious
spheres. No ultimate separation between what might be called sacred and what
might be called profane can be sustained.[60] What is being looked for is a *synthesis*
where the Christian perspective is neither *juxtaposed*, that is, simply put alongside a
secular curriculum, nor is it *superimposed*. Any attempt at theological imperialism,
where all aspects are taught under the direction and scrutiny of religious principles,
is a misinterpretation of the nature of the synthesis envisaged.[61] Study of secular
realities is not to be adulterated by nor subordinated to contact with a religious
perspective on life that is all-consuming, suffocating, distorting or constricting.[62]
Nor is religion itself to be absorbed within a secular world-view: the transcendent
should not be described as if it refers merely to the term of our continuing and
natural development, thereby being rendered as immanent.

An interesting comparison might be made between the approach advocated here
and that argued for by some Reformed Christian writers.[63] Nelson distinguished
three approaches to faith-discipline integration: compatibility, reconstruction and
transformation. The first of these places a premium on the effort to locate and to

integrate *compatible* elements indigenous both to the scholar's Christian faith and to his discipline. Academic knowledge is independent of faith, but can be related to it. The second sees no common ground and aims for a complete rebuilding of the discipline from biblical foundations and Christian assumptions. Claims to disciplinary autonomy, according to this view, are attempts to do without God and they build on 'epistemological sand'. The third approach recognises that between Christian faith and the secular disciplines there are at least *some* shared assumptions and concerns, but also a need to transform the academic discipline in order to do justice to the sovereign and comprehensive claims of Christ.

In this transformationalist approach, the elements of secular academic disciplines, which do not depend on biblical foundations or on Christian assumptions, are neither dismissed nor suppressed; but they do need to be re-shaped in the light of the converted person's transformed view of self and world. The reconstructionist campaigns 'from outside', in an assault on the false priorities and inadequate methods of secular disciplines. He or she seeks to expose their folly and to tear down their temples of distortion. The transformationist works from within them, in a much less drastic way, to bring them gradually closer to a biblically inspired understanding of that discipline.[64]

The approach I have advocated is much closer to transformation than to reconstruction. I believe that the reconstructionist allows too little scope for the operation of the (admittedly derived) autonomy of the academic disciplines. It denies their positive insights and exaggerates their distortions. It stifles their capacity to be creative and constructive and prevents the healthy friction von Hügel describes (see 4.3.3, below) as one of the contributions of the non-religious dimensions of life to our spiritual development. Together with writers of the reformed tradition, I am qualifying the notion of the autonomy of the disciplines, not in service of any theological imperialism, which is always to be resisted, but in acknowledgement of God as the source and goal of all truth. One must allow for the limitations of human penetration of truth and recognise the complementarity of various perspectives on truth.

Several implications follow from such a view. First, the methodology and findings of any particular discipline are to be considered, despite their construction by human 'instruments' or agents, as potential avenues towards an understanding of God's purposes for us, rather than merely as serving purposes we have arrived at for ourselves. Second, we should, in due humility, allow for the tentativeness or provisionality of the knowledge we think we have arrived at, this being as true of claims to religious knowledge as of any other kind. Third, the findings of one discipline are best appreciated in the light of complementary knowledge provided by other disciplines; none (including theology) is adequate on its own. Taken together, as a totality, the disciplines constitute a circle in which each one conditions, frames, challenges and illuminates the others.

Also in the Reformed tradition, Badley draws on Nelson's three broad categories and employs them to analyse alternative approaches to the integration in the curriculum of faith and learning. He argues that a Christian should aim for a combination of a perspectival and an incarnational form of integration. This means that one reviews every area of the curriculum from the perspective of a Christian worldview and also that the teacher personally exemplifies a congruence between content, methodology and lifestyle and where she embodies a harmony between the life of faith and the pursuit of academic study. *Both* these forms of integration are necessary educational implications of a Christian worldview. Any attempt to bring a transforming Christian perspective to bear upon an area of academic study needs the teacher's personal example to give it purchase and credibility and to make it sufficiently attractive to be worth serious consideration by pupils. Over-reliance on the good example of teachers, however, without the attempt to bring a Christian perspective to bear upon and to transform the disciplines, fails to engage with academic subjects adequately and leads to a juxtaposition between, rather than a synthesis of faith and culture.[65]

I have suggested that integral to a Catholic philosophy of education is a belief that the different areas of the curriculum have a relative autonomy and yet a mutual interdependence and that teachers should not separate religion from other aspects of school life. I have also described a religious perspective as having a crucial role in the curriculum if the pupils are to develop a synthesis between faith, life and culture. There are clearly pedagogic and curriculum implications that follow from such an emphasis for those Catholics who teach subjects other than religion in church schools. This situation is made more complex when teachers who are not Catholics work in Catholic schools and are expected to contribute to a (religiously based) holistic or integral approach. If harmony is to emerge from the various contributions to the curriculum of all staff, then all will wish to know who is conducting the orchestra, and from which score. It is certainly not a matter of one-way communication, but of mutual and reciprocal accommodation. For example, "the language of worship cannot escape the impact of all the other aspects of the civilisation within which it lives and changes...What happens in politics, philosophy, science, customs, art, fashions, affects the way believers perceive their faith."[66]

Such a view of the seamless web or the total interconnectedness of Catholic education is not new. In his *De Doctrina Christiana* Augustine had said that " all subjects (must) be surveyed in the light of being connected with one another, and they cannot be understood except in the light of those interconnections."[67] And Aquinas (for example, in *De Veritate*) had spoken of the synergy and interaction among our powers, such that anything happening to the body happens to the person and anything happening to the soul affects the body.[68] Joseph Evans comments that

> none of these powers proceeds on its own laissez-faire way independent of the others...Engaged in common are the intellect and the imagination and the powers of desire, love and emotion. In their operation they influence each other and involve one another.[69]

More recently Kevin Nichols has again articulated the importance of recognising the overall unity of the various constituent elements within a religious view of life. These include scripture, doctrine, liturgy and morality. He emphasises that the parts of a system cannot really be understood without reference to the wider whole in which they are situated.

> Elements in a system interact with each other, mesh, support, and affect each other. They stand in each other's light...Something which has a function within a system may be unintelligible outside it.[70]

A Catholic philosophy of education should promote among a school staff a concern for maintaining a unified approach to and vision of the educational enterprise. It should help them to avoid incoherence in the curriculum and fragmentation in the pursuit of separate spheres of knowledge, but it should combine this with a degree of sensitivity to the respective jurisdiction and scope of the various subjects within the curriculum. As Nichols comments, "it is not the business of religion or theology to go trampling over other people's gardens."[71]

This whole emphasis on the interconnectedness of a Catholic view of education still leaves unresolved several questions. Some of these echo questions posed by the philosopher of education Jane Roland Martin.

> Is a curriculum incomplete when it is not a unified whole or when it is not inclusive? Is it disconnected when its various subjects are unrelated to one another or when it does not connect up with student needs and purposes? Does it lack meaning when there is no unifying principle or theme to give the various subjects significance or when the subjects are not meaningful to students? Does it lack integration when the various parts are not tied together or when new knowledge and different perspectives are not incorporated in it?[72]

It will be difficult to hold together the three themes already referred to earlier, the integral development of the human person, the autonomy of the disciplines, and the synthesis of faith and culture, without a deep appreciation of the interconnectedness and the organic nature of all aspects of education. In response to Martin's questions I attempt in chapters six and seven to relate the interconnectedness aspect of a distinctively Catholic approach to education to the openness and inclusiveness she mentions. In these two chapters I argue for both an inclusive pedagogy and an appropriation by pupils of living tradition as essential elements within a Catholic education.

Before that, in the next chapter, I will show that an appreciation of the notion of personhood in the light of Christ will help my response to Martin's questions. Such a view of persons also facilitates a coherent understanding of the three key principles that have been at the heart of this chapter. It will be further suggested that the distinctive features of a Catholic philosophy of education necessarily involve a degree of exclusivity. For, built into the holistic and integrated approach within Catholicism, there is also a dialectic between accommodation and openness to the world on the one hand and, on the other hand, resistance to and struggle against it. This dialectic, which involves a constant creative tension between development and discipline in our lives, helps to clarify both the distinctiveness and the exclusiveness within Catholic educational philosophy. By clarifying what Catholic education is for, it will be easier to see how - and why - it must resist some alternative perspectives which are incompatible with it, for example, those implicit within the philosophy of the "market", with its attendant features of individualism, utilitarianism and materialism.

4.3.1   Von Hügel

In anticipation of my claim that it *is* possible to combine distinctiveness with inclusiveness and as an exemplification of how this chapter's key themes (integral human development, autonomous disciplines, a synthesis of faith, life and culture and the need for interconnectedness) can be interpreted and understood in such a way that they mutually support and illuminate one another, I draw upon the personal example and writings of Baron Friedrich von Hügel (1852-1925).[73]   With an aristocratic Scottish mother and an Austrian diplomat as father, von Hügel spent his early life in various European cities, gaining a cosmopolitan perspective and a facility in several languages before settling down for most of his adult life in England. He did not study at university, although he was a dedicated scholar. This well-connected layman combined several roles in his wide range of contacts and through his many interests and extended span of correspondence. He was a biblical critic, a religious historian, a philosopher of religion, a spiritual director and an ecumenist. Unfortunately, he has been almost completely neglected in the literature on Catholic education despite the fact that he has a wealth of insights worth drawing upon.   Despite the great respect with which he was held, especially among Christians beyond his own communion, it is only fair to record that he failed in his own lifetime to convince many of his fellow Catholics to attend carefully to his version of an integrated and well-rounded Catholicism.

   This may be due, in part, to the fact that, although a devout and loyal member of the church, he prized his independence from any particular party line. He also participated significantly, both in his own right and in a mediating role, in the very lively debates of his time, especially those relating to the church's difficulties in establishing a satisfactory accommodation with the insights of modern thinking. The modernist movement in the Catholic Church at the beginning of the twentieth century sought to reinterpret Catholic thought in the light of current theories from historical, biblical, scientific and philosophical studies.   Von Hügel, being a polymath, delved into all these areas and applied them to his reflections on the church and religious life. In doing so, he did not confine himself to the familiar categories employed by specialists in any particular discipline, thereby making himself suspected, either of religious unorthodoxy or of not being a serious scholar. This was compounded by his evident sympathy for several figures in the modernist movement who were condemned by the Catholic Church for jettisoning too readily traditional concepts and categories and for slipping into heresy as a result.[74] Perhaps another reason for von Hügel's lack of influence on Catholics in England has been his convoluted and Teutonic style of writing, which showed the influence both of his being brought up in a cosmopolitan and multi-lingual household and of his multi-disciplinary studies.   But, if his mind was "laborious, many regarding, fully weighing, slow, deep ploughing,"[75] it certainly yielded insights from which we can still derive much benefit.

Throughout his writings we find a picture of what might be meant by an integral human formation, though this was not a phrase he used himself. The synthesis of faith, culture and life that he hints at is one that displays a dynamic and deep equilibrium. He shows how wholeness, holiness and humanity can be held together, indeed, how they need each other. The themes of richness, fullness, growth, infinite expansion, abundance, balance and inclusiveness pervade his works. By demonstrating in his own life and writings the importance of balancing the institutional, intellectual and mystical elements of religion, allowing each of these to supplement, stimulate and to purify the other two, and not allowing one element to dominate, he managed to inject warmth, vitality, depth and genuine openness into the picture of what an educated Catholic could be like.[76]

Von Hügel stressed that the church does not have a monopoly of truth and grace, and that God is to be found, and that truth, beauty and goodness are present, in all religions. Such a view was not characteristic of the Catholic Church of his own time, although it was fully in harmony with previously neglected elements of its history. Drawing upon the thought of the Spanish theologian de Lugo (1583-1660), he brought out the universalist side of Catholicism and showed that tolerance did not mean indifference.[77] Von Hügel's tolerance was based first on a humble recognition that we can neither trace nor confine the operations of God's grace in individuals and also in institutions, and second on a trust in the essential good faith and sound religious instinct of people everywhere. Tolerance, then, it might be said, is owed to others because of their basic goodness. It is advisable because Catholics do not possess a monopoly of truth and so should be ready to learn from and be enriched by the insights of others. Finally, it is incumbent on all if we are to be open to the universal and inscrutable ways of God. He opposed the heresy-hunting mentality that prevailed in his church in the first few years of this century and set himself resolutely against the narrowness, suspicion, timidity and controversial spirit which he deplored among his fellow Catholics. He had learnt from the Parisian priest Huvelin that it is possible to remain deeply believing while remaining realistic about difficulties.[78] He did not water down the church's teaching on the transcendence of God, the divinity of Jesus, the need for institutional adherence, the objective claims for doctrinal truth, or the cost of religious life. But he did manage to combine this embrace of the 'otherness' of religious faith with an openness to the non-religious dimensions of life.

4.3.2. Our need of the non-religious dimensions

One of the most important and pervading themes in von Hügel's works is the fact that we need, for the sake of our religious health, as much as for the health of the rest of our personality, all the other, non-religious dimensions of our being, to be fully developed. These include our physical, emotional, aesthetic, social and intellectual growth. The multiplicity of our inner life provides the necessary materials, stimulants, interactions and obstacles from which richness, balance and harmony can emerge.[79]

> Catholicism will have to recognise, respect, love and protect the non-religious levels and complexes of life, as also coming from God as occasions, materials, stimulations, necessary for us men towards the development of our complete humanity, and especially of our religion...These various stages and ranges possess their own immanent laws and conditions of existence and growth, and deserve our love and service in this their nature and development.[80]

The body and the senses have a crucial role here for von Hügel. In his view epistemology and psychology combine in showing us that we need the stimulation of the senses for the awakening of our spiritual awareness.[81] God is only apprehended only in, with, and on occasion of, yet also in contrast to, other realities. Von Hügel believes that this obtains in knowledge of any kind that we claim to have. If this is so, then we must fill our lives with a wide range of interests, for their own sake and for our spiritual development.[82] The body is not the enemy of the spirit, but "the stimulator and spring-board, the material and training ground" for it. Through its agency we must "strive to awaken and utilise" every aspect of life, with its special characteristics, "in its right place and degree, for the calling into full action of all the rest."[83]

By taking the Incarnation of Christ as a model for our appreciation of how the human and the divine can coexist, rather than be seen as opponents, von Hügel combines belief in sacramentality, mediation and communion, features later identified by McBrien as constituting the essence of Catholicism. "Typical growth in religious depth and fruitfulness is not a growth away from the stimulations, occasions, concomitants, vehicles and expressions of sense."[84] Nature is not driven out or destroyed by grace; it is built on and transformed.

The different spheres of life all have their part to play. It is right and proper to encourage people to cultivate, rather than to deflect their attention away from, an interest in politics, economics, language, history, science and philosophy.[85] These various levels in life contribute to each other. Therefore we should study religion both together with and apart from them, since the presence of God "underlies, environs, protects and perfects all the lesser realities."[86]

Presumably von Hügel wished to preserve two values here. There is the mutual illumination and stimulus offered when subjects are studied together or in each other's light. Yet it is also necessary to protect the separate identity and relative autonomy of each one, so that it can be truly itself rather than merely the auxiliary or the servant of another discipline. He jealously defended the rights of historians and scientists to operate freely and according to their own methodology, with a right to their own sphere of jurisdiction, and without interference from theologians or church authorities.

> Religion is not directly either Ethics or Philosophy, Economics or Art, yet at the peril of emptiness and sterility, it has to move out into, to learn from, to criticise, and to teach, all these other apprehensions and activities.[87]

Theology may well be the crowning discipline but this does not entail crippling or distorting the others; rather it means adopting an open and inclusive attitude towards them. Such openness, while recognising the genuine insights, values and truths contained in other disciplines, does not disallow theology the right to indicate their limitations or where they might need complementing. Similarly theologians will benefit from the perspectives and insights gained through deep immersion in other disciplines. In von Hügel's view we should neither

> sacrifice religion to these activities or these activities to religion...God is the God of the body as he is of the soul; of science as he is of faith; of criticism and theory as of fact and reality.[88]

Furthermore,

> This source and sustenance [God] of the other realities is apprehended by us ever with, and in, and over against, those other, various realities that impinge upon our many-levelled lives...Religion has the...task of ever respecting, whilst ever more harmonizing, purifying, and utilizing, each and all of these various realms.[89]

In my treatment of post Vatican II thinking on Catholic education I have noted the tension that exists between the three principles; holding together a concern for the autonomy of the disciplines, the synthesis between culture and faith and development of the critical faculties of students as part of their integral formation is not easy. A study of the works of von Hügel provides a welcome filling out of these principles and an example of their application. No one brings out more clearly than he does the essential interconnections between these principles.

As von Hügel is keen to remind us, "man is not a mere sum-total of water-tight compartments." For, although the various areas of knowledge "have to be discovered and treated according to the principles and methods immanent and special to that department," their insights must be brought to bear upon each other.[90] For example,

> science will help to discipline, humble, purify the natural eagerness and wilfulness, the cruder forms of anthropomorphism, of the human mind and heart. (It) will help to give depth and mystery, drama and pathos, a rich spirituality, to the whole experience and conception of the soul and of life, of the world and of God...Crush out, or in any way mutilate or deautonomise this part, and all the rest will suffer.[91]

There will be similar gains that flow from serious study of all the disciplines, since they offer insights into real and essential aspects of our nature and our world.

> However much man may be supremely and finally a religious animal, he is not only that; but he is a physical and sexual, a fighting and an artistic, a domestic and social, a political and philosophical animal as well.[92]

4.3.3. Friction

Von Hügel was well aware that it would be no easy task to bring all these different parts of our personality into some kind of harmony. Integral human development could not happen without much friction, cost and pain.[93] He treated the 'midwifery of pain' as 'inseparable from the birth and rebirth of a personality'.[94] He was convinced, to a degree that puzzled his closest friends, that to experience our nature as internally discordant was both normal and necessary for our human and spiritual growth.[95] The different energies and needs within us and the various opportunities and environments pressing upon us were bound to conflict with one another, to cause friction, tension and to co-exist in an uneasy rivalry.[96]

The theme of friction and its place in our development recurs frequently throughout all of von Hügel's writings. The friction within us that is caused by the mutual chafing of the different parts of our personality serves several functions. Sometimes it prevents religion from overstraining us by forcing us to develop another part of ourselves, perhaps a part that had been neglected in our attempts to meet religious requirements.[97] Sometimes the sheer 'non-fit', the 'otherness' of, for example, science or religion, one to another, forces us to make room within us for a perception which transcends our previous categories or exceeds the bounds of inadequate language.[98] At other times, the purpose of the inner friction that we experience stems from the fact that "the primary function of religion is not the consoling of the natural man as it finds him, but the purification of this man, by effecting an ever-growing cleavage and contrast between his bad false self, and ...his true good self."[99]

Clearly von Hügel has a rich understanding of the complexity of our inner lives and of our need for guidance which will ensure that we do not become unbalanced by particular enthusiasms of our own or by the demands of others. Among the various possible avenues we could travel in life we must be prevented from pursuing any path, including the religious one, too far or too soon, lest we be ill-equipped or unready for the journey and its eventual rigours. Some of the tensions and frictions from which we suffer will be experienced as the conflicting calls of the senses versus the spirit, or of the past versus the present, or of the institutional versus the individual.[100] No matter, for we need all of these tensions to enter into us, to recognise the call, which comes from beyond our own little worlds, through these experiences, to wake up and to allow ourselves to be enlarged in consciousness and character. In this process, which is part of what continual conversion entails, there will be a combination of correction and confirmation: some elements in our nature and habits need to be either curbed or reshaped, while others deserve and will receive a strengthening or boosting of their natural powers.

One of the ways that von Hügel's perspective reflects an emphasis more prevalent in his own era than in ours is the notion of life as a testing ground for the growth of personality, as a seedbed for the emergence of spirit, as a training school of sanctity.[101] In the scheme of things heroism is called for and this only comes through facing real struggle.

> Real temptation, true piercing conflict, heavy darkness, and bewildering perplexity...risks of failing and falling: all this forms an essential part of this painful-joyous probation and virile, because necessarily costing and largely gradual, self-constitution of man's free-willing spirit.[102]

Some of this is reminiscent of Teilhard de Chardin's language on the need for God to work in us through our passivities as well as through our activities, through what we undergo as well as through what we achieve via effort. Teilhard was no more being morbid than was von Hügel in making allowance for the dark side of life.[103] Von Hügel acknowledges a role for asceticism as a valid and, indeed, essential and constituent part of the Christian outlook, despite the apparent hardness of this viewpoint and despite the combat and concentration it requires of us to follow this way.[104] Without temptation and struggle, virtue could not develop within us. Heroic virtue, together with adoration, is, for him, the very essence of religion.

Finally, there is another, perhaps somewhat surprising, dimension to the role of friction in our lives. Part of its value lies in the challenge it throws out to the religious dimension in us. Our very church allegiance will find itself checked, purified, steadied and sobered - and therefore made more wholesome - by the struggles faith has with the institution of the church.[105] For the church needs to learn from and to be enriched by our tussle with it, just as we will benefit enormously by being ready to receive the wisdom and training it offers to us. And this is where those other, non-religious, elements of life come into their own. For

> religion will have to come to see that it cannot attain to its own depth, it cannot become the chief thing, if it does not continually renounce to aspiring after being everything.[106]

4.3.4. *Church affiliation and inclusiveness*

Von Hügel has shown - although he does not use these terms - some of the depths of what might be meant by integral human development and also the contributory role played in this development by both the autonomy of the different subjects or disciplines and the synthesis of faith and culture. He also exemplifies how one can combine a firm commitment to a church with a genuine openness to people with different convictions and institutional affiliations.

The first mistake to avoid, he would claim, is any attempt at complete identification of the visible with the invisible church. This would be incompatible with Catholicism.[107] Only God can read men's hearts; no earthly institution, even the church, has yet reached perfection; and God's Spirit may dwell in, but it also transcends his church.

A second mistake would be to have an unbalanced or excessive veneration for the authority of the church. Von Hügel is convinced that such authority is an absolutely essential factor assisting in the soul's growth, but, even so, it still only constitutes part, not the whole, of our religious life. One must also be realistic, open and honest about the shortcomings of that authority.

> Official Authority is ever repetitive of something past and gone; is the voice of the average thoughts of the many; aims at limiting the action of its subjects to a passive reception and more or less mechanical execution of its commands; is essentially timid; cares necessarily more for the outward appearances and material output, than for the interior disposition and form of the soul's activity; maps out the very phenomenal world into visible, mutually exclusive regions of spiritual light and darkness.[108]

This recognition of such shortcomings does not seem to have undermined von Hügel's loyalty to his church in any way. In his view, with the combination of features that co-exist within the church, our spiritual lives will benefit from both the prudent and the daring sides of her character. This is true even if we are not able to appreciate it at the time when we experience either her conserving or her creative actions. And, of course we must acknowledge, von Hügel points out, that

> church officials are no more the whole church...than Scotland Yard or the War Office or
> the House of Lords, though admittedly necessary parts of the national life, are the
> whole, or average samples, of the life and fruitfulness of the English nation.[109]

Thus we have a concept of von Hügel's commitment to the church, which is firm and unwavering, alert to the riches she offered and ready to accept the discipline she imposed, but also well aware of her limitations. He was also open-minded about and ready to learn from other faiths which he recognised and appreciated as having elements of truth and light in them even though he could not accept that they were all equally true. The claim to universality of the Catholic Church should in no way lead to intolerance.[110]

Von Hügel's open and sensitive approach to people of other Christian denominations led him, when they asked his advice, to take great care not to pressurise them to become Catholics. They must feel ready for this. Without that readiness, premature pressure could disturb their equilibrium and they might end up in a worse state than they were in before leaving behind their former religious affiliation. Souls outside the church were not lost; they were safe with God, wherever they were. Instead of an excessive urge to win converts as rapidly and in as large numbers as possible, rather he sought to strengthen and deepen whatever beliefs (however tentative) and whatever religious practice (however tenuous a hold in their lives) they already had.[111] Part of his caution against too zealous an attempt to proselytise others stemmed from the harm he felt he had done, the confusion he had sown and the disturbance he had caused for some of his friends and even to members of his own family by sharing too readily and forcefully his own religious position and convictions.

This caution led him to adopt a balanced approach to others who were seeking religious guidance. He advocated a way that was "fervent without fanaticism," one that combined an encouraging and a sympathetic approach without displaying an indifference to the claims of his own faith.[112] In this openness to people who were not fellow Catholics, von Hügel was out of step with the prevailing ethos of his church. It can justifiably be claimed that he was a forerunner of that more positive and ecumenical attitude towards other Christians and to adherents of other faiths that emerged at Vatican II. A fortress Catholicism, with its temptation to exert a military discipline over its members and to display a closed and defensive mentality in the face of criticism, was uncongenial to him.

Von Hügel did not use either of those phrases which we have seen are central to the current Catholic understanding of the goal of education, namely 'integral development of the human person' and 'synthesis of faith, culture, and life.'

Nevertheless, it will be apparent, from the presentation I have given of his thought, that he offers a rich and nuanced appreciation of their meaning. In his own work it is clear that both integral development and the desired synthesis depend upon those other features to which he gave such emphasis: openness to the truth wherever it was to be found, respect for the autonomy of the disciplines and a nurturing of the critical faculties of both the already committed faithful and those who still sought a religious home. If we are open to the differences between people and ourselves, if we welcome their 'otherness' and the particularity they present to us, if we are genuinely inclusive, we will adapt ourselves to their needs.[113] Such inclusiveness and openness, together with the freedom of manoeuvre, flexibility and responsiveness that follow from them, are built upon the confidence, the inner sense of security and stability and the settled conviction of one who stands on firm ground. Von Hügel demonstrates in his work that it is possible, within the parameters of a Catholic perspective, to combine distinctiveness and inclusiveness. These two qualities are not mutually exclusive, but maintaining a creative tension between them will be a complex and costly exercise.

Notes for Chapter 4

---

[1] *Gravissimum Educationis*, in Abbott, Walter, (ed), *The Documents of Vatican II*, London, Geoffrey Chapman, 1967, p.639.

[2] *Ibid.*, p.645. (in a footnote)

[3] The primacy given to parents in the education of their children was a prominent theme in papal teachings of the inter-war years, in response to collectivist and totalitarian ideologies of both the right and the left.

[4] I say more on salvation in chapter five.

[5] *Gravissimum Educationis*, pp. 641, 646, 648.

[6] *Ibid.* p.639.

[7] Gregory XVI stated in *Mirari vos* (1832) that "from the most foul well of indifferentism flows that absurd and erroneous opinion, or rather delirium, of liberty of conscience...But what death is worse for the soul than the freedom to err?" quoted in Kamen, H, *The Rise of Toleration*, London, Weidenfeld and Nicolson, 1967, p.241. Pius IX, in 1864, completely rejected the idea that "the Roman pontiff can, and ought to, reconcile himself to, and agree with, progress, liberalism, and modern civilization." quoted in Dulles, Avery, *Models of the Church*, Dublin, Gill and Macmillan, 1974, p.84.

[8] The Sacred Congregation for Catholic Education, *The Catholic School*, London, Catholic Truth Society, 1977, pp.10, 11.

[9] Anthony Bryk, Valerie Lee and Peter Holland, *Catholic Schools and the Common Good*, Cambridge, Massachusetts, Harvard University Press, 1993; Marcellin Flynn, *The Culture of Catholic Schools*, Homebush, (Australia), St Pauls, 1993; Ross Keane & Dan Riley (eds), *Quality Catholic Schools*, Archdiocese of Brisbane, 1997; Catholic Education Service, (i) *Quality in Catholic Schools*, London, 1995; (ii) *Learning from OFSTED and Diocesan Inspections*, London, 1996; (iii) *A Struggle for Excellence*, London, 1997; (iv) *Foundations for Excellence*, London, 1999. Andrew Morris's five articles also provide evidence for the relative success of Catholic schools: (i) 'The academic performance of Catholic schools', *School Organisation*, vol. 14, 1994, pp.81-89, (ii) 'The Catholic school ethos; its effect on post-16 student academic achievement', *Educational Studies*, vol. 21, no. 1, 1995, pp.67-83, (iii) 'Same Mission, Same Methods, Same Results?', *British Journal of Educational Studies*, December 1997, pp.378-391, (iv) So Far, So Good: levels of academic achievement in Catholic schools', *Educational Studies*, vol. 24, no. 1, 1998, pp.83-94, (v) 'Catholic and other secondary schools: an analysis of OFSTED inspection reports', *Educational Research*, vol. 40, no. 2, 1998.

[10] *The Catholic School*, pp. 8,13.

[11] *Ibid.*, pp. 7, 12, 13.

[12] *Ibid.*, p.14.

[13] *Ibid.*

[14] *Ibid.*, p.15.

[15] For example, see Walbert Buhlmann, *With Eyes to See*, Slough, St Paul Publications, 1990, chapters 5 - 7, which deal with Latin America, Africa, Asia and Euramerica respectively. Also, see Aylward Shorter, *Toward a Theology of Inculturation*, London, Geoffrey Chapman, 1988. A penetrating analysis of the task of inculturation is offered by Michael Paul Gallagher, in *Clashing Symbols*, London, Darton, Longman & Todd, 1997.

[16] In 1997 the Sri Lankan theologian Tissa Balasuriya was excommunicated as a result of criticisms of his attempt to re-interpret aspects of Christian theology and to relate them to the thought forms of Asian cultures and experience. This excommunication was lifted a year later.

[17] I explore further the relevance of differentiation applied to the religious realm within Catholic schools and the educational implications of appropriating living tradition in chapters six and seven.

[18] For recent guidance which exemplifies that combination of distinctiveness and inclusiveness, as constituent features of Catholic education, which I am advocating in this book, see Bishops' Conference of England and Wales, *Catholic Schools & Other Faiths*, Chelmsford, Matthew James Publishing, 1997.

[19]*The Catholic School*, p. 15.

[20]On the autonomy of the secular, see *Gaudium et Spes*, para 36, and Patrick Hannon, *Church, State, Morality & Law*, Dublin, Gill and Macmillan, 1992, p.55.

[21]Haldane, 'Philosophy and Catholic Education', *The Sower*, April 1995, p.30.

[22]*Ibid.*

[23]For a collection of essays exploring a Catholic understanding of history, see *Eternity in Time*, edited by Stratford Caldecott and John Morrill, Edinburgh, T & T Clark, 1997.

[24]Paddy Walsh clarifies of some of the issues at stake here, in *Education and Meaning: Philosophy in Practice*, London, Cassell, 1993.

[25]*The Catholic School*, p.18.

[26]John Paul II, *Catechesi Tradendae*, London, Catholic Truth Society, 1979, para 5.

[27]*Ibid.*. paras 43, 67.

[28]*Ibid.*, para 69.

[29]*Ibid.*, para 15.

[30]*Ibid.*, 7, 13, 18.

[31]See section 4.3.3 on von Hügel and friction.

[32]*Catechesi Tradendae*, para 17.

[33]*Ibid.*

[34]*Ibid.*, para 47.

[35]*Ibid.*, paras 29, 32.

[36]*Ibid.*, paras 38, 49, 53, 59, 92.

[37]The Sacred Congregation for Catholic Education, *Lay Catholics in Schools: Witnesses to Faith*, (London, Catholic Truth Society, 1982), pp. 8, 9, 11, 12, 13, 14, 17.

[38]*Ibid.* pp.17,18.

[39]*Ibid.* pp. 22, 24, 33, 34, 35, 41.

[40]*Ibid.*

[41]Newman, J.H., *An Essay in Aid of a Grammar of Assent*, introduced by Nicholas Lash, London, University of Notre Dame Press, 1979, p.89.   In *University Sermons*, (introduced by D. M. MacKinnon and J. D. Holmes, London, SPCK, 1970, p. 93.) Newman devotes a whole sermon to the theme of 'Personal Influence, the Means of Propagating the Truth'.

[42]*University Sermons*, p.94.

[43]The Congregation for Catholic Education, *The Religious Dimension of Education in a Catholic School*, (London, Catholic Truth Society, 1988), p.26.

[44]*Ibid.*, quoting from a 1982 speech by Pope John Paul II.

[45]*Ibid.*, pp. 26, 29, 30, 56.

[46]*Ibid.*p.43. See also p.48. For a more detailed treatment of the human person, see chapter five.

[47]*Ibid.* p.49.

[48]*Ibid.* p.3.

[49]For a powerful push in this direction, one which challenged Catholic schools to be more humane places which reflect the Gospel spirit of freedom and love, see Purnell, P, *Our Faith Story*, London, Collins, 1985.

[50] Congregation for the Clergy, *General Directory for Catechesis*, London, Catholic Truth Society, 1997.

[51] Congregation for Catholic Education, *The Catholic School on the Threshold of the Third Millennium*, Boston, Pauline Books, 1998.

[52] On this topic, see sections 2.2., above and 9.5., below.

[53]This is discussed further in 4.3.2, 4.3.3 and in chapter 5.

[54]David Konstant, *Signposts and Homecomings*, Slough, St Pauls, 1981, p.121. For further biblical references asserting the centrality of Christ in a Christian's understanding of self and world, see Matthew 28: 18-20; the prologue to John's Gospel; John 14:6; Ephesians 1:9-10; 1 Timothy 2:5.

[55]Konstant, *ibid.*

[56]G. K. Chesterton, *The Common Man*, (London, Sheed and Ward, 1950), pp.167-8. *cf.* Newman on the interconnectedness of knowledge in *Idea of a University*, London, Longmans, Green & Co, 1912, pp. 50, 51, 134, 137.

[57]Michael Himes, 'Catholicism as Integral Humanism: Christian Participation in Pluralistic Moral Education,' in *The Challenge of Pluralism*, edited by F. Clark Power and Daniel K. Lapsley, (University of Notre Dame Press, 1992), p.130.

[58]See Himes, *loc. cit.*, p.132.

[59]Himes, *loc. cit.*, p.133. For an indication of how Christianity can be related to the curriculum and how many subjects can be open to a religious dimension, see Kevin Williams, 'Religion, Culture and Schooling,' in *From Ideal to Action*, edited by Matthew Feheney, Dublin, Veritas, 1998.

[60]See Patrick Hannon, *op. cit.*, p.33 on there being no ultimate separation between service of God and social behaviour.

[61]The true nature of this synthesis is outlined by Gemma Loughran in 'The Rationale of Catholic Education' in *Education and Policy in Northern Ireland*, edited by R. Osborne, R. Cormack & R. Miller, Belfast, Policy Research Institute, 1987, pp.115-122. Loughran argues that a Catholic view of education differs from a secularist philosophy "which insists on an exclusively this-world interpretation and explanation of reality and which therefore dismisses as irrelevant any religious belief", and that it also differs from a philosophy of education which "distinguishes between secular knowledge and a separate realm of religion." She points out that, in contrast with these two views, "the Catholic understanding is of the unity of all knowledge, of the oneness of truth in Christ." *ibid.*, p.117.

[62]Teachers of different curriculum areas should expect their work to be receptive to the religious atmosphere and worldview on which the school is founded. In this sense they cannot claim to be uninfluenced by it. *The General Directory for Catechesis*, (1997) strongly emphasises the importance of interdisciplinary dialogue in Catholic schools being prompted by religious instruction. (London, Catholic Truth Society, 1997, p.74.)

[63]Ronald Nelson's essay 'Faith Discipline Integration: Compatibilist, Reconstructionalist, and Transformationalist Strategies' (from *The Reality of Christian Learning*, edited by H. Heie and D. Wolfe, Grand Rapids, Michigan, Eerdmans Publishing, 1987, pp.317-339) has influenced several other recent Reformed critiques of Christian education, including, for example, some of the work of Ken Badley ('The Faith/Learning Integration Movement in Christian Higher Education: Slogan or Substance?', *Journal of Research in Christian Education*, vol. 3, no. 1, Spring 1994, pp.13-33) and 'Two "Cop-Outs" in Faith-Learning Integration', (*Spectrum*, vol. 28, no. 2, 1996, pp.105-118) and several of the essays in *Agenda for Educational Change*, edited by John Shortt & Trevor Cooling, Leicester, Apollos, 1997.

[64]On these three approaches see Nelson, *loc. cit.*, pp.317, 325, 329 and *Agenda*, pp.13, 88, 175. It is interesting to note that, in this analysis, Nelson relies heavily on Lonergan: first, with regard to his epistemology, in his treatment of the conditions of our knowing; second, borrowing Lonergan's analysis of how our mental horizons are modified by the flooding into our lives of the unearned and unconditional love of God; and third, drawing heavily on Lonergan's analysis of the nature and effects of conversion and how this relates to our capacity for knowledge. The use of 'reconstruction' by Christian writers from the reformed tradition is quite different from that of Dewey or Freire, which refers to reflection upon and interrogation of experience, to processing of knowledge and to consideration of its application in personal and social projects.

[65]Badley, (1996), *loc. cit.* For a constructive approach to interaction between different curriculum disciplines, see Fachtna McCarthy's chapter, 'The Mind of God: Science and Theology Today', in *Faith and Culture in the Irish Context*, edited by Eoin Cassidy, Dublin, Veritas, 1996, especially pp. 38-39, 42-46.

[66]Leszek Kolakowski, *Religion*, (Glasgow, Fontana, 1982), p. 183.

[67]Quoted by E. Kevane in *Philosophy and the Integration of Contemporary Catholic Education*, edited by G. McLean (The Catholic University of America Press, Washington, 1962), p.233.

[68]I acknowledge that Augustine and Aquinas differ in significant ways in their holisms. Thus Augustine *disconnects* body and person by comparison with Aquinas. And Aquinas insists on a *distinction* between philosophy and theology, between reason and revelation, in a way that is not characteristic of Augustine.

[69]J. Evans, (ed) *Jacques Maritain: The Man and His Achievement*, (New York, Sheed and Ward, 1963), pp.193-196.

[70]K. Nichols, in *Religion and Education: Islamic and Christian Approaches*, edited by Syed Ali Ashraf & Paul Hirst (Cambridge, The Islamic Academy, 1994), p.213.

[71]*Ibid.*, p.205. Nichols acknowledges his indebtedness to Newman's major study on the epistemology of religious belief, *A Grammar of Assent*.

[72]J. R. Martin, in *Beyond Liberal Education*, edited by Robin Barrow and Patricia White (London, Routledge, 1993), pp.116.

[73]For a comprehensive and concise summary of von Hügel's life and thought, see Kelly, James J, *Baron Friedrich von Hügel's Philosophy of Religion*, Leuven University Press, 1983. Alternative accounts are provided by Ellen Leonard, *Creative Tension: The Spiritual Legacy of Friedrich von Hügel*, Fordham University Press, 1997 and Joseph Whelan, *The Spirituality of Friedrich von Hügel*, London, Collins, 1971.

[74]On the condemnation of modernism, see chapter three, note 36.

[75]According to Bernard Holland, who introduced and edited von Hügel's *Selected Letters*, (London, Dent, 1927), p.13.

[76]Von Hügel, *The Mystical Element of Religion*, vol. 1, London, Dent, 1908, pp.59, 61, 70. According to von Hügel, each of the three elements is open to abuse, imbalance or distortion, but they are each capable of providing for one another a powerful and constant check and opposition within the complete spiritual life. See also Bernard Holland (ed), *Selected Letters* (of von Hügel)), London, Dent, 1927, p.191.

[77]von Hügel, *The Reality of God & Religion and Agnosticism*, edited by Edmund Gardner, London, Dent, 1931, pp.149-50; *Eternal Life*, Edinburgh, T&T Clark, 1913, pp.350-1; *Selected Letters*, pp.39, 250.

[78]As one reference, among many, to von Hügel's sense of indebtedness to and esteem for Huvelin, see *Eternal Life*, pp.374-7.

[79]*Mystical Element of Religion*, vol. 2, pp.281, 283, 371, 393, 395.

[80]Von Hügel, *Essays and Addresses on the Philosophy of Religion*, London, Dent, 1921, pp.238-9. On the need for attention to the various levels and needs of life, see von Hügel, *Essays and Addresses, Second Series*, London, Dent, 1926, pp.59-60.

[81]*Selected Letters*, p.349. "We never begin (or in the long run keep up) the apprehension of things spiritual except on occasion of the awakedness and stimulation of the senses...There is no such thing as an exclusively spiritual awakening to, or apprehension of spiritual Realities."

[82]*Ibid.*, p.260. See also p.289.

[83]*Essays and Addresses*, p.238. *cf.* also *Essays and Addresses: Second Series*, pp.98, 107. and von Hügel, *Eternal Life*, p.329.

[84]*Essays and Addresses,*. p.230. See also p.283.

[85]*Essays and Addresses: Second Series*, pp.38, 229.

[86]von Hügel (1931), *The Reality of God and Religion & Agnosticism*, pp.33, 36.

[87]*Eternal Life,* p.330.

[88]*Ibid.*, p.332.

[89]*Ibid.*, pp.368,394.

[90]*Mystical Element of Religion*, vol. 1, pp.xxvi, 44.

[91]*Ibid.*, p.45.

[92]*Ibid.*, p.47.

[93]*Eternal Life*, p.357.

[94]Albert Cock, *A Critical Examination of Von Hügel's Philosophy of* Religion, p.77. (No date is given, but from internal evidence the study was clearly published in either 1948 or 1049. Instead of a publisher, only the distributors are mentioned: Hugh Rees, London.)

[95]John McGrath, *Baron Friedrich von Hügel and the Debate on Historical Christianity*, San Francisco, Mellen Research University Press, 1993, pp.157, 158.

[96]*Essays and Addresses*, p.xii.

[97]*Essays and Addresses: Second Series*, p.219.

[98]*Selected Letters*, p.94.

[99]*Ibid.*, p.72.

[100]*Essays and Addresses: Second Series*, pp.62, 246-7.

[101]"The essential, the most indispensable of the dimensions of religion is, *not breadth, but depth*, and

above all, *the insight into sanctity and the power to produce saints.*" Letter from von Hügel to Norman Kemp Smith, 3/1/1922. See *The Letters of Baron Friedrich von Hügel and Professor Norman Kemp Smith*, edited by Lawrence Barmann, New York, Fordham University Press, 1981, p.162. (emphasis in the original.)

[102] *Mystical Element*, vol. 1, p.369.

[103] Teilhard de Chardin, *Le Milieu Divin* (London, Collins, 1972) speaks of the passivities of diminishment, the place of asceticism , resignation and detachment. There is also in this work by Teilhard a reflection of von Hügel's emphasis on the value of all dimensions of life as vehicles on our heavenly journey: "By virtue of the Creation and, still more, of the Incarnation, nothing here below is profane for those who know how to see." (p.66.)

[104] *Selected Letters*, p.275.

[105] *Selected Letters*, p. 201.

[106] *Ibid.*, p.95.

[107] *Essays and Addresses,* p.230.

[108] *Essays and Addresses: Second Series*, pp.10, 12, 23. cf *Eternal Life*, p.324. In *Letters to a Niece* (pp.165-6) von Hügel refers to his efforts to make the church intellectually more inhabitable, since at this time he claimed it was less strong on the needs, rights and duties of the mental life than it was on promoting spiritual insights. Authority was one part, but a necessary one, within his Catholicism. "I believe because I am told," he said, but he then immediately went on to add, "because it is true, because it answers to my deepest interior experiences and needs." (*Mystical Element*, vol. 1, p.54.)

[109] *Essays and Addresses, Second Series,* p.17.

[110] *Reality of God*, pp.13, 21. and *Letters to a Niece*, pp.xxxiv, 56.

[111] *Letters to a Niece*, p.x. *cf.* "I find myself inclined to be very zealous to help souls to make the most of what they already have; and, if they come to think of moving, to test them to the uttermost." *Selected Letters*, pp. 346-7.

[112] *Reality of God*, p.151. *Eternal Life*, p.352. He was convinced that "the persuasiveness of the church is in inverse ratio to her coercive character and action." p.352. cf. *Mystical Element*, vol. 1, p.xxvi.

[113] *Mystical Element*, vol. 1, p.34.

CHAPTER 5

DISTINCTIVE WORLDVIEW

If Catholic schools are to be distinctive, then much of this distinctiveness will rest upon their displaying an appreciation firstly, that the whole curriculum has a religious dimension, and, secondly, that all the disciplines, although autonomous, have a part to play in promoting the integral development of the whole person. One would need to add to such an appreciation a desire to integrate faith with both culture and life. This distinctiveness will also depend upon a shared world-view and a shared concept of the sort of person that education should be aiming to develop, with Christ being taken as the prime role model. No attempt to articulate a consistently thought through approach to education could avoid implying at least a view of the nature of persons and their place in the general order of things, including some ideas about what it is important for them to be like. As Philip May has pointed out, "behind every educational system, its aims, curricula, teaching methods and organization, lie assumptions about the nature of man and the purpose of life."[1] From a rather different perspective, Fred Inglis comments, "by implying a view of what to do with knowledge, the curriculum, like the culture, implies a picture of how to live and who to be."[2]

5.1   Shared view of life

Behind a Catholic philosophy of education there is an anthropology, a theology of creation, a Christology and an ecclesiology. I do not claim that the *content* of all these is distinctively Catholic. Many of the central elements within a Catholic worldview, for example, doctrines of the Trinity, Incarnation and salvation, are shared by other Christians.[3] The official Catholic position is that these shared doctrines are more fundamental for Christian faith than areas of doctrinal differences among Christians. Furthermore, many elements within a Christian worldview are also shared by people of other faiths.[4] As examples of these shared elements, apart from belief in God, I will refer in this chapter to the voice of conscience, the notion of the soul, the interconnectedness of intellectual, moral and spiritual qualities, the acknowledgement of sin, the need for a disciplining of our powers and a receptivity to grace.

With so much of importance held in common, both with fellow Christians and with people of other faiths, a powerful case could be made for ecumenical Christian schools and also for inter-faith education shared between, for example, Christians, Jews and Muslims. Despite being sympathetic to, indeed enthusiastic about, such projects, I intend to leave them on one side, for my aim here is to explore the internal coherence of the claim that (separate) Catholic education can combine distinctiveness with inclusiveness. Given my particular focus, I do not consider here why some other Christians, who share substantially a great many beliefs with Catholics, do not think separate schooling is either necessary or desirable. This interesting and important question would have to be addressed if one sought to provide a comprehensive exploration of the relationship between Christian philosophies of education and particular forms of schooling, or if one aimed for a critical and well-founded justification for separate, faith-based schooling. Both of these aims are beyond the scope of my narrower exploration here.

It is not essential to my argument that the elements within a Catholic Christian worldview that I pick out should lead inexorably to a desire for separate schooling even on the part of all Catholics. This would require a marked degree of uniformity among Catholics in their understanding of and commitment to these elements and it would depend upon an approach by the church that was monolithic in its stance and pronouncements. There is no evidence of such uniformity among believers and much evidence of a high level of diversity within the church as a whole and within Catholic education in particular. This becomes clearer as soon as the context, composition and functioning of Catholic schools in other countries is examined.

There is, however, a central or 'mainstream' position within Catholicism that defends the right of the church to maintain schools under its aegis and guided by its own educational philosophy. Of course, there are alternative viewpoints on both the composition and weighting of the 'ingredients' of a Catholic worldview. There are also different views about the need for, and indeed essential nature of, Catholic schools. Despite, this, for the purposes of my argument I assume that the 'mainstream' position described here is representative and authoritative. The *salience* of the elements referred to in this chapter is so highly marked within Catholicism and their implications for education are so strongly emphasized, that a Catholic interpretation of them has *often in practice* been the foundation for a policy of separate schooling. It has frequently been assumed that Catholic education is to be provided to ensure that these elements receive due attention and appropriate treatment. Without the opportunity to provide such a religiously informed context for education, the Catholic Church believes that prevailing assumptions in society and education will undermine her teaching, hinder a sufficiently rounded development of persons and even distort in some way an understanding of those truths and values held in common with others.

Within Catholic theology, ecclesiology, an understanding of church, plays a key role in the distinctive configuration and weighting of these elements. In ecumenical dialogue it is often different understandings of church which prevent agreement, rather than theological differences over personhood, creation or Christ. There is not scope here to analyze the multiple, complementary, mutually correcting and sometimes conflicting models of church which are available within Catholicism, for example, models of the church as institution, as herald, as Body of Christ, as sacrament, as servant or as mystical communion.[5] However, I would contend that her ecclesiology provides Catholicism with a particular way of bringing together thinking about human nature, the person of Christ and God as the source and goal of creation. It also establishes a context for understanding the relationship between the material and the spiritual, nature and grace, faith and reason, freedom and authority, discipline and development, and the individual and the community.[6] These polarities are important elements of a Catholic worldview. Any attempt to grasp the meaning, scope and significance of Catholic doctrine, morality and spirituality is likely to be deficient if these are not interpreted in the context of a Catholic ecclesiology. The overall shape of Catholic education, likewise, can only be appreciated if it is related to a Catholic understanding of the church and its mission. In the light of my claim about the importance of ecclesiology, it should not be surprising if I seek to resolve some of the problems arising from an ambivalence within Catholic education - the twin imperatives to be both distinctive and inclusive - by retrieving in a later chapter a deeper sense of church, specifically through drawing upon the notion of living tradition.[7]

It is because the Catholic understanding of human nature, purpose and destiny differs in crucial respects from some other accounts that are predominant in society, that many Catholics seek a separate context for the education of their children. Within the friendly space provided by separate schooling, there is an opportunity to educate for a different world than that envisaged by secular society to aim for a different ideal of what persons are meant to become. From the perspective of a Catholic approach to education, alternative worldviews are deficient in one or other respect in their 'reading' of human nature and destiny: perhaps through omission, imbalance, exaggeration or under-emphasis. This position does not directly *contradict* certain Catholic beliefs that might be considered essentially inclusive, but it does co-exist in some tension with them. This inclusive dimension of Catholicism embraces the following beliefs. First, there is much truth and value in worldviews outside the church. Second, the church herself is damaged by sin and should always be open to reform. Third, the church should always be ready, not only to communicate her message but at the same time ready to learn from others in order to augment and penetrate more deeply into what she already possesses.

The presentation of any set of beliefs is bound to be influenced by the prevailing assumptions of the people being addressed; that is, it will not be 'free-standing' in the sense that it is irrelevant who the debating partners are. What they are for and what they neglect will both frame and modify the presentation, what is emphasized and omitted, the 'shape' or ordering of the presentation and the implications drawn from it. *Recent* arguments for the continuation of an educational policy of separate Catholic schooling within England and Wales have been conducted with the perceived shortcomings of liberal, secular and market-led ideologies principally in mind, rather than any perceived shortcomings of other Christian or religious groups.

In the light of this my focus on conscience, soul, the interconnectedness of intellectual, moral and spiritual qualities, sin, discipline and grace as key aspects of a Catholic worldview which provide a foundation for those key elements of Catholic education which were outlined in chapter four, may appear less strange. They will *not* add up to an adequate summary of Catholic beliefs. Nor will they distinguish clearly Catholicism from other parts of the Christian church. They should, however, display *important features of the worldview* which underpins the key concepts analyzed in the previous chapter and in casting light on the *distinctiveness* of the worldview Catholic education, some of its parameters and requirements, they should *signal the problematical relationship between distinctiveness and inclusiveness.*

In order to bring into focus some of these key aspects of a Catholic worldview which underpin a Catholic philosophy of education, I take the following steps. First, I draw upon the thought of Newman in emphasizing the importance of conscience and the moral dimension of the search for truth. Second, I consider the central role of religion in education. Third, I identify elements that contribute to the integral development of persons. Fourth, I explore some of the connections between an understanding of human persons, the personhood of Christ and the formation of character. Fifth, I comment on some of Maritain's work in seeking to achieve a deeper understanding of personhood by relating this concept both to individuality and to our relations with others. Sixth, I draw out some of the implications of the belief that we are made in God's image. Seventh, I distinguish several aspects and implications of the belief that all people have a vocation from God.

5.2   *Newman and Christian education*

Newman, writing in the nineteenth century, interpreted some of the intellectual assumptions of his time as implicitly undermining of a Christian understanding of the relationship between religion and education and between faith and reason. He anticipated the threat to religious believers caused by the tendency within liberal education towards both reductionism and apparent neutrality which in reality marginalised religious considerations and priorities.

In *The Idea of a University* Newman argued forcibly, not only for comprehensiveness in the range of disciplines available for study in a university and for the preservation of a sense of the unity of knowledge, but also for the essential presence of theological study within that unity. Theology is required, not only as a subject which offers worthwhile academic knowledge in its own right, but also as a necessary condition for the development among students of a holistic understanding of the interrelationships between character formation and the acquisition of knowledge.[8] Newman analyses (among other topics) the mutual bearing on each other of theology and other knowledge and the corresponding duties (regarding intellectual development and spiritual growth) owed to one another by the church and the academy.[9] One might fairly paraphrase Newman's view of the role of theology and religion within the circle of knowledge as one which was simultaneously academic, edificatory (or existentialist) and architectonic. Although

Newman wished to preserve the freedom of the investigator (we all need 'elbow room' in the domain of thought), he stressed the real possibility that intellectual gifts will be abused if they are not disciplined by appropriate habits, lifestyle and formation.[10]

For Newman, one of the ways that secular and liberal approaches to education fail to do justice to a Catholic view of human nature and needs is their neglect of the voice of conscience in prompting us to look out for revelation.[11] He strongly emphasised the role of religious knowledge in building up the personality and also paradoxically the development that was necessary, before religious knowledge could be attained. He particularly dwelt on the working of conscience which, he claimed, makes humans aware of the presence in their lives of a divine Judge. His view was that there is something *in* us which is not merely *of* us, which points us beyond ourselves, if we can only discern its operations sufficiently clearly.

> It is more than man's own self. The man has no power over it, or only with extreme difficulty; he did not make it; he cannot destroy it;...he can disobey it, he may refuse it, but it remains.[12]

Not only does the conscience, according to Newman, represent for us the divine voice, but the more we follow its dictates and heed its warnings, so much the more clearly will we hear its tones, understand its message, love its commands and be more consciously present to the speaker.[13]

For some religious educators the apprehension of truth necessarily precedes the adoption of a religious life-style and the practice of a particular morality. The reverse is true, at least in the order of life, if not in the order of logic, for Newman. The attainment of truth in the religious sphere is the fruit rather than the root of virtue. Moral life makes possible the recognition of religious truth. In recent years there has been a stress in religious enquiry on the notion of a 'the long search'. Valuable though this has been in its implications for inter-religious dialogue and ecumenism, for the development of a historical perspective and for encouraging greater openness to and respect for the views of other people, it needs to be balanced by the reminder that the journey is also a moral one. It is not an intellectual game. As Newman says: "no enquiry comes to good which is not conducted under a deep sense of responsibility, and of the issues depending on its determination."[14]

The search for religious truth that has been tested for its reliability will be dependent in part at least for its success upon the moral state of the searcher. The search will sometimes be painful, because it will necessarily involve scrutiny of the self, not merely the observation of other religious persons. According to such a view, the search will entail interrogation of our own consciences; access to truth is only made possible through moral living and a right state of heart.[15] Newman states that the right state of heart both gives birth to faith and also disciplines it. The right state of heart protects faith "from bigotry, credulity, and fanaticism."[16] While we live under the sovereignty of sin our minds are clouded and our discernment of truth cannot be clear, confident or consistent. It is only in the wake of a faithful existence, after a conversion that is simultaneously intellectual, moral and spiritual, and which frees us from the noetic implications of sin, that we attain to objectivity in knowledge in the moral, spiritual and religious order.[17]

Clearly some of Newman's ideas present problems for educators in a pluralist society where schools do not have a mandate to conduct themselves on the lines he suggests. They cannot assume prior commitment to a substantial understanding of the good, nor can they meet his requirement that Christian education embrace character formation, the nurturing of conscience and the habits of religious disciplines alongside of intellectual enquiry. Far from religious beliefs shaping the educational process, as Newman would have wished, they have frequently been marginalised both in society generally and in schools in particular.

5.3.   *Religion in education: marginal or central?*

Two examples of such argument are those provided by Stephen Carter and George Marsden respectively.[18]   Carter's thesis is that in the public square (in the USA), religion meets not with hostility, but rather with trivialisation, being treated "as an unimportant facet of human personality."[19] As a result, the free exercise of religion is inhibited and too many constraints are put in its way in order to prevent the baleful effects of either religious exclusivity or excessive influence.[20]

In the context of higher education (again in the USA) Marsden laments the marginalisation of religious belief and practice and accuses the academy in general of privileging 'methodological atheism' and cultural relativism.[21] Marsden shows how religious faith can have an important bearing on scholarship and, by implication, suggests that to suppress awareness of this bearing is to diminish the quality of scholarship at work.[22] He argues that religious beliefs "shape not only our overt ways of valuing things, but also our priorities". [23] They affect what we select as worthy of study, the questions we ask and the theories that appear to possess explanatory power. Religious beliefs, according to Marsden, will affect our motivation for study, the application of our research, how we interpret its wider implications and how we relate these to our overall picture of the world.[24] As examples of (Christian) religious doctrines that have a bearing on scholarship, he cites those relating to creation and to the incarnation. He argues that belief in creation has implications for how we think about human rights, moral principles and even epistemology. Similarly, belief in the incarnation has implications for our understanding of the possible relationships between the supernatural and the natural realms and how the contingent can be a vehicle of access to the transcendent.[25]

It does not really matter if the various charges levelled by Carter and Marsden against the prevailing social and academic culture of society in the USA are fully justified. Nor does it matter if their diagnosis is not fully transferable to other contexts. What does matter is that at least some religious believers in many countries *perceive* the social and educational arrangements of their society as being inhospitable to the nurturing of religious faith and lifestyle. The desire of the Catholic community for a distinctive form of education rests on a substantial, comprehensive and integrated view of the human person and a particular worldview which are contested in our society and held by only a minority of the population. If the charges levelled by Carter and Marsden are warranted, the desire for a distinctive form of education cannot be satisfied without the provision of separate schooling. Only in such a protected arena could the Catholic view of personhood be adequately attended to and appropriately promoted throughout the curriculum and school community.

My argument thus far does not, of course, entail state support for such separate provision. Additional arguments are needed if state support is to be indicated. In chapter eight I consider several of the charges levelled against separate Catholic schooling. In response to these charges I supply a seven strand argument in defence of the claim that Catholic schools contribute to the common good and therefore, by implication, the claim that they deserve support from the public purse. Public support would be conditional upon guarantees that certain social safeguards are in place and that certain educational conditions are met. In this chapter I focus on those aspects of personhood which are essential to a Catholic worldview and which are foundational for Catholic education.

5.4.   Integral development

There are many aspects to understanding human beings which have, over the centuries, surfaced as significant: that they are embodied, that they have the use of reason, can laugh, imagine what is not there in front of them, can communicate and create, and that they have free will.[26] Of these human characteristics, the capacities for the use of reason and the exercise of free will have traditionally been seen as absolutely crucial in identifying what distinguishes humanity from the rest of creation. Reason and free will make it possible for human beings to transcend mere 'givenness' in their lives, where they are simply being acted upon. These qualities enable persons to display a degree of intelligent agency where they contribute something original, in the sense that it is not automatically programmed into them or laid down in advance as part of their nature. Both rationality and freedom of the will have been held to reflect features of divinity.[27]

Alternative emphases have stressed that human beings are sinful, flawed, finite and self-defeating creatures, in need of redemption, conversion, transformation and salvation. A humble recognition of the harsh reality of this weaker side of human nature, with its proneness to negativity, cowardice, contradiction, confusion, isolation, social violence and self-destruction prevents too optimistic a view of human nature from being held and it suggests the need for salvation from a source beyond humanity. The power of sin has a bearing on internal obstacles to learning, in that "deceit, the violation of intellectual honesty, the resistance to reality, and the fear of truth are all very much with us." [28] Christian moral principles have a significantly different configuration from much contemporary secular morality, even on those occasions when what is enjoined or forbidden appears similar in content within their respective codes of conduct.[29] One way this is so is shown through their recognition, not only of human limitations and fallibility, but also of the 'dark' side of ourselves, the capacity, not only to miss the best but also to pursue the worst and to fall into evil ways.

Stanley Hauerwas points out that "the language of spiritual growth, holiness and perfection directs attention to the development of the moral self in a manner quite different from the contemporary concern with moral development."[30] He picks out several features of Christian morality that distinguish it in important ways from its secular counterparts. These include several notions: life is to be treated as a gift; we are called to imitate a master; this entails accepting that we need to be rescued from ourselves; this requires conversion, followed by obedience and faithfulness. Christians also describe the self as subject to sin, a theological term which does not simply mean that we are capable of wrongdoing but that we are estranged from God who is the source and goal of our being.[31] It will immediately be clear that this is very different from an emphasis on autonomy, development of our powers and rational decision making.

In one of the rare textbooks outlining a Catholic philosophy of education, written more than forty years ago, Redden and Ryan claim that Catholic education takes into account the 'whole man', because it embraces the "development and discipline of all the powers of body and soul, and essentially is, therefore, religious, moral, liberal, cultural, and universal."[32] Two things should be noted here. First, the use of the word 'discipline' with regard to our powers is significant. They are not simply to expand in a way that is a natural unfolding. They will have to face some degree of curbing, of constraint. Our energies have to be harnessed and transformed under a set of norms.[33] Secondly, the 'soul' - also to be developed and disciplined - is a concept that is mysterious, even alien in a secular society, where lack of consensus about religious matters has meant that neutrality or silence on 'the soul' must be the order of the day.

Yet omission of a sense of the soul, from a Catholic perspective, distorts entirely our understanding of persons, their development and their destiny. As Redden and Ryan say, "it makes a great difference in the theory and practice of education whether or not one admits the existence of the soul...the freedom of the will, and the doctrine of original sin."[34] For tied up with an understanding of what might be meant by soul, other concepts come into view, for example, unrepeatability and incommunicability.[35] If education is based on a false picture of human nature and of its final end, such education will inevitably be seriously deficient. It will not take proper account of either our weaknesses and needs or of our strengths and potentialities. In 1929 Pope Pius XI challenged contemporary educational theories thus: "every method of education founded, wholly or in part, on the denial or forgetfulness of Original Sin and of grace, and relying on the sole powers of human nature, is unsound."[36]

There are several elements hinted at in that quotation. They could perhaps be put as follows. There is the longer-term perspective offered from within religious faith: it is not sufficient to prepare people for life on earth; this is not our final resting place, our ultimate destination. This-worldly concerns are, of course, very important; but, of themselves, they are not enough; indeed, they can be misinterpreted if not read *sub specie aeternitatis*.[37] Original sin is a reality that must be taken into account; human beings are flawed; the nature, cause, effects of and remedy for human defects must be acknowledged. This will necessarily involve opening humanity up to resources which come from beyond its own powers, however much these have been developed. These powers, good in themselves, are condemned to distortion, sterility or misuse through the effects of sin. Because of the prevalence of sin in human beings, the intellect is less able to attain truth, the will less able to seek for the good and human nature is more inclined towards evil.[38] *The Catechism of the Catholic Church* points out that conscience can be almost blinded by inappropriate habits or by sin:

> Ignorance of Christ and his Gospel, bad example given by others, enslavement to one's passions, assertion of a mistaken notion of autonomy of conscience, rejection of the Church's authority and her teaching, lack of conversion and of charity: these can be at the source of errors of judgement in moral conduct. [39]

From a Christian perspective, all the help we need is freely available from God if we are ready to receive it. The work of education entails preparing in us an active receptivity.

If I have extrapolated more than is contained in the letter of that quotation from Pius XI, I do not think that I have strayed from the spirit contained within it. What is clear is that a Catholic philosophy of education rests upon a particular view of the human person and of the purpose of life, a view that embraces a dialectic of development and discipline, one which leads, not only to full humanity, but also to divinisation. In this chapter some key aspects of the Catholic understanding of the person are explored further, since an understanding of these is integral to the case for a distinctive approach to education.

5.5. *Identity and character*

An understanding of the human person is of such importance for Christians that one might justifiably claim it is a focal point in their theology. What is the meaning and significance of this claim? I offer five considerations. First, a reflection on the nature, meaning and destiny of human persons is at the centre of much theological writing. Second, I expect, by concentrating on the notion of person, to find an entry into what is at the very heart of theological concerns: the difference God makes to our lives, to the way we see them and to the way we live them. Third, although Christians do not believe that God is only concerned about the place of humanity in the cosmos, they do hold that in some mysterious way the secret of God's purposes and, indeed God's very nature, is implicated in and revealed through the emergence of humanity. Fourth, a better understanding of our own being - and its possibilities for becoming - will prompt us towards a more adequate appreciation of the world in which we find ourselves and our relationship with the beings and Being which surround us. Finally, Christians believe that there is a special connection between the person of Jesus the Christ and the personhood of humans.

There are many scriptural references to the role of Christ in changing us so radically that we put on a new nature.[40] Certainly for Christians the answer to the question "who do you say that I am?" put by Jesus to his disciples[41] relates intimately to the answer we might each give to the question "who am I?" For Christ's understanding of himself and his mission has decisively influenced the way many human beings have come to understand themselves. This influence is brought out by theologian Michael Himes in the following way. Himes suggests that the Church's reflection on the significance of what God was doing in Jesus the Christ and the belief that in him there was revealed 'true God *and* true man' - where the '*and*' might with justification be rendered 'in the light of' or 'because of' - is an attempt to bring out the conviction that "the fuller the expression of God, the richer the humanity which receives the impression, *and* the more fully and richly human one is, then the more perfectly one receives God who is always self-gift."[42] In other words, Christ shows us that divinity and humanity are not in competition; indeed the more fully human we become, the more aptly we express divinity (although I stress in this chapter that this does not imply a belief in a natural 'unfolding' or 'expansion' of our nature).[43]

The connection between our understanding of the person of Christ and of human personhood more generally has two related aspects. The first aspect stems from the conviction that Jesus came to show us the true nature and potential of humanity (not only to *reveal* what we can be, but also to enable us to *realise* that potential). Belief in the Incarnation leads to a new picture of humanity, one that is open to the divinising grace of Christ and union with God. This entails a re-ordering, indeed a transformation of our lives, our powers and aspirations. The second aspect of the connection stems from the belief that the more understanding we have of the nature, purpose and work of Jesus the Christ, the more light will be cast on our lives. As a coda we might add that the more we can enter with insight into the depths of our lives and their manifold dimensions, the better we shall come to appreciate what was going on and what was revealed for our salvation in the life of Jesus.

In short, a study of the human person is central to the concerns of Christian theology. It allows us to see how God`s grace and call affect all that we are and do. Christians believe that they have a distinctive perspective on human nature. If we ignore or work against this understanding of human personhood, they would claim, we are likely to defeat our own projects, to damage creation and to diminish all life, including our own. On the other hand, if we allow ourselves to grapple with, to be illuminated by and to be nourished within a Christian appreciation of and perspective on personhood, life will be, not merely enhanced, but exalted.

A Christian perspective on personhood may differ in crucial respects from alternative views, but this does not rule out aspects of continuity and of common ground. Christian teaching is not that grace works to suppress or to destroy nature, but rather that it embraces, enlivens, reorders and reintegrates and, in so doing, elevates it. I have already mentioned (as part of my comments on Newman) concern for the formation of character as an integral part of education. The idea that character is central to an understanding of personhood and therefore also of education would be shared by people of many different faiths and worldviews. Even a brief analysis of character reveals both similarities and differences of emphasis between Christians and others. The notion deserves more exploration than I can devote to it here.[44] At this point I merely pick out four of its aspects which, when taken together, have a bearing on the main line of argument being pursued in this chapter.

Joseph Dunne describes the self in three ways.[45] First, there is the 'sovereign' self, where we have a stable centre and a secure anchorage. Second, in reaction against this way of speaking, there is the 'deconstructed' self. Under the influence of, for example, Marx and Freud, and taking into account the effects of alienation, the subconscious and false consciousness stemming from the various types of oppression and repression in life, the deconstructed self loses its security. The third self is the 'storied' or the 'historical' self, where "we make sense - or fail to make sense - of our lives by the kind of story we can - or cannot - tell about it."[46] This third self, with the notions of narrative and accountability which are central to it, is important for the particular understanding of character which I am reaching towards. For it brings out the need to make sense of life as a whole, that is, to see the "whole picture," and not merely settle for understanding life as a series of isolated episodes. Without suppressing the questioning and critique required by the deconstructed self, a Christian educator might wish to develop further and to give special emphasis to several features suggested (but not spelt out) by Dunne's analysis. Each person's own intimate 'anchorage' in God, the sacredness of the selfhood of every other person, human participation in an ongoing narrative of both individual and community-based receptivity and responsiveness to God's communication, and to the notion of our stewardship of the gift of creation.

The second contribution towards a better understanding of character I take from Nicholas Dent, who reminds us that the kinds of ends we aim for in life will make all the difference to the kinds of virtues and vices we develop. He turns our attention away from the powers at our disposal and directs it instead towards our goals.[47] Again, a Christian educator might develop this further by advocating a transcendent rather than a subjective humanism as a developmental goal. Education should focus our attention on the worthiness and coherence of our goals, the nature of their authority and the kind of discipline they impose on us if we are to attain them. More than self-realisation is required for healthy growth of character.

Picking up this point about character being related to the ends we pursue and the attachments towards which we feel drawn, Michael Sandel provides a third clarification. He points out that, not only can such aims and attachments be transformed, so that the very person that I am is called into question, but we can come to be possessed by those things - including those qualities - we think we own. "As my attachment to [something] grows, it gradually becomes attached to me...[and] constitutive of my identity; it becomes more and more *me*, and less and less *mine*...the less I possess it, and the more I am possessed by it."[48] In order to prevent our being over-controlled by those things we are attached to, the Christian educator might wish to stress here the role of self-examination and self-denial as integral elements in any form of education that claimed to liberate students from whatever might threaten or diminish their humanity.

Fourthly, Craig Dykstra puts the development of character in the context of the worshipping community. Only in such a context can a Christian form an adequate understanding of the moral growth and education of persons. Without the presence of "worship and prayer, confession and repentance, biblical and theological study and interpretation, fellowship and discipleship," we will operate with inadequate concepts, we shall miss key elements in our stories, we shall fail to strive for the right ends and we shall not be appropriately transformed.[49] A Christian does not find out who he or she really is by introspection or in isolation from the practising faith community. Here the Christian educator stresses the value of an ecclesial context for character formation and self-knowledge.

Of course, knowing who I am cannot be separated either from finding out whence I have come, (my origins and history), or whither I am going (my future development and destiny). I find that my identity is partly given and partly still a task to be carried out. It is already there to be discovered and yet also still to be constructed. One of the paradoxes of personhood is that, even when I accept, through faith, that God is constantly present to me, offering support and constant love, nevertheless I still experience my identity as both guaranteed and yet fragile. An exploration of who I am opens up certain polarities within me. Along with continuity and sameness I recognise change within me, whether I resist or welcome it. With the stability and shaping brought about externally by context, culture and constraint, and internally by habit, decisions and inertia, I also find within myself an openness, a lack of imprisonment by the past, a readiness to go beyond current parameters and expectations, my own and those of others. Despite limitations, constraints and past commitments, there is still an element of freedom available to me. In the midst of much familiarity the strange and the striking can prompt me to wonder and to question, perhaps even to change direction, or at least to see things differently.

This very element of freedom is double-edged. It can be used positively. I can also use it to resist the good and to run the risk of falling into sin.[50] Some causes of falling into wrongdoing, for example, "ignorance, inadvertence, duress, fear, habit, inordinate attachments,"[51] may appear to offer me some excuses or to reduce part of my responsibility. Nevertheless, even some of these may develop a hold on me due to culpable neglect, neglect either of appropriate sources of help and guidance, or neglect of good habits and sound attachments. My freedom then constitutes a mixed blessing for me, since it leaves room for errors in both lifestyle and in particular moral judgements. It leaves open the possibility that conflicting or inappropriate allegiances will gain a foothold in my life. The Christian educator may at this point wish to stress our need for forgiveness, for conversion and for receptivity to the redemptive work of Christ.

5.6.   *Individuality, personhood and otherness*

In my brief analysis of character several implications for Christian education have emerged. I indicated that human development involves much more than a mere natural unfolding of the tendencies latent within me. Questions about the possibility of God as transcendent source and goal of human existence have been put on the educational agenda. I warned against both an over-emphasis on, and an unwarranted optimism about, the individual. I expressed caution about any notion of human self-sufficiency and highlighted the fragility of freedom. Taken together, these reflections are indicative of some aspects of the tension that exists between a Christian understanding of personhood and the language of much contemporary education.

This tension can be clarified further by considering the difference between individuality and personality. In recent years, across a wide range of writing, including philosophy, political theory, sociology, ecology and economics, there has been a growing challenge to what is felt to be an over-emphasis on individualism and its attendant narrowness, competition, exploitation and destructiveness.[52] A return to a more relational understanding of the person, informed by a Christian perspective, might assist us in seeing how an imbalanced picture of individuality has contributed to the expression of selfishness, ingratitude, despair, isolation, mistrust, fear, apathy and possessiveness often castigated by advocates of a more communitarian approach. Too often, as Colin Gunton remarks, "such features of our humanity that have sometimes been taken to represent the sole or chief quality of personhood, such as consciousness, subjectivity, conscience, will, reason, creativity are all capable of -- indeed, positively encourage   individualistic and non-relational views of the person in society and the world."[53] These are constituent and essential features of humanity. They need to be placed in a context where the notions of spirit, otherness and relationship are taken seriously if they are not to distort our reading of personhood.

Jacques Maritain, writing during the Second World War, identified the error behind much of this misreading of human nature, the confusion between individuality and personality. For Maritain the foundation for individuality is matter, whereas the foundation for personality is spirit.[54] Given the psychological associations which have gathered around the word 'personality' and its connotations of inner drives, subconscious motivations and superficial idiosyncrasies, we might now prefer to employ instead the word 'personhood', a term which conveys more *gravitas*. 'Personhood,' rather than 'personality,' also suggests something we have exercised more control over, both in terms of moral decision-making and in terms of the degree of rationality displayed. Both individuality and personhood are key aspects of our total being and what they each rest upon, matter and spirit respectively, are vital elements in the composite being that we are.

In distinguishing these aspects Maritain says that personality - or, as I prefer, personhood - is about the "mastery and independence of my spiritual self", whereas individuality is about "the letting loose of the tendencies which are present in me by virtue of matter and heredity."[55] We might distinguish these two poles of our being in the following way. Individuality is what will "unfold" naturally and inexorably from us, given the initial material deposit that we inherit and subject to the usual battery of natural forces and external influences and pressures which human beings encounter and which impinge upon their development. Personhood will only emerge through a deliberate and conscious engagement of our will and reason in decisions and a moral life which transcend our origins in the sense that they are not totally governed by our natural inheritance. If we contrast nature and person, we may say that nature relates to what happens *in* us, the person relates to what we do with what is in us. In the first we are passive objects of experience; in the second we are agents in our own right. When Maritain speaks of personality, he refers to something interior to us. "This internal selfhood grows in proportion as the life of reason and freedom dominate over the life of instinct and sensual desire."[56] On the other hand, to speak of individuality is to refer to the material ego. "The ego is in reality scattered among cheap desires or overwhelming passions, and finally submitted to the determination of matter."[57]

Maritain's intention was not the downgrading of individuality but its inclusion, deployment and enhancement in the development of personhood. Individuality for him is heavily associated with the different but related notion of individualism. A focus on either individuality or individualism could tempt us into isolation and a more diminished life. Maritain had also seen that an overemphasis on individuality opened the way to the apparently opposite danger of collectivism. Only a life tempered by discipline, sacrifice, self-control and spirituality could stand against the crowd, whether in Nazi Germany or in Communist Russia.

Excessive emphasis on self-reliance and a reduced sense of community are side-effects of an imbalanced stress on the importance of the individual, as opposed to the person. Christianity has not escaped accusations of an exclusive preoccupation with individual salvation, as if this was a one-to-one transaction between the individual and God. Recent reflection on education in the English Catholic Church has reiterated the social nature of human beings and stressed the essential solidarity required of Christians.[58] It could be argued, from a faith perspective, and on a wider plane than education, not only that we owe each other mutual support and consideration, but that we need each other, with our mutual differences and our stimulation, our chafing and challenges to one another, to learn who we are and how we can become what we would like to be. We also need each other to get to heaven - and not simply as occasions of earning grace.

The importance of solidarity has sometimes been neglected in previous articulations of the meaning of the image of God in humanity. If we concentrate too much on an individualistic interpretation of this image of God in us, we might surrender to the cult of self-sufficiency advocated in our society. In doing so we might then slip into falsely valuing people according to their achievements. We might fail to recognise that "people's worth does not come from their ability, beauty, or goodness."[59] In the context of Catholic education, pupils are not to be judged as more or less worthy of attention, according to their capacity for contributing to the economy or according to their academic ability.[60] The twin beliefs, that every human person, being made in the image of God, possesses an ineradicable dignity, and that in relieving our neighbour's suffering we are serving Christ, are central to Christian teaching. These beliefs have major implications for school policies, for example, those relating to pupil admissions, discipline, resource allocation, community service, personal and social education, support for those with special needs, the evaluation and celebration of pupils' work, pastoral care and teacher appraisal.

One way of showing respect for the dignity of pupils and a concern for their flourishing is the establishing by the teacher of an appropriate distance. By this I mean three things. First, the uniqueness of each person and his or her special gifts must be acknowledged. This will entail providing opportunities for the exercise of choice, responsibility, initiative and decision-making. Such psychological 'space' for each pupil is an aspect of the distance to which I am referring.

Second, in the process of teaching, pupils should be encouraged to avoid the temptation to 'domesticate' too quickly what appears strange to them. The assimilation into their own categories of describing and evaluating should be balanced by an openness to what is 'other' than them, in terms of people, problems and situations. Admitting what is alien, uncomfortable and demanding into our lives is important for our spiritual growth. This second aspect of distance refers to the space between pupils and the subject matter they engage with.

Third, the maintenance of a certain distance between teachers and their pupils ensures that teachers avoid two types of excess in their classrooms. The first of these is the danger of domination over pupils, which prevents their empowerment. The second is the contrary risk of subordinating the role of the teacher to meeting pupils' current wants and interests. On the one hand, manipulation and coercion rob pupils of freedom. On the other hand, if the teacher yields too readily to pupils' current immaturity and fails to challenge them with what appears at first as 'foreign' or 'other', this will prevent their growth.

My comments on the implications for education of a Christian understanding of human beings suggest that freedom is related more to personhood than to individuality. Christian freedom should not be confused with the individualism and self-expression that are encouraged in our contemporary culture. In such a context, freedom means removal of constraints and self-sufficiency. Seen this way, freedom might seem to be threatened by any (or all) of the following: tradition, community, authority, the discipline of accepting objective morality, the possibility of permanent commitment, the notion of divine revelation, all of which are integral to Catholic Christianity.

Christian freedom, in contrast, takes seriously our social nature, our interdependence and our duty to preserve the common good; it expects our decisions to be taken in the light of an informed conscience and guided by a truth which comes from beyond ourselves. A Christian interprets freedom as best developed in a theonomous and Christocentric way. We are oriented to salvation. We do not thrive by emphasising our autonomy. A Christian believes that humans flourish best only by accepting God's authoritative guidance and grace and by following the path of discipleship laid down by Jesus the Christ and witnessed to in the New Testament. This kind of freedom, far from inducing passivity, narrowness or exclusiveness on the part of learners, requires from them an active receptivity, an openness to the unfamiliar, an energetic engagement with the world and an inclusive reaching out to others.

In some respects my attempt here in the context of Catholic education to resolve a dichotomy between two polarities echoes parallel work by the philosopher Richard Pring. In exposing and challenging false dichotomies between the academic and the vocational, between theory and practice and between education and training,[61] his critique aims to retrieve the best features of both ends of each of these polarities and to achieve an integration of the worlds of learning, of work and of everyday life. In the same way I hope to bring out the false dichotomy of an inadequate understanding of distinctiveness and inclusiveness in Catholic education and to show that these features can, to a significant degree, be reconciled. It is interesting to note that in his analysis Pring offers a catholic treatment of the whole person which is in close harmony with a more explicitly Catholic understanding of persons. He depicts the whole person as one who combines knowledge and understanding, intellectual virtues, imagination, intellectual skills, self-reflection, moral virtues and habits, social and political involvement, integrity and authenticity.[62] He criticises liberal education for being insufficiently inclusive, for example, of the world of work, the political dimension, personal relationships and for excluding the less academic. He also criticises the vocational tradition in education for being too narrow in its concerns (and thereby excluding too much).[63]

5.7. God's image

Christians commonly say of human beings that they are precious because they are made in the image of God. This is not meant to separate them from, or to downgrade, the rest of creation. If we are made in the image of God, this does not mean that we do not need the world and other creatures to become truly ourselves. God does not invite us to bypass creation, but to plumb its depths and to journey through it. Nor does it mean that we have nothing to give to it. Indeed, as moral theologian Kevin Kelly points out, not only are we dependent upon the rest of the material world, but also, increasingly, "the rest of the material world is becoming dependent on us for its survival."[64]

When unpacked, we find that believing we are made in the image of God entails a further belief. According to this, we have a task to carry out on behalf of the rest of creation, as its priests, mediators, or bridge-builders; we are to name it, that is, to recognise its particularity, to bless it, to work in harmony with it and to bring it to God. This does not imply a simple acceptance of the world as it is, any more than it means merely an acceptance of the way we are. Not only is personal conversion required, following criticism and judgement of those elements within us that need to be confronted.[65] We are also called upon to confront unjust social situations, to remedy the damaging side-effects of some natural processes and to alleviate suffering wherever it occurs, whether this stems from nature, from divisive and destructive social structures and institutions, or whether it is self-inflicted.

These implications of the Christian belief that human beings are made in the image of God are relevant to Catholic education. They indicate how the promotion of critical rationality, scientific knowledge and technological skill through the curriculum should be underpinned by moral values and a concern for ecological harmony, environmental health, reduction of unnecessary suffering and the promotion of social justice. The stimulus of intellectual enquiry and the development of academic knowledge, valuable though these are in themselves, should also be directed towards the service of others, concerned for flourishing of all God's creatures, guided by the path of discipleship and aimed at a personal relationship with Christ.

5.8.   Vocation

In emphasising the importance of a personal relationship with Christ, we need to stress that this does not entail the surrender of a subject to an overlord, although this is indeed how such a relationship has often been described in the past in more hierarchical societies. A relationship with Christ leads not to the subordination of the real and particular 'me' but rather to its strengthening, enhancement and elevation. As put by Alistair McFadyen, "God relates with what is other in a way which guarantees its independence, but which calls it into free relation with God; calls it to join in the fullness of divine life in a manner appropriate to its own existence."[66] True union does not dissolve but differentiates. This is seen in the work of the Spirit at Pentecost, which led to the apostles speaking, not in one (either heavenly or earthly) language, but in the various other languages of the people around them at that time. Just as those who heard Peter and friends then were amazed to be spoken to in their native languages, so we too will find that we are spoken to in all the specific conditions and particular situations of our lives.

Of course, the various parts of our nature can serve both as obstacles to, as well as building blocks for, a fully rounded relationship with God through the person of Christ. We are called, with the help of God's grace working in our soul, to mediate a spiritual vocation to the body and, on the broader canvas of life, to mediate a divine vocation to the world as a whole.[67] This double-sided calling or vocation, which it is our task to carry out, comes to us in two ways: firstly, externally, as it were, mediated by the living tradition of the Church; secondly it emerges internally, from within us and from our encounter with the world. In our response to these forms of God's communication there follows a third type of calling, which comes through us, and is directed towards creation. We are familiar with the first; it focuses particularly on the preaching of the Gospel, sacramental celebration and the reception of the Church's teaching and life. We are less familiar with the second source, not so much in the experiencing of it but in the recognition of it as coming from God. It is often experienced as a lack, a hunger or a desire, a never-ending drive or search or restlessness, a permanent dissatisfaction with the things of this world. This absence of, yet unquenched desire for, substantiality in life is an indication of the divine signature that pervades everything we seek to rely on. "The desire is God's summons. God is the source of our desire as well as its term."[68]

As for the third type of call, that which is given out from us to the world, we have scarcely begun to acknowledge it, let alone explore its meaning for us. Despite the uncertainties that surround it, we can be sure that it starts from exactly where we are now, with all the limitations and also the opportunities afforded to us by this situation. John Sachs expresses this powerfully in the following way:

> I myself, as this particular, unique creature, in the totality of my being, with my particular talents, in the reality of my freedom, both its limitations and possibilities in this particular time and place in history, in the abiding significance of my past actions and the open-endedness of the future, and not merely some added task or action which I can accept or refuse, am God's 'specific will.'[69]

This specific will is not predetermined; it arises out of the countless possibilities open to us in the responsible exercise of our freedom. Our blessing of the world and our call to it, start from our admitting God into our lives. As the recently deceased Buber scholar, Pamela Vermes, puts it,

> God takes up his abode wherever he is admitted. And the only dwelling-place which every individual is qualified to prepare for God, and into which he can admit him, is the place, the situation, in which he himself stands.[70]

This admittance is not like grudgingly permitting the immigration of an alien into a foreign land, but welcoming a homecoming, a restoration of right relationships. For just as "Christ's call recontextualises persons into a new meaning-frame,"[71] so our mediating God's call to creation reassembles silent or separate fragments into a symphonic whole. God's spirit has a way of opening up systems that formerly seemed closed, and luring them into new possibilities. If we are in the process of composing a life in partnership with God, on the many levels of our existence, physical, aesthetic, social, intellectual, moral and spiritual, and if we are opening ourselves up through enquiry, wonder, patience and, above all, suffering, then this openness will allow the current of God's grace to pass through us and to permeate all we touch and undergo.

From within a perspective of responding to God's call, conversion, then, is neither an escape from 'lower' levels of our lives, nor a mere addition to them. It requires the transformation of *all* things in our lives and does not allow for a form of Christianity that can be practised, as it were, 'on the side'. In the context of Catholic schools therefore, it follows from this view of vocation that acknowledgement of God as our source and goal must inevitably have a central place in their public life and that religion will have an architectonic role within their curriculum. Church schools in this sense strive to minimise the relegation of religion to the realm of the private option and to counter that marginalisation and trivialisation referred to by Marsden and Carter.[72]

This notion that we are called by God, and that this calling is constitutive of our being and decisive for our destiny is a central theme within Christian thinking and an element which clearly distinguishes a Christian view on humanity from a secular one. Firstly, this is because the Christian view of the person is one that is theocentric, that is, "it sees human dignity as flowing from the person's relationship with God and not as the result of some quality that human beings possess independently."[73]   The theocentric world-view differs from the purely anthropocentric one in that it recontextualises our desire for autonomy, rationality and control, preventing these from being assumed by us to be of absolute and always overriding importance.

Secondly, the notion of a calling reminds us that God expects more of us than is simply 'natural'. Human nature begins with a given structure but it is one that is essentially inchoate and incomplete. Any adequate response to God's call is one that actively collaborates in the ongoing task of transcendence. The Christian view of the person goes beyond the secular in that it upholds as the ultimate goals of life not merely development and wholeness but also holiness and perfection.

Thirdly, the theocentric view of the human person deepens our understanding of freedom. It is necessary, but not sufficient, to aim for a level of inner stability, harmony and control so that we are not driven by forces, for example, fears, repressed desires, or an excessive need for the approval of others, when we exercise choices or make decisions. Furthermore, it follows from such a view that it is necessary, but not sufficient, for real freedom to be exercised, that we are not subject to external interference or coercion from other individuals or social pressures. However, if, in the exercise of choice, we insist that the self must be completely 'untrammelled' and unconstrained, we may fail to take account of the cumulative effect on us of acts already chosen or of the ends that we pursue or to which we are drawn. As Dwyer says,

> in our decisions we respond to God's offer and demand, and in them we either create the selves we are called to be or lose our way. Our decisions are not merely choices of how to act; they are choices of who to be. The person is not a changeless being who makes decisions about objects or things; rather, we ourselves change profoundly in the decisions we make.[74]

There is another implication of an understanding of the notion of calling as constitutive of personhood, one that introduces an element that could not be accepted from a non-theistic perspective. This is the notion that, within the context of God's call to each of us, we each have a purpose and a mission which is given to us by God, rather than purpose being interpreted as something imposed on our circumstances by us. The strong commitment to autonomy that is advocated as a principal aim within secular education is undermined by this notion of calling. A Christian understands the concept of mission as something intrinsic, and not accidental, to the concept of person. In this way, our very being depends on what we are called and commissioned to be. Freedom is thereby set in the wider context of a theonomous orientation. We are called to participate in the mission of Christ and our own identity is found in relation to the divine will for us. With Christian educators, this participation in the mission of Christ will express itself in a ministry of witness which enables others "to receive, understand and appropriate the

Christian tradition as a means of grace for their own lives, and to join in turn in its witnessing work."[75]

From this Christian perspective which I have just outlined, it would be both short-sighted and self-defeating for us to seek to impose on our lives an overall purpose, or even worse, a series of disconnected purposes or projects, without reference to or even in defiance of their divine source. But

> when the power of reason is placed within the context of Creation, when 'the whole' toward which we orient ourselves is seen to exist through God's free decision, the sense of the 'I' that we express through our reason is changed. We now understand ourselves as chosen to be, and if we are chosen to be, then the divine wisdom behind that choice defines who we are in a more profound way than any other interaction or determination that could follow.[76]

There are important indications here of the priority which should be given in Catholic education to the notion of vocation, in the various senses which I have outlined above. This notion of vocation clearly goes beyond any secular mandate for careers education and it offers a serious alternative to prevailing perspectives on autonomy. Furthermore, it has the potential to re-orient curriculum content and to govern community priorities. By being set in the context of a comprehensive narrative with application to the multi-dimensional character and social nature of human persons, it also has the capacity to provide for staff and students alike a significant challenge, one which is pedagogic and professional, at the same time as being both personal and political.

5.9.   Conclusion

In this chapter I have identified several elements of a worldview informed by Catholic beliefs which, when taken together, provide a foundation for a distinctive approach to education. Central to this worldview is an understanding of the human person interpreted in the light of the Church's teaching about Jesus Christ. In articulating a Catholic perspective on the human person, I have picked out certain features for comment: the voice of conscience, the formation of character, the notion of the soul, the need for conversion and the offer of salvation. I have considered the interconnectedness of intellectual, moral and spiritual qualities, acknowledged the implications of a Catholic view of the effect of sin on our understanding and freedom of action and suggested a corresponding need in us for a disciplining of our powers and a receptivity to grace. I have noted some implications of the belief that we are made in God's image and I have explored some aspects of what is entailed by a belief in vocation. Let me draw out one implication of this last point. I would expect a Catholic school to ensure that, in the course of its personal and social education programme, proper consideration is given to the notion of vocation. This notion has both a specifically religious sense and a broader, work-related sense. Pupils should be encouraged to explore the possible interconnections between their talents and inclinations, the needs of others and God's particular call to each of us. Clearly, when the different components of this chapter are taken together, they suggest that religious beliefs play a crucial and central role in Catholic education. To such a degree is this so, separate religious schooling is advocated for their proper operation and efficacy.

Underlying the Church's desire to maintain separate schools, which allow adequate attention to the elements outlined in this chapter, is a belief that metaphysics, morality and spirituality all need to be integrated into the educational process. As different realms of discourse these should, for purposes of academic analysis, proceed in different ways and at different levels. But, in the context of a holistic education, they should not be totally separate operations. Pupils should be encouraged, according to their maturity and capacity, to discern the truth about reality, to discover a pattern of behaviour which meets their needs and is in tune with that reality, and to be receptive to a relationship with its source. Without such interconnections our metaphysics is difficult to verify; our morality cannot be a proper response to reality, for it falls into the trap of confusing shallow with deeper needs, and blindly seeks to impose itself in a world without ultimate meaning or purpose; and our spirituality can slide into something optional, private, uncritical and ineffective.[77]

Chapters four and five have sought to clarify the key concepts within a Catholic philosophy of education together with the world-view and accompanying understanding of human nature which this philosophy presupposes.[78] Some features of this worldview do not fit in with a secular approach to education, for example, the 'scandal' of Christianity, the necessity for salvation, the role of the church, the call to conversion, the life of prayer and the place of self-sacrifice. Such unfamiliar notions as these can be expected to modify radically the understanding in Catholic schools of key educational notions such as integral human development, rationality and autonomy. The view of human nature outlined here will also have implications for the overall coherence of the curriculum and the culture and ethos of schools.

This set of foundational beliefs and the pattern of educational arrangements currently in place for promoting them are highly contestable in our society. Criticism, both of the theory and of the practice of Catholic education, should prompt Catholic educators to consider carefully the justification and coherence of their claim to a distinctive approach to education. It should also challenge them to address inconsistencies between rhetoric and reality and to attend to any possible side-effects of such a distinctive approach to education, for example, that it is liable to slip into an exclusiveness which contradicts its own philosophy. I explore further, in the following chapters, a possible response to the contested nature of the Catholic philosophy of education as outlined in chapters four and five. The particular concern of the next chapter is to investigate the implications of this claim to distinctiveness for those who work in church schools and to consider what bearing the claim has on both inclusiveness and exclusiveness.

Notes for Chapter 5

---

[1]Quoted by V. A. McClelland in *Society in Conflict: The Value of Education*, edited by Elizabeth Ashton and Brenda Watson, *(Aspects of Education,* Number 51, The University of Hull, 1994), p.28.

[2]Fred Inglis, *The Management of Ignorance*, Oxford, Blackwell, 1985, p.47.

[3]See Stanton Jones, 'Recovering the Person', in *Agenda for Educational Change*, edited by John Shortt and Trevor Cooling, Leicester, Apollos, 1997, especially pp. 110-115. Jones articulates an evangelical Christian analysis of the human person that closely matches the one I present here.

[4]For a comparison of Islamic and Christian approaches to understanding personhood, aspects of the curriculum and the purpose of education, see *Religion and Education*, edited by Syed Ali Ashraf and Paul Hirst, Cambridge, The Islamic Academy, 1994, especially pp. 218-236.

[5]A landmark study of these models is that by Avery Dulles, *Models of the Church*, Dublin, Gill & Macmillan, 1974.

[6]For a major reinterpretation of Catholic ecclesiology, critical of both neo-conservative and liberal Catholic approaches, see David Schindler, *Heart of the World, Center of the Church*, Edinburgh, T & T Clark/Grand Rapids, Eerdmans, 1996.

[7]See below, chapter seven.

[8]John Henry Newman *The Idea of a University*, London, Longmans, Green & Co, 1912 (originally published 1852). See especially pp. xvi, 50-51, 70, 113, 137, 441.

[9]*Ibid.*, Discourses III, IV, VIII, IX.

[10]*Ibid.*, pp.471-6; 398.

[11]Newman, *Sermons Preached on Various Occasions*, London, Longmans, Green & Co, 1921, pp.64-68.

[12]*Ibid.*, pp.64-65.

[13]*Ibid.*, p.65. *Cf.* Newman, *University Sermons*, edited and introduced by D. M. MacKinnon and J. D. Holmes, London, SPCK, 1970, p.18.

[14]Newman, *A Grammar of Assent*, introduced by Nicholas Lash, Notre Dame, University of Notre Dame Press, 1979, p.331. (originally published 1870)

[15]*Ibid.*, pp.9, 247.

[16] Newman's *University Sermons*, p.234.

[17]For the relation between conversion and objectivity in our knowledge, see my two articles in *Theology*, *'Subjectivity and Religious Understanding*,' November 1982, pp.410-417 and *'Lonergan, Conversion and Objectivity*,' September 1983, pp.345-353.

[18]Stephen Carter, *The Culture of Disbelief*, New York, Doubleday/Anchor, 1993; George Marsden, *The Outrageous Idea of Christian Scholarship*, New York, Oxford University Press, 1997.

[19]Carter, p.xv.

[20]Carter, *passim*.

[21]Marsden, *op. cit.*, pp.20, 35, 84, 86. 'Methodological atheism' means acting (and theorizing) as if God does not exist, bracketing out the question of the truth of God's existence and relying in one's studies solely on data which can be verified empirically.

[22]*Ibid.*, pp.63-64. Such influence will not exert any predictably direct or uniform effect, for, as Marsden says with reference to Christianity, "influences vary with the type of Christianity, the type of individual, the field and sub-field of scholarship, and the types of traditions of interpretation currently available." (p.70)

[23]*Ibid.*, p.63.

[24]*Ibid.*, p.64.

[25]*Ibid.*, pp.88, 90.

[26]For some useful analyses of human nature from a theological perspective, see John Macquarrie, *In Search of Humanity*, London, SCM Press, 1982; Rene Latourelle, *Man and His Problems in the Light of Jesus Christ*, New York, Alba House, Society of St Paul, 1983; John Crosby, *The Selfhood of the Human Person*, Washington DC, Catholic University of America Press, 1996.

[27]For example, by that most authoritative Catholic philosopher and theologian, Thomas Aquinas, in his *Summa Theologiae*. However, the equally influential Christian theologian Augustine was much less confident about the power of human reason and freedom to withstand the urges of desire and the

demands of a flawed will.

[28]Edward Farley, 'Can church education be theological education?' in Jeff Astley, Leslie Francis and Colin Crowder, *Theological Perspectives on Christian Formation*, Leominster, Gracewing, 1996, p.38.

[29]There have been and are, of course, some secular thinkers, for example, Hobbes in the seventeenth century, Freud at the beginning of the twentieth century, who held 'lower' views of human nature, although in both of these cases it could be argued that within their secularism there is a residual element of a Judaeo-Christian mind-set.

[30]Stanley Hauerwas, *A Community of Character*, Notre Dame, University of Notre Dame Press, 1981, p.130.

[31]*Ibid.*, pp. 130, 131, 271.

[32]John Redden and Francis Ryan, *A Catholic Philosophy of Education*, Milwaukee, The Bruce Publishing Company, 1956, p.vii.

[33]*Ibid.*, p.29.

[34]*Ibid.*, p.22.

[35]John Crosby, *op. cit.*, pp.41, 65.

[36]See Pope Pius XI, *On Christian Education of Youth (Divini Illius Magistri)*, in *Selected Papal Encyclicals & Letters*, vol. 1, 1896-1931, London, Catholic Truth Society, 1939, p.29.

[37]For an intimation that the sense of the eternal and the infinite are not merely brought *to* human lives (as foreign imports, as it were) through the medium of certain religious beliefs, but are rather already *immanent within* human experience, as revealed in an endless restlessness and questioning, a passion for ultimacy and a sense of the infinite, see Crosby, *op. cit.*, pp. 161, 162, 164. Catholic liberation theologians (for example, Leonardo Boff or Gustavo Gutierrez,) might wish to 'up-grade' the importance of this-worldly concerns by comparison with some traditional emphases.

[38]Redden and Ryan, *op. cit.*, p.56.

[39] London, Geoffrey Chapman, 1994, p.398.

[40]Among others we could cite here: Colossians 3. 10, on having to put on a new nature; 2 Corinthians 3: 18 on being changed into God's likeness; (cf Romans 8: 29); 2 Corinthians 5:17 on identification with Christ helping us to overcome our sinful nature and our self-destruction, 1 Corinthians 2:16 on having the mind of Christ; 2 Peter 1:4 on being sharers in the divine nature.

[41]Matthew 16:15; Mark 8:29; Luke 9:20.

[42]Michael Himes, 'Catholicism as Integral Humanism: Christian Participation in Pluralistic Moral Education', in *The Challenge of Pluralism*, edited by F. Clark Power and Daniel Lapsley, Notre Dame, University of Notre Dame Press, 1992, p. 123.

[43]*Ibid.*

[44]For a detailed analysis on this topic, see Joel Kupperman, *Character*, Oxford, Oxford University Press, 1991.

[45]Joseph Dunne, "Philosophies of the Self and the Scope of Education", in Papers of the Philosophy of Education Society of Great Britain Conference, Oxford, 1995, pp.170-180; see particularly pp.171-4.

[46]*Ibid.*, p.174.

[47]Nicholas Dent, *The moral psychology of the virtues*, Cambridge, Cambridge University Press, 1984, p.12.

[48]Michael Sandel, *Liberalism and the Limits of Justice*, Cambridge, Cambridge University Press, 1982, p.179; quotation from p.56.

[49]Craig Dykstra, *Vision and Character*, New York, Paulist Press, 1981, p.3.

[50]St Paul, Romans 7:15, 20, 22-23.

[51]*Catechism of the Catholic Church*, p.389.

[52]See, for example, H. Skolimowski, *Living Philosophy*, London, Arkana, 1992); R. Bellah et al, *Habits of the Heart*, London, Hutchinson, 1988; D. Selbourne, *The Principle of Duty*, London, Sinclair Stevenson, 1994; A. MacIntyre, *After Virtue*, London, Duckworth, 1985.

[53]C. Gunton, *The One, The Three and The Many*, Cambridge University Press, Cambridge, 1993, p.187.

[54]J. Maritain, *Education at the Crossroads*, Yale University Press, 1943, pp. 8-9.

[55]*Ibid.*, p.34.

[56]*Ibid.*

[57]*Ibid.*

[58]See, for example, The Catholic Bishops' Conference of England and Wales, *The Common Good and the Catholic Church's Social Teaching*, Manchester, Gabriel Communications, 1996 and Catholic Education Service, *The Common Good in Education*, London, 1997.

[59]Jane Kopas, *Sacred Identity*, New York, Paulist Press, 1994, p. 145.

[60]*The Common Good and the Catholic Church's Social Teaching*, para 13.

[61]Richard Pring, *Closing the Gap: Liberal Education and Vocational Preparation*, London, Hodder & Stoughton, 1995, p.134.

[62]Richard Pring, *op. cit.*, pp.128-130.

[63]These last two sentences summarise the carefully argued essay, 'Liberal & Vocational Education: A conflict of value', in the Victor Cook Lectures, 'Education, Values and the State', edited by John Haldane, University of St Andrews, 1994, pp.7-41.

[64]Kevin Kelly, *New Directions in Moral Theology*, London, Geoffrey Chapman, 1992, p. 38.

[65] If we accept that we are made in the image of God, and that this includes the notion that we are offered friendship with God and a share in divine life, then treating our life purely as a personally constructed work of art, as an act of self assertion or self-realisation, is no longer a tenable option. We need the truth to set us free. For these implications of believing that we are made in God's image, see John O'Donnell, 'Theological Anthropology in the Encyclicals of John Paul II', in *Continuity and Plurality in Catholic Theology*, edited by Anthony Cernera,1998 and Louis Dupre, 'On the Task and Vocation of the Catholic College', in *Examining the Catholic Intellectual Tradition*, edited by Anthony Cernera and Oliver Morgan, 2000, both Fairfield, Connecticut, Sacred Heart University Press.

[66]A. McFadyen, *The call to personhood*, Cambridge University Press, Cambridge, 1990, pp.29, 30.

[67]Aidan Nichols, *Byzantine Gospel: Maximus the Confessor in Modern Scholarship*, Edinburgh, T & T Clark, 1993, p.168.

[68]Stephen Duffy, *The Graced Horizon*, Collegeville, Minnesota, The Liturgical Press, 1991, p.106. The theme of human restlessness requiring God as the only source of satisfaction was expressed most powerfully and memorably by Augustine in his *Confessions*.

[69]J. Sachs, *The Christian Vision of Humanity*, Collegeville, Minnesota, The Liturgical Press, 1991, p.106.

[70]P. Vermes, *Buber on God and the Perfect Man*, Scholars Press, 1980, p.180.

[71]A. McFadyen, *op. cit.*, p.57.

[72]See note 18, above.

[73]John Dwyer, in *The New Dictionary of Catholic Social Thought*, edited by J.A. Dwyer and E.L. Montgomery, Collegeville, Minnesota, Liturgical Press, 1994, p.724.

[74]*Ibid.*, p.731.

[75]Charles Wood, 'Theological education and education for church leadership' in Astley, Francis and Crowder (1996), *op. cit.*, p.304. (see note 28)

[76]Robert Sokolowski, *Eucharistic Presence*, Washington, DC, The Catholic University of America Press, 1994, p. 130.

[77] For two very different, yet richly rewarding and sophisticated analyses of the bearing of a Christian ontology and worldview on an understanding of education, see Robert Martin, *The Incarnate Ground of Christian Faith*, Lanham, University Press of America, 1998, and Signe Sandsmark, *Is World View Neutral Education Possible and Desirable?* Carlisle, Paternoster, 2000.

[78] For an alternative, complementary interpretation of the relationship between key aspects of a Catholic worldview and the educational endeavour, see Anthony Cernera and Oliver Morgan, *Examining The Catholic Intellectual Tradition*, Fairfield, Connecticut, Sacred Heart University Press, 2000, pp.208-214.

CHAPTER 6

INCLUSIVENESS AND EXCLUSIVENESS

In chapters three to five I focused on central features of the *content* of the claim that there is within Catholicism a distinctive philosophy of education and of life. It must be acknowledged that there can be no *absolute* demarcation between the content of a claim and what its adherents believe should follow from it. Nevertheless, I intend to draw out some of the *implications* of this claim by focusing on various ways that this distinctiveness might be expressed in broad policy issues or in particular practices in Catholic schools. The main aim of the chapter is to explore how the claim to be distinctive coheres with the parallel claim that Catholic education is essentially inclusive. Different meanings of the term 'inclusiveness' and its correlative 'exclusiveness' will be analysed. I shall indicate in the process some of the factors that have had a bearing on a deepening understanding of and commitment to inclusiveness in education. Then I shall argue that many aspects of inclusiveness are compatible with Catholic principles; that some aspects are essential to such principles, but that other aspects present problems for Catholic educators.[1] Some kinds of inclusiveness necessarily follow from a Catholic perspective and are intrinsic to Catholic education. Other aspects are accepted as part of a set of liberal principles that do not depend upon Catholic beliefs, but which do not contradict them either.

This situation also applies to practices that should be *excluded* from Catholic schools: some of these would be excluded in any school which seeks to exemplify liberal principles; others would be excluded because they conflict with a Catholic worldview. Some kinds of exclusiveness are necessarily entailed by the claim of Catholic education to be distinctive. Many kinds of exclusiveness would, however, be quite incompatible with Catholic principles.

These points might be outlined more schematically. In relation to Catholic Christianity, forms of inclusion may be (1) distinctively (i.e. exclusively) required: *only* Catholics must include this feature; (2) essentially, but not exclusively, required: Catholics and others must include this feature; (3) compatible with, but not required: an acceptable, but not a necessary inclusion; (4) incompatible. Similarly, with regard to Catholic Christianity, forms of exclusion may reflect any one of these four types. Such an analysis would require extensive justification and exemplification. However, my aim here is not provide a detailed and comprehensive mapping of *all* the various forms of inclusion and exclusion possible in Catholic education. Instead I merely wish to demonstrate that a Catholic philosophy of education is compatible with *a sufficient number* of forms of inclusiveness (considered normative from religious and educational perspectives) to justify the claim that *in several respects a Catholic education can be (and should be) both distinctive and inclusive.* For the purposes of my argument, therefore, I do not need to allocate specifically each form of inclusion (or exclusion) referred to into the precise categories outlined above.

6.1.1. *Inclusive and exclusive language*

In contemporary society the terms 'exclusive language' and 'inclusive language' are sometimes employed to distinguish modes of speaking to and about others which have either negative or positive intentions or effects. If someone is accused of using exclusive language, it is implied that such a person is guilty of one or more of the following faults. They ignore or downgrade the experience of their audience. They use pronouns, metaphors or examples that refer too narrowly to the experience of some of those to whom or about whom they are speaking, as if they were either invisible or unimportant. They make assumptions about roles, qualities and insights that are unduly limiting in their provenance and scope. This could apply in matters of different race, gender, religious faith, class, ability, nationality, sexual orientation or political persuasion.

If you use language which excludes me in some way, for example, in the contexts of church liturgy or preaching, school assembly or classroom, political speeches, or even in informal conversations at parties or in public houses, then you leave out part of what is essential to me. You have assumed, prematurely and in a prejudicial manner, something about me that is inaccurate, incomplete or simply unjust. In that process I feel diminished and your message is made more alien to me than it might appear otherwise. You have distanced yourself from me and at the same time reduced the relevance to me of your communication. By granting, at least implicitly, a privileged position to some perspective that does not include me, you have made it more difficult for me to enter into this area of discussion as an equal. You prevent me from feeling that I have anything worth contributing (or at least anything that I anticipate will be taken seriously by you). You have made me more of an 'outsider', an inferior, of less account. As a result of your stance I may then be tempted, in order to become acceptable, to omit or even to deny crucial aspects of my experience and identity, or to concede principles which I do not really hold to, thereby slipping into inauthenticity.

Part of what is entailed by being inclusive, then, seems to be the displaying of certain attitudes to others: respect, openness, welcome, acceptance and the desire to provide access to what we have on offer and also protection against discrimination. A positive view of difference is built into the idea of inclusiveness: those who are different will be recognised and responded to in a positive way.

6.1.2. Inclusiveness normative from a Christian perspective

Many kinds of inclusiveness, like those just mentioned, do not derive directly from a particular faith perspective. I shall explore more of these later in the chapter, especially when I analyse the teacher-pupil relationship. In the particular context of Catholic education I believe that many kinds of inclusiveness are entailed by the distinctive worldview which I outlined in chapter four. Among these I pick out ten forms of openness or inclusiveness which stem from a broadly Christian religious perspective and which should be considered normative for Catholic education. I list these without assuming that they are all actually present in particular schools.

First, there is openness to the grace of God (on the basis that we are not self-sufficient, either individually or communally). Second, there is openness to the promptings of the Holy Spirit, who leads us continually and more fully into truth and who cannot be confined to the working of the visible church. Third, there is an awareness of and response to the needs of others, whoever and wherever they are, including all types of needs, this inclusiveness demonstrating a concern for the well-being of others in all the diversity of their needs. Fourth, there is an inclusiveness of sinners, which involves an avoidance of premature judgement and of elitism, in favour of patience, forgiveness and tolerance (all under the aspect of compassion, not of justification). Fifth, there is an openness to and a respect for the autonomy of different sources of knowledge, that is, an avoidance of theological imperialism and an acknowledgement that reason is not contradicted by revelation but rather is both complemented and reframed in its light. Sixth, there is openness to political realities and recognition of the need to co-operate with others of different persuasions. Seventh, there is a willingness to engage in inter-religious dialogue and ecumenism and to equip others to do so as a central aim of education. Eighth, inclusiveness is shown by inculturation, taking cultures seriously, distinguishing culture from the heart of religion and being ready to adapt the cultural expressions employed by the Church, thereby facilitating a synthesis between faith and cultures. Ninth, there is openness to the need for ongoing internal reformation of the Church. Part of this aspect of openness is recognition of the need for constant development in our understanding of doctrine. Fresh expressions of faith are encouraged in order to link up more effectively with, and to cast more light upon, the different aspects of peoples' lives and thereby facilitate a synthesis of faith and life. Tenth, inclusiveness is demonstrated not only by the facilitation of a harmonious internal pluralism in the life of the Church (as against the enforcement of uniformity or a premature polarisation of views) but also by a level of trust which allows subsidiarity to be taken seriously within the Church.

All of these forms of inclusiveness, except those indicated in points six and ten, are implicit either within one or more of the key elements of Catholic education (as outlined in chapter four) or in one or more aspects of the Catholic worldview (as articulated in chapter five). The sixth form of openness, shown in a pragmatic willingness to co-operate with 'outsiders', can be said to have dictated the Church's acceptance of the dual system in England and Wales (described in chapter three). Collaboration with other citizens in the public domain is a theme that is repeated in several of the Bishops' documents on Catholic education. It is addressed further in chapter eight, below, when I consider the possible contribution of Catholic schools to the common good in the context of a plural and largely secular society. The tenth form of inclusiveness is, to a degree, implicit in my treatment of living tradition and subsidiarity in later chapters.

It will be apparent that some of these forms of openness will be fully endorsed by people who do not consider themselves religious. Those described under my third and sixth headings come into this category. Conversely, however, people without religious affiliations or sympathies are likely to assess the forms of openness described under my first, second, seventh, ninth and tenth headings as a matter of supreme indifference. As for the other forms of openness outlined, those under my fourth, fifth and eighth headings, these will probably meet with a cautious welcome, mingled with a degree of perplexity. All of these forms of inclusiveness, in one way or another, have a bearing upon both school policy and classroom practice.

6.1.3   Differentiation

In the context of education the idea of differentiation is familiar: a planned process of intervention in the classroom to maximise potential based on individual needs. Teachers approach differentiation in several ways. They make allowances for individuals' difficulties and handicaps to learning, whether these are academic, social or personal. They provide different resources, set different tasks and provide differing levels of support. They look for different responses or outcomes in order to increase the chances that the learning needs of all their pupils will be met and that all pupils have an opportunity to have access to and make progress through the curriculum. It is possible to speak of

> differentiation in teaching styles, in the pacing of lessons (i.e. allowing different pupils to work at different speeds), in the level of the curriculum goals, in the type of response expected of pupils, in the curricular sequence, in the structure of lessons, in grouping arrangements and in the time devoted to different pupils.[2]

Such efforts have been boosted since 1994 by the Code of Practice on the identification and assessment of Special Educational Needs.[3] Teachers are also encouraged (through school policies relating to equal opportunities and through inspection) to demonstrate how they are matching their plans, resources, approaches and procedures to the diverse needs of pupils, taking into account differences in academic ability, age, gender, physical disability, ethnicity, religious belief and socio-economic circumstances.[4]

The notion of differentiation has not often been applied to religious differences in the context of a church school. Differentiation in religious education, and further, with regard to the permeation of the religious ethos throughout the curriculum and the life of the school, presents one of the greatest challenges for Catholic schools at the end of the twentieth century. As religious educator Jim Gallagher points out, 'in most groups there will be a variety of levels of interest, understanding, practice and commitment.'[5] Instead of focusing on the *universal* nature of God's revelation, as mediated through the teaching, worship, service and community life of the church, differentiation draws attention to the fact that it is addressed to the diversity of *particular* lives.

This is why rhetoric as well as logic is required. For rhetoric, as an art of moral communication, entails taking particular audiences into account, and without seeking to manipulate them, takes account of their circumstances, priorities, concerns and values in an effort to 'move' them and to make the Gospel accessible and attractive. In the context of the church's capacity to apply the principles of differentiation to her communication of the message of salvation, the notion of rhetoric is linked closely with that of 'reception'. Concern about 'reception' of the church's teaching acts as a moderating influence on the usual focus on 'promulgation' and brings out the need for the church to be a listening and learning church.[6]

The more inclusive attitude displayed in the practice of differentiation stems partly from greater respect for the dignity and uniqueness of each person and partly from recognition of incompleteness within the church. There is less presumption of a radical separation between the members of the church who have authority to teach in its name and those who are expected to learn from this teaching. Teachers who do not recognise the uniqueness of each pupil and the gift that she or he has to bring to the classroom are likely to obstruct learning. Presumptive language, which assumes, for example, that all pupils have the same level of faith-commitment, can be exclusive, alienating and anti-educational. As Jim Gallagher says, "we have to recognise that each journey of faith is unique and we have to respect that each pupil has a different starting place and will have his or her own pace for the journey."[7] This recognition merely echoes the comment in *Catechesi Tradendae* that "Catholic establishments should respect freedom of conscience" and that they have a duty "to offer a religious training suited to the often widely varying religious situations of the pupils."[8] Pupils will be at different levels of readiness for and responsiveness to or even rejection of faith. Catholic schools should seek to adopt an inclusive approach to all of them. This inclusive approach will build on and express those features of inclusiveness already listed as normative from a faith perspective[9] and those required pedagogically by differentiation. These two sources mutually reinforce one another in the respect shown to and the attempt to meet the needs of pupils.

A highly inclusive response by the Bishops' Conference of England and Wales to religious pluralism in Catholic schools is the recently issued *Catholic Schools & Other Faiths*.[10] Here a close connection is suggested between fidelity to tradition and the nurturing of faith, the promotion of dialogue and openness, and service to the community. These three aims for Catholic education are seen as intimately interrelated. Such an emphasis implies a radical re-thinking of the purpose of Catholic schools, one that differs considerably from the more inward-looking and protective form of Catholic education predominant earlier this century.

The more inclusive emphasis requires an education that develops the attitudes, insights and skills which facilitate dialogue and encounter with people of a variety of faith stances and partnership with their respective communities. This emphasis derives not from an abandonment or loss of confidence in the clear identity and distinctive features of Catholic education, but rather from an interpretation of these which requires, as an essential and constituent element of them, a high degree of openness to the perspectives and needs of others. *Catholic Schools & Other Faiths* makes a strong case for sensitivity to be shown to people of other faiths and for careful safeguarding of their interests in the drawing up of school policies. In the guidance notes accompanying the document the practical implications of such concern are drawn for Catholic schools. These include arrangements for assemblies, personal and social education, religious education, the content and treatment of other curriculum areas, admissions criteria, support for the culture and values of families from other faiths, for instance, with regard to feasts, fasts, prayer, diet, dress, and co-operation with their spiritual leaders.[11] This kind of sensitivity is founded upon principles originally articulated in the documents emanating from the Second Vatican Council.[12] *Catholic Schools & Other Faiths* might be said to represent a direct application of these conciliar documents to the context of Catholic schools in late twentieth century England and Wales and a deliberate attempt to promote a more inclusive style of involvement in the world.

This emphasis on differentiation has recently been applied quite specifically to the task of religious formation, wherever it takes place. 'Personalised accompanying' and sensitive attention to the particular stage of growth that each student has reached in their unique journey of faith is advocated.[13] Inclusiveness as shown by a willingness to acknowledge the differences between people and to stand back from an imposed uniformity is very much in evidence in some recent statements from the Bishops' Conference of England and Wales. *Valuing Difference* (1998) challenges Catholics to ensure that schools and parishes make their institutional and community arrangements much more hospitable to people with varying forms of disability.[14] It evaluates recent steps in responding to the needs of people with diverse handicaps and argues for renewed efforts to welcome into the Catholic community those who face particular obstacles to full participation, to acknowledge their gifts and to learn from their insights and experience.

On the Threshold (*OT*) demonstrates the same desire to implement a more inclusive interpretation of Catholicism.[15] This report on sacramental initiation takes seriously the fact that some people do not feel at home in a church situation (*OT*, p.5). It acknowledges the pull of the two polarities that are the subject of this book, when it asks: 'should we welcome them [would-be recipients of the sacraments] with open arms and no pre-conditions or should we make certain demands?'(*OT*, p.5) In exploring the terms of church membership, it steers a path that seems to combine concern for the distinctive character of the Catholic faith with recognition of its essentially inclusive nature. The tone of the report is positive, gentle, pastoral and non-judgemental. It acknowledges that seekers do not come to the church as 'blank pages in a book' and it urges that 'we should look at the experiences of life, the values and the ideas they are bringing with them' (*OT*, pp.10-11). 'We cannot simply put people through a programme regardless of their previous experience' (*OT*, p.58). Learning in the church is not a one-way affair; those who already belong may have something of value to learn from outsiders; they may even need to change in the light of the perceptions of people who are currently 'at the margins', not yet incorporated into the (visible) church. Two complementary roles are described as equally necessary if the Church is to respond adequately to seekers: custodian of the Church's riches and an explorer. 'Custodians want to stand still and be protective; explorers want to move on and discover new avenues' (*OT*, p.37).

6.1.4. *Inclusiveness: influences and constraints*

The practice of labelling language as 'exclusive' or 'inclusive' stems from a range of changes in our society. Among other factors one might attribute such labelling to an ever-deepening penetration of our understanding of liberal democracy, and the sources and contexts which enhance or obstruct its operations. In order to grant others an appropriate degree of freedom and to treat them as of equal worth one must listen to their stories, enter into their perspectives, learn from their experiences, be challenged by their 'otherness' and be enriched by their differences. Progress in the social sciences[16] helps us to appreciate the various rationales behind differing ways of doing things, 'seeing' things and prioritising among them.

Yet among the sources contributing to a growing emphasis on inclusiveness one can justifiably claim that some come from within the life of the church.[17] There have been fresh insights into the implications of the Gospel, alternative interpretations of what is meant by church and new understandings of what is required for a properly educational relationship in school settings.[18] Developments since Vatican II have led to various shifts in emphasis. Among these one could cite the 'preferential option for the poor', liberation theology, modifications in the church's social teaching and an increasingly inclusive theology of religions. Cumulatively, these mean that greater emphasis is now placed on the all-embracing scope of the Gospel and its application to people of all races, classes, and conditions.[19] Feminist theology is, in this context at least, part of a wider move to interpret the Gospel as a story which liberates us from all that enslaves us and as a text which liberates us for a life that is more fully human.[20]

Taken together, these secular and religious factors contribute to a greater emphasis on inclusiveness. In a truly educational relationship that displays the quality of inclusiveness, there will be room for dialogue and reciprocity. The influences I have mentioned which emphasise the importance of inclusiveness within education have prompted fresh understandings of equal opportunities, of the community dimension of schooling and of the kind of curriculum to be pursued by pupils.

There cannot, of course, be an unqualified kind of openness or inclusiveness in education. This is for several reasons. First, there are other qualities competing for our allegiance as aspects of good education. Among these we could expect to find clarity in communication. There should be stability and persistence in the values pursued. Accuracy in scholarship and the attainment of nationally agreed standards will remain priorities. Certain kinds of curriculum content will be privileged in terms of the resources made available to them and the weight that they carry. This is because they have both high value in the eyes of the general public (which pays for education through their taxes) and they have strong epistemological warrant for being conveyed as valid knowledge. To these must be added critical distance and objectivity and a degree of detachment from being swamped by current feelings and fashions and local circumstances. One cannot expect inclusiveness to override all these, but instead to take its place alongside them. Indeed, it might be argued that 'inclusiveness' is based upon them.

Second, and related to the first point, as Siegel points out, "there is no necessary connection between inclusion and epistemic worthiness, or between exclusion and epistemic defectiveness."[21] Epistemology and social justice are separate issues and operate on different levels, although it may well be the case that sometimes an exclusive outlook which disregards social justice has been a factor in the failure to take proper account of the full range of potential evidence relating to a question. Teachers must demonstrate the authority of truth and of objective criteria in their classroom exchanges if they are to help their pupils to develop. To accept any view which is put forward by pupils as valid, on the basis of a superficial understanding of inclusiveness, may cause a child to remain in ignorance or with a distorted view when this could have been avoided. It is necessary to heed Siegel's reminder that, "treating a person with respect is compatible with regarding his or her views as unjustified or false."[22]

Third, when teaching and assessment seek to take account of objective standards and criteria of appropriateness, then it becomes relevant to ask questions about competence, expertise and qualifications. It is not a fundamental attack on anyone's dignity to say that, on particular issues, which require prior training, particular experience or specialist knowledge, not all views can count as equal or even receive serious consideration.

A fourth constraint on the degree of inclusiveness in the classroom comes from the inability of teachers to escape entirely from the limitations of their own setting and worldview.[23] There will be some things they cannot envisage because of particular features in their upbringing, education and training, their mandate (from government and governors) and in the prevailing assumptions of their time and culture. Much of this will influence their conduct without their being conscious of it. In addition, having deliberately committed themselves to certain principles and values as having overriding authority over them, (perhaps inclusiveness being one of these) teachers will rule out some topics as too trivial to deserve time in school. They will consider that some views should be denied scope for articulation on the grounds that they are demeaning of human dignity or endanger communal harmony. Some kinds of behaviour will be forbidden as inherently damaging both to those who indulge and to others who are affected by such indulgence. Hence, tiddlywinks, bestiality, racism, bullying and drug-taking are not promoted in the curriculum.

These limits to inclusiveness do not undermine its importance in education. Any deepening in our understanding of its nature and role in education is likely to be influenced by a growing realisation that our openness to God cannot be separated from our openness to others.   In his influential Reith lectures Jonathan Sacks commented:

> I believe that our capacity to recognise the 'wholly Other' that is God is measured by our ability to recognise the image of God that resides in the person who is not like us: the human 'wholly other.'...To have faith in God as creator and ruler of the universe is to do more than believe that God has spoken to us. It is to believe that God has spoken to others, in a language which we may not understand.[24]

The argument might be that God is fully open to all and so, if we wish to be open to God, then we will need to display openness to all, without reservation or resentment.   Furthermore, if we are taking our cue from what we believe about God's way with us and with others, then there will be a sense in which this openness is simultaneously discriminating and non-discriminating. It is non-discriminating in that all, without exception, are embraced by God's grace and invited by his call. Yet it is discriminating in the sense that God's universal invitation is adapted to the uniqueness of each individual, so that each is fed in a way that is proportionate to her or his capacities, aspirations and needs.

6.1.5. *The Gospel imperative for inclusiveness and its challenge to Catholic schools*
The imperative from the Gospels is both universal and all-embracing: the call is to all nations; and everything which Jesus taught is to be conveyed.[25]   The inclusiveness that flows from such a universalism should be treated, according to Michael Barnes, a leading Catholic spokesperson on inter-faith relations, less as a system than as an 'instinct'.[26]   Continuities and discontinuities between different faiths should be recognised and an allowance made for the mysterious workings of the Holy Spirit within and beyond all faiths. Such an inclusive instinct will avoid any patronising.[27]   Our seeking for a link between Christ's Word and the 'other words' which come from God in various ways entails neither a lack of loyalty to nor a compromise with our own tradition.[28]   Our main priority should surely be to exhibit a constant openness to the activity of God rather than faithfulness to the tradition, even if we believe that this tradition articulates definitively our understanding of the nature and purpose of God's ways.[29]
The tension within Christianity between an exclusive and an inclusive emphasis stems from the combination of the universal and the particular. The Gospel might be addressed to all peoples and might touch upon all aspects of their existence. Nevertheless, as a continuation of the incarnational principle, it is carried forward through particular traditions and embedded in particular communities that are located in time and space. If faith has an eternal dimension, yet it is rooted in history. Of course, there are constant foundations or principles that withstand the test of time, for example, the person of Jesus Christ, the teaching of the Gospels, the accumulated moral and spiritual wisdom of tradition and the carefully worked out and intricately intermeshed body of doctrine. Nevertheless the circumstances of the people to whom the 'story' is addressed are constantly changing. Our context and culture, our predicament and problems remain in a state of flux.

Inclusiveness is also required, then, because the 'story' is 'unfinished', open to further development.   For the ongoing completion of creation and redemption, which remains for us in the future, not only do we need tradition and heritage, communities of memory, but also innovation and creativity, communities of anticipation.[30]   There will be a creative tension between these two, with memory cherished for the sake of the future and with anticipation fostered as the rightfully to be hoped for harvest from the past.   Another way of putting this is to refer to the need for a double form of hermeneutics, the first requiring 'retrieval' and the second requiring 'hospitality'.   'Retrieval' preserves a heritage; it rescues what is essential from the particular historical tradition and ensures continuity.   'Hospitality' prevents insularity; it ensures that a concern for memory and heritage does not slip into a backward-looking, inflexible or exclusivist stance.   It displays a "readiness to welcome strange and unfamiliar meanings into our own awareness, perhaps to be shaken by them, but in no case to be left unchanged."[31]

One important educational implication here is that the whole curriculum has the potential to provide a context for an encounter with God.   Religion is not to be confined to one aspect of the curriculum; it must reach out beyond a protected 'slot'. Yet religion is also to be challenged and enriched by dialogue with other curriculum areas.   As Nicholas Lash puts it,

> If Christianity is a school for the production of persons in relation to the unknown God through discipleship of the crucified, then there is *nothing* (his emphasis) that we do and suffer, think, or feel, or undergo, which may not contribute to such schooling.   It follows that there is no single activity, or cluster of activities, which alone counts as 'Christian teaching.'[32]

Such a holistic approach to the curriculum entailed by Catholicism's inclusive spirituality would rule out as deficient the dualistic kind of Catholic school described by James Arthur.[33]   If there is no sustained attempt to integrate faith and culture in the religious and secular curriculum, then a school is, from a Catholic point of view, insufficiently inclusive in its approach.

Another dimension of that inclusiveness which should be a constitutive feature of Catholic education is indicated in the Gospels.   A recurring theme there is Jesus's ministry to outsiders, the poor and the rejected.   Likewise Catholic education should include those who are deviants, sinners, unorthodox, unpopular, unsuccessful, disabled, that is, the poor, interpreted broadly.   Pupils with learning difficulties and behaviour problems, those who are non-conforming, critical or dissenting, all have an important part to play in a Catholic school.   If a Catholic school is to be true to its Gospel roots, such pupils should experience acceptance and affirmation as persons with an inalienable dignity.   Their uniqueness should be cherished, their talents nurtured, their questions taken seriously, their capacity for redemption never lost sight of, nor their spirits crushed.   This does not mean that bad behaviour is condoned, explained away, ignored or downplayed; nor does it mean that the school should not strive for worldly success in terms of examination passes, sporting results, entry of pupils into higher education or into a variety of vocations.   But it does imply that the school should seek to treat these aims as subordinate to other goals, ones that relate more directly to the spread of the Gospel, acceptance of its message, and furtherance of the Kingdom of God.

It follows from a Christian perspective on life that "a person's significance is not determined by the value of what he or she contributes to other people's experiences....The fundamental worth of each human being lies neither in what a person achieves nor in what a person makes possible for others to achieve, but in God's love for that person."[34] Although this is easier to recognise in the context of the home, it applies also in the context of school. The unconditional acceptance and love experienced by children at home will provide a powerful foundation, indeed it is a prerequisite for later recognition of God's love for us.[35] Such inclusiveness forms the human soil in which the Gospel message can be sown.

Those on the margins of acceptability, the semi-committed, the half-believers, the occasional participants, the lapsed or 'resting' church members - all can be only too easily excluded from admission into church schools. There is a danger here of a contradiction between values which are espoused and those which are upheld in practice. Kenneth Wilson has recently pointed out that whereas church schools were originally set up in the nineteenth century to provide educational opportunities for the poor, now they tend to cater principally for those who could not be considered poor at all.[36]

Wilson is particularly critical of church school admission policies that require evidence of religious commitment. "Those who are able to satisfy this criterion tend to be those who would be educationally rich anyway - religion having become a minority middle class pastime."[37] The desire in church schools to ensure that they contain a high proportion of pupils who come from religiously committed families undermines, for Wilson, their gospel imperative of service and has several other damaging side-effects:

> [First] it would deprive many children of the everyday contacts with those of different faiths and cultures which could help prepare them for adult life in a multi-faith community. [Second] excluding non- Christian children from one of the borough's better schools [gives] a disquieting message about the church's attitude to equal opportunities. [Third] it indirectly [tells] the other faith communities that they should make their own arrangements for the education of their children - suggesting a future of segregation with possibly unthinkable consequences.[38]

These are important criticisms of church school admission policies, which should not operate in a way that compounds anyone's disadvantage. But while they should cause governors of church schools to review very carefully the implications of their admission policies, and while the application of religious criteria is notoriously difficult to manage with consistency and justice, this does not mean that there is no place for such criteria. A crucial barrier to admittance in Catholic schools would relate to whatever makes Catholic education very difficult to carry out. Some kinds of behaviour are incompatible with its central tenets, purpose, and atmosphere. This stipulation is vulnerable to the criticism that such judgements are merely subjective. How committed must a Catholic school be to inclusiveness in the range of senses indicated earlier? While a school may decide (with regret) that it could no longer cope with certain kinds of misbehaviour, in the face of activities which undermined its purpose as a Catholic school, this might better be decided *after* it had tried and failed, not before.

I am prescinding from this argument the special case of those pupils who have severe learning, physical or emotional difficulties and for whom the school is inadequately equipped to provide a suitable education. In such cases the cost of additional provision might be prohibitive. However, the burden of proof in this case would rest with the school. The assumption must be in favour of inclusiveness, rather than the other way about. It is only too easy to seek to justify non-acceptance of pupils on spurious grounds which relate more closely to the perceived reputation and desired results of the school than to its *raison d'être*.

However, if it *is* accepted that there is a legitimate place for separate church schools, it is not illogical to seek to preserve their special character by ensuring that they contain a proportion of Catholic pupils which is sufficiently high to constitute a critical mass. It will be even more important to ensure that there is a significant proportion of staff who are committed to a Catholic approach to education, if the distinctiveness of such schools is to be maintained.

Part of what is meant by the inclusiveness of Catholic schools is the role they *share with* other agencies within the community. Education in general, and Catholic education in particular, is not the exclusive preserve of schools. It is a collective endeavour which is shared with parents, the parish, the wider church community (deanery, diocesan, national and even international - many religious orders which play an important role in Catholic education have an international membership), Christian associations, youth clubs and charitable organisations.

Government educational policy throughout much of the 1990s encouraged schools to 'opt out' from their Local Education Authority and to receive funding directly from national government. In the case of Catholic schools who adopted the more independent Grant Maintained status this decision often distanced them from the diocesan system of schools, even when it did not flout diocesan policy. Any attempt to make schools operate as independent 'islands' undermines co-operation, community and co-responsibility for the common good. It encourages the use of education as a positional good for the benefit of an elite, rather than as transformational of personal experience and as constitutive of the good life to be shared in common. It would be unfortunate if, after only recently shedding hierarchical features which were reinforced by pre-Vatican II models of church - now complemented by alternative models[39] - Catholic schools were to become less democratic internally and less accountable to their local communities - through an increase in internal, self-management, chief executive-style authority and a decrease in the influence of intermediate institutions. Despite counter-currents, the Catholic church is seeking ways to be a more participative community, with greater power-sharing, especially with the laity.[40] It would be difficult now to reverse the trend towards greater integration between Catholicism and democratic modes of decision making and working.[41]

6.1.6. *Inclusiveness as an educational virtue*

In seeking to be sensitive to the different nuances of the word 'inclusive' I have so far referred to a developing understanding of the implications for Catholic schools of the Christian Gospel. In order to deepen my exploration of these implications, I now turn to those dimensions of inclusiveness that should be reflected in the educational relationships prevailing in schools. One dilemma facing Catholic schools relates to knowledge of other faiths and worldviews. When and how should this be done? Should teachers include the beliefs of those opposed to any form of religion? It is clear that such knowledge *should* be promoted, first, in the interests of social harmony and mutual understanding, second, in order to address the spiritual needs of pupils who are not Catholics and third, to enhance, through the opportunity afforded by comparison, the critical self-awareness of all pupils. A difficulty for some people might be how to relate an understanding of other life stances to an appreciation of and commitment to Catholicism itself. The Catholic school would seem to be simultaneously both advocating a particular view of life (as I outlined in chapter five), giving it a privileged position in the life of the school, and calling it into question by the degree of its openness to and respectful treatment of other perspectives. This problem is considerably alleviated in principle, I believe, through my recasting of a Catholic philosophy of education by focusing on the intimate *relationship* between distinctiveness and inclusiveness.

If it were to be argued that there is within Catholicism itself an ecumenical imperative,[42] agreement has been reached neither as to the timing nor as to the degree at which such knowledge of the positions of others should be imparted. Deciding these matters is not merely a matter of pedagogical prudence, resting on empirical findings about notions of psychological 'readiness' or of conceptual development. The relative weight to be attached to the differing roles of Catholic schools in fostering identity-formation and in promoting the capacity for dialogue and mutual understanding between people of different faiths and cultures is still open to debate. Sandsmark says that the challenge for schools is to find the right balance.[43] But any work undertaken in service of such a balance between (religious) self-confidence and openness will be influenced, in part at least, on what are perceived to be the constitutive elements of a Catholic view of human nature, development and destiny and the key features of a Catholic education. It will also depend upon which kind of theology of religions is held, however implicitly, by the teacher, as well as on local circumstances.

John Stuart Mill more than a century ago in *On Liberty* expressed the belief that we *cannot* understand our own point of view properly until we have considered other points of view, for without such understanding we have no grounds for preferring our own. This belief merely echoes a statement made even earlier.[44] In 1644 John Milton argued in parliament against censorship of printing:

> what wisdom can there be to choose, what continence to forbear without the knowledge of evil?...I cannot praise a fugitive and cloistered virtue, unexercised and unbreathed, that never sallies out and sees her adversary, but slinks out of the race, where that immortal garland is to be run for, not without dust and heat...[T]hat which purifies us is trial, and trial is by what is contrary.[45]

More recently, Larry May has shown the benefits of being exposed to a plurality of views which challenge us to reflect critically upon our own beliefs and which open up the possibility of better understanding the perspectives of others.[46] The early fathers of the church debated hotly the merits and dangers of engaging with sources beyond their faith. If openness to other points of view has not always been a leading virtue among Catholics, such openness indicates no lack of commitment to Catholicism.

A rather different approach to stressing the importance of inclusiveness is to show that it is at the very heart of the act of teaching. Martin Buber speaks of education as having an ascetic character, where the teacher seeks to separate herself from the instinct to dominate and to experience the person 'on the other side' of the teaching relationship, the pupil.[47] He says that "inclusiveness is the complete realisation of...the partner;" but this is not merely a matter of empathy; it is something more full-bodied than that.[48]

Buber depicts an educational relationship that is based on dialogue. In this relationship there is an awareness of the other's legitimacy, and the act of inclusion (by the teacher, of the pupil) is not merely regulative (as an act of moral restraint or self-discipline on the part of the teacher) but is also constitutive of the teacher-pupil relationship. There has to be a 'reaching over' by the teacher. "Only when he catches himself 'from over there', and feels how it [the child's individuality] affects one, how it affects this other human being, does he recognise the real limit of the situation."[49] But the experience of inclusion is one-sided in that the teacher "experiences the pupil's being educated, but the pupil cannot experience the educating of the educator. The educator stands at both ends of the common situation."[50]

For Buber then, teaching involves inclusion in so far it entails an effort to avoid the temptation to dominate another, and in so far as the teacher seeks to enter into the pupil's perspective and thereby to identify with his or her needs. Dialogue will be the hall-mark of the encounter, but the type of inclusion possible in teaching can only be one-sided, in that the dialogue partners are unequal in status and role; for only in friendship can we find a full experience of mutuality and reciprocity.

Two recent writers have commented helpfully on aspects of inclusiveness, developing Buber's insights further. The first comes from the field of spirituality. Henri Nouwen, describing the type of inclusiveness (which he calls 'hospitality') to be exercised by teachers within the classroom, says that they should create a free and friendly space, which will allow students to grow and reveal to them that they have something to offer as well as to receive.[51] "We will never believe that we have anything to give unless there is someone who is able to receive...[Students need] teachers who can detach themselves from their need to impress and control, and who can allow themselves to be receptive."[52] Nouwen invites teachers to think of their students as guests in their classrooms, guests who need affirmation, encouragement and support, but also a degree of unambiguous confrontation and challenging witness from the teacher. "Receptivity without confrontation leads to a bland neutrality that serves nobody. Confrontation without receptivity leads to an oppressive aggression which hurts everybody."[53]   Nouwen's emphasis on 'hospitality' as an aspect of the teacher's role implies neither paternalism nor any failure to recognise the importance of encouraging student 'ownership' of their classrooms. It does suggest, however, that the primary responsibility for developing this rests with the teacher, especially with younger students and in the context of compulsory schooling.

I take it that the kind of inclusiveness being spoken of here by Nouwen is one that invites learners in classrooms to share their experiences, insights, and questions. Their contributions are to be accepted as gifts to be welcomed, respected and valued. True classroom 'hospitality' or inclusiveness, however, goes beyond this. It offers an encounter, through the teacher, with the insights and values of another world, a world that transcends the one currently envisaged by the pupils. This kind of inclusiveness involves openness and receptivity on the part of the teacher, but this should be a discerning receptivity, displaying no abdication of responsibility. If the teacher is to reach out to pupils, starting from where they are, if she is to 'embrace' their needs, to accept their concerns and perceptions, nevertheless she is not to leave them at this point but instead to encourage them to 'travel' further. In the context of a Catholic school a particular sense of the direction of the travel, its goal and the pitfalls and helps along the journey, will be given normative status.

The second writer whose work illuminates the importance of inclusiveness within the practice of teaching is Max van Manen. In a sense the whole of his book *The Tact of Teaching* is about the building blocks of inclusiveness.[54] He asks the teacher to reflect on children's lives and he points out that pupils need security so that they can take risks and they need support so that they can become independent. They also need direction from us if they are to find their own direction in life. Tact means for van Manen the practice of being oriented towards others and in teaching to be tactful is to 'touch' someone. This tact will manifest itself as holding back (compare Buber's point, above, about resisting the temptation to dominate) and it will be manifested as openness to the child's experience and as attunement to his/her subjectivity. During the subtle influence exerted by the teacher on the pupil the child's space will be preserved, what is vulnerable in him or her will be protected and what is good will be strengthened, yet at the same time personal growth and learning will be sponsored. All this will be achieved through the mediation of speech, silence, the eyes, gesture, atmosphere and example. Such tact, however gentle, will still leave a mark on the child; the teacher should seek to make a difference.

These insights from van Manen, together with those from Nouwen, deepen our understanding of the nature of inclusiveness that is described by Buber as being at the heart of the educational relationship. Such inclusiveness should be especially evident in the language used by teachers:[they] "should avoid words and language patterns that disvalue or degrade; that shame or demean; that are chauvinistic, oppressive or exclusive;...that are mechanistic, controlling or manipulative."[55] Two further comments are apposite here. First, the kinds of qualities indicated by these three writers as constituting pedagogical inclusiveness are not the monopoly of teachers working in Catholic schools, for they would be displayed by teachers of a wide range of persuasions, religious and non-religious alike. There may, however, be additional motivational reasons for Christian teachers to embrace these inclusive qualities in their pedagogy. These motivational reasons stem from their religious beliefs. Such beliefs can be summarised briefly. Each pupil has a divine origin and an eternal destiny. Each pupil is made in the image and likeness of God. In responding to the needs of their pupils a teacher encounters Christ. By opening oneself to pupils' 'otherness', gifts and insights, one's appreciation of God's ways is likely to be enriched.

Second, a key element of the tact to be deployed in the context of a Catholic school is the response of teachers to pupils who come from families where either no religion is practised or where there is a commitment to a faith other than Catholicism. An inclusive response in this context should display the same human and moral sensitivity which Buber, Nouwen and van Manen have reminded us is a feature of all good teaching. The teacher will avoid "offensive or stigmatising comments about non-believers"[56] or about people whose beliefs differ from those which the school is specifically mandated to represent. Furthermore, in situations where there is integration between religious material and other subjects, this will be carried out "in a manner which avoids proselytism and indoctrination."[57]

This point is of particular importance in the context of a Catholic school since I have already shown, in chapter four, how the integration of faith, culture and life is to be striven for as a key feature of Catholic education. The integration of faith, experience, attitudes and lifestyle to be aimed for in the classroom must display the kind of openness indicated over the last few paragraphs. There should be no undue pressure on pupils to reach 'appropriate' conclusions in that process of integration, nor any premature closure of discussion which might imply that there is not still more which could be explored.

Kevin Williams mentions two issues that arise in the context of a religious school seeking to provide an integrated approach to the curriculum, that is, where religion is treated as an integrating principle and where religion is reinforced through the teaching of other subjects.[58] The first issue relates to how we envisage religion might exercise an integrating role within the curriculum. The second issue relates to how we identify the respective rights of parents, pupils, the school and the community, and the tensions between these rights.

The two questions, although distinct, are connected, for the more religion is integrated into other curriculum subjects, the less possible it is either to withdraw from indirect religious education or to resist its message. It could also be claimed that too successful an integration of religion into the rest of the curriculum might prevent pupils from gaining a suitable degree of detachment. They would not be able to enjoy a vantage point from which to think critically about the religious principles put before them. This could weaken the autonomy of the disciplines which we have seen (in chapter four) is frequently upheld in the central guiding documents on Catholic education.

Williams brings out clearly that there is some tension between the attempt to use religion as an integrating principle in the curriculum and the respective rights of pupils, parents and others. Parents have rights to bring up their children according to their own conception of the good. An over-dominant religion holding sway throughout the curriculum puts this right in jeopardy for some parents, even as it implements the wishes of others by demonstrating the all-pervasive relevance of religion.[59] There will also be implications for staff, if religion is acting as an integrating force, since such an integration cannot happen without the whole of the staff contributing in a coherent way towards a common endeavour, "in the light of an agreed educational and Christian vision."[60]

If we accept that the features of inclusiveness outlined already in this chapter should be considered essential elements in any healthy pedagogy, an over-dominant religion as integrating principle of the curriculum will lead to several risks. We might fail to show the tact asked for by van Manen. We might give in to the temptation to dominate, in just the way that Buber warned us against. We might undermine the atmosphere of hospitality required of teachers by Nouwen. However, an insufficiently strong emphasis on the integrating role of religion in the teaching and life of a Catholic school will lead to an erosion of that distinctiveness which is the *raison d'être* of its existence *as* a separate school. A careful balance has to be maintained, one that promotes the centrality and potentially integrative force of religion in education, while at the same time exercising constraint and sensitivity with regard to its limits and potentially damaging side-effects.

If the preceding analysis is valid, Catholic schools should exhibit several features of inclusiveness. Firstly, the educational needs of pupils who are not Catholics but who find themselves, for a variety of reasons, in Catholic schools will be met satisfactorily. Secondly, members of staff who are not Catholics will be able to contribute both positively and with integrity in such schools. Thirdly, there will be sustained dialogue with external perspectives. Fourthly, the plurality of views within Catholicism itself will be given room for expression.[61] Fifthly, a spirit of tolerance of and respect for people with differing views will be fostered. Sixthly, there will be a promotion, wherever feasible, of the capacity to enter into co-operation, joint action and ecumenical endeavour with people of a variety of stances (ones that are not inimical to the school's values). Seventhly, the critical faculties of pupils will not be neglected or suppressed in an attempt to enforce orthodoxy, but instead they will be nurtured and strengthened by an open, sympathetic yet rigorous treatment of doubts, difficulties and objections which might be raised either by believers or by unbelievers.

6.2.1. *Exclusiveness on educational grounds*

I have touched upon many dimensions of inclusiveness, including those which stem from a religious perspective on life and from the Gospel imperative, those which relate to our use of language, those which arise from the practice of differentiation and in the course of educationally felicitous teacher-pupil relationships. Some of these aspects of inclusiveness are not only in harmony with distinctively Catholic principles; they are required by and integral to Catholicism. Other aspects of inclusiveness are accepted as part of a set of liberal principles that do not depend upon Catholic beliefs, but which do not contradict them either.

This situation also applies to practices which should be *excluded* from Catholic schools: some of these would be excluded in any school which rests upon liberal principles; others would be excluded because they undermine a Catholic worldview. It will not always be easy to distinguish clearly the grounds on which some practices are to be excluded, for example whether or not these reasons depend on the adoption of religious doctrines. This will often stem from a combination of reasons, some primarily faith-based, while others are primarily based on more general principles of rationality, liberty and equality.

What sort of thing might be excluded? Indoctrination will be one of these excluded practices, on the grounds that it offends against some of the features of inclusiveness integral to good teaching which I referred to in 6.1.6, for example, tact, mutuality and reciprocity, an atmosphere of freedom for pupils and a fostering of their critical faculties. Similarly, bullying, humiliation and practices that demean dignity or diminish self-esteem should be excluded from any educational setting. If we are to proclaim and to protect the value of each individual and his/her culture, any form of racism should also be ruled out.[62]

An overbearing role for the school as institution in relation to the individuals, both pupils and staff, who attend it, will also be excluded as incompatible with the purposes of liberal education. If healthy growth is to be fostered, there is a need to avoid both under- and over-protection. There is always a danger that, for the sake of preserving the purity of the gospel of salvation from possible contamination, and in order to protect the faithful from alternative and confusing messages, the church may seek to regulate variety too zealously. An excess of control works against the creation of an ethical environment, for it reduces room for initiative or responsibility, for the development of a sense of agency and the opportunity to learn from mistakes. Before the Second Vatican Council, limits to variety were intended to promote obedience and conformity. After it, an acceptance of the need to demonstrate that inclusiveness which is at the heart of the Christian gospel meant attention should be paid to differences among people, as well as to what they have in common.

In the context of a church school, where the transmission of a 'thick' tradition is part of its *raison d'être* or mission, undue weight given to the institution sometimes shows itself in too heavy an emphasis given to the past over the present. I shall explore this defect (in chapter seven) in the context of a discussion of living tradition. Such a concern to protect the individual from undue institutional pressure does not necessarily entail an individual*ism* that neglects community. Rather it seeks to allow for the confident development, measured growth and disciplined expression of individuality, where there is room for the pupils' own experience and perceptions to be taken seriously and for the teachers' particular 'pedagogical signature'[63] to be written into the 'script' or drama of school affairs.

There would be several other candidates for exclusion. Some forms of competition - both between and within schools - would offend against both a liberal and a Catholic spirit, since they might lead to inadequate protection for the unsuccessful, especially those who are disadvantaged, and over-concern for public image or for the trappings of success. Within the curriculum an excessive emphasis on academic programmes of study or on vocational preparation would be inappropriate, since they could lead to an imbalanced education or to a reduction in opportunities. There should be no denial to pupils of the chance to encounter and reflect upon alternative (accurately and fairly represented) worldviews.

This open treatment of a variety of worldviews would stem partly from recognition of the contested nature of all 'thick' descriptions in our pluralist society and partly out of a desire to do justice to those whose views differ in significant ways from those promulgated by the school. It would rely, too, on the expectation that such open treatment would contribute positively to the securing of better understanding and the establishment of more harmonious relations between different groups in society.

If pupils are to develop a worldview of their own, then a consideration of how other worldviews are both similar to and also different from theirs should aid them in reaching a deeper understanding of its characteristics, grounding and implications. Such serious consideration of alternative worldviews does not imply that teachers should adopt a neutral stance towards any and every ideology, for, as I have already suggested, some stances will be ruled out as undermining of human flourishing, or as antithetical to the educational endeavour. So long as viewpoints are described fairly and accurately, their shortcomings should be pointed out, as well as their strengths.

Some emphases in society are likely to be subjected to criticism in the context of a Catholic school, even if this occurs only at the level of staff discussion about how to respond to external pressures. Two examples here would be the use of technical rationality and the desire for self-fulfilment.[64] Each of these has a place but both can mislead us into thinking that we have understood a situation adequately or that we have adopted an appropriate strategy, and both can slip easily into activities which do less than justice to the complexities of human nature, motivation, learning and achievement. Technical rationality, if adopted uncritically, can lead to an overemphasis on managerialism, thereby falling short of key elements of leadership, the questioning of ends, as well as means, the exploration of values, the importance of vision and the exercise of practical judgement. The stress on self-fulfilment, on the other hand, opens up the way to individualism, fails to count the cost of commitment, neglects the needs of community, relies too readily on therapy for readjustment and downplays the need for continuing conversion.

6.2.2   Compatibility and tension between Catholic and liberal principles
Catholics have incorporated into their social teaching many principles held dear within liberalism, interpreted broadly. These would include an increased respect for the rights of minorities and of individual conscience. If the existence of their

separate schools in England and Wales is to continue, Catholics depend upon a social and political context that allows minorities the right to protect and to promote their own way of life. This rests on the condition that they do not threaten the way of life of the majority. But much is entailed by that condition. Schools must promote rationality. They must prevent any attempt at indoctrination. They must accept equal opportunities as of central importance. They must not threaten harmony within the community. Nor must they fail to provide for their pupils at least a minimum level of competence in a fairly prescribed national curriculum. Unless they meet these requirements, they will receive neither the approval nor the support of the wider community. Unless they are prepared to stay in line on these issues, permission to continue will be denied to them, no matter how they are funded.

Immediately it will be clear that there is some tension between the attempt to hold together the distinctiveness of Catholic education with openness to the liberal principles mentioned above. This tension would arise even if it were not the case that Catholic schools contain large numbers of pupils and staff who are not Catholics. The fact that they are so populated adds to the practical difficulties and poses moral dilemmas which perplex policy makers. I will explore this tension in more detail.

It arises partly from the difficulties of combining principles which emerge from radically different conceptual backgrounds. An example of this is the notion of human rights. In his analysis of the (1963) papal encyclical *Pacem in Terris*, John Langan draws out three subtle differences between a Catholic and a liberal understanding of human rights.[65] First, for Catholics, these rights do not exist prior to the duties to which they are correlative. One cannot exercise freedoms without acknowledging a parallel range of obligations. In liberalism obligations often receive a much lower profile than rights. Second, when rights are formulated, the goals toward which they are to be directed must be morally acceptable; the rightness of the use to which they are put is relevant to considerations of the validity of the rights themselves. The rights must be exercised within moral limits and for the sake of the common good, rather than as an act of self-expression. Third, much greater emphasis is given within a Catholic perspective to the role of family and church as safeguards of both dignity and freedom in the social order and as vital agencies which have group rights themselves. Taken together, these points tend to reduce the usually overriding, even if not absolute, status often attributed to rights by liberals.

One difficulty for Catholic educators in a liberal society is that society has become accustomed to the advocacy of a 'thin' rather than a 'thick' description of what constitutes the 'good' to be pursued and to be protected, in the public sphere at least. By a 'thick' description of the good I mean one with the following six general features. First, its several interlocking parts jointly constitute a system (rather than a loose collection of disconnected elements). Second, it will be far-reaching in its scope and explanatory power. Third, it will have been highly developed over a substantial period of time. Fourth, it will be embedded in a particular community. Fifth, it is transmitted in the context of traditions, narratives and prescribed actions.

Sixth, it possesses normative status for its adherents.[66]   In contrast, a 'thin' conception of the good relies on procedural principles which command a very wide level of acceptance within society, partly because they are envisaged as not being founded on any one particular, more substantive view of life. These principles need not necessarily be so interrelated that they constitute any coherent system. They do not attempt to articulate a philosophy of the good that covers all major dimensions of life, concentrating on those aspects required for peaceful co-operation. The 'thin' conception of the good is also held to be normative, although more for its instrumental than for its intrinsic value.

The justification for relying on a 'thin' view of the good comes partly from a supposed reduction in the level of consensus within society as to which values should receive public support, in terms of law, taxation and social approval. It depends also on a heightened awareness of the presence within our society (largely through immigration since the end of the Second World War) of people with a plurality of worldviews and cultures that differ significantly from both Christianity and from western political liberalism.

In public and in our legislation we have adjusted to a situation where a 'thin' understanding of the 'good life' prevails and those who hold a 'thick' understanding are permitted to express this in private, in their homes, churches, specific associations, and, for some, with certain limitations, in their schools.   Catholic schools operate out of a 'thick' framework, while being part of a society that restricts itself to operating out of a 'thin' framework.   Not all parents, pupils and staff associated with Catholic schools accept the 'thick' framework.   Catholics who do accept it are not all agreed as to the attitude they should take towards people who adopt policies which appear to arise from the 'thin' framework.

6.2.3. Wine, water and acid: exclusiveness as protective of integrity

Another aspect of the tension caused by the combination of principles from conceptually different family backgrounds can be brought out by introducing the metaphors of wine, water and acid. It might be said, from a faith perspective, that the combination of elements which make up a distinctively Catholic reading of the human condition and an education appropriate to that condition blend together in such a way as to be available for us as 'wine': fortifying, nourishing, palatable and capable of lifting our spirits. The metaphor of wine can, of course, be double-edged; for wine can also stultify our thinking, divert us from reality, slow down our reactions and damage us internally. However, for the purposes of this comparison, let wine represent the 'proper article', a liquid which is ideal for our present condition and which at the same time provides a foretaste of heaven, our future destination.

When mixed with some elements, the effects are to 'water down' the distinctively Catholic wine on offer. This 'watering down' could be envisaged as coming about in at least two ways. First, this may happen because of the sheer presence in schools of significant numbers of pupils, parents and staff who are not committed to Catholic education.   Second, it may occur through the accommodation of principles which, although not themselves directly hostile to Catholicism, stem originally from a liberal society which seeks to be neutral as between religions and agnostic as to what constitutes the 'good' life. Among these might be included freedom of conscience and of speech, equality of opportunity, toleration of difference, the priority given to (a particular interpretation of) both rationality and autonomy, the rejection of indoctrination and a stance in the face of pluralism which seems to be accepting of relativism. Some of these elements, for example, freedom of conscience and the importance of rationality, though historically associated with liberalism, could arguably be seen as implicit in Christianity, that is, their relationship is closer than a mere compatibility with it. Certainly Aquinas, in the thirteenth century, underlined the central importance of rationality in the Christian life, for example, in identifying, interpreting and following the natural law. He also connected the operation of conscience very closely with the exercise of rationality.[67]

Similarly, if the school has adopted, to any significant degree, the drive to succeed in league tables and to survive in a market-oriented approach to education, and if it so emphasises the importance of customer satisfaction (whether these customers are seen as the pupils or the parents) and the meeting of individual preferences, then, to some degree, less time and energy might be devoted to the promotion of central Catholic messages about education. In such circumstances it will sometimes be difficult to avoid watering down the priorities and practices that are central to Catholic education.

It is not that these possible additional elements are all inimical to Catholic education, (although some are), or that they are all equally damaging (for some are more likely than others to undermine the Catholic ethos of a school). A school might try to combine the key concepts in Catholic education with some interpretations of autonomy, choice, rationality, and the contested nature of the good or with the market oriented approach to education. Without this being an inevitable outcome, it could, however, find itself in danger of watering down its message, dissipating its energies, confusing the members of its community and preventing the attainment of its main goals.

This is partly because there is a limit to the number of principles that can be taken on board as overriding and all-pervasive. Such principles need constant clarification, dedicated exemplification, nurture and celebration, if they are to permeate every aspect of school life. The greater the diversity of 'messages' sent to pupils, staff and parents through the many aspects of the workings of a school, the less powerfully the central 'message' will appear to be communicated. Any attempt to pursue several different goals in a school makes it less likely that some of them will be properly heard, let alone receive strong commitment.

This watering down effect also partly comes about because there is some tension, if not direct contradiction, between some of the possible additional features which Catholic schools may be tempted to adopt. For example, if the drive to be top of local or national league tables of examination results is pursued too vigorously, this may conflict with alternative priorities in Catholic schools, such as salvation of souls or caring for the poor. Some kinds of punishment of wrongdoing and some forms of condemnation of failure may conflict with the imperative to display Gospel values and the spirit of forgiveness. Some expressions of school promotion in the 'market-place' may undermine the notion of the common good by damaging other schools or by preventing internal critical voices from being heard. This is not to say that caring and effectiveness cannot be found together, nor is it to imply that success necessarily implies exploitation. But there has to be coherence and compatibility among school values. The kinds of success which are to be striven for, the means used to achieve school aims, the allocation of resources to priorities, all need to be guided, ordered and brought into harmony by reference to core principles which articulate the mission of the school. Perhaps greater clarity about these core principles will assist leaders in the task of discerning when the adoption of additional priorities might weaken the school's mission.

If some combinations lead to watering down the 'wine' of Catholic education, others have a much more serious effect: the 'liquid' that is left is more like acid than either water or wine. If principles are adopted which are incompatible with the Catholic 'core' themes, they may end up being corrosive of the mission of the school. Vigilance with regard to the principles that are espoused within a school is always necessary. A critical awareness of their roots, implications and effects is needed, whether they are expressed in government policies, other political or social priorities or in the ideologies that contest for allegiance in our culture. Somewhere a line has to be drawn. Such and such a principle is incompatible with a Catholic view of education. While it can be discussed, it cannot be *promoted* in a Catholic school. Those who seek to do so will be subject to constraint or even to sanctions, depending on the degree to which (and the deliberateness with which) they seek to undermine the ethos of the school. In a community which aims to be distinctive, the advocacy of some kinds of principles or priorities is ruled out as incompatible with the *raison d'être* or mission of that community. For example, an atomistic' individualism, methodological atheism, a distorted interpretation of autonomy and rationality lacking guidance from grace or conversion, subjectivism and relativism in morality, all of which were treated in chapter four, are incompatible with the mission of Catholic schools. This is true also of excessive accommodation to political pressures for a market-led, competitive approach to education, where education is dominated by economic priorities, and also of some of the assumptions implicit in 'managerialism', briefly critiqued in chapter two.

6.2.4. Dangers of exclusiveness

To some extent, then, the claim to distinctiveness necessarily involves a degree of exclusiveness. If it is to avoid slipping into elitism, such exclusiveness needs constant vigilance; it should be kept to a minimum and conducted with humility. If too 'strong' a conception of distinctiveness is operative, pupils and staff who do not share this view could be seen as a potential threat. There are three different types of criticism which can be envisaged if exclusiveness is perceived to be a *dominant* feature of Catholic education.

The first of these could arise from within a certain understanding of Catholic tradition itself. It might be put like this. Inadequate room is left in the 'strong' model for proper attention to be given to either the autonomy of the disciplines or to the synthesis between faith, culture and life. Behind this accusation might lie the belief that the model of orthodoxy at work is too closed, too certain, too dominant and too prescriptive to allow room for the development of doctrine or growth in moral understanding. What is 'outside' the bounds of acceptability is decided too soon and what is 'inside' is accepted too readily, with insufficient examination. Such a view of the tradition to be conveyed lacks openness to the notion that the Holy Spirit is still calling us more fully into truth. It assumes that we already possess everything that is needed, so that any adjustment made within the tradition to allow a closer co-operation with those 'outside the gates' would be interpreted as a retreat. In short, this response would be based on the assumption that tradition is *living* and that the 'strong' interpretation of the distinctiveness of a Catholic education is in fact restricted and that it constitutes a reduction of the fullness of Catholicism.

The second type of criticism might also emerge from among supporters of Catholic education. It might be expressed in the following way. To uphold the 'strong' interpretation of Catholic education with full rigour in a context where the continued survival of Catholic schools depends in practice upon the presence and the contribution of both pupils and staff who are not Catholic would be a suicidal policy. It would lead to the closure of many such schools, and therefore to a massive reduction in the availability of Catholic education for Catholic children, let alone any possibility of witnessing to Catholic education and values for other children. This criticism might be developed further. A reduction in the number of Catholic schools, if it were on a large scale, would leave far less room for the expression of parental choice in educational matters. There would be fewer alternatives to a monolithic state educational system. At the moment this is based on a range of values that are either unsupportive of or in some cases inimical to Catholic principles, for example, with regard to perceptions of objective truth or values, or in matters relating to sexual behaviour, social welfare, or medical ethics.

A third type of criticism has come from those outside the Catholic tradition. It relies on one or more of the following fears. First there is a fear that separate education for Catholics will allow indoctrination, and as a result will undermine children's rights.[68] Second, there is a fear that religious segregation, (sometimes associated with ethnic and class segregation) will lead to isolation and elitism and so damage social cohesion. Third, with increasing demands from other minority groups, for example the Muslim community, for separate schools, there is a fear that national educational policy will have to choose between the alternatives of allowing increasing fragmentation within the national culture by conceding a much higher number of separate schools with a distinctive ethos, or of perpetrating an injustice by refusal to extend rights currently held by Catholics, among others.

6.3. *Conclusion*

In this chapter I have explored how the Catholic claim to offer a distinctive approach to education relates to its parallel claim that such an education must be inclusive if it is to be consistent with the key principles which provide a *raison d'être* for separate Catholic schools.   I have identified several features of inclusiveness and exclusiveness and considered their relevance for Catholic schools.   In this analysis I have argued that many characteristics of inclusiveness are both intrinsic to and essential for Catholic education.   I have also shown that, although many kinds of exclusiveness are incompatible with Catholic principles, some kinds of exclusiveness are necessarily entailed by the claim to be distinctive.   Establishing the right balance, where distinctiveness is maintained in such a way that the maximum of inclusiveness is promoted and the minimum of exclusiveness is permitted, is a delicate and complex task.   In the next chapter I examine the notion of 'living tradition' for the light it can cast on the project of combining distinctiveness with inclusiveness in a manner which avoids the dangers that can accompany such an association.

Notes for Chapter 6

[1]For an interesting treatment of inclusive and exclusive forms of secularism in schools, one which contrasts with my treatment of inclusive and exclusive forms of Catholic education, see Graham Haydon, 'Conceptions of the Secular in Society, Polity and Schools', *Journal of Philosophy of Education*, vol. 28, no. 1, 1994, pp.65 - 75. For a treatment of the open and closed aspects of Catholic school culture, see also Kevin Williams, 'Religion, Culture and Schooling' in *From Ideal to Action*, edited by Matthew Feheney, Dublin, Veritas, 1998. Williams argues that one of the most distinctive features of a Catholic school should be its openness. He shows (p.50) that "a Christian school which is clear sighted about its *telos* does not have to be intolerant, ungenerous and illiberal in its culture."

[2]J. Quicke, 'Differentiation: a contested concept', *Cambridge Journal of Education*, vol. 25, no. 2, 1995, p.214.

[3]*Code of Practice on the Identification and Assessment of Special Educational Needs*, Department for Education and Welsh Office, 1994; Circular 6/94: *The Organisation of Special Educational Provision*, Department for Education, 1994.

[4]See Robert Stradling and Lesley Saunders, *Differentiation in Action*, London, NFER/HMSO, 1991, and also National Council for Educational Technology, *Differentiation: A Practical Handbook of Classroom Strategies*, Coventry, NCET, 1993. Catholic Education Service, *Differentiation: A Catholic Response*, London, 1997.

[5] Jim Gallagher, *Soil for the Seed*, Great Wakering, McCrimmons, 2001, p.100.

[6]There is also a close connection between the notions of reception and inculturation. On inculturation, see chapter four, note 15. For two important studies on 'reception', see Frederick Bliss, *Understanding Reception*, Milwaukee, Marquette University Press, 1994, and Daniel Finucane, *Sensus Fidelium: The Uses of a Concept in the Post-Vatican II Era*, San Francisco, International Scholars Publications, 1996.

[7]Jim Gallagher, in *The Contemporary Catholic School*, edited by T. H. McLaughlin, J. O'Keefe and B. O'Keeffe, London, Falmer Press, 1996, p.292.

[8]John Paul II, *Catechesi Tradendae*, London, Catholic Truth Society, 1979, section 69, p.92. For the theme of respect for religious freedom in Catholic education, see also *The Religious Dimension of Education in a Catholic School*, para 6.

[9]Especially forms one to four, seven and eight, as listed in 6.1.2., above.

[10]Bishops' Conference of England and Wales, *Catholic Schools & Other Faiths*, London, Catholic Education Service, 1996.

[11]*Ibid.*, pp.4, 6.

[12]In particular, *Nostra Aetate*, on relations with other faiths, *Dignitatis Humanae*, on religious freedom and *Gaudium et Spes*, on positive acceptance of the modern world.

[13] Congregation for Catholic Education, *Directives Concerning the Preparation of Seminary Educators*, Boston, St Paul Books, 1994, p.25. See also Congregation for Institutes of Consecrated Life and for Societies of Apostolic Life, *Inter-Institute Collaboration for Formation*, Boston, St Paul Books, 1999, p.25. For a careful analysis of differentiation in the school context of religious teaching, see 'Le cours de religion, un carrefour?' by Monique Foket, in *L'Enseignement de la Religion au Carrefour de la Théologie et de la Pédagogie*, edited by Camille Focant, Louvain-la-Neuve, Peeters, 1994.

[14] Bishops' Conference of England and Wales, *Valuing Difference*, Chelmsford, Matthew James Publishing, 1998.

[15] Bishops'Conference of England and Wales, *On the Threshold*, Chelmsford, Matthew James Publishing, 2000.

[16]For example, anthropology, sociology, psychology and politics.

[17] On inclusivity in ecclesiology, see Dennis Doyle, *Communion Ecclesiology*, New York, Orbis, 2000, pp.172-174.

[18]See Owen O'Sullivan, *The Silent Schism: Renewal of Catholic Spirit and Structures*, Dublin, Gill & Macmillan, 1997, p.109, on the integration of the feminine for a greater completeness in the church and p.175, on the attitudes prerequisite for ecumenism: tolerance of diversity, a spirit of dialogue,

respect for the person, recognition of the role of reception and working in *communio* (all drawn from Pope John Paul II's 1995 encyclical *Ut Unum Sint.*)

[19]On the option for the poor, see Bishops' Conference of England and Wales, *The Common Good and the Catholic Church's Social Teaching*, Manchester, Gabriel Communications, 1996, paragraphs 12-15. For a direct application of such teaching to education, see Bishops' Conference of England and Wales, *The Common Good in Education*, Chelmsford, Matthew James Publishing, 1997. The priority to be given to the disadvantaged has been given official status as a core principle in Catholic education. See *Principles, Practices and Concerns*, p.3, and *Learning from OFSTED and Diocesan Inspections*, pp.20-21, both Catholic Education Service, 1996.

[20]For examples of feminist theology, see *Women's Voices: Essays in Contemporary Feminist Theology*, edited by Teresa Elwes, London, Marshall Pickering, 1992; *Feminist Theology: A Reader*, edited by Ann Loades, London, SPCK, 1990; and Elizabeth Johnson, *She Who Is*, New York, Crossroad, 1992.

[21]Harvey Siegel, 'What Price Inclusion?', *Teachers College Record*, vol. 97, no. 1, Fall 1995, pp.10, 25.

[22]*Ibid.*, p.25.

[23]*Ibid.*, p.14.

[24]Jonathan Sacks, *The Persistence of Faith*, London, Weidenfeld and Nicolson, 1991, p.106.

[25]Matthew 28.18. The Gospels as a whole show Jesus being inclusive of sinners, outcasts, women, people of other races, the unpopular and the sick.

[26]Michael Barnes, SJ, 'Catholic Schools in a World of Many Faiths,' in *Contemporary Catholic School*, p.236.

[27]*Ibid.*

[28]Barnes, *Religions in Conversation*, London, SPCK, 1989, pp.8, 35.

[29]See Barnes, *ibid.*, p.49.

[30]See Mike Golby, (unpublished) 'Communitarianism and Education' in Papers of Philosophy of Education Society of Great Britain Conference, Oxford, 1996, p.152.

[31]Thomas Ogletree, quoted by Lucien Richard in Jeff Astley, Leslie Francis and Colin Crowder (eds), *Theological Perspectives on Christian Formation*, Leominster, Gracewing, 1996, p.159.

[32]Nicholas Lash, *Easter in Ordinary*, London, SCM Press, 1988, pp.258-9. Such an all-embracing approach will be guided, for Lash, by what he calls the 'identity-sustaining rules of Christian discourse and behaviour'. See pp.259, 271, 272.

[33]See *The Ebbing Tide*, pp.227-8.

[34]David Pailin, *A Gentle Touch*, (London, SPCK, 1992), pp.13, 95.

[35]See John Bradford, *Caring for the Whole Child*, London, The Children's Society, 1995, p.37.

[36]Kenneth Wilson, *Education,* 23 February 1996, p.12.

[37]*Ibid.*

[38]*Ibid.*

[39]Avery Dulles, *Models of Church*, (Dublin, Gill and Macmillan, 1974) has provided one of the most influential summaries of a changing ecclesiology.

[40]See Leonard Doohan, *The Lay-Centered Church*, Minneapolis, Winston Press, 1984, Edmund Hill, *Ministry and Authority in the Catholic Church*, London, Geoffrey Chapman, 1988 and Terence Nichols, *That All May Be One: Hierarchy and Participation in the Church*, Collegeville, Minnesota, The Liturgical Press, 1997, for three examples of a less hierarchical emphasis in post Vatican II ecclesiology.

[41]*The Sign We Give,* a report on collaborative ministry produced for the Bishops' Conference of England and Wales, Chelmsford, Matthew James Publishing, 1995, argues (p.20) for inclusiveness to be treated as a central feature of Catholicism.

[42]See, for example, *Ut Unum Sint*, encyclical of Pope John Paul II, London, Catholic Truth Society, 1995.

[43]Signe Sandsmark, 'Religion - Icing on the Educational Cake?', *Religious Education, Vol.* 90, No3/4, Summer/Fall 1995, p. 427.

[44]John Stuart Mill, *On Liberty*, quoted by Tony Jackson, *Discipleship or Pilgrimage? The Educator's Quest for Philosophy*, State University of New York Press, 1995), p.143.

[45]John Milton, *Areopagitica & other tracts*, London, Dent, 1907, p.22.

[46]Larry May, *The Socially Responsive Self*, Chicago, The University of Chicago Press, 1996, pp.17, 18, 22, 41.

[47]Martin Buber, *Between Man and Man*, London, Fontana, 1974, p.123.

[48]*Ibid.*, p.124.

[49]*Ibid.*, p.128.

[50]*Ibid.*

[51]Henri Nouwen, *Reaching Out*, London, Collins/Fount, 1980, p.81.

[52]*Ibid.*

[53]*Ibid.*, pp.82, 91, 92.

[54]Max van Manen, *The Tact of Teaching: The Meaning of Pedagogical Thoughtfulness*, London, Ontario, The Althouse Press, 1993.

[55]Thomas Groome, *Educating for Life*, Allen, Texas, Thomas More Press, 1998, p.197.

[56]Kevin Williams, 'The Religious Dimension of Secular Learning: an Irish dilemma', *Panorama*, 1996, p.12.

[57]*Ibid.*

[58]*Ibid.*, p.2.

[59]It should be noted that Williams is referring, not to the kind of Catholic schools there are in England and Wales, where they constitute only a minority (about 10% of schools in total), but to the rather different context of Catholic schools in Ireland, where they are the common form of schooling.

[60]Dermot Lane, 'Catholic Education and the School: Some Theological Reflections', in *The Catholic School in Contemporary Society*, Dublin, Conference of Major Religious Superiors, 1991, p.92.

[61]Examples of the plurality of views within Catholicism include: (1) the practice of contraception, (2) the merits of intercommunion, (3) the standing of the divorced in relation to reception of sacraments, (4) the scope of church authority in relation to theological expression, (5) the relative emphasis to be given to social justice or to spirituality in the life of the church, and (6) the respective weight to be given to local, national and to Roman decisions, for example, in episcopal appointments. Some of these impinge directly on schools and require sensitive handling.

[62]Leela Ramsden (in *The Contemporary Catholic School*, p.206) quotes from Walsh and Davies' (1984) collection, *Proclaiming Justice and Peace: Documents from John XXIII to John Paul II*, London, Collins Liturgical Publications: "Every form of social or cultural discrimination in fundamental personal rights on the grounds of sex, race, colour, social conditions, language or religion, must be curbed and eradicated as incompatible with God's design."

[63]Elliott Eisner, *The Enlightened Eye*, New York, Macmillan, 1991.

[64]N. Brennan, 'Christian Education, Contestation and the Catholic School', p.10. in Conference of Major Religious Superiors (Ireland), *The Catholic School in Contemporary Society*, Dublin, Conference of Major Religious Superiors, 1991.

[65]John Langan, 'Catholicism and Liberalism', in *Liberalism and the Good*, edited by R. Bruce Douglass, Gerald Mara and Henry Richardson, New York, Routledge, 1990, pp.110-111.

[66]Michael Walzer (in *Thick and Thin*, Notre Dame, University of Notre Dame Press, 1994) traces the idea of thickness (with regard to interpretations of morality and of life generally) to Clifford Geertz's *The Interpretation of Cultures*, New York, Basic Books, 1973. Bernard Williams discusses thick concepts of morality in *Ethics and the Limits of Philosophy*, London, Fontana, 1985, pp.129, 140, 143-145. Charles Taylor discusses the problematic nature of frameworks and strong evaluation which feature as central aspects of thick accounts of the good in *Sources of the Self*, Cambridge, Cambridge University Press, 1989. T. H. McLaughlin has discussed thick and thin theories of the good in 'Values, Coherence and the School', in *Cambridge Journal of Education*, Vol. 24, no. 3, 1994, pp.453-470.

[67]See Brian Davies, *The Thought of Thomas Aquinas*, Oxford, Clarendon Press, 1992, pp.235-7.

[68]On the need for balance between parental rights, children's rights and the requirements of education, see Eamonn Callan, 'The Great Sphere: Education against Servility', *Journal of Philosophy of Education*, vol. 31, no. 2, July 1997, pp.221 – 232. On the need for a liberal state to restrict parental rights in the interest of promoting autonomy in students as a necessary foundation for responsible citizenship, see Meira Levinson, *The demands of liberal education*, New York, Oxford University Press, 1999.

CHAPTER 7

LIVING TRADITION

Separate schooling based on a distinctive educational philosophy, one informed throughout by religious beliefs, might be called a holistic form of education. Such holistic education has to face a number of criticisms. These criticisms can be divided into two broad categories, those relating to the effects of this kind of education within schools, and those relating to its effects within society. In this chapter I seek to address the first type of criticism.

My main aim is to show that there are intellectual resources within Catholicism which facilitate the promotion of an education with the capacity to combine distinctiveness with inclusiveness (within the limits indicated in chapter six). Some of the (school-focused) criticisms which can be levelled against Catholic education become much less convincing, even if they cannot be totally rebutted, once account is taken of the potential role of an appropriation of 'living tradition'. In order to achieve my aim, first, I acknowledge that the emphasis on a distinctive approach to Catholic education can be criticised for the potentially malign aspect of its 'total' nature as well as for being narrow and inward-looking. Second, I explore the notion of 'living tradition' as offering a way of responding positively to these criticisms. Third, I summarise the immensely influential contribution of the French philosopher Maurice Blondel (1861-1949) to the Catholic Church's understanding of 'living tradition'. My summary is based on the whole corpus of Blondel's diaries, essays, correspondence and major philosophical volumes. His work is almost unknown in England, largely because it remains (with only two exceptions) untranslated into English. Fourth, I draw out the implications for Catholic schools today of a Blondelian interpretation of living tradition and at the same time I show the relevance of these implications to my argument.

7.1   Criticisms of holistic approach

The holistic approach to Catholic education has been criticised on the grounds that it leads to an authoritarian educational environment.[1] Cooper makes two important points which should cause Catholic educators to look carefully at their practice and its unintended side-effects. First, the rights of older adolescents could be jeopardised by being subordinated to the wishes of their parents with regard to religious schooling, if this is conducted in too 'strong' an atmosphere. Second, "the maintenance of this [religious] community accentuates the exclusion of others; the articulation of school with Christian faith reproduces the other as outsider."[2] I do not think that these are automatic or necessary side-effects; they can certainly be minimised. One of Cooper's concerns about efforts on behalf of religion in education is that "faiths are seen as discrete phenomena that (should) remain pure, simple and relatively unchanging."[3] My treatment of living tradition should go some way towards alleviating this concern since it shows the capacity for a Catholic school to respond to its pupils as if they were subjects and partners, not merely objects and recipients of its work.

Thiessen acknowledges the possibility of an unhealthy form of Christian nurture which must be guarded against.[4] This would "fail to have as its goal the freeing of the child to make an 'independent' choice for or against Christian commitment". It would 'force' children to become Christians in a way that made sacramental initiation 'automatic', thereby "discouraging growth towards normal rational autonomy." Such unhealthy nurture "fails to cultivate a rational grounding for Christian convictions," and it also "fails to encourage children and students to grapple with the questions that inevitably arise." Other shortcomings include those of failing to "expose the maturing child to alternate belief systems" and neglecting "to teach students to respect people who are committed to other worldviews."[5] While Thiessen accepts that such failures would be serious defects, he argues that it is possible to nurture young people in a Christian environment in ways that protect and advance their sense of freedom and their rational powers, together with promoting their knowledge about and respect for others.[6]

There are other difficulties which follow from the holistic approach to Catholic education. Some of these difficulties have already emerged from my analysis of inclusiveness and exclusiveness, for example, the challenge presented by a holistic approach to the notion of the autonomy of the disciplines, a concept which we have seen is part of that central core of key principles underpinning Catholic education.

The interpretation of an integral and inclusive spirituality, as seen in von Hugel, (chapter four) should help in removing fears that religion will necessarily play an over-dominant role in relation to the autonomy of the different areas of the curriculum. It will not, however, remove fears on the part of some teachers that their expected exemplification of such an inclusive spirituality will be experienced as a constraint on their freedom of action and interpretation. Teachers working in a Catholic school which has articulated the nature of its distinctiveness might well feel that there is some tension between the collective view they are expected to promote and their own individual interpretation. Those who do not share the collective view will find it much harder to 'plough their own furrow' where explicit clarification of a school's Catholic nature has been carried out. Will they feel able to contest the institution's view of truth on grounds that it is unhealthily narrow, inflexible, intolerant, or in some other way deficient? It might also be argued that there is a problem as to which holistic view is being promoted, since there are important differences which flow from the various models of church, revelation and faith which are available within the Christian churches and within the Catholic Church in particular.

Other criticisms have been levelled recently against the emphasis on distinctiveness within Christian education. These include the accusations that such a concern leads to schools being inward-looking, over-concerned with boundaries, reifying Christianity, over-valuing beliefs, idealising theology and being blind to pluralism.[7] Hull suggests that there is a danger that the concern for wholeness can slip into a form of totalitarianism. Adrian Thatcher also warns of the danger of over-emphasising religious differences.[8] He argues that, by their focus on religious difference, Christians might neglect other kinds of difference.[9] Both Hull and Thatcher rely on a retrieval of emphasis on the Holy Spirit rather than the person of Jesus Christ. This leads them to argue for a degree of openness which puts church schools under some strain and challenges them to display a much greater solidarity with the wider human race, especially those most in need.

A renewed consciousness of the universal presence of God, the call for greater sensitivity to differences other than religious and the challenge to demonstrate greater solidarity with the whole of humanity are all to be welcomed. None of these necessarily undermine the very *raison d'être* of church schools, although they do place onerous - and appropriate - expectations on them. Two comments are in order here. I accept the positive case put forward by Hull and Thatcher for a more open and inclusive approach by Christians in education, but I reject the negative implications of their argument.

First, Hull's view seems to me to trade on something which depends on the institutional preservation (admittedly plural in form) of Christianity. Unless there exist 'identity-sustaining rules of Christian discourse and behaviour',[10] that is, unless there is tradition which is embodied in some way, with a degree of stability and continuity, rooted in texts, practices and institutions which prevail over time, our reconstruction and application of Christian faith to changing circumstances and needs will not be possible. The emphasis on distinctiveness may be carried too far; Hull's warning here is salutary. But it does not have to be a distraction from fulfilling the Christian mission to live for others. Clarifying distinctiveness can serve instead as a necessary preliminary to and accompaniment of an outward-looking approach. We need to be clear about the nature of the task and the direction to be taken. We also need to recognise temptations which might lead us astray and to allow for readjustment of direction if wrong routes have been taken.

Hull describes a particular pattern of development in Christian approaches to education. This involves a move from education for Christendom to education for Christianity, and from there to education for Christianness.[11] This last move depends upon a supporting structure and an institutional embodiment which facilitates, stimulates and guides the practice of a critical yet faithful reflection on the implications of the Gospel and its relationship to the changing circumstances of our lives. Hull and Thatcher's trenchant criticisms of those who are too concerned with defending distinctiveness and integrity within Christian education run the risk of cutting the ground from under Christian educators. As Christian educators widen the focus of their attention and extend the scope of their efforts, the foundations on which they stand could be neglected.

These two writers helpfully remind us of several important things: God's universal salvific concern, the unpredictable and unbounded operation of the Holy Spirit, the tendency among Christians to be both inward-looking and defensive, the neglect of important aspects of difference and the need for Christians to be more open to the presence of God in people of other faiths - and of no explicit religious faith. They also challenge their fellow Christians to be more generous with their talents and resources and to travel more lightly in regard to their tradition. But there is the danger that in so concentrating on widening the scope of *who* we are *for,* we neglect the sources of our faith, and forget *where* we stand and *why* we face in this direction and have these priorities.

My first response to Hull and Thatcher's critique of some features of church schools, then, is to draw attention to the need for a living tradition which preserves the 'identity-sustaining rules of Christian discourse and behaviour' mentioned by Lash. My second comment is related to this. It is possible to so emphasise taking down boundaries, in order to demonstrate openness, that the substance of our message about salvation gets dissipated. It would be like seeking to keep up performances of a play or a piece of music while being careless about the foundation text on which they draw. In so attending to the needs of the differing audiences we face, (which is commendable), we might forget or distort the original 'score'.[12]

Trevor Cooling draws on an extended image of New Testament theologian Tom Wright to show how creativity and flexibility with regard to interpreting a text and rendering it relevant and applicable to new contexts must be balanced by fidelity and consistency to that which is drawn upon. He uses the model of the finding of a new Shakespeare play, where we have to construct the fifth Act, which is not in our possession, in such a way that it fits in with and develops further the first four Acts which we do possess. In such a context, creativity is not ruled out; indeed it is called for; but this will be a creativity which is constrained by the existing (incomplete) text.[13]   According to Nicholas Lash, "there is a creativity in interpretation which, far from being arbitrary, (the players cannot do whatever they like with the score,) is connected in some way with the fidelity, the 'truthfulness' of their performance."[14]   This is quite different from the kind of solidarity advocated by Hull and Thatcher, which could, as Kevin Nichols puts it, "easily result in total assimilation; with church schools surviving only as the smile on the face of the tiger."[15]

7.2.   *Living tradition*

The notion of living tradition, as articulated by several of the writers mentioned below, allows Catholics to avoid two possible dangers in the process of educating from a religious worldview: ossification as well as assimilation. The first danger is that tradition will be held to so inflexibly and with such little attention to the changing circumstances of each age that it becomes ossified.[16] Its borders will be protected from perceived threats so effectively that contact with what is 'other', perplexing, or challenging will be prevented. Loyalty to the past might be given such importance that it becomes almost idolatry. The status attributed to past teaching is so high that little room is left for independent judgement on the part of learners and no opportunity offered to engage with new situations that have not already been addressed by the tradition. Questioning is seen as betrayal.

Such 'immobility' is often a feature of a 'classicist' outlook, where the agencies and criteria for controlling tradition are thought of as both 'universal' and 'fixed for all time'.[17] This does not leave sufficient room for the input or contribution of the learner to the transformation of what he or she is learning. It prevents "the very activities which can keep a tradition alive, namely, those exercises of judgement and imagination by which it can be cleansed and renewed and fitted to new circumstances."[18] Such a 'classicist' outlook also obstructs communication with those from different cultures, since it refuses to accept the legitimacy of using resources from outside its own 'borders'. It fails to do justice to history, to changing contexts or to pluralism. Lonergan calls such a classicism "the shabby shell of Catholicism", for it relies too little on the love of God and the multiple dimensions of conversion.[19]

Nichols points out that tradition is not the handing on of something inert, like a 'baton in a relay race', nor is it something into which we are moulded indiscriminately.[20] Rather we are to understand tradition as 'the transmitted life of a community'. Nichols' point here is that 'life' is suggestive of something much more dynamic, expansive and multi-dimensional than the handing on of beliefs. To live tradition, as opposed merely to repeat it, involves, for Nichols, innovation and creativity as well as respect for the past and loyalty to it. The art of living a tradition demands a 'creative fidelity'.[21]

Fidelity and creativity do not have to be seen as opposed to one another; they can be held together. This is important in the context of Catholic schools, where a balance has to be struck between faithfulness to tradition and openness to the experience and insights of present members of the school community.[22] In the attempt to put the Gospel into practice, fresh interpretation, not mere repetition, can be a form of bearing witness and making a contribution. On the other hand, in the context of encouraging pupils and staff to engage with the missionary imperative of the Gospel, we may find that the effort of appropriating a text which at first appears to be alien to us, if followed by appreciation of its meaning, can lead us to a deeper self-discovery and a sense that life is both enhanced and liberated, rather than diminished and constrained.

In order to guard against the second danger, that of assimilation, where secularisation is "bleaching the Catholic character out of that church's educational institutions",[23] there will be a degree of moulding, or formation, and this will be a forming of "faith, character and consciousness".[24] This formation is expected, within a Christian perspective, to convert us from self-seeking, misguided orientations and valuing what is unworthy of our vocation to holiness. The horizons that are available at any one time to the learner depend on the extent to which he or she has undergone previous conversions. What will appear as problematical or what will appear as offering a solution will depend on these conversions and their effects on our horizons.

Those, like Westerhoff and Nichols, who emphasise formation in the process of living a tradition, intend to prevent that total assimilation to secular culture which they fear might be a possible outcome of engaging openly with the questions that culture puts to Christians. They expect Christian education to be carried out in the ambience of an active communion within a church. Otherwise there is a danger that the openness that is part of avoiding ossification will slide into emptiness, so that there is no distinct Christian identity being maintained. Burtchaell makes a complaint about Catholic higher education in the USA that some might extend further. "What was first intended unreflectively as an act of denominational ecumenism devolves into interdenominational vagueness and then into nondenominational secularism."[25]

In the spectrum of commitment which may be expected within a church school the notion of living tradition can help us to see that "there is no incompatibility between whole-hearted faith and openness to criticism"[26] and that we can find an appropriate stance "between non-betrayal and maximum devotion".[27] If 'immobility' is impossible for authentic Christianity, a retrieval of the notion of living tradition should remind us that so too is 'radical novelty'; if the former is 'infantile', the latter is scarcely an improvement in being 'adolescent'.[28] The first danger I have mentioned, that of the ossification of tradition, runs the risk, in the context of education in general and of church schools in particular, of leading teachers to forget that they have not been young in *these* circumstances, in the current situation facing pupils, with its own, new opportunities and temptations. Furthermore, it might mislead them into thinking that they can pass on to their pupils the wisdom derived from past experience, without an ability to learn from the present. This would prevent the young from growing up properly into a discerning religious understanding and a responsible moral maturity. They would be kept in a childish condition.

The second danger, where there is an excess of openness and critical questioning and where the readiness to forget or to modify tradition in the face of the new can slide into assimilation, also prevents proper development beyond the stage of adolescence. By favouring change always at the cost of continuity, such an approach undercuts the necessary stability of perspective and the personal foundation needed for constructive action and decision-making on the part of pupils. Schillebeeckx puts the need for a balance to be struck in the following way:

> The Christian *perception of* the meaning of the offer of revelation comes about in a creative *giving* of meaning: in a new production of meaning or a re-reading of the Bible and the tradition of faith within constantly new situations of every kind....Our 'situations' or contexts have new insights and particular sensitivies but also their own blindspots, one-sidedness and prejudices.[29]

My treatment of the notion of living tradition as a possible way of combining distinctiveness with inclusiveness can be seen to fit in well with the wider epistemological and hermeneutical movement of which Gadamer is a leading proponent.[30] I say this despite criticisms of Gadamer's position (for example, by Habermas) for being excessively optimistic about the benign role of tradition. A tradition can be critiqued on the ground that it functions on behalf of an ideology, with beneficiaries and those who suffer on its account. But the possibility of such critique does not invalidate my treatment of the notion of 'living tradition', a distinctive form of life (and interpretation) which has the capacity to be open, self-critical, inclusive and to allow for both continuity and change. Gadamer shows the intimate connections between the kinds of knowledge we arrive at and the situations in which we find ourselves, the prejudgements and assumptions fed to us by the traditions we inherit, from which we draw and to which we contribute. Our interpretations and understanding of life do not start from a blank sheet. Nor do they do emerge from a position of pure detachment. They build upon some prior (if provisional) commitment. They are always already oriented and guided by some form of anticipation built up in us. This anticipation is filtered through the categories provided for us in the 'texts' which inform our conceptual inheritance. Although we always remain inextricably part of one tradition or another, in our use of the mental 'tools' it offers we are able to modify it, sometimes significantly. The attempt to engage the tradition, whether to live it out or to reject it, inevitably influences its development.[31] Our conversations with tradition and our attempts to 'apply' it to our circumstances will in turn also change us, in that they will confront us with its strangeness as well as its familiarity; this strangeness will surprise us, "bring us up short" and cause us to revise our earlier views.[32] .

I think one can justifiably claim that Blondel (whose work is referred to in 7.3) anticipated (by sixty years) central Gadamerian concerns, although I have found no evidence of any direct influence. In my treatment of Blondel and living tradition I take the view that a focus on the 'text' of the tradition and a capacity to 'see' more clearly the meaning of one's experience are so intimately related that one cannot have one without the other. This despite the fact that the 'text' and one's 'seeing' are each vulnerable to distortion.

7.3. Blondel and living tradition

Probably no one has contributed more effectively to the notion of living tradition in the Catholic church than the French philosopher Maurice Blondel (1861 -1949). He pointed the way to a notion of tradition which serves not only to conserve but also to discover. It is possible to detect his influence on the thinking of key twentieth century Catholic theologians, such as Karl Rahner (via Maréchal), Henri de Lubac (via Valensin), Yves Congar and Teilhard de Chardin. We can thereby trace his imprint on the Second Vatican Council, an imprint which was indirect since it passed through the intermediary work of others.[33] One of the leading American contemporary theologians, Avery Dulles, comments positively on Blondel's

> dynamic and expansive notion of tradition, in which believers are prepared to achieve
> new insights through the pursuit of discipleship and engagement in the practices
> characteristic of committed Christians,[34]

and he welcomes Blondel's contribution as a way forward from the one-sided and inadequate view of tradition which prevailed at the beginning of this century. Drawing upon a range of Blondel's work, I shall first summarise his key insights and illustrate his contributions to Catholic thinking on the notion of living tradition. Then I shall briefly indicate some of the educational implications which follow from such a Blondelian emphasis together with their particular relevance to the thesis being argued here.[35]

The essay which provides several of Blondel's seminal ideas on living tradition is *History and Dogma*. This originated in a number of articles that appeared in 1904 as a contribution to the controversy about the role of historical criticism in the Church's life. Blondel claimed to point a way forward which both avoided the pitfalls of those who fixed the Church in a restricting and narrow immobilism, and also escaped the dangers stemming from those who yielded too much to contemporary scholarship. Blondel believed that God's last word has not been spoken; Christ is still communicating as he promised he would: "I still have many things to say to you but they would be too much for you now. But when the Spirit of truth comes, he will lead you to the complete truth" (John 16, 12). This truth cannot be contained in a purely intellectual manner, for this would bypass those who find this difficult. Furthermore, the truth that comes from God lies always beyond mere human formulations and cannot be captured in them. "There can be no given moment of history when the mind of man has exhausted the mind of God."[36]

The only way we can enjoy the truth is by drawing upon the collective experience derived from faithful action by the church's members. Tradition makes it possible for something to pass from the implicitly lived to the explicitly known.[37] The overall way of life of the Church carries more riches than can be unpacked and passed into circulation at any one particular epoch of its existence. Tradition is a

> living synthesis of all the speculative and ascetic, historic and theological forces...It
> embraces the data of history, the efforts of reason and the experiences of faithful
> action.[38]

In this synthesis we all have a contribution to make, for tradition is to do with the whole body of the Church, not just any particular privileged section of it.

> Without the Church, the faithful could not detect the true hand of God in the Bible and
> souls; but, unless each believer brought his little contribution to the common life, the
> organism would not be fully alive and spiritual.[39]

Blondel feared that some scholars had exaggerated the power of historical investigation, while other scholars had overrated the efficacy of philosophical reasoning. In accessing the truth about God's ways and purposes, these two forms of human enquiry are inadequate. Despite the need for both, something more is required: "the mediation of collective life and the slow progressive labour of the

Christian tradition."[40]   There is a certain light shed by the orderly and repeated performances of Christian practices:

> faithful action is the Ark of the Covenant where the confidences of God are found, the Tabernacle where he perpetuates his presence and his teaching.[41]

There is, for Blondel, a kind of meaning and verification carried in our action which goes beyond the competence of our powers of reasoning. As he says,

> a man can carry out completely what he cannot entirely understand, and in doing it he keeps alive within him the consciousness of a reality which is still half hidden from him. To 'keep' the word of God means in the first place to do it, to put it into practice.[42]

According to Blondel, a dialectic between devotions and truth operates in such a way that the humble faithful can benefit from a profound intuition more penetrating than that enjoyed by the most erudite of intellectuals.[43] Furthermore, he thought that dogmas and the practices enjoined on us by the Church, when put together, make one body and it would be 'murderous vivisection' to try to separate them.[44] The constant theme echoing throughout Blondel's writings comes from St John: he who does the truth comes to the light. In *History and Dogma* he puts it thus: "the miracle of the Christian life is that from acts at first difficult, obscure and enforced, one rises to the light through a practical verification of speculative truths".[45]

Following this presentation of faithful action as the focus of tradition, Blondel reminds us that there can be no doctrinal unity without a prior common discipline and conformity of lifestyle.[46] Joint action (and even more, shared suffering) would open the way for greater unity than could ever be achieved by a theological vanguard or pioneer elite group. To pay attention to tradition as a whole, rather than giving emphasis to only part of it, enables us not only to preserve what is valuable from the past (this much at least about tradition is commonly appreciated) but to move forward, for

> its powers of conservation are equalled by its powers of conquest. (Tradition) discovers and formulates truths on which the past lived, though unable as yet to evaluate or define them explicitly.[47]

We should, therefore, be wary of shedding too quickly or casually those aspects of the Christian tradition which do not easily 'make sense' to us, features which jar on our understanding or sensibilities. It may be that through an uncomfortable confrontation between the expectations of a living tradition and the individuality of our own experience there is an opportunity to avoid illusion and to widen our horizons.

Blondel did not advocate an uncritical acceptance of all features of the Church. He was well aware of many defects in the Church he loved and he realised that purification was necessary as part of the process of building a new synthesis for his time. He could be scathing about some aspects of church life and especially a distorted view of authority then operative in the higher echelons of the clergy. Coming from such a man, from the centre, these criticisms have all the more force.

The predominant party in the church (at the beginning of the twentieth century), Blondel believed, was wrong to exercise a power that was political, rather than spiritual in style, for this was incompatible with the Gospel. The Church was supposed to serve, not tyrannise over souls.[48] It seemed to Blondel that the face of the Church too often presented to the world was a serious aberration from the ideal: "a Catholicism without Christ, religion without a soul, authority without a heart".[49] It was wrong to think that God could be served by making him reign in society without preparing souls to receive him.[50] The emphasis on ecclesiastical imperialism and prestige, which he decried, is a far cry from the strength that comes from weakness; the former smacks of paganism, whereas the latter comes closer to Christianity. Blondel insisted first, that authority is assisted but not inspired, and second, such authority must consult and be clarified and joined by the prayer and study of the faithful; it should not flow just one way, from above to below. Authority is an organ of tradition, not a replacement for it.[51] Though he did not minimise the principle of authority, Blondel certainly rejected authoritarianism in the Church, because it exalts a part of tradition above the whole in a most unhealthy manner for the body which shares Christ's life.

Nothing illustrated the misuse of authority more for him than the dangerous distortion of clericalism. This was endemic in the church at the beginning of the twentieth century, inherent in the one-way thinking which saw everything in terms of from above to below, an over-hierarchical conception of the Church. He saw rule by clergy was a kind of guardianship over minors who were never allowed to grow up, take risks or show any initiative. "Clericalism", said Blondel,

> is founded on an objectivism which identifies the human container with the divine content'; it is behind the immobile mentality prevalent within the Church and also responsible for much of its fanaticism and lack of humanity.[52]

He considered it

> the most dangerous of traitors, the most false-hearted and deadly of the enemies of Catholicism, since it contradicts the essence of the Church and makes of it a sect, something unilateral, formal, intellectual, neither good, loving, nor loveable.[53]

The stress given by Blondel to the contribution of the whole body of the faithful in his treatment of living tradition differed greatly from the distinction which was too sharply made earlier this century between the teaching and the learning church, the clergy and the laity. If the laity were always treated like children, he wondered, how could candidates for the teaching Church ever be recruited; from such juvenile and inexperienced sheep, how could wise pastors be found?[54]

In 1946, at the age of eighty-five, Blondel returned again to the topic of tradition and the need to balance the risks of growth with the need to safeguard the church against specious novelties.[55] He continued to emphasise that the transmission of truths, functions and powers involved in tradition requires from the faithful more than a simple acceptance.   He remained supremely confident about the "unquenchable power of enriching invention" which resided within tradition.[56] It is not a chain which has to be dragged along, weighing us down; rather it should be thought of as an umbilical cord, providing lifeblood and nourishment.[57] In these last comments on tradition he reiterated his earlier themes: tradition and innovation are not opposed to one another; responding to the prompting of the Spirit and submission to authority are not incompatible; revelation is inexhaustible; the church lives through growth; every generation has its trials, its mission and its effective fruitfulness in adapting what is permanent and what is moving in the church to one another.[58]

7.4. Educational implications

Some of the concerns about the promotion of a strong ethos in Catholic schools might be alleviated by Blondel's interpretation of living tradition. On the one hand, there might be concerns about a certain rigidity, immobility or fixedness within the church and therefore also in its approach to education. Following Mitchell, I called this the danger of ossification. How could fidelity to tradition be combined with both an openness to criticism (from within as well as from beyond those committed to the faith) and also a creativity and flexibility in adapting to the changing circumstances and questions of each new generation? Too fixed an understanding of tradition would leave little room for the contribution of pupils or staff and could even invite too authoritarian an approach to education which cramped the development of pupils and undermined the possibility of their growing into a mature and responsible autonomy. Such an emphasis might also, I suggested, unduly restrict teachers in church schools, make excessive demands on them in their role as exemplars of faith and even give inadequate attention to their rights to freedom of conscience and self-expression.

On the other hand, an excess of openness and modification of tradition in order to meet the needs and priorities of each new age might dissolve the distinctiveness of the Catholic identity and undermine the mission of church schools. I called this the danger of assimilation. In several respects the outline I have given of the Blondelian approach to living tradition offers guidance for church schools on how to address these concerns and suggests a nuanced understanding which allows Catholic educators to avoid these dangers. Let me draw out some of the implications for schools of Blondel's comments on living tradition.

First, undue weight is not to be given to the past. Rather than being backward-looking, seeking always to preserve, to repeat, to transmit, church schools should, in the light of a rich appreciation that tradition is living, respond to the changing circumstances and new questions facing pupils and staff. What kind of balance is struck, in the course of each year's work, to ensure that pupils are invited, not only to enter into the educational and ecclesial heritage from the past, but also to respond to the concerns and questions thrown up by new circumstances through their own contributions and projects?

Second, Blondel reminds us that, if tradition is to flourish and to be welcomed, there must be due emphasis given to the experience, insights, problems and questions of the particular members of the school community, both pupils and staff. Furthermore, each person should be able to feel that his or her contribution is needed and valued by the school community. How hard do our schools try to communicate to all pupils that their questions are taken seriously and that they have particular talents which both the school and the wider society (including the parish) is in need of?

This leads into the third implication of Blondel's analysis of living tradition, which is that the church's representatives cannot be credible or effective teachers if they are not simultaneously still learners. They must not give the impression of having 'arrived' or of being 'complete' and therefore of having stopped developing. They should be models, not only of life-long learning in academic terms, but also of life-long growth in faith and an ever-deepening appreciation of the mysteries of God's world and ways. One aspect of this point is that Blondel believed that the church could not claim to teach if she was not prepared to go on learning. The other aspect is that the church cannot expect her members to receive what she has to offer if at the same time she does not allow learners to make a contribution, so that there is reciprocity about the teaching and learning process. It follows from this that teachers will elicit and respond positively to feedback from their pupils about the helpfulness of their endeavours. They will also model commitment to devotional practices. And they will demonstrate to these pupils a familiarity with the discipline, lifestyle and feelings associated with being a pupil (for example, excitement in finding new ideas and a desire for feedback on their own progress).

Fourth, Blondel's comments warn against the church school adopting an overbearing attitude in its efforts to convey the truth, even salvific truth. Its tutelary role should never slip into tyranny. There must be room for questioning, for disagreement, for learning by mistakes, for exploration, even when this appears to stray from orthodoxy. The church school should seek to serve its pupils, not keep them in a state of servility. This will require an atmosphere which facilitates discussion and debate, which invites pupils to exercise responsibility and to show initiative in a variety of forms and contexts, and which also allows them to withdraw (without reprimand) from these if they choose.

If in this point Blondel warns against too premature closing of argument, this is related to a fifth implication of his thought, namely that church schools should take care to avoid an excessive reliance on a narrow interpretation of rationality as the only means to arrive at truth. In addition to the usual modes of detached and impartial academic reasoning there should be an openness to broader forms of rationality, for example, a readiness to learn from poetry and the arts, from personal experience and collaborative action, from spirituality and worship. According to Blondel, we move slowly from the implicitly lived to the explicitly known. We must attend to the multiple dimensions of life and to the integral development of the human person. These comments should guard us against any over-intellectual emphasis or any compartmentalisation of knowledge or separation of the curriculum from the devotions, problems and practices experienced by members of the school community. We will succeed in relying excessively on rationality if the curriculum is broad and balanced. It helps if pedagogy allows for pupil input, as well as reception. Teachers should respond sensitively to pupil feedback. They should praise many forms of achievement and encourage all pupils to experiment, to co-operate and to offer and to receive help. Again, if the school community shares its sorrows, highlights its concerns, values and priorities, and celebrates its achievements through sacred and secular rituals, this too will help in the process of promoting a richer experience of the diverse modes of rationality.

This brings us to a sixth implication. If there is to be no sharp separation of academic from more 'existential' concerns within a school, the school should expect to train its members in faithful action, both in its devotional expression and in social action. There would be formation in spirituality and in community service and these would be seen as mutually supportive strands. In support of training in faithful action the school should be prepared to retain those aspects of the tradition which might appear at first to be uncomfortable for its members. Instead of relying on what readily appeals or what is easily understandable, the school should offer opportunities for pupils to experience the call to self-denial, to on-going and ever-deepening conversion, to loyalty to and engagement with the *whole* liturgical cycle and its constitutive elements.

Seventh, not only did Blondel display in his own teaching all the qualities of inclusiveness which I touched upon in chapter six, in his writing he urged a sensitivity to the differing spiritual, intellectual and personal needs of learners. His comments about the need for adaptability on the part of the teacher echo contemporary calls for attention to differentiation in approaches to teaching and learning. Blondel advocated patience in the face of misunderstanding, confusion, error and shortcomings. In avoiding an overbearing atmosphere the school will not seek too quickly to uproot the weed growing alongside of the wheat.[59] Blondel always displayed a high degree of both patience and precision in pointing out mistakes and distortions, but he also advocated that searchers needed a friendly space in which to develop and to try out their ideas. Teachers in Catholic schools should be noted for this form of 'hospitality'.

Such patience did not imply an undiscriminating tolerance. The eighth implication of Blondel's understanding of living tradition is that a degree of vigilance is required in order to safeguard the church, and, by extension, also the school, against the corrosive effects of what I called in 6.2.3 'acid'. By that I meant thought or practices which either directly or more subtly undermine the mission of the church school. Some priorities in the educational world will appear in the light of such vigilance to damage the carefully nurtured 'wine' of Catholic education, either by 'watering it down' or by mixing it with 'acid'. Threatening elements might be forms of competitiveness within and between schools; unbalanced kinds of curriculum, pedagogy or policies for assessment and behaviour; distorted expressions of egalitarianism; or concessions to pluralism or to a liberal view of education. The exercise of vigilance in the face of these threats should be maintained by each particular school, but always in harmony with the safeguarding role played by the wider church. Our openness to the continuing unfolding of truth made accessible to us by the Holy Spirit entails remaining in communion with the wider church. No Catholic school, therefore, should act as if it were an island, operating in isolation from the rest of the church. Our nurturing of living tradition is not for the sake of ourselves alone, but it is to be exercised on behalf of the whole church. In this light, a Catholic school will engage positively with the oversight and inspection which is carried out on behalf of the church.

I have shown how Blondel's treatment of living tradition offers helpful guidance for the task of combining fidelity and creativity in the context of a Catholic school. If real contact with active minds is to be made, then new intellectual creations are necessary. Blondel said this, not because former ways of expressing the faith are easily dispensable but because further explorations of the riches of the faith are essential for effective communication with outsiders, indeed often extremely helpful for promoting deeper understanding of the legacy of faith for insiders too.[60]

In seeking to combine fidelity with creativity, students can be considered 'living documents' who engage in dialogue with the documents of tradition. Not only are students expected by teachers to become familiar with and to interrogate the official 'texts' (here interpreted in the broadest sense) mediated by the church. The church, through its teachers, also 'consults' students both about the effectiveness of the church's attempt to communicate the message contained in the 'texts' and about the significance, scope and potential of these 'texts' in their own lives. The church cannot understand itself adequately without a serious effort to understand students. An authentic sense of identity on their part depends on continuity with the past, together with authorship of their own lives. This sense of personal identity is partly comprised of a feeling of belonging and partly of the appreciation that each person is unique. The General Directory for Catechesis echoes this point when it speaks of the balance to be maintained between gift and response, between 'handing over' and 'giving back'[61] The first of these is *traditio*, that which we receive from the church. Without being balanced by *redditio*, the personal response and additional contribution of recipients, in this case students, the tradition will remain inert, infertile, perhaps even oppressive, rather than life-giving.

Theologian Philip Endean argues that, rather than being backward-looking, our fidelity to tradition should be future-oriented.

> The central focus of our fidelity is not what is already established, but rather the catholic unity that will come into being when God is all in all. We only understand our tradition aright when we see it as pointing us toward a reality that is even greater. ... Christianity [is] permanently generative of new response; our primary responsibility is to the new. Our fidelity to existing tradition, however, absolute, is always only in function of that primary responsibility.[62]

This comment is likely to alarm traditionalists, who tend to emphasise our primary loyalty is to the past, to what has been handed on. Endean, however, does not envisage the relationship between fidelity and creativity as being basically one of conflict; nor does be believe, despite his preference for a future orientation, that either fidelity or creativity should dominate the other as a priority.

The relationships between fidelity and creativity, between the word of doctrine and the response which is holiness of life – between rootedness in tradition and sensitivity to the other – these are relationships of mutual dependence.[63]

If teachers in school are conscious of the mutual dependency of fidelity and creativity, then they are more likely to model for their students a continuing openness and willingness to learn and to grow in understanding of the tradition and its bearing on the world. At the same time, in responding seriously to the questions and criticisms that emerge from 'consultation' with the students, they are more likely to facilitate a 'renegotiation of the Christian tradition'.[64] I believe that my application here to the educational sphere of Endean's views about the relationship between fidelity and creativity would have been fully endorsed by Blondel.

In this chapter I have also brought out some of the features which would make Catholic schools both distinctive and inclusive, without being totally 'open' in the some of the senses entailed by a more liberal view of education which prevails in secular schools. If we adopt a Blondelian perspective, there are limits to the extent to which we are able to mark the boundaries of distinctiveness, either of the church or of the church school. The reason for this is that no definition of pure Christianity is possible since it is a living reality, not a concept or theory. Introducing someone to the faith is bringing them into a way of life, not to a mere acceptance of a formula.[65] Ossification and immobility are incompatible with living tradition, a notion that implies a church on the move. Blondel considered that the capacity for movement was integral to the church's nature and mission. His view was that if we wish to win souls and to spread the good news of Christ (as opposed to defending institutions), this is best done from a moving vehicle, not from a fortress.[66]

In order to pass on a faith in the context of living tradition, according to Blondel, a blend of docility and initiative is required; docility to tradition and also to the needs of others, initiative to adapt the life of tradition to the needs of individuals. He employed the imagery of music and text to bring out this blend. Faith as docility on its own is like music that is written but remains on the page unplayed; faith as confidence and trust and initiative is like music that is played, but without the text is in danger of rambling away pointlessly and getting lost.[67] An appreciation of living tradition provides several pointers as to how a Catholic school might attempt to promote in its pupils an active receptivity, a critical solidarity and a discerning openness. An appropriation of living tradition, along the lines suggested by Blondel, makes it possible for Catholic schools to maintain their distinctiveness while displaying an openness to the insights and questions of pupils and to the changing needs of the times.

Blondel was, of course, not the only major exponent of living tradition to have influenced modern Catholic thought. Both Möhler and Newman in the nineteenth century highlighted key aspects which contributed to later thinking on living tradition; thus Möhler stressed the role of the Holy Spirit in the experience of the faithful, while Newman significantly advanced our understanding of the development of doctrine.[68] But by bringing together reason, experience and faith, by giving emphasis to the collective experience of the faithful, by showing the relationship between devotion and arriving at the truth, by describing a more healthy role for authority than prevailed in the church of his time, and by showing how tradition can facilitate a meeting place for what is permanent and what is changing in the life of the church, Blondel powerfully enhanced the Catholic Church's ability to appreciate and to apply the notion of living tradition to its own self-understanding.[69] In doing so he has bequeathed a legacy which can assist Catholic educators in guarding against at least some of the risks to which any substantive worldview and any associated 'strong' school ethos are prone.[70]

7.5.   Conclusion

The notion of 'living tradition' has been examined for the light it can cast on the task of combining distinctiveness with inclusiveness in such a way as to avoid the dangers of either ossification or assimilation. Key insights from Blondel, a major and influential exponent of the notion of 'living tradition', have been retrieved and applied to my consideration of the coherence of the claim of Catholic education to be both distinctive and inclusive.

The analysis so far has concentrated mainly on the implications *within* Catholic schools of a distinctive philosophy of education. I now address potential criticisms of the effects of distinctive and separate Catholic schools in terms of their place in a liberal and pluralist society. My response to these criticisms will lead me to argue that Catholic schools can be shown, both in principle and in practice, to contribute to the common good.

Notes for Chapter 7

[1] Padraig Hogan is critical of those who entertain "strong proprietorial designs on the emergent identities of learners...who have a right to be different...without fear of discrimination." Although his target is much broader than Catholic education, this form of education does not escape unscathed. ('Identity, Difference and the Epiphanies of Learning', unpublished paper delivered at Philosophy of Education Society of Great Britain, Oxford, April, 1997, pp.213, 214. On authoritarianism as a feature of more general attempts (beyond Catholic schools) to restore the position of Christianity in education, see Davina Cooper, 'Strategies of Power: Legislating Worship and Religious Education', in *The Impact of Michel Foucault on the Social Sciences and Humanities*, edited by Moya Lloyd and Andrew Thacker, London, Macmillan, 1997.

[2] Cooper, *ibid.*, p.164.

[3] *Ibid.*, p.159.

[4] Elmer Thiessen, 'Fanaticism and Christian Liberal Education', *Studies in Philosophy and Education*, vol 15, 1996, pp.293-300.

[5] Thiessen, *loc. cit.*, pp.298-299.

[6] For a more detailed defence of this argument see Thiessen, *Teaching for Commitment*, Leominster, Gracewing, 1993.

[7] John Hull, unpublished paper given at an International Symposium on Church Schools, Durham University, 1996, 'The Holy Trinity and the Mission of the Church School'.

[8] Adrian Thatcher, unpublished paper at International Symposium on Church Schools, Durham University, 1996, 'Making the Difference - Theology of Education and Church Schools'.

[9] *Ibid.*, pp.4, 5.

[10] Nicholas Lash, *Easter in Ordinary*, London, SCM Press, 1988, pp. 259, 271, 272.

[11] Hull, *loc. cit.*, p.1.

[12] For two helpful discussions on the notions of 'score' and 'performance' in the context of preserving both fidelity and creativity, see R.M. Rummery, *Catechesis and Religious Education in a Pluralistic Society*, Sydney, Dwyer, 1975, p.195, and N. Lash, *Theology on the Way to Emmaus*, London, SCM, 1986, chapter three.

[13] See Trevor Cooling's chapter in J. Astley & L. Francis (eds), *Christian Theology and Religious Education: Connections & Contradictions*, London, SPCK, 1996.

[14] Nicholas Lash, *Theology on the Way to Emmaus*, London, SCM, 1986, p.40.

[15] K. Nichols, 'Theology and the Dual System', unpublished paper for International Symposium on Church Schools, Durham University, 1996, p.5.

[16] Basil Mitchell, *Faith and Criticism*, Oxford, Clarendon Press, 1994, p.3.

[17] Nicholas Lash, *Theology on the Way to Emmaus*, London, SCM, 1986, pp.20, 53. and also Bernard Lonergan, *Method in Theology*, London, Darton, Longman & Todd, 1972, p.29.

[18] Charles Wood, 'Theological inquiry and theogical education' in Astley, Francis and Crowder (eds), *Theological Perspectives on Christian Formation*, Leominster, Gracewing, 1996, p.354.

[19] Lonergan, *op. cit.*, p.327.

[20] K. Nichols, 'Imagination and Tradition in Religion and Education', in Astley and Francis (eds), *Christian Theology & Religious Education*, 1996, p.189.

[21] *Ibid.*, pp.190-1.

[22] On the dual task for living tradition of faithful transmission and ongoing development, see Anthony Cernera and Oliver Morgan, *Examining the Catholic Intellectual Tradition*, Fairfield, Connecticut, 2000, p.201.

[23] James Burtchaell, in *Schooling Christians*, edited by Stanley Hauerwas & John Westerhoff, Grand Rapids, Michigan, Eerdmans, 1992, p.181.

[24] See John Westerhoff, in Hauerwas & Westerhoff, *op. cit.*, p.267.

[25] Burtchaell, *loc. cit.*, p.179.

[26] Mitchell, *op. cit.*, p.139.

[27] George Fletcher, *Loyalty*, Oxford, Oxford University Press, 1993, p.60.

[28] Lash, (1986) *op. cit.*, p55.

[29] Edward Schillebeeckx, *Church: The Human Story of God*, translated by John Bowden, London, SCM,

1990, pp.44, 35.

[30] H-G. Gadamer, *Truth and Method*, translated by Joel Weinsheimer & Donald Marshall. 2nd rev. ed., New York, Crossroad, 1989, especially pp.291-297.

[31] Gadamer, *op. cit.*, pp. 307-11; 324-41; 373.

[32] Gadamer, *op. cit.*, 268.

[33] For the influence of Blondel on twentieth century Catholic (especially but not only French) thought see, for example, Aidan Nichols, *From Newman To Congar*, Edinburgh, T & T Clark, 1990, pp.154, 196, 250-1, 253. Yves Congar, *Tradition and the Life of the Church*, London, 1964. Etienne Fouilloux, *Une Église en quete de liberte*, Paris, Desclee de Brouwer, 1998. Gerald McCool (ed), *A Rahner Reader*, London, Darton, Longman & Todd, 1975, pp.xiv, 73, 259. Henri de Lubac, *At The Service of the Church*, translated by Anne Elizabeth Englund, San Francisco, Ignatius Press, 1993, pp.19, 65, 101-2. *Henri de Lubac et le mystère de l'Église*, Actes du colloque du 12 octobre 1996 a l'Institut de France, Paris, Cerf, 1999. H. de Lubac (ed), *Maurice Blondel et Auguste Valensin. Correspondance* [in 3 volumes] (Paris, Aubier, 1957-65); *idem.*, (ed) *P. Teilhard de Chardin et Maurice Blondel. Correspondence*, translated by William Whitman (New York, Herder and Herder, 1967); see also *P. Teilhard de Chardin, Lettres Intimes à Auguste Valensin, Bruno de Solage, Henri de Lubac, André Ravier, 1919-1955. Introduction et notes par Henri de Lubac* (Paris, 1974). Henri de Lubac (ed), *Correspondance Blondel-Wehrlé*, Paris, Aubier-Montaigne, 1969 (two volumes). Pierre Gauthier, *Newman et Blondel*, Paris, Les Éditions du Cerf, 1988.

[34] Avery Dulles, *Models of Revelation*, Dublin, Gill & Macmillan, 1983, p.50.

[35] For this section I develop further J. Sullivan, 'Living Tradition', *The Downside Review*, vol. 105, January 1988, pp.59-66.

[36] Maurice Blondel, 'Histoire et Dogme', in *Les Premiers Écrits de Maurice Blondel*, Paris, Presses Universitaires de France, 1956, p.213.

[37] *Ibid.*, p.205.

[38] Blondel, quoted in Dru and Trethowan's introduction to *Letter on Apologetics and History and Dogma*, London, Harvill Press, 1964 (reissued 1995, Edinburgh, T & T Clark), p.215.

[39] *Ibid.*, p.277.

[40] *Ibid.*, p.269.

[41] *Ibid.*, pp.277, 279.

[42] *Ibid.*, pp.273-4.

[43] Blondel, *Carnets Intimes*, vol I, Paris, Les Éditions du Cerf, 1961, pp.339-40.

[44] Blondel, *Carnets Intimes*, vol II, Paris, Les Éditions du Cerf, 1966, p. 279.

[45] *op. cit.*, p.274.

[46] Blondel, *L'Action*, Paris, Presses Universitaires de France, 1973, p.413.

[47] *History and Dogma*, p.267.

[48] Blondel, *Carnets Intimes*, II, p.259.

[49] *Ibid.*, p.158.

[50] *Ibid.*

[51] Blondel, *Exigences Philosophiques du Christianisme*, Paris, Presses Universitaires de France, 1950, p. 203.

[52] Blondel-Wehrlé *Correspondance*, op.cit., p.288.

[53] *Ibid.*

[54] *Blondel-Laberthonnière: Correspondance Philosophique*, Paris, Éditions du Seuil, 1961, p.181. Associated other criticisms which Blondel levelled against the church of his time included inferior preaching, claiming a monopoly of grace, debasing the sacramental life, a blunt and crude approach to apologetics and too much emphasis on (and an inappropriate exercise of) the rights and powers of the church. See *Carnets Intimes*, vol. I, p. 219 and vol II, pp.242, 254, 257, 277; also *Blondel-Wehrlé Correspondance*, op.cit., vol II, p.531.

[55] Blondel, *La Philosophie et L'Esprit Chrétien*, vol II, Paris, Presses Universitaires de France, 1946, pp.77-88.

[56] *Ibid.*, p.81.

[57] *Ibid.*, pp.81-2.

[58] *Ibid.*, pp. 81, 83, 84, 87.

[59]Matthew 13: 24-30.

[60]Blondel, *Carnets Intimes*, op. cit., vol. II, p.41.

[61]Congregation for the Clergy, *General Directory for Catechesis*, London, Catholic Truth Society, 1997, p.80.

[62] Philip Endean, 'The Responsibility of Theology for Spiritual Growth and Pastoral Care', *New Blackfriars*, vol. 81, No. 947, January 2000, p.49.

[63] *Ibid.*, p.52.

[64] *Ibid.*

[65]Blondel, *Carnets Intimes,* II, pp.282, 290.

[66]*Ibid.*, p.273.

[67]Raymond Saint-Jean, *L'Apologétique philosophique: Blondel 1893 - 1913*, Paris, 1966, p.298.

[68]J.A. Möhler, *Unity in the Church or the principle of Catholicism*, edited and translated by Peter Erb, Washington, DC, The Catholic University of America Press, 1996; J.H. Newman, *The Development of Christian Doctrine*, London, Sheed and Ward, 1960. Among his disciples, at least in some elements of their thought, might be included Gregory Baum, Yves Congar and Charles Curran. See Baum, *Man Becoming*, New York, Herder & Herder, 1970; Congar, translated by A. N. Woodrow, *Tradition and the Life of the Church*, London, Burns & Oates, 1964; Curran, *The Living Tradition of Catholic Moral Theology*, Notre Dame, Indiana, University of Notre Dame Press, 1992.

[69]Blondel, *Carnets Intimes*, vol. II, op. cit., pp.284, 339. For imaginative re-appropriations of living tradition in recent Catholic ecclesiology, see John Thiel, *Senses of Tradition*, New York, Oxford University Press, 2000 and Terrence Tilley, *Inventing Catholic Tradition*, New York, Orbis, 2000.

[70]I have drawn heavily in parts of this last section on my article 'Blondel and a Living Tradition for Catholic Education', *Catholic Education: A Journal of Inquiry and Practice*, vol. 1, no. 1, September 1997, pp.67 -76.

CHAPTER 8

CATHOLIC SCHOOLS AND THE COMMON GOOD

In the previous chapters I have argued that there is a distinctive Catholic approach to education, one that is substantive, comprehensive and integrated. The worldview it is based on and the priorities which emerge from its educational philosophy are contestable, held by a minority of citizens and conflict, in some respects at least, with views widely shared among the public at large. Unless Catholics can show that their desire for a distinctive form of education is not vulnerable to accusations of being inward-looking, isolationist and unconcerned about the common good, their schools will neither deserve nor attract the support of a wider society.

Yet, if one extreme to be avoided is the kind of emphasis on distinctiveness that leads to exclusiveness, there is also an inverse difficulty for Catholic schools. Too great a concern to display inclusiveness might leave Catholic schools open to the criticism that they merely duplicate 'secular' schools and do not warrant special support, funding or legal protection from the state, nor continuing self-sacrifice from the Catholic community itself. A balance has to be struck, where it can be shown that Catholic schools combine distinctiveness with belonging to the wider community and promoting the common good. This will entail displaying all the positive and humane values which are jointly accepted by society and the church, for example, equal opportunities, due process and those features of inclusiveness which were outlined in chapter five. Far from being inward-looking, Catholic schools aim to develop in pupils the desire and ability to contribute constructively to worldly affairs simultaneously with their readiness to respond to the call to conversion and to perfection. Such a positive contribution entails not only a willingness to give themselves wholeheartedly and energetically to the common tasks of safeguarding human welfare, but also the capacity to criticise prophetically prevailing priorities and power structures where these seem misguided and undermining of the common good. Individuals and communities outside the church will also, of course, contribute in significant ways to the critique of social policies, thus upholding the common good. Their challenges will sometimes be allied to those of the churches against secular (or other religious) decisions and sometimes they will be directed against the churches where these are perceived to lose sight of the common good, perhaps in seeking to protect their own interests at its expense. In this chapter I intend to show that a concern for the common good is an integral feature of a

Catholic philosophy of education and that Catholic schools can be shown to contribute to this common good.

As an acknowledgement of the contested nature of Catholic education, I consider first in this chapter a range of possible objections to the existence of separate church schools in contemporary society. Secondly, I explore how a particular understanding of the relationship between church and world provides a foundation for a positive approach to the issue in question here, namely whether separate Catholic schools can be justified in a pluralist society. Thirdly, I provide an exposition of a Catholic understanding of the notion of the common good. Fourthly, I show how Catholic schools can contribute to the common good.

8.1. *Catholic schools and contemporary society: some concerns*

The continuing existence of - and, as in the UK, state support for - separate Catholic schools within a multi-cultural and multi-faith society is open to several possible objections. Such objections might be categorised as economic, social, political and educational. Two other types of objections could also be considered. First, there is the claim that the maintenance of separate Catholic schools fails to give due priority to the ecumenical imperative. Second, there is the claim that alternative pastoral strategies for the Catholic faith community would serve it better.[1] Pope John Paul strongly underlined the absolutely central importance of ecumenism to Catholicism.[2] However, there has more than once been serious controversy among English Catholics regarding the appropriateness of maintaining Catholic schools as a major pastoral strategy for the faith community.[3] All of these objections deserve careful consideration. However, I shall treat them only briefly here because my main concern is to clear the ground for the construction of a case for the continued existence of separate Catholic schools in the context of a pluralist society. This case is sufficiently broadly based to merit the attention of those who are not 'insiders' to Catholicism.

Even though the Catholic community in England and Wales is still expected to pay what amounts to a substantial additional levy for its denominational schools, these are nevertheless very heavily supported from public funds, through taxation.[4] On economic grounds a complaint could be made that the existence of the dual system unnecessarily complicates the overall provision of schooling, leading in some areas to duplication of provision (which is a burden to the economy), or to prolonged wrangling over the allocation of school places. Resource management of the education system could be streamlined if no account had to be taken of the different demands of particular minority groups for separate schooling.

On social grounds it might be argued that the existence of separate Catholic schools unnecessarily reinforces existing divisions within society, exaggerates the differences between people, reduces the level of mutual understanding and thereby undermines social cohesion. Various criticisms have been levelled against Catholic schools. Owing to their tight control over admissions, they are able to avoid taking their fair share of really difficult pupils. Because of the rigidity of the set of values they espouse, they do not prepare their pupils for the real world. They do not adequately meet the needs of the increasing number of non-Catholic pupils who attend Catholic schools. They damage the interests of education in some localities.[5] Support for church schools could be interpreted as anachronistic, perpetuating the social influence of the established churches at the expense of many other types of churches, in a way that is out of proportion to the real number of their adherents. Because the admission policies of many church schools require evidence of church affiliation and attendance, it might be argued that the demand for places in some areas leads to spurious claims to religious belonging, which work to the disadvantage of those who are already socially disenfranchised.[6] Pupils who could benefit most from church schools are thereby prevented from enjoying such features as small, homogeneous communities, the use of more traditional teaching styles, high standards of behaviour and the confident advocacy of more traditional virtues and values.

Concerns about the social effects of separate schooling lead in some cases to political anxieties. I pick out four examples of potential political concerns. First, one might focus on the justification for allowing certain privileges to (mainly) Catholics and Anglicans but refusing other groups the right to set up their own schools with support from the public purse. Evidence of inequality of treatment might lead to loss of faith in the just distribution of goods provided by our political system. Second, it could be argued that the existence of a plural system of schools undermines the effectiveness of a consistent and nation-wide approach to schooling and it siphons off from the state sector the support of some parents. It also reduces the quality of education provided and thereby disadvantages the nation in comparison with its competitors. Third, the concern for separate schooling might, to some observers, indicate a withdrawal from rather than a full involvement in society. Does the emphasis on discipleship in church schools undermine the development of citizenship? Fourth, if, in an effort to be even-handed, the state were to concede more minority faith-groups the right to run their own schools, with public funding, this might lead to social fragmentation and increased political turmoil[7]

On educational grounds Catholic schools are vulnerable to criticism on several fronts. One of these is neglect of the development of pupils' autonomy and exercise of free choice. Connected to this is the danger of indoctrination. Another possible deficiency is giving inadequate attention to pupils' rights in relation to their parents. A fourth potential weakness is allowing a distortion of the curriculum towards religious perspectives. If the focus of these is too narrow, Catholic schools could fail to contribute to mutual understanding. Each of these defects show insufficient attention to the imperative to be inclusive that I have argued is an essential pole within Catholicism.

There are other criticisms on educational grounds that could be levelled against Catholic schools. One of these is the inculcation of an unhealthy sense of guilt (as a consequence of emphasising sin and the need for forgiveness). Another is a failure to attend to the differing spiritual needs of pupils, (through assuming too readily that they all share the same faith). Undue reverence for traditional authority and the past, instead of an openness to the questions, insights and needs of the present would constitute a third weakness. Yet another deficiency could be the distortion brought about if a school treated religious, spiritual and moral development as if these were absolutely intertwined. The differences between these three aspects of personal growth should be respected, and failure to do so is potentially damaging to pupils. A further criticism here might be that Catholic schools, in their ideology at least, if not in their actual practice, expect too much of the teacher-pupil relationship. The teacher is required to be a moral exemplar and model of faith. If this role is over-emphasised, there is the danger of casting young people more in the role of disciples than of pupils or students. My treatment of inclusiveness and of living tradition in Catholic schools in chapters six and seven sought to show that such dangers could be avoided and these particular criticisms met.

8.2.   *Church-world relationship*

A Catholic understanding of the relationship between church and world underpins the desire to maintain both the distinctive and the inclusive dimensions of Catholic education. In addition, it provides a basis for ensuring that such inclusiveness is not only a feature *within* Catholic schools, in the various senses outlined in chapter six, but also that such inclusiveness is expressed in openness to the world. An essential part of Catholic teaching relates to the promotion of the common good of society as a whole. It follows from a Catholic understanding of the church-world relation that Catholic schools should have it as a major goal to equip their pupils with the knowledge, skills and motivation to contribute to the societies of which they are members.

An understanding of the relationship between the church and the world is itself drawn from an understanding of the relationship between sacred and secular, between divine and human. This was explored in chapter four. From this it follows that there is an essential *compatibility* between church and world, since, from the perspective of faith, God is never absent from creation. God is its source, sustainer, redeemer and goal. However, the word 'redeemer' itself warns us against too easy an *identification* of church and world. It should also remind us not to identify too readily church and kingdom. Both church and world are called to ceaseless conversion, to grow ever more fully into the stature of the children of God; neither have 'arrived'; the process of transformation must penetrate all aspects of our actions, feelings and thoughts, as well as our communities and their institutions and practices. If, from the point of view of faith, the church believes herself to have received irrevocably the communication of God's message, this does not exhaust the scope of God's Holy Spirit or restrict Her operations to the church. The church still has to 'receive' more deeply the implications of God's saving message and still has to grow more fully into both the kind of society (in its community aspect) and into the kind of people (as individuals) that God is calling for. Some of the 'lessons' will come from 'outside' the church, for God is working throughout the world as well as from within the church itself. Thus, in a sense, both church and state need each other for their mutual completion. This is a view put forward by the English Catholic historian Christopher Dawson in a series of lectures given in the USA. "The Church is socially incomplete unless there is a Christian society as well as an ecclesiastical congregation, and the State is morally incomplete without some spiritual bond other than the law and the power of the sword."[8]

For much of the nineteenth century there was antagonism between the two ideologies of Catholicism and liberalism.[9] Various elements contributed to the body of liberal views, not all of which were equally represented in all forms of liberalism. Among these we find a desire for "parliamentary government, regular elections, a free press, an independent judiciary, separation of church and state", together with a belief that "progress, leading to final perfection, could be achieved by means of free institutions".[10] Perhaps one can speak of liberalism as a 'family' of ideas, which embrace, in different combinations, "a political programme, an economic outlook, a view of human nature, a social theory, an ethics, an epistemology, even a metaphysics".[11]

Weaknesses in liberalism are recognised from within the western liberal community itself. The rise of communitarianism is testimony to perceived shortcomings. There is too much emphasis on the individual at the expense of the community, and too much emphasis on rights, to the neglect of corresponding duties. Such a focus on the individual invites self-absorption on the part of citizens. This leads to reckless and conspicuous consumption because of an ineffective sense of restraint or of limits, and a debilitating denigration of the authority and necessary demands of moral principles. Without sufficient attention to tradition and to the community, there can be too cavalier a response to novelty and a failure to generate the qualities of loyalty and public-spiritedness[12]

Weaknesses in their own position have also been accepted by many Catholics. Nineteenth century triumphant apologetics, militant isolationism, ultra-orthodox sectarianism, refusal to allow any accommodation, adaptation or innovation are not advocated by mainstream Catholicism today. Vatican II's *Gaudium et Spes* displays a much more positive attitude: the church has not only something to teach and to give the modern world; it has something to learn and to receive as well.[13]   The modern world is not to be demonised any more than it is to be deified. Such a change of emphasis, which amounts to a rapprochement with the modern world, as well as an *aggiornamento* or renewal of the church itself, has been strengthened by several factors. These include the decline of neo-scholasticism as the prevailing form of Catholic philosophy, an appropriation of insights from historical, biblical, psychological and social studies, an engagement with 'secular city' theology and the development of political and liberation theology. In addition, there has been a fresh articulation of Catholic social teaching and a new confidence in commentary on public affairs relating to a whole range of issues. Catholic commentary relates to such issues as nuclear weapons, overseas aid, housing and family policies, immigration, the plight of refugees, the depiction of violence and sex in the media and the operations of the economy.[14]

In the nineteenth century the Catholic Church retreated in the face of revolutionary movements, the process of secularisation and the growing power of nation states. She adopted, sometimes in the face of persecution or in response to hostile legislation, an oppositional and isolationist stance in her relationship to the world, fearing that any adaptation would lead, via dilution and indifference, to assimilation to and then elimination by the world. Every effort was made to ensure that, in the face of an increasing diversity within society, the church presented itself not only as universal, but also as uniform.

Adaptations became necessary during the twentieth century because of cultural changes, leading to a different understanding and new expression of the faith. As already described in chapter two, the Second Vatican Council (1962-65) gave legitimacy to a new emphasis in the church's stance toward the world, so that the language became much more positive, with the tone being suggested by terms such as 'invite', 'encourage', 'promote', 'respect' and 'dialogue'.[15] Accompanying this move away from isolation, the institutional church appears to have displayed a much more positive attitude, one of greater humility, openness, a desire to show involvement and willingness to take risks.[16]

In the first article of its Constitution on the Church, the Second Vatican Council declared that by virtue of its relationship with Christ, "the Church is a kind of sacrament of intimate union with God and of the unity of all mankind; that is, she is a sign and instrument of such union and unity."[17] Associated with the notion of the church as sacrament is the view that it mediates God's grace in a symbolic way, making available for us what is otherwise inaudible, intangible and invisible. This does not entail the view that, outside such a body, God does not communicate, offer grace or redeem the world. God cannot, for a believer, be confined in any way. However, our appreciation of God's ways can be focused and made more vivid by an understanding of the mediating role of sacramental experiences.

This mediating or bridge-building role of the church belongs to it as part of its nature as an *interim* body, which should neither be too closely identified with the world nor with the idea of the Kingdom of God. Too close an identification with the Kingdom might lead to isolation and elitism. Too close an identification with the world might lead to so many compromises that contamination is a result. As the Brazilian theologian Leonardo Boff puts it: "ecclesiological health depends on the right relationship between Kingdom-world-Church."[18] The church must take institutional realities into account, both their positive and their negative features, in order that its central messages can be heard and welcomed, rather than merely imposed. This calls for a way of relating to the world that neither automatically legitimates established political regimes nor automatically calls them in question. The church must not be reduced to focusing on merely temporal concerns; but they must not be ignored either. The Kingdom of God, as taught by Jesus, has been inaugurated but it has not yet reached completion. The church as an interim body is to bring into focus, in a distinctive or pre-eminent way, the work to be done in between the 'already' and the 'not yet' of this Kingdom.

The church's move, from an oppositional stance to a more positive reading of the world and a call for greater involvement in its concerns, is closely connected to a growing acceptance by the church that both limited government and constitutional democracy are beneficial to society. *Gaudium et Spes* is at pains to argue that the state

> must take care not to put obstacles in the way of family or cultural groups, or of organisations and intermediate institutions...Citizens...should take care not to vest too much power in the hands of public authority nor to make untimely and exaggerated demands for favours and subsidies.[19]

Kenneth Grasso, a political scientist, has recently commented on what he calls the church's "preferential option for constitutional democracy" and he identifies six features of this preference: [1] human rights; [2] limited government; [3] subsidiarity; [4] freedom; [5] "constitutions specifying the scope of government and the rights of individuals"; [6] "opportunities to play an active part...in the political community".[20]

The acceptance by the church of limited government and constitutional democracy is related both to a prudential response to historical developments and to an appreciation of the implications of traditional Catholic social teaching. Key concepts within that teaching, some of which are original to the church, include (a) the notion of the common good, (b) the dignity of the human person, (c) natural law, (d) subsidiarity and (e) solidarity. It has to be admitted that popes in the twentieth century warmed to democracy and the notion of human rights not only because of the internal logic of their own tradition but also in the face of totalitarian regimes and a massive increase in the powers available to the state (of whatever political persuasion), powers which have threatened Catholic communities. The pragmatism of the papal response does not, however, contradict its principled rationale; the papal reading of political realities and their attendant rights and duties is drawn from a perspective which envisages a transcendent point of reference for society, with supernatural destiny as the goal of humanity. Such a teleology tends to relativise the importance of purely political considerations and suggests the necessity of separating spiritual and temporal authority and roles.

The American Jesuit, John Courtney Murray, has been credited with influencing significantly the Catholic church's change of emphasis with regard to the secular world during the period immediately prior to and throughout the Second Vatican Council, especially in relation to freedom of conscience.[21] Many of Murray's themes were to permeate key texts of the Council: the 'compenetration' of Church and world, the eschatological character of Christian existence, which looks to the future, the coming-to-be of the Kingdom, the distinction between classical and historical consciousness (an idea which Murray had borrowed from Lonergan and integrated into his political theology), the dialectic between freedom and authority, the mutual need of the individual and the community for each other, the church's call to service, and the requirement that the church remain a visible community. I will comment on two of these points which are relevant to the development of my argument.

Firstly, Murray clarified how authority is needed for freedom to flourish. Its purpose is not to be self-serving but to enable freedom to grow healthily. He considered that a creative tension between freedom and authority is inevitable and that each is open to distortion. His view was that authority does not "stand *over* the community as a power to decide and command' but rather that it 'stands *within* the community, as a ministry to be performed in the service of the community."[22] The church should witness through service; by meeting needs it should seek to draw all into the ambience of the kingdom, the communion of love, to "gather into one the children of God who are scattered abroad" (John 11:52). Such missionary work requires from the church some preservation, but it will be preservation without possessiveness, a treasury of truth held in trust without a turning inward. This will involve a combination of reverence for the past and openness to the concerns of today.

Secondly, the visibility of the church in society that Murray called for is intended not for the sake of self-aggrandisement or for worldly status. It is required instead in order that the source of salvation be acknowledged and properly responded to, with no delusions about the costs of commitment and no disguising the conflicts both internal to self and within society that will be entailed in accepting. Murray wanted to ensure "that the work done is the work of the Church", rather than some mere human construct which bends too readily to the whims of the world.[23] In this way the cutting edge of truth would be felt. The visibility of the church as an organisation within society is necessary, according to Murray, "both for the sake of its own unity as an interpersonal communion and also for the sake of its action in history."[24] This visibility implies that distinctiveness is to be maintained so that authority can exercise a corrective function necessitated by our sinful tendencies.

In a book published while the Second Vatican Council was still meeting, Murray made another distinction which casts light on the attempt within Catholic education to be both distinctive and inclusive. This was the distinction between evangelism and proselytism. This distinction reflects the boundary between the legitimate influence of the church in society and its unwarranted interference. The difference between evangelism and proselytism is less to do with the final goal intended than with the style and spirit that can be discerned in the activity. Among the characteristics of proselytism Murray identified "self-assertive aggressiveness,...language or action offensive to the religious sensibilities of the community; the employment of means of seduction...Proselytism does not stand at the door and knock; it rushes rudely into the house."[25] Like those who proselytise, evangelists will also aim for conversion by communicating the gospel, but they will be less domineering or concerned for 'conquest'. They will display a gentler and more patient spirit, being more open to the work of the Spirit, more respectful of the dignity of the individual and more sensitive to the needs of those with whom they enter into dialogue.

The attempt to combine distinctiveness with inclusiveness in Catholic schools can be assisted by drawing on several of Murray's points, even if some of them have to be developed further in ways which he did not envisage. For the purposes of this chapter, however, his main contribution is to challenge the church to take a responsible public role in society. This public role is partly for the sake of truth. It is also offered as a service, to promote the common good, and to prevent the state from exercising an excessive influence over matters where it is not best placed to pronounce with authority, for example, marriage, the family, the relation between parents and children and the realm of education.

8.3.   *Catholic understanding of the common good*

The notion of the common good, as taught within the Catholic tradition, has a lengthy history. It draws upon both classical (especially Aristotelian) and scriptural roots.[26] I take the broad meaning of the phrase the 'common good' to refer to "the sum total of those conditions of social living, whereby men are enabled more fully and more readily to achieve their own perfection".[27] An understanding of the common good is not one that the church arrives at ready-made, complete and applicable thereafter to all times and situations. The common good will depend on an understanding of many things: human nature, the possibilities and constraints afforded by the level of our scientific 'reading' of and technological capacity to 'manage' the world around us, the possible elements required for individual and social flourishing, the available values which can be realised and the potential threats against which we should guard ourselves. For example, earlier twentieth century Catholic defences of the common good were directed against totalitarian belief systems such as communism and fascism, which completely subordinated the individual to the needs of the collective.

Jacques Maritain, who dominated the intellectual scene of Catholic philosophical commentary on social and political issues for more than thirty years in the middle of the twentieth century, had in view especially these totalitarian threats to faith and humanity. He also took into account the apparently less extreme but equally insidious threats from liberal, materialist capitalism. One kind of threat over-valued the collective and destroyed the basis of responsible individuality; the other over-valued individualism and neglected the common good.

In *The Person and the Common Good* Maritain showed that there is no real conflict between what is good for society and what is good for individuals.[28] Between the person and the common good we should envisage not an opposition but rather "a reciprocal subordination and mutual implication".[29] He saw two contrasting threats to the harmony that should exist between the good of society and that of individuals. First, there was the ambition of totalitarian politics to control all aspects of life and to form persons in such a way as to rob them of their rightful freedom. Second, he lamented the exaltation of a shallow individuality and an indisciplined free choice within the liberal West. Because of these twin threats, Maritain was concerned to protect the priority of religious values from social interference. Some of the most important aspects of our nature, Maritain believed, transcend political society, and therefore should be free from undue state influence.[30]

"Man is constituted a person, made for God and life eternal, before he is constituted a part of the city".[31]

It would be in keeping with Maritain's general view to claim that totalitarian regimes sought deliberately to destroy parental responsibility and authority as potential threats to the state, while liberal capitalism (more benignly) neglected and undermined such responsibility and authority by exalting individualism. His emphasis on the importance of the family, both as a contributing factor in serving the common good and as an element in human flourishing, is closely related to the development of the notion of subsidiarity, which I examine below. According to Maritain, the notion of the common good serves to protect individuals and yet it also exacts from them the price of responsible co-operation. Crucially, the domain of religion must not be subordinated to the priorities of the state.

The notion of the common good has recently become the focus of both scholarly and public debate.[32] The most recent authoritative, if brief, statement of the Catholic Church's position on the common good in this country is that issued in the autumn of 1996 by the Bishops of England and Wales.[33] I will take this document as a significant indication of the (English and Welsh) Catholic Church's position on the common good, even though it does not do more than hint at the implications for education of the principles which are enunciated there.[34]

The common good is defined as "the whole network of social conditions which enable human individuals and groups to flourish and live a fully human life, otherwise described as 'integral human development'".[35] Underpinning the understanding of the common good that pervades this document there are two particular ideas which are given prominence: these are subsidiarity and solidarity. "If subsidiarity is the principle behind the organisation of societies from a vertical perspective, solidarity is the equivalent horizontal principle."[36] Central to subsidiarity is the desire to disperse authority and to foster the healthy development of a range of institutions and communities which serve as intermediary bodies between the state and individuals.[37] The classic definition and assertion of subsidiarity upon which the bishops draw is that of Pope Pius XI:

> Just as it is gravely wrong to take from individuals what they can accomplish by their own initiative and industry and give it to the community, so also it is an injustice and at the same time a grave evil and disturbance of right order to assign to a greater or higher association what lesser and subordinate organisations can do.[38]

Solidarity, on the other hand, is meant to indicate the virtue of acting in the light of our mutual responsibility for one another. It underlines our interdependence. Far from reducing morality to a private, simple or sentimental response, it engages with the complexity of the systems in which we are all enmeshed, economic, cultural, political and religious.[39] Subsidiarity and solidarity are seen to be intimately related, each serving the common good, although in different ways. Subsidiarity should serve to protect and to promote the particular and the local interests of intermediary bodies. Solidarity should ensure that such interests do not lead to excessive narrowness of concern, fragmentation, division, lack of cohesion or a denial of those features of our existence that we hold in common.

There will be some tension between these two, for if a concern to protect subsidiarity is carried too far by any group, this will undermine the concerted decision-making and action by representatives of the whole community. In such circumstances the group might adopt a counter-cultural mode of relating to the wider society. This has sometimes been the stance adopted in secular societies by the Catholic Church. It can also happen that little room is left for the operation of subsidiarity because of a too dominant pressure to institutionalise and promote solidarity through collective action. Then there is a danger that local communities and groups will be stifled, over-dependent on the state and prevented from exercising initiative. If they were forced to confine the practice of their traditions to the private and domestic domain, this would emasculate entirely their claims to offer something of public significance, even to those who are not adherents.

Subsidiarity and solidarity are closely associated, in the minds of the bishops, with other basic principles or emphases: the importance of listening to ideas from others, natural law, the 'option for the poor' and the importance of recognising our social responsibilities.[40] This last is given a broad interpretation:

> Christ taught us that our neighbourhood is universal: so loving our neighbour has global dimensions. It demands fair international trading policies, decent treatment of refugees, support for the UN and control of the arms trade. Solidarity with our neighbour is also about the promotion of equality of rights and equality of opportunities.[41]

The Bishops stress that democracy depends on common values and an understanding of the common good. They deplore the ceaseless amplification of claims to rights in the name of an autonomy that operates without limits and in a vacuum. Instead, they emphasise, human rights derive from the nature of the human person made in the image of God.[42] They go on to apply these principles to the market place, social services, the mass media, the world of work, Europe, the global common good, the environment, ownership and property, with a recognition of the multiplicity of roles we play:

> [a] manager in one enterprise may be the consumer in another, the neighbour of a third, the supplier of a fourth, a shareholder in a fifth; and may subsequently become a redundant ex-employee, the victim of the very policies that as a manager he or she may have helped to create.[43]

There are both advantages and drawbacks in relying on religiously based arguments for the defence of human rights and the promotion of the common good.[44] A religious context for such arguments might provide for adherents of a faith some motivation and resources (in the form of guidance and discipline from the ecclesial community) in addition to that enjoyed by people outside such communities. However, if the grounds for defending rights and promoting the common good cannot be shared with 'outsiders' this can lead to difficulties in communication, in mutual trust and understanding, and in the willingness to engage in joint action. It is my intention in the next section to construct a case for Catholic schools that rests, to a large degree, on evidence or arguments which do not derive their plausibility from acceptance of the Catholic worldview described in chapter five.

8.4.   Catholic schools and the common good

In the preceding analysis of the Catholic understanding of the common good I have not drawn out sufficiently clearly the strong emphasis in Catholic thought on justice, the option for the poor and respect for the dignity and freedom of the individual.[45] These principles must be demonstrated *within* Catholic schools if advocates of separate church schools are to have any credibility. Such demonstration has not always been apparent. But I have indicated that the notion of the common good has an important place in Catholic thinking and that it has a wide application.[46] Far from wanting faith to be treated as a private affair, it is central to Catholic teaching that, along with spiritual values and moral teaching, scripture reading and study, personal prayer and collective worship, Catholic education should have social and civic functions; it should contribute to the development of the qualities necessary for citizenship. A broad and practical concern for the needs of others should be promoted within schools and society.[47] Even if the Catholic notion of the common good does not fully convince others, there may well be sufficient consensus, on non-religious grounds, about what is required for this good, to enable the argument that Catholic schools contribute positively to the common good to be taken seriously.

There are seven strands to the argument that Catholic schools contribute to the common good. These seven strands can be divided into three broad categories. The first three focus on the outcomes and popularity of Catholic schools. The second three are concerned with the 'safeguarding' role of Catholic schools - that is, safeguards from undue state influence, from defects in liberal education and from being closed to the possibility of the transcendent. The final strand is based on the notion of Catholic schools as 'constitutive communities'. It is not essential to my case that each strand will on its own withstand the strain of opposition or that it will pull waverers into the camp of the committed. But I believe that, when taken together, the seven strands I pick out jointly comprise a sufficiently cogent argument (in 'secular' terms) that the potential contribution of Catholic schools to the common good significantly outweighs any possible disadvantages of denominational education.

8.4.1. Outcomes and popularity
The first three of the seven strands to this argument would need to rely mainly on empirical evidence. Since this is not an empirical study I can only hint at what would have to be established, if these strands were to be developed. First, there would be the argument that Catholic schools meet the educational standards required by society (through its elected representatives) at least as well as if not more successfully than other schools. This would involve taking into account the catchment area, intake, resources and the academic progress made by pupils in their

passage through the school.

It is not part of the Catholic case for separate school provision that their schools should tolerate educational standards lower than those laid down for all schools, on the grounds that they claim to offer something different from these other schools. The Catholic community does not dispute the appropriateness of the curriculum requirements or the academic standards expected of all schools. It does, however, wish to supplement them, to place them in a broader context and, in some cases, to modify or to realign the priorities among them. One example is that more importance is to be given to preparing for life than to earning a living. Another example is a desire to bring out the essential interconnections, as seen from a faith perspective, between the moral, the spiritual and the religious dimensions of life.

There is substantial agreement in the Catholic community on the study skills, areas of learning and attainment targets that are expected in 'common' schools. Catholics ask for the right to go beyond this in their own schools. This 'going beyond', however, neither contradicts nor distracts from the substance of these academic expectations. It does cast them in a different light, in particular by viewing academic effort as part of the realisation of our God-given talents, as an element in our response to God's call and as an integral part of a more deep-seated striving for perfection.

If Catholic schools could be shown to have failed to promote educational standards this would count as a major obstacle to acceptance of their claim to be promoting the common good. I believe that there is evidence available which supports the claim that Catholic schools in general do meet or even exceed the educational standards expected of mainstream schools. Such evidence comes from various sources: from OFSTED, local education authority and diocesan inspection reports, from patterns of parental choice of schools for their children and from independent academic researchers.[48]

It should be noted that my claim is not that a Catholic school which ensures that its pupils succeed academically is *ipso facto* a good *Catholic* school. Other features would be looked for before this judgement could be made. My claim is, rather, that a Catholic school which did not ensure that its pupils made significant academic progress would be a poor school by Catholic as well as according to secular criteria. Furthermore, such academic progress is to be expected of all pupils, including those who suffer economic or social disadvantages. English, American and Australian research suggests that Catholic schools enable such pupils to make greater progress than they usually achieve in 'common' schools.[49]

The second strand in the argument that Catholic schools contribute to the common good would be evidence that they promote among their pupils a high level of concern and competence in moral and social issues, a sense of responsibility, a willingness and a capacity to contribute to public life and citizenship. For example, if a concern for justice and peace, for human rights and freedom, for the protection of the environment and conservation of the habitat of other creatures were marked features of the behaviour of those who attended Catholic schools, this would be relevant evidence. The gathering and analysis of such evidence would require a large-scale and longitudinal survey, one that is beyond the scope of my argument. But, in principle, two conditions would invalidate, or at least seriously weaken, the claim that Catholic schools contribute to the common good. One of these is if it could be shown that graduates from Catholic schools did not display a high level of awareness and understanding of a broad range of moral and social issues. The second is if it was demonstrated that they lacked the ability to act constructively on such awareness.

It should be noted that this strand of the overall claim on behalf of Catholic schools only requires evidence that they promote at least as high a level of awareness and competence in moral and social affairs as that shown by the products of other schools. My claim here is not the major one that Catholic schools contribute more than others to the common good, but the lesser one that they can be shown to contribute to this good in sufficiently numerous, diverse and significant ways that those who seek to defend them can justifiably declare that the objections levelled earlier in this chapter, far from being overwhelming, can, in principle at least, be satisfactorily answered.

A third part of the defence of Catholic schools in the context of a pluralist society is that they meet the wishes of very many parents that their children's education should be based on their own beliefs and values. This strand of the argument does not rest entirely on empirical grounds. There are two reasons for this. First, the principle that parents are to be acknowledged as the first and foremost educators of their children is absolutely central to Catholic teaching on education.[50] Second, the respect to be given to parental wishes and rights is considered an aspect of the principle of subsidiarity. This was examined in 7.3; it is also applied to the defence of separate church schools in the fourth strand of my argument.

It is very difficult for the state to adopt a neutral stance with regard to parental wishes regarding their children's upbringing. Either the state supports the provision of education according to parental wishes or it ends up by obstructing such education through the provision of schools which claim in principle to be neutral (or blind to differences). In practice such schools not only ignore parental wishes; they are perceived by some faith communities to be hostile to and corrosive of them.[51] Other things being equal, the satisfying of parental wishes is a good in itself. Of course, this good has to be balanced by other considerations, for example, concerns about costs or about educational standards. The provision of denominational schooling should not undermine the other educational goals held dear by society; nor should it lead to other schools being disadvantaged in any way.

Catholic families reflect the reduction in the birth rate shown by the rest of the population. Overt religious 'practice' in many Catholic families is considerably less than a quarter of a century ago.[52] Despite these facts, there is evidence from England and Wales that a higher proportion of children who have been baptised as Catholics are attending church schools than was the case up to 1975. Catholic schools suffer much less from falling rolls than other schools. This partly because they retain popularity with Catholic parent and partly because an increasing percentage of parents who are not Catholics want their children to attend church schools.

These parallel increases, in the proportion of baptised Catholic children attending church schools and in the proportion of non-Catholic pupils who attend these schools, are quite compatible. With a few exceptions, it appears that provision for Catholic schools has not historically matched the demand for places. Now, from within the reduced overall size of the 'practising' Catholic community, church schools continue to be popular in most areas, even though the sense of there being a moral duty to send children from Catholic homes to church schools seems much less marked than hitherto. It could be argued then that continued parental support for church schools, even from parents who 'practise' their faith in other ways less fervently, indicates a more deliberate and individual choice than when attendance at church schools was a cultural norm within the Catholic community.

Two conclusions might reasonably be drawn from a situation where there is increasing pressure on pupil admissions in Catholic schools exerted by parents from other Christian denominations, from other religious faiths and from non-religious backgrounds. The stronger conclusion might be that Catholic schools satisfy parental wishes for a congenial educational ethos more fully than is the case in many county schools. Alternatively, and expressed more weakly, even if such parents really desire a form of education which is not exactly the same as that provided within Catholic schools, their wishes are frustrated more often in county schools, which many find less attractive environments for the upbringing of their children.

8.4.2. Safeguarding role of Catholic schools
A fourth strand of the defence of separate Catholic schools relies on the principle of subsidiarity described in 8.3. The relative autonomy of their schools is seen by Catholics as an expression of subsidiarity, whereby 'intermediate' communities exercise initiative in areas where they have competence and a direct interest. According to Catholic teaching, this application of subsidiarity to schools helps to limit the incursion of intrusive governments and it functions as an enabling condition for human flourishing, facilitating individual growth, healthy community life, responsible choice and scope for creativity.

Two comments might be made here about subsidiarity. First, the principle of subsidiarity, although advocated as an important element in Catholic social thinking, does not depend on belief in revelation, and its employment entails neither acceptance of the church's magisterium nor reliance on any of its theological presuppositions. In a sense it could be said to be a purely secular principle of social organisation, derived from human experience. It is, after, all, accessible to reason and open to believers and unbelievers alike, even if, as a principle, it can be additionally buttressed by religious beliefs about the human propensity to sin and the salvific mission of the church. Second, there is some tension between the church's advocacy of subsidiarity as a general principle to be employed in social and political affairs and the centralising tendency displayed in the exercise of authority within the church itself.

As a result, where the Catholic Church is a leading exponent of the argument for subsidiarity, and in so far as the principle is seriously compromised by the church's own practice in 'internal' affairs, its advocacy in the school context lacks conviction. This does not invalidate the principle itself. It does, however, present a twin challenge to the church. On the one hand, greater integrity and consistency must be demonstrated in applying the principle within church organisations, including dioceses, parishes and schools. On the other hand, the Church must strive more energetically to engage in dialogue with others and to communicate the nature and scope of the claim for subsidiarity more effectively in the public forum.

A fifth strand in the separate schools case draws on a cluster of ideas that rely on a more general religious perspective, one that goes beyond the scope usually allowed by a liberal education. This cluster of ideas could be shared with people from a variety of religious and moral stances. It does not depend directly on Catholic principles. From the perspective of many religions and also from the perspective of some forms of moral philosophy there are possible dangers to the common good that might arise from current forms of liberal education. Such dangers might include too subjective a view of morality, too anthropological a view of nature, too narrow a view of rationality, and too optimistic a view of human capacities.

To guard against these dangers, it might be argued that at least some schools in society should maintain a stance which is explicitly open to the possibility of receiving revelation and which displays a reverence for the 'givenness' of nature, a search for the 'discovery' (rather than the 'construction') of (objective) morality, and a realistic recognition of the proneness of the human will to self-deception and evil. This cluster of ideas modifies and perhaps constrains the promotion of critical and independent thinking encouraged within liberal education, but it does not contradict such thinking. It seeks to serve the common good by a more realistic acknowledgement of the dialectic between development and discipline that I outlined in chapter five as an essential feature of human nature.

By extension of the fifth strand we are led into the sixth, which also relies on a faith perspective: the acknowledgement of a transcendent point of reference for society with an accompanying sense of accountability to a higher source of authority than that supplied by the state or even by international bodies such as the United Nations Organisation. Such a view suggests that the state is not self-sufficient, and it encourages the state to be more humble in its aspirations and more self-limiting in its actions.

On the one hand, acceptance of God as the transcendent point of reference should prompt in us receptivity to resources beyond our 'normal' capacity (in Christian terms, grace). This is related to the point in my fifth strand about the 'givenness' of nature. Such a view implies that nature as 'gift' (understood to embrace the 'new' nature offered in the baptism, forgiveness, conversion and transformation implied by a life open to God's call) is the source of our interrelated salvation, not nature as 'grasped' in a self-propelled journey in search for individual happiness.

On the other hand, acceptance of God as the reference point for society gives us a reason not to enforce all the goodness we can. The state is not the supreme authority. We are riddled with the very weaknesses we seek to eradicate in others, and therefore we must be wary of setting ourselves up in judgement over them. We do not have an adequate understanding of God's purposes and ways. Such views qualify our temporal ambitions and priorities. For it sees a connection between 'soulcraft' and statecraft, between the formation and transformation of our spiritual and moral development and the art of politics, social policy and community building. Those who accept God as their supreme authority and as their guide to true life should remember that they need to address dimensions of their nature and calling other than (and alongside) the social and political. In a religious perspective, each of us is envisaged as a 'project' of ultimate and eternal significance, a project to be pursued together with and on behalf of others.

If, in this scheme of things, all are of eternal significance, none can be sacrificed for the sake of the collective. The 'relativising' of the importance of the state might be argued to be one weapon in defence of the sacred dignity of the individual. This is one form of contribution to the common good supplied by schools that proclaim the authority of God over our lives. Once this authority is acknowledged, we should be more conscious of the futility and destructiveness of a selfish individualism. It should also make us more fully aware of both the attractiveness and the cost of commitment through the education and formation provided by faith-based schools. Such formation should then enable us to see, beyond the limitations of individualism, how the 'demands' of love require that our priorities and actions are modified by discipline, sustained by sound habits and facilitated by a supportive culture.

8.4.3   'Constitutive' communities

The seventh strand to my argument is based on the role of the church school as a 'constitutive' community, one that provides for its pupils a concrete example of the burdens and benefits and the conditions and processes involved in community life. A 'constitutive' community is one that is identity-building. It is fundamental to our self-description. It provides the narrative which initially and provisionally makes sense of our lives, telling us where we have come from, who we belong to and where we are headed. It provides the moral 'building blocks' and training for the development of personal qualities which form the basis of our character. In the minds of those who participate in such constitutive communities there will be a close association between community, culture, character and conscience. Memory, membership and responsibility will be integrally related, although this does not entail any neglect of critical thinking, imagination and creativity, all of which are also needed to enable pupils to transcend the limitations of memory and membership.[53]

This seventh strand of my argument assumes that the 'thin' view of the good allowed by liberal education pays insufficient attention to the need for identity to be fostered and to the part played in our development by both memory and membership. At the same time as failing to recognise the necessity of both memory and membership as conditions which facilitate the growth of a sturdy independence and sense of responsibility, such a 'thin' view exaggerates their limitations, treating cultural attachment as potentially imprisoning.[54] The concern not to over-determine the direction of someone's life must be shared by advocates of a 'thicker' view of life such as Catholicism. Since this concern is required by their own principles about the dignity and essential freedom of the human person, they will wish to ensure that the necessary 'space' needed for individual initiative and choice does not become empty.

Through her schools the church aims to foster both the institutions and the personal values which support and sustain liberty. The two are intimately connected, for persons and their individual 'life-plans' do not emerge from a vacuum. Pupils cannot even consider such 'life-plans' without encountering concrete examples to engage with and to react against. They also need to be taught principles that are embodied in practices. If principles are to make sense, pupils should be confronted with signs of their potential scope and their effect on decisions. They need to know the sources and grounding of principles, as well as their demands and their promises. They also need to see their operation in the context of some integrating vision. Constitutive communities, conveying through their teaching and ethos a 'thick' view of the good, might be described as necessary conditions for sustaining the possibility of truly autonomous lives.[55] At the same time, it is believed, they contribute to the building of society by providing first-hand experience of and comprehensive training in community life.[56]

8.5. Conclusion

My comments on Catholic schools as constitutive communities have culminated in a very strong claim, one which there is no room either to develop or to substantiate here: Catholic schools, insofar as they are constitutive communities, provide necessary conditions for the development and exercise of autonomy. Stated thus, this claim presents a major challenge to the common school ideal, integral to which is a concern for the promotion of autonomy. It is, however, not part of my purpose to argue that only Catholic schools can be constitutive communities; many other forms of schooling, those which are faith-based and indeed some kinds of common schools, given certain conditions, can also function as constitutive communities. Furthermore, it has not been suggested that constitutive communities, simply on the basis of their being constitutive, provide sufficient conditions for the development of autonomy. One would have to add many of the features of inclusive pedagogy outlined in chapter six, augmented by considerations of how to foster critical thinking.

Rather, I have tried to show that, when they are true to the logic of their own philosophy and mission, Catholic schools, far from being sectarian or parochial, have a concern for the common good as a high priority in their aims. It has also been suggested here that evidence of the importance of the common good in

Catholic schools might be considered in the light of their academic and social outcomes, the safeguarding role they play in counteracting prevailing imbalances or omissions in current educational assumptions and practices, and their positive, community-building role. According to the norms of a Catholic philosophy of education, an inward-looking and isolationist form of schooling would represent a serious distortion, rather than an adequate reflection, of the universal and inclusive imperative within Catholicism.

Notes for Chapter 8

[1] While there is little dispute about the claim that high standards of education are provided by many Catholic schools, there remains considerable uncertainty as to their effectiveness in promoting a commitment to Catholicism.

[2] See John Paul II, *Ut Unum Sint*, London, Catholic Truth Society, 1995. Priscilla Chadwick analyses progress and prospects for an ecumenical approach to Christian education in *Schools of Reconciliation*, London, Cassell, 1994.

[3] See correspondence on this topic published in *The Tablet* during May and June 1997, especially pp.707, 737, 771-2. The issue flared up again three years later. See *The Tablet* for May 20th and 27th May and for June 3rd, 10th and 17th, 2000, pp.663, 674-5, 699-701, 720-721, 735, 752-3, 767-8, 791, 824, 840. The theme recurred again in response to Annabel Miller's 'Why Catholic Schools?' in *The Tablet* of 12 May 2001, pp.689-690. See following correspondance 19th May, p.733.

[4] The church community has to provide 15% of building costs for its voluntary aided schools.

[5] James Arthur, in *The Ebbing Tide*, Leominster, Gracewing, 1995, pp.105, 113, 119.

[6] Bishops' Conference of England and Wales, *A Struggle for Excellence*, London, 1997.

[7] For a range of arguments *pro* and *contra* the extension of voluntary status for minority faith schools, see Commission for Racial Equality, *Schools of Faith*, 1990, pp.8-19.

[8] Christopher Dawson, *The Crisis of Western Education*, London, Sheed and Ward, 1961, pp.107-8.

[9] For a concise treatment of three 'moments' in the relations between Catholicism and liberalism, (rejection, acceptance and criticism) see John Langan's chapter, 'Catholicism and Liberalism - 200 Years of Contest and Consensus', in *Liberalism and the Good*, edited by Bruce Douglass, Gerald Mara and Henry Richardson, New York, Routledge, 1990.

[10] Peter Steinfels, in *Catholicism and Liberalism*, edited by Bruce Douglass and David Hollenbach, Cambridge University Press, 1994, pp.23-4.

[11] *Ibid.*, p.23.

[12] Bruce Douglass' chapter 'Liberalism after the good times', In *Catholicism and Liberalism*, p.118. .

[13] See sections 40-45 of *Gaudium et Spes.*

[14] Cf Joseph Komonchak (1994) in *Catholicism and Liberalism*, p.98.

[15] Desmond Ryan, *The Catholic Parish: Institutional Discipline, Tribal Identity and Religious Development in the English Church*, London, Sheed & Ward, 1996, p.19.

[16] *Gaudium et Spes* (Pastoral Constitution on the Church in the Modern World), paragraphs 1, 42, 43. (from Walter Abbott (ed), *The Documents of Vatican II*, London, Geoffrey Chapman, 1967.)

[17] *Lumen Gentium*, paragraphs 9 and 48.

[18] Leonardo Boff, *Church, Charism & Power*, London, SCM Press, 1985, p.2.

[19] *Gaudium et Spes*, loc.cit, paragraph 75.

[20] Kenneth Grasso, Gerard Bradley and Robert Hunt (eds), *Catholicism, Liberalism & Communitarianism*, Lanham, Maryland, Rowman & Littlefield Publishers, 1995, pp.31-2.

[21] For this section I rely principally on the collection of selected writings of J. C. Murray, *Bridging the Sacred and the Secular*, edited by Leon Hooper, Washington, DC, Georgetown University Press, 1994. A critical commentary on the continuing relevance of Murray's work is provided by Thomas Hughson: *The Believer As Citizen*, New Jersey, Paulist Press, 1993.

[22] *Bridging the Sacred and the Secular*, p.216.

[23] *Ibid.*, p.218.

[24] *Ibid.*, p.216.

[25] J. C. Murray, *The Problem of Religious Freedom*, London, Geoffrey Chapman, 1965, pp.44-5.

[26] In sacred scripture there is a developing theology of creation, of history, of stewardship and of covenant, all of which have a bearing on the common good, the sense of a communal relationship with God, and, through God, with each other. The legal and liturgical elements in scripture also reinforce the strong emphasis on community and the common good.

[27] Pope John XXIII, quoted by Canavan (1995), in *Catholicism, Liberalism & Communitarianism*, p.25.

[28] Jacques Maritain, *The Person and the Common Good*, London, Geoffrey Bles, 1948, pp.43, 53.

[29] *Ibid.*, p.46.

[30] *Ibid.*, p.51.

[31]*Ibid.*, p.52.

[32]For an extremely brief attempt to articulate a minimal foundation of common values for schools and society, see School Curriculum and Assessment Authority (London, 1996), *Consultation on values in education and the community*. See also David Hollenbach, 'The Common Good, Pluralism and Catholic Education', in *The Contemporary Catholic School*, edited by McLaughlin et al, 1996, pp.89-103.

[33]Catholic Bishops' Conference of England and Wales, London, 1996, *The Common Good and the Catholic Church's Social Teaching.*

[34]In May 1997, after the General Election, the Catholic Bishops' Conference of England and Wales issued a follow-up document, *The Common Good in Education.*

[35]*The Common Good and the Catholic Church's Social Teaching*, p.12.

[36]*Ibid.*, p.8.

[37]*Ibid.*, p.13.

[38]Bishops' Conference, *The Common Good and the Catholic Church's Social Teaching*, p.13, quoting Pius XI, (1931), *Quadragesimo Anno.*

[39]Bishops' Conference, *The Common Good and the Catholic Church's Social Teaching*, p.14.

[40]Ibid., p.3.

[41]*Ibid.*, p.7.

[42]*Ibid.*, p.10.

[43]*Ibid.*, pp.17-27.

[44] On the potential contribution of Catholic thought to building community in a liberal society, see Brian Stiltner, *Religion and the Common Good*, Lanham, Rowman & Littlefield, 1999.

[45]On the centrality of concern for social justice within a Catholic approach to education, see Thomas Groome, *Educating For Life*, Allen, Texas, Thomas More Press, 1998, chapter 8.

[46]For evidence of constant reference by the Catholic Bishops of England and Wales to concern for the common good in educational matters in recent years, see *Partners in Mission*, Catholic Education Service, 1997, pp. 67, 70, 124, 127, 129.

[47]See The Congregation for Catholic Education, *The Religious Dimension of Education in a Catholic School*, London, Catholic Truth Society, 1988, art. 45, p.22. See John Coleman in *Education for Citizenship*, edited by Mary Boys, New York, The Pilgrim Press, 1989, p.35. "What citizenship adds to discipleship [is]: a wider solidarity, a humbler service, a new reality test for responsibility; what discipleship adds to citizenship [is]: [the ideas of] utopia, counterculture and vocation."

[48]See chapter four, note 47, for details of five articles by Andrew Morris that chart the success of Catholic schools.

[49]For the USA, see Andrew Greeley: *Catholic High Schools and Minority Students*, New Brunswick, N.J, Transaction Press, 1982; Bryk (ed), *Catholic Schools and the Common Good*, Harvard University Press, 1993, and Charles Glenn, *The Ambiguous Embrace*, Princeton University Press, 2000. For Australia, see Marcellin Flynn, *The Culture of Catholic Schools*, Homebush, St. Pauls, 1993. For England, see *The Struggle for Excellence* (1997) and *Foundations for Excellence* (1999), both Bishops' Conference of England and Wales, together with Morris articles listed in note above.

[50]See Declaration on Christian Education, issued in 1965 and published in *The Documents of Vatican II*, edited by Walter Abbott, London, Geoffrey Chapman, 1967, arts. 3 & 6, pp.641, 644.)

[51]See Mark Halstead, 'Voluntary Apartheid? Problems of Schooling for Religious and Other Minorities in Democratic Societies', *Journal of Philosophy of Education*, Vol. 29, No. 2, 1995, pp.257-272.

[52]See note 15, above, for Desmond Ryan (1996).

[53]See James Fowler, 'Character, Conscience and the Education of the Public', especially pp. 236-240, in *The Challenge of Pluralism*, edited by F. Clark Power and Daniel Lapsley, Notre Dame, Indiana, University of Notre Dame Press, 1992.

[54]Alasdair MacIntyre provides a highly positive and optimistic view of sub-communities within the wider *polis* in *After Virtue*, London, Duckworth, 1981. Eamonn Callan suggests that the developmental antecedents of mature liberal virtues might possibly be better served in separate schools. (See Callan, *Creating Citizens*, Oxford, Oxford University Press, 1997, p.181.)

[55]See Patrick Riordan, (*A Politics of the Common Good*, Dublin, Institute of Public Administration, 1996, pp. 120, 125, 135, 150) on the role of institutions in sustaining the conditions which promote

autonomy and how protecting the role of such institutions is an element in the common good. Kevin Williams, 'State Support for Church Schools: Is it Justifiable?', in *Studies in Education*, Vol. 11, No. 1, 1995, pp.37-47 and J. M. Halstead, *The Case for Muslim Voluntary-Aided Schools*, Cambridge, The Islamic Academy, 1986 offer alternative justifications, parallel to my own, for faith-based education in the context of a pluralist society. My argument that Catholic schools are constitutive communities, if it has any cogency, applies to other faith-based forms of education such as Islamic schools.

[56]*The Catholic School*, art. 13, p.9.

CHAPTER 9

CONCLUSION

As part of the church's mission to spread the gospel, Catholic schools need to make their 'story' attractive, credible and even compelling. If they do not preserve their distinctive identity, there will be no special reason for their separate existence. A community that lacks a strong sense of self-awareness, of shared values and of common goals will not have the resources or the motivation with which to be inclusive. But if it seeks too energetically to be distinctive, it can slip into appearing exclusive, either in membership or in tone, thus preventing many pupils from 'receiving' the gospel. Throughout this book I have grappled with key aspects of the problematical relationship between distinctiveness, inclusiveness and exclusiveness in the philosophy of Catholic education.

In this final chapter, first I provide a summary of the main outcomes of my exploration, acknowledging some aspects of the problem that received less prominence than they deserved. Second, key stages in the argument are shown to be closely-inter-related. Third, there is an indication of some of the further work that needs to be done in Catholic schools if the 'story' of Catholic education told here is to bear fruit in practice and so render my argument credible. Fourth, possible directions for building on the argument are suggested. Finally, I anticipate, in hope, a change of emphasis within the wider debate about the nature of Catholicism, a modification which might take at least some of its bearings from the limited treatment here of the dialectic between distinctiveness and inclusiveness in Catholic schools.

9.1   Main findings

Theological and educational literature are often studied quite separately and without reference to one another. Here they have been brought together in a dialogue, showing the bearing of theological thinking on educational philosophy and both the constraints on and opportunities for the outworking of theology in relation to educational practice and contexts. I have commented extensively on the principles enunciated in the key Roman documents on Catholic education. In relating these to the particular context of Catholic schools in England and Wales, I exposed an ambivalence in the documents and in the purposes of Catholic schools, an ambivalence that applies to all Catholic schools. I have suggested a way for Catholic schools to avoid the ambivalence and to be both distinctive and inclusive. This analysis could serve a mediating function between the global expression of key Catholic principles for education and their local application. It could also provide a resource for teachers who work in Catholic schools (or those who intend to do so), to assist them in engaging with the rationale of these schools.

The degree to which this relationship between distinctiveness and inclusiveness is problematical has been insufficiently acknowledged in past studies of Catholic education. Yet, central to the future of educational policy for Catholic schools will be a satisfactory resolution of this relationship, even if such a resolution has to be revised in each generation. If Catholic schools are to be true to their foundational principles, they must be both distinctive and inclusive. Distinctiveness and inclusiveness are correlative terms: one implies the other; they are integrally related. While these terms represent essential (and compatible) polarities within a Catholic philosophy of education, there are certain limits on the degree of inclusiveness possible.

There are proper constraints, too, on the expression of distinctiveness, although they have been given less prominence here. These constraints arise partly from the compulsory nature of school, which, especially for older pupils, reduces the scope for worship and service, neither of which can be imposed without undermining their integrity. Although both are possible in the school context, for their fullest expression they require other contexts, for example, the family, the community and the church. Another constraint arises from the fact that Catholic schools receive public support, in return for which they must attend to legitimate non-religious educational purposes, priorities and standards, as part of the common good.[1] To the extent that these aims are pursued there may be less scope for the fullest expression of the distinctive Catholic worldview in Catholic schools. However, I have shown that the concern to promote the common good, far from being a mere concession to political realities, is an integral feature of Catholic education.

In the process of examining the coherence of the claims of Catholic education to be both distinctive and inclusive, major features of a Catholic philosophy and theology of education have been clarified and re-presented. In particular, the notion of 'living tradition' has been retrieved and its potential for showing how Catholic education can be both distinctive and inclusive has been demonstrated. Key insights from the writings of Blondel have been appropriated and applied to this task. Again, central themes from the Catholic Church's recent official philosophy of education, the integral development of the human person, the autonomy of the disciplines and the synthesis between faith, culture and life, have been illustrated by reference to the work of another neglected thinker, Friedrich von Hügel. His work shows how these three themes can co-exist creatively and it offers a fertile source for understanding how the institutional, intellectual and spiritual dimensions of Catholicism mutually reinforce and correct each other. If Catholic schools are to be both distinctive and inclusive, they will need to do justice to all three of these dimensions and in the attempt to do so they could find inspiration and guidance from von Hügel.

9.2.   Unity and interconnectedness of the argument

The first five chapters were intended progressively to map the contours of a problematical and previous unexamined feature within Catholic education. First, I highlighted the potential of an understanding of two polarities within Catholicism to serve as an interpretative key that opens up issues crucial to that faith community and to others. Second, these polarities were brought into sharper focus to show how they relate to an unresolved problem in Catholic philosophy of education. Third, my enquiry was set in the particular context of Catholic schools in England and Wales. Fourth, key Catholic educational principles were analysed. Finally, an outline was given of the underlying worldview that 'colours' or shapes these principles.

In chapter one I suggested that the two polarities, distinctiveness and inclusiveness, offer a way of penetrating below the surface of controversies and debates about the nature of Catholic education. I argued that an understanding of the relationship between these polarities offers a valuable resource for regenerating a rationale for Catholic education, a task made necessary by new social circumstances. This was my main purpose. However, a subordinate aim has been to contribute to wider discussions about the relationship between liberalism and faith communities in a plural society.

In chapter two it was suggested that the polarity distinctive/inclusive, although historically deeply rooted within Catholicism, has been freshly highlighted and subjected to new pressures through recent educational developments in this country, such as the managerial imperative. In my review of contrasting studies of Catholic education, I argued that, despite their valuable insights, they failed to address the problematical nature of the relationship between distinctiveness and inclusiveness. After situating the argument in the particular social and political context of England and Wales, where a dual system of education exists, with responsibility shared, though unequally, by church and state, chapter three related educational changes to wider theological developments within the Catholic Church. It was shown how educational and theological changes combined to require of Catholic educators both a reinterpretation of the *raison d'être* of separate schooling and a fresh urgency in clarifying the relationship between distinctiveness and inclusiveness in such schools.

Taken together, chapters four and five seek to bring out the parameters of the claim that Catholic education is distinctive. With regard to Catholic educational principles, several features were shown jointly to constitute this distinctiveness: (a) the insistence on treating the secular and sacred in the curriculum as intimately and mutually implicated; (b) the creative tension to be maintained between the integral development of persons, the autonomy of the disciplines and the synthesis between faith, life and culture; (c) the centrality of Christ, both as teacher of salvific truth and as model for human development, leading to a view of education which forms, informs and transforms learners; and (d) the priority given to a particular interpretation of interconnectedness between all elements in education, (message, community, worship and service).   Underpinning these features a distinctive worldview was identified, the 'economy' of which combined elements of anthropology, theology of creation, Christology and ecclesiology. In marking out some of the contours of this worldview I discussed the bearing on education of a Catholic understanding of conscience, conversion and character, of sin, salvation and the soul, of being made in God's image and of the implications of a personal vocation.

The interpenetration of intellectual, moral and religious dimensions and perspectives, as presented in these two chapters, cumulatively brought out some of the difficulties inherent in the distinctive pole of Catholic thought. To emphasise distinctiveness thus 'goes against the grain' of many taken-for-granted views, for example, those relating to human nature and development, morality, rationality and freedom. It represents a 'thick' view of the good that is contestable in the wider society. It seems to rely on the assumption that this view is fixed within and receives unanimous support from the Catholic community, whereas in practice it is open to further development, fresh interpretations and alternative accounts from within that faith community. It could be criticised for paying too little attention to the ecumenical imperative within Christianity and for being insufficiently trusting of the influence of individual Christians formed by scripture and prayer. It gives priority to religious concerns to a degree that threatens to undermine the autonomy of the secular sphere, and this despite Catholic teaching about nature and grace. It constitutes an interconnectedness which, while pointing towards separate schooling as a desirable educational environment, is also vulnerable to the criticism that it paves the way for an all-embracing ethos which some might experience as suffocating or totalitarian.

I have highlighted here, in a rather one-sided manner, the 'uncomfortable' aspects of the 'story' of distinctiveness in order to bring out the challenges it presents in the educational context. That this is an inadequate representation of the claim to distinctiveness has already been anticipated in my treatment of von Hügel. I drew upon his work in order to demonstrate that, built into the key educational principles that are normative for Catholic schools and deeply integral to the worldview which underpins them, there is a capacity for, indeed, an imperative towards, inclusiveness. Chapters six, seven and eight relate the claim to distinctiveness to the claim to inclusiveness. In chapter six, I considered several dimensions of inclusiveness and exclusiveness *within* Catholic schools and teased out how these cohere with the distinctiveness previously outlined. Then, in chapter seven, the notion of 'living tradition' was developed as a way of fruitfully combining distinctiveness with inclusiveness in such schools. Finally, in chapter eight, I defended Catholic schools from the accusation that they are prone to exclusiveness because they fail to promote the common good.

In chapter six I showed that the Catholic claim to offer a distinctive approach to education was not only *compatible* with the notion of inclusiveness; I argued further that many of the characteristics of inclusiveness which I had identified were *intrinsic* to a Catholic philosophy of education. A creative tension, rather than an incompatibility, was shown to exist between the two poles. Their reciprocal interrelationship is such that one is intimately implicated in the other, with both polarities simultaneously reinforcing and qualifying their correlates.

Like other close relationships, the connections between distinctiveness and inclusiveness in Catholic education cannot be precisely predicted, definitely determined, comprehensively charted or finally fixed. Their 'cohabitation arrangements' are always subject to revision, modification and adjustment in the light of fresh understandings, new challenges, experiences of achievement, the availability of resources and the stresses arising from shortcomings (or excesses) on both sides. No authority can legislate for relationships or prescribe in advance the way they must inevitably develop. This will depend upon the day-to-day interpretations and actions, the flexibility of the partners and their mutual sensitivity and responsiveness. So too the ongoing (and constantly provisional) working out of the relationship between distinctiveness and inclusiveness within Catholic education will depend, in large part, on the day-to-day interactions and interpretations of teachers and pupils, rather than on edicts from the hierarchy of the church, or from any other source.

However, Catholic schools do not engage in the dialectic between distinctiveness and inclusiveness as if it has just arisen; they enter a debate that has a long history and they belong to a tradition from which it is wise to seek guidance. Thus (in chapter seven) the notion of living tradition was examined for the light it cast on the task of addressing this dialectic. With the help of insights from Blondel I showed that a retrieval of this notion offers a way to combine fidelity to the past and openness to the present. It also assists in the process of avoiding the opposite dangers of ossification or assimilation. If living tradition is critically appreciated and creatively appropriated, Catholic education can be distinctively holistic without undermining the autonomy of the disciplines or of pupils; it can also be inclusively open while neither abdicating its responsibility to proclaim truth nor compromising on essentials.

In chapter eight I reviewed a range of possible objections to the maintenance of separate Catholic schools. I then explored how developments in the Catholic understanding of the relationship between church and world provide a platform for a defence of the positive role which may be played by Catholic schools in society. After an exposition of a Catholic understanding of the common good I constructed a seven strand case to support the claim that Catholic schools contribute significantly to that good. A concern for the common good was shown to be an integral feature of a Catholic philosophy of education.

A creative tension, paralleling that between distinctiveness and inclusiveness, exists also between church and world and between the twin foundational principles which have received more prominence in Catholic social thought in recent years, solidarity and subsidiarity. In this context it may be argued that Catholic schools which reflect in practice their own distinctive educational philosophy will reflect this tension. On the one hand, they will offer a counter-cultural witness, one which fosters a critique of society and which prevents an over-identification with the world on the part of their pupils. On the other hand, they will avoid being elitist, divisive, isolationist or withdrawn from society. They will seek to promote among their pupils a strong sense of social responsibility, together with the understanding, capacity and commitment to build up the wider community and to strive, along with others, for the furtherance and flourishing of the common good. In supporting the maintenance of this creative tension, the use of Roman authority within the church is double edged. It can serve as a counterweight against tendencies to accommodate too readily to the various and particular secular pressures faced by Catholics. It can also, when used in a heavy-handed way, increase the secularising trends by adding to the fear and suspicion of ecclesially based forms of education and authoritarian defences of orthodoxy.

The notion of 'constitutive' communities and the principles of solidarity and subsidiarity, taken together, provide essential guidance for Catholic schools on how living tradition is to be constructed, sustained, communicated and developed. As constitutive communities, Catholic schools aim to provide a coherent curriculum which is given unity and focus by the integrating perspective of Christian faith and powerful examples of the nature, scope and costs of commitment. They do this in the context of a highly developed partnership between school home and church. By engaging pupils with a 'thick' view of the good, a coherent and comprehensive account of the world, and a living tradition, teachers in Catholic schools hope to provide a firm foundation for developing a sense of identity and belonging. They also nurture in pupils the ability and willingness to reflect critically on this tradition and to reach out to and work with others outside it.

It follows from the arguments developed throughout this book that Catholic schools should aim to promote among their pupils both a critical solidarity with tradition and a critical openness to society. Appropriation of and solidarity with the tradition should necessarily lead to a determination to extend that initial solidarity much further and to contribute positively to the wider society as well as an awareness of its shortcomings and dangers. Openness to others will entail an embracing of the many dimensions of inclusiveness which were outlined in chapter six and it will also require that the criticisms and shortcomings identified by those outside the tradition (as well as those which emerge from within it) are taken seriously.

9.3.   *An agenda for Catholic schools*

As examples of further work to be done within Catholic schools on this account one might include the following. First, the principle of subsidiarity should be applied more consistently within the church and her schools. Second, pupils in Catholic schools could be better equipped to engage effectively in a pluralist society. Third, there must be exploration of how differentiation can be applied to the area of religious differences. Fourth, Catholic schools need to reflect more rigorously on the extent to which they display a preferential option for the poor, for example, with regard to pupil admissions and exclusions and provision for pupils with special needs. Fifth, Catholic schools should examine how successfully they develop in pupils the capacity for critical questioning, both of their own tradition and of practices and philosophies in the wider society. Sixth, they must question whether sufficient 'space' is provided and respect shown for the individual freedom of pupils (for whom, unlike their parents or the teachers, school is not a voluntary community).

Part of the agenda, then, will be the application of the principles outlined here to teaching and learning, for example, in differentiation, assessment, attention to special needs and the permeation of a Catholic perspective throughout the curriculum and in pastoral care. There will be implications in several other areas too. These include the management style adopted in Catholic schools, approaches to staff development, appraisal and in-service training, modes of communication, for example with parents and governors, and the outreach work of the school to parishes and the local community.[2] If the principles of subsidiarity and solidarity outlined in chapter eight are to have credibility, further investigation of the advantages and disadvantages of an overall co-ordination of Catholic education within England and Wales would be beneficial as would further study of the possibilities of closer collaboration between Catholic schools.

9.4.   Further research needed

I suggest four additional possible directions for building on the work carried out here. First, one could explore the implications of different models of the church for Catholic schools and for the working out in them of the relationship between distinctiveness and inclusiveness.[3] Second, one might investigate the bearing of this study on non-school forms and contexts for Catholic education in faith. Third, the relevance of my treatment of distinctiveness and inclusiveness to Catholic schools in other countries could be considered. Fourth, other Christians, and indeed people of other faiths, may wish to apply my approach in this study to their own forms of faith-based education. In 1998 some Muslim schools have begun to receive official recognition and acceptance within the state system of education in the UK, as have some Christian schools which are not part of mainstream, institutional Christianity. These schools will need to give serious consideration to how many of the issues considered here: identity and diversity distinctiveness and inclusiveness, tradition and inculturation, engaging with legitimate secular educational and social requirements and promotion of the common good.

9.5.   From promulgation to reception

In exposing part of the anatomy and dynamics of the relationship between distinctiveness and inclusiveness in Catholic education I have revealed some of the tensions which exist between a Catholic and a liberal approach to education. Catholic educators might accuse liberal educators of displaying too subjective a view of morality, too anthropological a view of nature, too narrow a view of rationality and too optimistic a view of human capacities. Liberal educators, on the other hand, might challenge Catholic educators to beware of theological imperialism in their curriculum theory, to guard against indoctrination in their classroom practice, to be more inclusive in pupil admissions and staff appointments and to encourage more critical thinking when reflecting on their tradition.

The issues explored also represent wider social tensions between preserving identity and avoiding exclusion and between universalism and particularism. However, the exploration here of the problematical nature and possible coherence of distinctiveness and inclusiveness has not been exhaustive; many aspects have not been adequately examined, for example, those relating to gender, poverty, and to cultural and religious differences.[4]   Furthermore, even a more comprehensive treatment of distinctiveness and inclusiveness would still leave many unresolved issues which require attention in Catholic education, for example, issues relating to control, content, communication and evaluation.   Nevertheless, I hope that my identification and treatment of one problematic area does cast light on the spirit, sensitivity, purpose and style which should pervade Catholic education, not only in schools but in other contexts.

In chapter two I set this investigation in the context of a feature of contemporary education (and of other public services) that has the potential to damage teaching and to distort the use of authority in all schools and which poses a particular threat to Catholic schools. I called this phenomenon managerialism. A weakness of managerialism, I claimed, is an overemphasis on establishing mechanisms of control and measurement, accompanied by a failure to harness the techniques of management to an overarching and transformative 'story' that frames, inspires and directs educational and communal endeavour in the school context. In contrast, leaders liberate the talents and energies of staff and students through their ability to witness to and to embody a vision for life and learning that goes beyond personal advantage or even social welfare. This vision is not merely imposed by a person who is above or outside the school. However important and vigorous the contribution of the leader is, always there is a need to draw upon the experience and insights of others, within and beyond the school, if the vision is to be catholic or inclusive.

My attempt to regenerate a rationale for Catholic education offers one particular route towards such a 'story' or vision. The transcendent view of life inherent in that 'story' has the capacity to liberate education from the limiting perspectives and blunt tools of managerialism. It suggests that Catholic schools can be both distinctive and inclusive. I have also cited evidence suggesting that they can be effective in both religious and secular terms.[5] The qualities of distinctiveness, inclusiveness and effectiveness meet the requirements of a recent American analyst of the key issues facing Catholic schools at the start of the third millennium: 'Authenticity, access, and leadership – what are Catholic schools about, whom do they serve, and who will lead them? In my view, these are the most important issues for the future of Catholic schools.'[6]   Although I have concentrated on authenticity and access, interpreting authenticity in this book as distinctive purpose, identity and character, and interpreting access in terms of various types of inclusiveness, implications for

Catholic school leaders will have been apparent throughout various chapters. Catholic school leaders should, as a result of my articulation of the double imperative or two polarities examined here, feel clearer about what their leadership is *for*, what they should advocate, promote and defend. They should also feel clearer about *how* it should be conducted.[7]

The exercise of leadership in Catholic schools should reflect the shift in approach to authority that has been seen in the Church more widely, from an emphasis on the power of office to a more participative and inclusive style. At the start of the twenty-first century, schools in particular and the Church in general need leaders who listen, empower others to share in leadership, release the gifts of others, learn from their experience, serve and are self-giving. This is in stark contrast with the mentality that prevailed at the beginning of the twentieth century.

In the hierarchy alone resides the power and authority necessary to move and direct all the members of the society to its end. As for the many, they have no other right than to let themselves be guided and so follow their pastors in docility.[8]

A hundred years on, we need to ensure, not only that a clear vision illuminates our work, but also that this vision is constantly informed, re-interpreted and, where appropriate, adapted, through 'feedback' from those who try to implement it. In this way there will be a dialogical and reciprocal relationship between precept and practice. As an Australian expert on Catholic education puts it, 'It is only when the community as a whole is able to share in the leadership of the school, that the school community can start to grow in the image of Christ.'[9]

My contention has been that the nurturing of inclusiveness and the promotion of the common good both can and should be well served by Catholic schools that are inspired by a distinctive philosophy of education. I have also argued that the distinctive approach to education, arising from a Catholic philosophy of life, itself needs to be retrieved, preserved and articulated with clarity, confidence and charity by those who work in Catholic schools in order that it can be applied with greater consistency and effectiveness.

Until now the emphasis in 'official' and normative statements on Catholic education has been on *promulgation* of church teaching: the assertion, reiteration, clarification and defence of its distinctive nature. It follows from the argument developed here that in future much more attention will have to be given, within Catholic educational circles, to *reception* of church teaching: to attending to and learning from the experience and perspectives of those 'on the ground', trying to put the principles into practice. If that happens, then it will become clearer that distinctiveness and inclusiveness are integrally related, mutually qualifying and reciprocally interactive features of Catholic education.

Notes for Chapter 9

[1] See Kevin Williams, 'Education and human diversity: the ethics of separate schooling revisited', *British Journal of Educational Studies*, vol. 46, no. 1, 1998, pp.26-39.

[2] On issues to be addressed in Catholic schools of the future, see *From Ideal To Action*, edited by Matthew Feheney, Dublin, Veritas, 1998, chapters 13 to 15 (by Andrew Greeley, Gerald Grace and Matthew Feheney respectively). See also John Sullivan, *Catholic Schools in Contention*, Dublin, Veritas, 2000.

[3] See Sullivan, 2000, *op. cit.*

[4] On feminism in the Catholic school, see the chapter of that title by Bernadette Flanagan in *From Ideal To Action*. On issues of social justice and on the potential impact of liberation theology for the practice of Catholic education, see Thomas Oldenski, *Liberation Theology and Critical Pedagogy in Today's Catholic Schools*, New York, Garland Publishing, 1997.

[5] In addition to references provided for chapter eight, see John Convey, *Catholic Schools Make a Difference*, Washington, DC, National Catholic Educational Association, 1992.

[6] Michael Guerra, in *Catholic School Leadership*, edited by Thomas Hunt (et al), London, Falmer Press, 2000, p.88.

[7] On new understandings of authority and leadership within the Church, see David Stagaman, *Authority in the Church*, Collegeville, Minnesota, The Liturgical Press, 1999.

[8] Pope Pius X, *Vehementer Nos*, 1906, quoted by Denis McLaughlin in *Leading the Catholic School*, edited by John McMahon, 1997, p.12.

[9] Denis McLaughlin, ibid., p.25.

BIBLIOGRAPHY

Abbott, W, (ed) *The Documents of Vatican II*, London, Geoffrey Chapman, 1967

Achtemeier, P. M, `The Truth of Tradition: Critical Realism in the Thought of Alasdair MacIntyre and T.F Torrance`, *Scottish Journal of Theology*, Vol.47, No.3, 1994, pp.355-374

Akhtar, S, 'Muslims and their schools', *The Tablet*, 14/2/98, p.208.

Almond, B, `Alasdair MacIntyre: the virtue of tradition`, *Journal of Applied Philosophy*, vol. 7, No. 3, 1990, pp.99-103

Amilburu, M, (ed) *Education, the State & the Multicultural Challenge*, Pamplona, Ediciones Universidad de Navarra, 1996

Anglican - Roman Catholic International Commission, *Life in Christ*, London, Catholic Truth Society and Church House Publishing, 1994

Angus, L. B., *Continuity and Change in Catholic Schooling*, London, Falmer, 1988

Archard, D, *Children: Rights and Childhood*, London, Routledge, 1993

Archard, D, (ed) *Philosophy and Pluralism*, Cambridge, Cambridge University Press, 1996

Archer, A, *The Two Catholic Churches*, London, SCM, 1986

Aretin, K.O. von, *The Papacy in the Modern World*, London, Weidenfeld and Nicholson, 1970

Arthur, J, 'Catholic Responses to the 1988 Education Reform Act: Problems of Authority and Ethos', *British Journal of Religious Education*, vol. 13, No. 3, 1991, pp.181-189

Arthur, J, 'The Ambiguities of Catholic Schooling', *Westminster Studies in Education*, vol. 19, 1994, pp.65-77

Arthur, J, 'Admissions to Catholic Schools: principles and practice', *British Journal of Religious Education*, vol. 17, No. 1, 1994, pp.35-45

Arthur, J, 'Teaching and Employment Conditions in Catholic Schools', *Law & Justice*, no.124/125, 1995, pp.40-53

Arthur, J, *The Ebbing Tide*, Leominster, Gracewing, 1995

Arthur, J, 'A Catholic Policy on Teachers?', *Educational Management & Administration*, vol. 23, No. 4, 1995, pp.254-259

Arthur, J, 'Government Education Policy and Catholic Voluntary Aided Schools 1979-1994', *Oxford Review of Education*, vol. 21, No. 4, 1995, pp.447-455

Arthur, J, Walters, H, and Gaine, S, *Earthen Vessels*, Leominster, Gracewing, 1999

Ashraf, S. A. and Hirst, P, (eds) *Religion and Education: Islamic & Christian Approaches* Cambridge, The Islamic Academy, 1994

Ashton, E, & Watson, B, (eds) *Society in Conflict: The Value of Education*, The University of Hull (*Aspects of Education*, no 51), 1994

Aspin, D, `Church Schools, religious education and the multi-ethnic community`, *Journal of Philosophy of Education*, vol. 17, no. 2, 1983, pp.229-240

Astley, J, and Day, D, (eds) *The Contours of Christian Education*, Great Wakering, Essex, McCrimmons, 1992

Astley, J, and Francis, L, (eds) *Critical Perspectives on Christian Education*, Leominster, Gracewing, 1994

Astley, J, and Francis, L, (eds) *Christian Theology and Religious Education: Connections & Contradictions*, London, SPCK, 1996

Astley, J, and Francis, L and Crowder, C, (eds) *Theological Perspectives on Christian Formation*, Leominster, Gracewing, 1996

Audi, R, *Religious Commitment and Secular Reason*, Cambridge, Cambridge University Press, 2000

Aviram, A, 'Autonomy and Commitment: compatible ideals', *Journal of Philosophy of Education*, vol. 29, no. 1, 1995, pp.61-73

Badley, K, 'The Faith/Learning Integration Movement in Christian Higher Education: Slogan or Substance?', *Journal of Christian Education*, vol. 3, no. 1, 1994, pp.17-33

Badley, K, 'Two 'Cop-Outs' in Faith-Learning Integration', *Spectrum*, vol. 28, no. 2, 1996, pp.105-118

Ball, S, *Education Reform*, Buckingham, Open University Press, 1994

Ball, S, Gewirtz, S and Bowe, R, *Markets, Choice and Equity in Education*, Buckingham, Open University Press, 1995

Bailey, C, *Beyond the Present and Particular*, London, Routledge & Kegan Paul, 1984

Barmann, L, (ed) *The Letters of Baron Friedrich von Hügel & Professor Norman Kemp Smith*, New York, Fordham University Press, 1981

Barmann, L, 'Friedrich von Hügel as Modernist and as more than Modernist', *The Catholic Historical Review*, 1989, pp.211-232.

Barnes, M, *Religions in Conversation*, London, SPCK, 1989

Barnett, R, *The Limits of Competence*, London, Open University Press, 1994

Barrow, R, and White, P, (eds) *Beyond Liberal Education*, London, Routledge, 1993

Barrow, R, 'Denominational Schools and Public Schooling', *Interchange*, vol. 24, no. 3, 1993, pp.225-232

Baum, G, *Man Becoming*, New York, Herder and Herder, 1970

Baxter, M, and Bauerschmitt, F, '*Eruditio* without *religio*?: The dilemma of Catholics in the academy?', *Communio*, vol..XXII, no. 2, 1995, pp.284-302

Bayldon, M, '*Gravissimum Educationis* 30 years on', *New Blackfriars*, March, 1996, pp.131-136

Beavis, A, and Ross Thomas, A, 'Metaphor as Storehouses of Expectation', *Educational Management & Administration*, vol. 24, no. 1, 1996, pp.93-106

Bellah, R., et al, *Habits of the Heart*, London, Hutchinson, 1988

Bellah, R, et al, *The Good Society*, New York, Vintage Books, Random House, 1992

Benestad, B, 'Catholicism & American Public Philosophy', *Review of Politics*, 53 (Fall), 1991, pp.691-711

Bernadin, J, 'The Common Ground Project - Called to be Catholic', *Doctrine & Life*, vol. 46, October, 1996, pp.490-496

Berger, P, *The Sacred Canopy*, New York, Doubleday, 1969

Berger, P, *A Rumour of Angels*, London, Penguin, 1970

Berger, P, *The Social Construction of Reality*, London, Penguin, 1971

Berger, P, with Berger, B, and Kellner, H, *The Homeless Mind*, London, Penguin, 1974

Berger, P, *The Heretical Imperative*, London, Collins, 1980

Bernstein, R, *Beyond Objectivism and Relativism*, Oxford, Basil Blackwell, 1983

Bishops Conference of England and Wales, *The Sign We Give*, Chelmsford, Matthew James Publishing, 1995

Bishops Conference of England and Wales, *Education in Catholic Schools and Colleges: Principles, Practices and Concerns*, Manchester, Gabriel Communications, 1996

Bishops Conference of England and Wales, *The Common Good and Catholic Social Teaching*, Manchester, Gabriel Communications, 1996

Bishops Conference of England and Wales, *Religious Education: Curriculum Directory for Catholic Schools*, London, 1996

Bishops Conference of England and Wales, *Catholic Schools & Other Faiths*, London, 1997

Bishops Conference of England and Wales, *Partners in Mission*, Chelmsford, Matthew James Publishing, 1997

Bishops Conference of England and Wales, *The Common Good in Education*, London, CES, 1997

Bishops' Conference of England and Wales, *A Struggle for Excellence: Catholic Secondary Schools in Urban Poverty Areas*, London, Catholic Education Service, 1997

Bishops' Conference of England and Wales, *Foundations for Excellence*, Chelmsford, Matthew James Publishing, 1999

Blake, N, 'Church Schools, Religious Education & the multi-ethnic community: a reply to David Aspin', *Journal of Philosophy of Education*, vol. 17, no. 2, 1983, pp.241-250

Bliss, F, *Understanding Reception*, Milwaukee, Marquette University Press, 1994

Blondel, M, *La Philosophie et L'Esprit Chrétien*, vol. II Paris, Presses Universitaires de France, 1946

Blondel, M, *Exigences Philosophiques du Christianisme*, Paris, Presses Universitaires de France, 1950

Blondel, M, *Les Premiers Écrits de Maurice Blondel*, Paris, Presses Universitaires de France, 1956

Blondel, M, *Blondel - Laberthonnière: Correspondance Philosophique*, Paris, Éditions du Seuil, 1961

Blondel, M, *Carnets Intimes*, vol. I, Paris, Les Éditions du Cerf, 1961

Blondel, M, *Carnets Intimes*, vol. II, Paris, Les Éditions du Cerf, 1966

Blondel, M, *Letter on Apologetics and History and Dogma*, edited by A. Dru and I Trethowan, London, Harvill Press, 1964 (reissued Edinburgh, T & T Clark, 1995)

Blondel, M, *L'Action*, Paris, Presses Universitaires de France, 1973

Blondel, M, *Oeuvres Complètes*, Paris, Presses Universitaires de France, 1995, 1997

Board of Education of the General Synod of the Church of England, *Tomorrow is Another Country: education in a post- modern world*, The National Society, London, 1996

Boff, L, *Church, Charism & Power*, London, SCM Press, 1985

Bottery, M, 'Education and the Convergence of Management Codes', *Educational Studies*, vol.20, no.3, 1994, pp.329-343

Boys, M, *Educating in Faith: Maps and Visions*, San Francisco, Harper & Row, 1989

Boys, M, (ed) *Educating for Citizenship & Discipleship*, New York, Pilgrim Press, 1989

Bradford, J, *Caring for the Whole Child*, London, The Children's Society, 1995

Brennan, J, *The Christian Management of Catholic Schools*, Northampton, The Becket Press, 1994

Bridges, D, & McLaughlin, T, (eds) *Education in the Market Place*, London, Falmer Press, 1994

Brinkman, B, 'Due Veduta di Roma', *The Heythrop Journal*, vol. 37, no. 2, April 1996, pp.176-192

Brown, D, *Boundaries of our Habitations*, New York, State University of New York Press, 1994

Bruner, J, *The Culture of Education*, Cambridge, Mass, Harvard University Press, 1996

Bryk, A, Lee, V and Holland, P, (eds) *Catholic Schools and the Common Good*, London, Harvard University Press, 1993

Buber, M, *Between Man and Man*, London, Fontana, 1974

Buchman, M, and Floden, R, (eds) *Detachment and Concern*, London, Cassell, 1993

Budziszewski, J, *True Tolerance: Liberalism and the Necessity of Judgment*, New Brunswick, New Jersey, Transaction Publishers, 1992

Buckley, M, *The Promise and Project of the Catholic University*, 1999

Buetow, H, *The Catholic School: Its Roots, Identity, & Future*, New York, Crossroad, 1988

Buhlmann,W, *With Eyes To See*, Slough, St Paul Publications, 1990

Burns, G, *The Frontiers of Catholicism: The Politics of Ideology in a Liberal World*, Berkeley, University of California Press, 1994

Burtonwood, N, 'Beyond Culture: a Reply to Mark Halstead', *Journal of Philosophy of Education*, vol. 30, no 2, 1996, pp.295-299

Burwood, L, 'How Should Schools Respond to the Plurality of Values in a Multi-cultural Society?', *Journal of Philosophy of Education*, vol. 30, no. 3, 1996, pp.415-427

Bush, T, and West-Burnham-West, J, (eds) *Principles of Educational Management*, Harlow, Longman, 1994

Cahill, L. S., 'The Catholic Tradition: Religion, Morality, & the Common Good', *The Journal of Law & Religion*, vol.50, no.1, 1987, pp.75-94

Cahill, W, 'Why Greenfield? The Relevance of T. B. Greenfield's Theories to Catholic Education', *Educational Management & Administration*, vol. 22, no. 4, 1994, pp.251-259

Caldecott, S, and Morrill, J, (eds) *Eternity in Time*, Edinburgh, T & T Clark, 1997

Callan, E, 'The Great Sphere: Education against Servility', *Journal of Philosophy of Education*, vol. 31, no. 2, 1997, pp.221- 232

Callan, E, *Creating Citizens*, Oxford, Oxford University Press, 1997

Carey, P, & Muller, E, *Theological Education in the Catholic Tradition*, New York, Crossroad, 1997

Carmody, B, 'A Context for the Catholic Philosophy of Education', *Lumen Vitae*, vol.36, 1981, pp.45-61

Carney, P, 'Black pride on Moss Side', *The Tablet*, 11/10/97, p.1294

Carr, D, 'Education & Values', *British Journal of Educational Studies*, vol. XXXIX, no. 3, 1991, pp.244-259

Carr, D, *Educating the Virtues*, London, Routledge, 1991

Carr, D, 'Questions of Competence', *British Journal of Educational Studies*, vol. XXXXI, no. 3, 1993, pp.253-271

Carr, D, 'Spiritual Education: Towards a Distinctive Conception', *Oxford Review of Education*, vol. 21, no.1, 1995, pp.83-98

Carr, D, *The Moral Role of the Teacher*, Edinburgh, Scottish Consultative Council on the Curriculum,

1996

Carr, D, 'Songs of Immanence & Transcendence', *Oxford Review of Education*, vol.22, no.4, 1996, pp.457-463

Carr, D, 'Rival Conceptions of Spiritual Education', *Journal of Philosophy of Education*, vol. 30, no. 2, 1996, pp.159-178

Carr, T, *Newman and Gadamer*, Atlanta, Georgia, Scholars Press, 1996

Carr, W, 'Education and Democracy: confronting the postmodern challenge', *Journal of Philosophy of Education*, vol. 29, no. 1, 1995, pp.75-91

Carr, W, and Naish, M, *Education and the Struggle for Democracy*, Buckingham, Open University Press, 1996

Carr, W, 'Professing Education in a Postmodern Age', *Journal of Philosophy of Education*, vol. 31, no. 2, 1997, pp.309-327

Carroll, D, (ed) *Religion in Ireland: Past, Present & Future*, Dublin, Columba Press, 1999

Carter, S, *The Culture of Disbelief*, New York, Doubleday, 1994

Cassidy, E, 'Irish Educational Policy in a Philosophical Perspective: The Legacy of Liberalism', in *Religion, Education and the Constitution*, edited by Dermot Lane, Dublin, The Columba Press, 1992

Cassidy, E, (ed) *Faith & Culture in the Irish Context*, Dublin, Veritas Publications, 1996

Catechism of the Catholic Church, London, Geoffrey Chapman, 1994

Catholic Education Service, *Governing a Catholic School* (1 & 2), London, 1992, 1994

Catholic Education Service, *The Mission Statement into Action*, London, 1992

Catholic Education Service, *Evaluating the Distinctive Nature of a Catholic School*, (4th edition), London, 1999

Catholic Education Service, *The Inspection of Catholic Schools*, London, 1994

Catholic Education Service, *Social and Moral Education in Catholic Schools*, 1994

Catholic Education Service, *Education in Sexuality*, London, 1994

Catholic Education Service, *What Are We to Teach?*, London, 1994

Catholic Education Service, *Induction of Teachers*, London, CES, 1995

Catholic Education Service, *Spiritual & Moral Development Across the Curriculum*, London, 1995

Catholic Education Service, *Quality of Education in Catholic Secondary Schools*, London, 1995

Catholic Education Service, *Partnership in the Training of Teachers for Catholic Schools*, 1995

Catholic Education Service, *Learning from OFSTED and Diocesan Inspection and The Distinctive Nature of Education in Catholic Primary and Secondary Schools*, London, 1996

Catholic Education Service, *Differentiation: A Catholic Response*, London, 1997

Cernera, A, (ed) *Continuity and Plurality in Catholic Theology*, Fairfield, Connecticut, Sacred Heart University Press, 1998

Cernera, A, and Morgan, O, (eds) *Examining the Catholic Intellectual Tradition*, Fairfield, Connecticut, Sacred Heart University Press, 2000

Chadwick, O, *The Secularization of the European Mind*, Cambridge, Cambridge University Press, 1978

Chadwick, P, *Schools of Reconciliation*, London, Cassell, 1994

Chadwick, P, *Shifting Alliances: Church and State in English Education*, London, Cassell, 1997

Chesterton, G.K, 'The New Case for Catholic Schools' in *The Common Man*, London, 1950

Cock, A, *A Critical Examination of Von Hügel's Philosophy of Religion*, London, distributed by Hugh Rees, no publisher indicated, 1948

Coleman, J, *High School Achievement*, New York, Basic Books, 1982

Coleman, J, *Public and Private High Schools*, New York, Basic Books, 1987

Comby, J, with MacCulloch, D, *How to Read Church History*, vol. 2, London, SCM Press, 1989

Commission for Racial Equality, *Schools of Faith. Religious Schools in a Multicultural Society*, London, 1990

Congar, Y, *Tradition and the Life of the Church*, translated by A. N. Woodrow, London, Burns & Oates, 1964

Congregation for Catholic Education, *Directives Concerning the Preparation of Seminary Educators*, Boston, St Paul Books, 1994

Congregation for the Clergy, *General Directory for Catechesis*, London, Catholic Truth Society, 1997

Congregation for Institutes of Consecrated Life and for Societies of Apostolic Life, *Inter-Institute Collaboration for Formation*, Boston, Pauline Books, 1999

Conrad, R, *The Catholic Faith: A Dominican's Vision*, London, Geoffrey Chapman, 1994

Convey, J, *Catholic Schools make a Difference*, Washington DC, National Catholic Educational Association, 1992

Cooling, T, *A Christian Vision for State Education*, London, SPCK, 1994

Cooper, D, 'Strategies of Power: Legislating Worship and Religious Education' in *The Impact of Michel Foucault on the Social Sciences and Humanities*, edited by Moya Lloyd & Andrew Thacker, Macmillan, 1997

Council for Catholic Maintained Schools, *Life to the Full: A Vision for Catholic Education*, Dublin, Veritas, 1996

Coutagne, M.J., *L'Action. Une dialectique du salut*, Paris, Beauchesne, 1994

Coutagne, M.J, *Maurice Blondel, Professeur*, forthcoming

Crosby, J, *The Selfhood of the Human Person*, Washington, DC, The Catholic University of America Press, 1996

Curran, C, *The Living Tradition of Catholic Moral Theology*, Notre Dame, Indiana, University of Notre Dame Press, 1992

Curran, C, 'The Catholic Identity of Catholic Institutions', *Theological Studies*, vol. 58, No. 1,March 1997, pp.90-108

Darling-Smith, B, (ed) *Can Virtue Be Taught?*, Notre Dame, Indiana, University of Notre Dame Press, 1993

Davie, G, *Religion in Britain Since 1945: Believing Without Belonging*, Oxford, Blackwell, 1994

Davies, B, and West-Burnham, J, (eds) *Reengineering and Total Quality in Schools*, London, Pitman, 1997

Davies, B, and Ellison, L, *School Leadership for the Twenty-First Century*, London, Routledge, 1997

Davies, B, *The Thought of Thomas Aquinas*, Oxford, Clarendon Press, 1992

Dawson, C, *The Crisis of Western Education*, London, Sheed & Ward, 1961

Dent, N, *The Moral Psychology of Virtue*, Cambridge, Cambridge University Press, 1984

Dent, R, *Faith of Our Fathers: Roman Catholic Schools in a Multi-Faith Society*, Coventry Education Department, 1992

Department for Education (& Welsh Office), *Code of Practice on the Identification and Assessment of Special Educational Needs*, 1994

Department for Education, Circular 6/94: *The Organisation of Special Educational Provision*, 1994

Donovan, P, 'The Intolerance of Religious Pluralism', *Religious Studies*, vol.29, no.2, 1993, pp.217-230

Doohan, L, *The Lay-Centered Church*, Minneapolis, Winston Press, 1984

Douglass, R.B., 'Public Philosophy & Contemporary Pluralism', *Thought*, 64, December, 1989, pp.344-361

Douglass, R.B., *et al.* (eds), *Liberalism and the Good*, New York, Routledge, 1990

Douglass, R B., and Hollenbach, D, (eds), *Catholicism and Liberalism*, Cambridge, Cambridge University Press, 1994

Doyle, D, *Communion Ecclesiology*, New York, Orbis, 2000

Duffy, S, *The Graced Horizon*, Collegeville, Minnesota, The Liturgical Press, 1992

Dulles, A, *Models of the Church*, Dublin, Gill and Macmillan, 1974

Dulles, A, *Models of Revelation*, Dublin, Gill & Macmillan, 1983

Dulles, A, *The Catholicity of the Church*, Oxford, Clarendon Press, 1985

Dulles, A, *Assurance of Things Hoped For*, New York, Oxford University Press, 1994

Dulles, A, 'Criteria of Catholic theology', *Communio*, vol. XXII, no.2, 1995, pp.303-315

Dunne, J, 'The Catholic School & Civil Society: exploring the tensions', in *The Catholic School in Contemporary Society*, The Conference of Major Religious Superiors, Dublin, 1991

Dunne, J, *Back to the Rough Ground: `Phronesis` & `Techne` in Modern Philosophy & in Aristotle*, University of Notre Dame Press, 1993

Dnne, J, 'Philosophies of the Self and the Scope of Education', in Papers of the Philosophy of education Society of Great Britain Conference, Oxford, 1995, pp.170-180

Dupré, L, 'Catholic Education and the Predicament of Modern Culture', *Living Light*, vol.23, 1987, pp.295-305

Dupuis, J, *Toward a Christian Theology of Religious Pluralism*, New York, Orbis, 1999

Dwyer, J, *Catholic Schools and Catholic Social principles: a comparative study of Australia, England & Wales , & the USA*, PhD thesis, London University Institute of Education, 1991

Dwyer, J, & Montgomery, E.L., (eds) *The New Dictionary of Catholic Social Thought*, Collegeville, Minnesota, Liturgical Press, 1994
Dwyer, J, *Religious Schools v. Children's Rights*, Ithaca, N.Y., Cornell University Press, 1998
Dykstra, C, *Vision & Character*, New York, Paulist Press, 1981

Eade, R, (1996) 'The Christian Ministry of Church School Headship', *Spectrum*, 28:1, pp.55-67
Eaton, M, Longmore, J, and Naylor, A, (eds) *Commitment to Diversity: Catholics and Education in a Changing World*, London, Cassell, 2000
Egan, Sr J, *Opting Out: Catholic Schools Today*, Leominster, Fowler Wright Books, 1988
Eisner, E, *The Enlightened Eye*, New York, Macmillan, 1991
Elwes, T, (ed) *Women's Voices: Essays in Contemporary* Theology, London, Marshal Pickering, 1992
Endean, P, 'The Responsibility of theology for Spiritual Growth and pastoral care', *New Blackfriars*, vol. 81, No. 947, January 2000
Etzioni, A, *The Spirit of Community*, London, Fontana, 1995
Evans, J, & Ward, L, (eds) *The Social and Political Philosophy of Jacques Maritain*, London, Geoffrey Bles, 1956
Evans, J, (ed) *Jacques Maritain: The Man and His Achievement*, New York, Sheed & Ward, 1963

Farber, P, 'Tongue Tied: On Taking Religion Seriously in School', *Educational Theory*, vol. 45, no. 1, 1995, pp.85-100
Farley, E, 'Can church education be theological education?', in *Theological Perspectives on Christian Formation*, edited by Jeff Astley, Leslie Francis and Colin Crowder, Leominster, Gracewing, 1996
Feheney, M, (ed) *Education and the Family*, Dublin, Veritas, 1995
Feheny, M, (ed) *From Ideal to Action: The Inner Nature of a Catholic School Today*, Dublin, Veritas, 1998
Ferguson, T, *Catholic & American: the political theology of John Courtney Murray*, New York, Sheed & Ward, 1993
Ferrari, J, *Recherches Blondeliennes*, Dijon, Éditions Universitaires de Dijon, 1994
Finucane, D, *Sensus Fidelium*: The Uses of a Concept in the Post-Vatican II Era, Catholic Scholars Press, 1996
Fletcher, G, *Loyalty*, Oxford, Oxford University Press, 1993
Flynn M, *The Culture of Catholic Schools* Homebush, New South Wales, Australia, St Pauls, 1993
Focant, C, (ed) *L'Enseignement de la religion au carrefour de la théologie et de la pédagogie*, Louvain-la Neuve, 1994
Folscheid, D, (ed) *Maurice Blondel: Une dramatique de la modernité*, Paris, Éditions Universitaires, 1990
Fortin, E, 'Thomas Aquinas & the Reform of Christian Education', *Interpretation*, vol.17, no.1, 1989, pp.3-17
Fossion, A, *La Catéchèse dans le champ de la communication*, Paris, Cerf, 1990
Fouilloux, E, *Une Eglise en quête de liberté*, Paris, Desclée, 1998
Francis, L, & Lankshear, D, (eds) *Critical Perspectives on Church Schools*, Leominster, Gracewing, 1993
Fraser, J, *Between Church and State: Religion and Public Education in America*, New York, Macmillan Press, 1999

Gadamer, H.G, *Truth and Method*, translated by Joel Weinsheimer & Donald Marshall, Second revised edition, New York, Crossroad, 1989
Gaine, M, 'Roman Catholic Educational Policy', in *Religious Education: Drift or Decision?*, edited by Philip Jebb, London, Darton, Longman & Todd, 1968
Gallagher, J, *Soil for the Seed*, Great Wakering, McCrimmons, 2001
Gallagher, M.P., 'The New Agenda of Unbelief and Faith', in *Religion and Culture in Dialogue*, edited by Dermot Lane, Dublin, The Columba Press, 1993
Gallagher, M.P., *Clashing Symbols*, London, Darton, Longman & Todd, 1997
Gallagher, S, *Hermeneutics & Education*, New York, State University of New York Press, 1992
Gallin, A, *Negotiating Identity*, University of Notre Dame Press, 2000
Garrison, J, and Rud, A, (eds) *The Educational Conversation*, Albany, New York, State University of New York Press, 1995

Garver, E, *Aristotle' Rhetoric: An Art of Character*, Chicago, The University of Chicago Press, 1994

Gauthier, P, *Newman et Blondel*, Paris, Les Éditions du Cerf, 1988

Gilkey, L, *Catholicism Confronts Modernity*, New York, Seabury, 1975

Gillis, C, *Roman Catholicism in America*, New York, Columbia University Press, 1999

Gleason, P, *Contending With Modernity*, Oxford, Oxford University Press, 1995

Glenn, C, *The Ambiguous Embrace*, Princeton University Press, 2000

Golby, M, 'Communitarianism and Education' (unpublished) in Papers of Philosophy of Education Society of Great Britain Conference, Oxford, 1996, pp.149-155

Grace, G, *School Leadership*, London, Falmer Press, 1995

Grace, G, 'Realising the Mission: Catholic approaches to school effectiveness' in *Effective for Whom? School Effectiveness & the School Improvement Movement*, edited by R. Slee *et al*, London, Falmer Press, 1997

Grace, G, 'Is the a sea-change in Catholic Education?' unpublished paper

Grace, G, 'Critical Policy Scholarship: Reflections on the Integrity of Knowledge and Research', in *Being Reflexive in Critical Educational and Social Research*, edited by Geoffrey Shacklock and John Smyth, London, Falmer Press, 1998

Grasso, K, Bradley, G, and Hunt, R, (eds) *Catholicism, Liberalism & Communitarianism*, Lanham, Maryland, Rowman & Littlefield Publishers, 1995

Greeley, A, *Catholic High Schools and Minority Students*, New Brunswick, N.J, Transaction Press, 1982

Greeley, A, 'What Use Are Catholic Schools in America?', *Doctrine and Life*, vol.47, 1997, pp.77-81

Green, T, *Walls: Education in Communities of Text and Liturgy*, University of Notre Dame Press, 2002

Groome, T.H., *Christian Religious Education*, San Francisco, Harper & Row, 1981

Groome, T.H., *Sharing Faith*, San Francisco, Harper, 1991

Groome, T.H., *Educating For Life*, Allen, Texas, Thomas More Press, 1998

Gruchy, J de, *Christianity and Democracy*, Cambridge, Cambridge University Press, 1995

Gula, R, *Reason Informed by Faith*, Mahwah, New Jersey, Paulist Press, 1989

Gunter, H, *Rethinking Education*, London, Cassell, 1997

Gunton, C, *The One, The Three and The Many*, Cambridge, Cambridge University Press, 1993

Hager, P, 'Relational Realism and Professional Performance', unpublished paper for Philosophy of Education Society of Great Britain Conference, Oxford, 1996, pp.163-170

Haight, R, `The Church as Locus of Theology`, *Concilium*, 1994/6, London, SCM, pp.13-22

Haldane, J, `Critical Orthodoxy `, *Louvain Studies*, vol. 14, 1989, pp.108-124

Haldane, J, `Chesterton`s Philosophy of Education`, *Philosophy*, vol. 65, 1990, pp.65-80

Haldane, J, (ed) *Education, Values & Culture*, University of St Andrews, Centre for Philosophy & Public Affairs, 1992

Haldane, J, and Carr, D, (eds) *Values and Values Education*, University of St Andrews, Centre for Philosophy & Public Affairs, 1993

Haldane, J, `Education: Conserving Tradition`, in *An Introduction to Applied Philosophy*, edited by Almond, B Oxford, Blackwell, 1994

Haldane, J, (ed) *Education, Values and the State*, University of St Andrews, Centre for Philosophy & Public Affairs, 1994

Haldane, J 'Philosophy & Catholic Education', *The Sower*, April, 1995, pp.30-31

Halstead, J.M, *The Case for Muslim Voluntary Aided Schools*, Cambridge, The Islamic Academy, 1986

Halstead, J.M., 'Voluntary Apartheid? Problems of schooling for religious & other minorities in democratic societies', *Journal of Philosophy of Education*, vol.29, no.2, 1995, pp.257-272

Halstead, J.M., ' Should Schools Reinforce Children's Religious Identity?', *Religious Education*, vol. 90, nos3/4, 1995, pp.360-376

Halstead, J.M., & Taylor, M, (eds) *Values in Education & Education in Values*, London, Falmer Press, 1996

Hannon, P, *Church, State, Morality & Law*, Dublin, Gill and Macmillan, 1992

Hanson, A & R, *Reasonable Belief*, Oxford, Oxford University Press, 1981

Hastings, A, *The History of English Christianity 1920 -1990*, London, Burns & Oates, 1986

Hauerwas, S, *A Community of Character*, Notre Dame, University of Notre Dame Press, 1981

Hauerwas, S, and Westerhoff, J, (eds) *Schooling Christians*, Grand Rapids, Michigan, Eerdmans, 1992

Hauerwas, S, *In Good Company: The Church as Polis*, Notre Dame, Indiana, University of Notre Dame

Press, 1995

Hay, D, 'Morals and religion', in *The Tablet*, 3/2/96, p.132.

Haydon, G, 'Conceptions of the Secular in Society, Polity and Schools', *Journal of Philosophy of Education*, vol. 28, no. 1, 1994, pp.65-75

Haydon, G, 'Thick or Thin? The Cognitive Content of Moral Education in a Plural Democracy', *Journal of Moral Education*, vol.24, no.1, 1995, pp.53-64

Haydon, G, *Teaching About Values*, London, Cassell, 1997

Hebblethwaite, B, *The Adequacy of Christian Ethics*, London, Marshall Morgan and Scott, 1981

Heft, J, *A Catholic Modernity?* New York, Oxford University Press, 1999

Heie, H, & Wolfe, D, (eds) *The Reality of Christian Learning*, Grand Rapids, Eerdmans, 1987

Hervieu-Léger, D, *La Religion Pour Mémoire*, Paris, Cerf, 1993

Heslop, R, 'The Practical Value of Philosophical Thought for the Ethical Dimension of Educational Leadership', *Educational Administration Quarterly*, vol. 33, no.1, 1997, pp.67-85

Heyd, D, (ed) *Toleration: An Elusive Virtue*, Princeton, Princeton University Press, 1996

Hick, J, and Hebblethwaite, B, (eds) *Christianity and other Religions*, Glasgow, Collins, 1980

Higgins, 'The significance of postliberalism for religious education', in *Theological Perspectives on Christian Formation*, edited by Astley, Francis and Crowder, 1996

Hill, E, *Ministry and Authority in the Catholic Church*, London, Geoffrey Chapman, 1988

Himes, M, & Pope, S, (eds) *Finding God in All Things*, New York, Crossroad Herder, 1996

Hogan, P, (ed) *Partnership and the Benefits of Learning*, Maynooth, Educational Studies Association of Ireland, 1995

Hogan, P, *The Custody and Courtship of Experience: Western Education in Philosophical Perspective*, Dublin, The Columba Press, 1995

Hogan, P, 'Identity, Difference and the Epiphanies of Learning', unpublished paper delivered at Philosophy of Education Society of Great Britain Conference, Oxford, 1997, pp.213-223

Hogan, P, & Williams, K, (eds) *The Future of Religion in Irish Education*, Dublin, Veritas, 1997

Hogan, P, 'Europe and the World of Learning: Orthodoxy and Aspiration in the Wake of Modernity', *Journal of Philosophy of Education*, vol. 32, (3), 1998

Holmes, D, and Bickers, B, *A Short History of the Catholic Church*, Tunbridge Wells, Burns & Oates, 1983

Holmes, M, *Educational Policy for the Pluralist Democracy*, London, Falmer Press, 1992

Holmes, M, 'The Place of Religion in Public Education', *Interchange*, vol.24, no.3, 1993, pp.205-224

Hooper, J.L., (ed) *Bridging the Sacred and the Secular: selected writings of John Courtney Murray*, Washington, DC, Georgetown University Press, 1994

Hornsby-Smith, M, 'A Sociological Case for Catholic Schools', *The Month*, October, 1972, pp.298-304

Hornsby-Smith, M, *Catholic Education: The Unobtrusive Partner*, London, Sheed & Ward, 1978

Hornsby-Smith, M, *Roman Catholics in England*, Cambridge, Cambridge University Press, 1987

Hornsby-Smith, M, *Roman Catholic Beliefs in England: Customary Catholicism & transformations of religious authority*, Cambridge, Cambridge University Press, 1991

Hornsby-Smith, M, 'Transformations in English Catholicism: Evidence of Secularisation?', in *Religion and Modernization*, edited by Steve Bruce, Oxford, Clarendon Press, 1992

Hornsby-Smith, M, 'The Catholic Church and Education in Britain: From the "Intransigence" of "Closed" Catholicism to the Accommodation Strategy of "Open" Catholicism', in *Catholicism in Britain and France Since 1789*, edited by Frank Tallett and Nicholas Atkin, London, Hambledon Press, 1996

Hornsby-Smith, M, *Catholics in Britain 1950-2000*, London, Cassell, 1999

Horton, J, (ed) *Liberalism, Multiculturalism & Toleration*, London, Macmillan, 1993

Hostetler, K, 'The Scope & Virtue of Educational Tolerance', *Philosophy of Education*, University of Illinois, 1995, pp.456-459

Hügel, F von, *The Mystical Element of Religion*, (in two volumes) London, Dent, 1908

Hügel, F. von, *Eternal Life*, Edinburgh, T & T Clark, 1913

Hügel, F. von, *Essays and Addresses on the Philosophy of Religion*, London, J. M Dent & Sons, 1921

Hügel, F. von, *Essays and Addresses*, Second Series, London, J.M. Dent & Sons, 1926

Hügel, F. von, *Selected Letters*, London, J.M. Dent & Sons, 1927

Hügel, F. von, *Letters from Baron von Hügel to a Niece*, London, J.M. Dent & Sons, 1928

Hügel, F. von, *Readings from Friedrich von Hügel*, selected by Alger Thorold, London, J.M. Dent &

Sons, 1928

Hügel, F. von, *The Reality of God & Religion and Agnosticism*, London, J. M. Dent & Sons, 1931

Hughes, G, 'Shades of the Ghetto', *The Tablet*, 7/10/92, pp.1396-7

Hughson, T, *The Believer as Citizen: J.C. Murray in a New Context*, New York, Paulist, 1993

Hull, J, 'The Holy Trinity and the Mission of the Church School', unpublished paper given at International Symposium on Church Schools, Durham, 1996

Hull, J, 'A Critique of Christian religionism in Recent British Education', in *Christian Theology & Religious Education*, edited by Jeff Astley and Leslic Francis, London, SPCK, 1996

Hunt, R, and Grasso, K, (eds) *John Courtney Murray and the American Civil Conversation*, Grand Rapids, Eerdmans, 1992

Hunt, T, Oldenski, T, and Wallace, T, (eds) *Catholic School Leadership*, London, Falmer, 2000

Inglis, F, *The Management of Ignorance*, Oxford, Blackwell, 1985

International Journal of Education and Religion, Leiden, Brill, vol. 1, (1), 2000

Jackson, T, *Discipleship or Pilgrimage? The Educator's Quest for Philosophy*, New York, State University of New York Press, 1995

Jacobs, R, *The Vocation of the Catholic Educator*, Washington, DC, The National Catholic Educational Association, 1996

Janosik, C, 'Catholic Identity in Catholic Higher Education', *Catholic Education: A Journal of Inquiry and Practice*, vol. 3 (1), September 1999

Jenkins, H. O., *Getting it Right*, Oxford, Blackwell, 1991

Jirasinghe, D, and Lyons, G, *The Competent Head*, London, Falmer, 1996

Johnson, E, *She Who Is*, New York, Crossroad, 1992

Johnson, J, *Teaching in Catholic Schools*, Maryvale Institute, Archdiocese of Birmingham, 1994

John Paul II, (Pope) *Catechesi Tradendae*, London, Catholic Truth Society, 1979

John Paul II, (Pope) *Ex Corde Ecclesiae*, Rome, 1990

John Paul II, (Pope) *Ut Unum Sint*, London, Catholic Truth Society, 1995

Jonathan, R, 'Liberal Philosophy of Education: a paradigm under strain', *Journal of Philosophy of Education*, vol. 29, no. 1, 1995, pp.93-107

Jonathan, R, 'Education and Moral Development: the role of reason and circumstance', *Journal of Philosophy of Education*, vol. 29, no. 3, 1995, pp.333- 353

Jonathan, R, *Illusory Freedoms: Liberalism, Education and the Market*, special issue of *Journal of Philosophy of Education*, vol. 31, no 1, 1997

Jordan, B, *The Common Good: Citizenship, Morality & Self-Interest*, Oxford, Blackwell, 1989

Jung, P.B., 'A Roman Catholic Perspective on the Distinctiveness of Christian Ethics', *The Journal of Religious Ethics*, vol.12, no 1, 1984, pp.123-141

Kamen, H *The Rise of Toleration*, London, Weidenfeld and Nicholson, 1967

Kay, W, & Hughes, F, 'Christian Light on Education', *Religious Education*, vol.80, no. 1, 1985

Keane, R, and Riley, D, (eds) *Quality Catholic Schools*, Archdiocese of Brisbane, 1997

Keenan, J, 'The Problem with Thomas Aquinas' Concept of Sin', *The Heythrop Journal*, vol. 35, no. 4, 1994, pp.401-420

Kekes, J, *The Morality of Pluralism*, Princeton, New Jersey, Princeton University Press, 1993

Kekes, J, *Moral Wisdom and Good Lives*, New York, Cornell University Press, 1995

Kelly, J.J., *Baron Friedrich von Hügel's Philosophy of Religion*, Louvain, Leuven University Press, 1983

Kelly K *New Directions in Moral Theology*, London, Geoffrey Chapman, 1992

Ker, I, & Hill, A, (eds) *Newman after a hundred years*, Oxford, Clarendon Press, 1990

Ker, I, *John Henry Newman*, Oxford, Oxford University Press, 1990

Ker, I, *Newman and the Fullness of Christianity*, Edinburgh, T & T Clark, 1993

Kerlin, M, 'Friedrich von Hügel: The Ultramontane as Ecumenist', *Cithara*, XIV, May, 1975, pp.3-17

Klaushofer, A, 'Faith Beyond Nihilism: The Retrieval of Theism in Milbank and Taylor', *The Heythrop Journal*, vo. 40, (2), April 1999

Kohli, W, (ed) *Critical Conversations in Philosophy of Education*, London, Routledge, 1995

Kolakowski, L, *Religion*, Glasgow, Fontana, 1982

Konstant, D, (ed) *Signposts and Homecomings* , Slough, St Paul Publications, 1981

Kopas, J, *Sacred Identity: Exploring a theology of the person*, New York, Paulist Press, 1994
Kotva, J, 'Christian Virtue Ethics and the "Sectarian Temptation"', *The Heythrop Journal*, vol. 35, no. 1, 1994, pp.35-52
Kupperman, J, *Character*, Oxford, Oxford University Press, 1991
Kymlicka, W, *Liberalism, Community and Culture*, Oxford, Clarendon Press, 1989
Kymlica, W, *Multicultural Citizenship*, Oxford, Clarendon Press, 1995

Lane, D, 'Catholic Education & the school: some theological reflections', in *The Catholic School in Contemporary Society*, Dublin, Conference of Major Religious Superiors, 1991
Lane, D, (ed) *Religion, Education and the Constitution*, Dublin, Columba Press, 1992
Lane, D, (ed) *Religion and Culture in Dialogue*, Dublin, Columba Press, 1993
Lash, N, *Theology on the Way to Emmaus*, London, SCM, 1986
Lash, N, *Easter in Ordinary*, London, SCM Press, 1988
Lash, N, *The Beginning and the End of 'Religion'*, Cambridge, Cambridge University Press, 1996
Latourelle, R, *Man and His Problems in the Light of Christ*, New York, Alba House, Society of St Paul, 1983
Leahy, M, and Laura, R, 'Religious "Doctrines" and the Closure of Minds', *Journal of the Philosophy of Education*, vol. 31, no. 2, 1997, pp.329-343
Leicester, M, & Taylor, M, (eds), *Ethics, Ethnicity and Education*, London, Kogan Page, 1992
Leonard, E, *Creative Tension: The Spiritual Legacy of Friedrich von Hügel*, New York, Fordham University Press, 1997
Lesko, N *Symbolizing Society*, Lewes, The Falmer Press, 1988
Levinson, B, review of Neil Postman: *The End of Education* (New York, Knopf, 1996) in *Harvard Educational Review*, vol.66, no.4, 1996, pp.873-878
Levinson, M, *The demands of liberal education*, Oxford, Oxford University Press, 1999
Little, S, *To Set One's Heart: Belief & Teaching in the Church*, Atlanta, John Knox, 1983
Loader, D, *The Inner Principal*, London, Falmer Press, 1997
Loades, A, (ed) *Feminist Theology: A Reader*, London, SPCK, 1990
Lobkowicz, N, 'Christianity and Culture', *Review of Politics*, vol 53, Spring 1991, pp.373-389
Lombaerts, H, *Management and Leadership of Christian Schools*, translated by Terry Collins, Groot Bijgaarden [Belgium], Vlaams Lassaliianns Perspectief, 1998
Lonergan, B, *Method in Theology*, London, Darton, Longman & Todd, 1972
Lonergan, B *Topics in Education, edited* by Robert Doran and Frederick Crowe, Toronto, University of Toronto Press, 1993
Long, F, 'Blondel on the Origin of Philosophy', *Philosophy Today* 33, 1989, pp.21-27
Long, F, 'The Blondel-Gilson Correspondence Through Foucault's Mirror', *Philosophy Today,* 35, 1991, pp.351-361
Long, F, 'The Postmodern Flavour of Blondel's Method', *International Philosophical Quarterly*, vol. 31, no. 1, 1991, pp.15-22
Long, F, 'Blondel's Religious Postulate in *Action'*, *The Irish Theological Quarterly*, vol.61, no.1, 1995, pp.57-69
Loughran, G, 'The Rationale of Catholic Education', *Education & Policy in Northern Ireland*, edited by R.D. Osborne *et al*, Belfast, Policy Research Institute, 1987
Lubac, H de, (ed) *Maurice Blondel et Augustin Valensin. Correspondance* (in three volumes), Paris, Aubier, 1957-65
Lubac, H de, (ed) *P. Teilhard de Chardin et Maurice Blondel. Correspondance*, translated by William Whitman, New York, Herder and Herder, 1967
Lubac, H de, (ed) *Correspondance Blondel-Wehrlé*, (two volumes) Paris, Aubier-Montaigne, 1969
Lubac, H de, *Petite catéchèse sur Nature et Grace*, Paris, Fayard, 1980
Lubac, H de, *At The Service of the Church*, translated by A. E. Englund, San Francisco, Ignatius Press, 1993
Henri de Lubac et le mystère de l'Eglise, Actes du colloque du 12 octobre 1996 a l'Institut de France, Paris, Cerf, 1999 [no editor indicated]

Macedo, S, 'Multiculturalism for the religious right?', *Journal of Philosophy of Education*, vol.29, no.2, 1995, pp.223-238

Macedo, S, 'Liberal Civic Education & Religious Fundamentalism', *Ethics*, vol. 105, April, 1995, pp.468-496

MacIntyre, A, *After Virtue*, London, Duckworth, 1993

MacIntyre, A, *Whose Justice? Which Rationality?*, London, Duckworth, 1988

MacIntyre, A, *Three Rival Versions of Moral Enquiry*, London Duckworth, 1990

Macpherson, E, 'Chaos in the Curriculum', *Journal of Curriculum Studies*, vol. 27, No. 3, 1995, pp.263-279

Macquarrie, J, *In Search of Humanity*, London, SCM Press, 1982

Manen, M van, *The Tact of Teaching*, London, Ontario, The Althouse Press, 1993

Manent, P, *The City of Man*, Princeton University Press, 1998

Manno, B, 'Catholic School Education: Providing Leadership in the Educational Reform Movement', *Living Light*, vol. 25, no. 1, 1988, pp.7-12

Maritain, J, *The Person and the Common Good*, London, Geoffrey Bles, 1948

Maritain, J, *Education at the Crossroads, New* Haven, Yale University Press, 1943

Maritain, J, 'On some typical aspects of Christian education' in *The Christian Idea of Education*, edited by D. Fuller, New Haven, Yale University Press, 1957

Maritain, J, 'Thomist Views on Education', in *Modern Philosophies and Education*, edited by Nelson Henry, Chicago, University of Chicago Press, 1955

Marquand, D, and Seldon, A, (eds) *Ideas That Shaped Post-War Britain*, London, Fontana, 1996

Marsden, G, *The Outrageous Idea of Christian Scholarship*, Oxford, Oxford University Press, 1997

Martin, R, *The Incarnate Ground of Christian Faith*, Lanham, University Press of America, 1998

Martin, S, *Cultural Diversity in Catholic Schools*, Washington, DC, National Catholic Educational Association, 1996

Marty, M, *Education, Religion and the Common Good,* San Francisco, Jossey-Bass, 2000

Maxwell, N, *From Knowledge to Wisdom*, Oxford, Basil Blackwell, 1987

May, L, *The Socially Responsive Self,* Chicago, University of Chicago Press, 1996

McBrien, R, *Catholicism*, two volumes, London, Geoffrey Chapman, 1980; 3rd edition, 1994

McBrien, R, 'Before and After Vatican II', *Priests and People*, August-September, 1996, pp.297-302

McClelland, V.A., '*Sensus Fidelium*: The Developing Concept of Roman Catholic Voluntary Effort in Education in England and Wales, in *Christianity & Educational Provision in International Perspective*, edited by Witold Tulasiewicz & Colin Brock, London, Routledge, 1988

McClelland, V.A (ed), *Christian Education in a Pluralist Society*, London, Routledge, 1988

McClelland, V.A (ed), *The Catholic School and the European Context*, University of Hull, Aspects of Education, vol. 46, 1992

McClelland, V. A., and Hodgetts, M, *From Without the Flaminian Gate*, London, Darton, Longman & Todd, 1999

McCool, G, (ed) *A Rahner Reader*, London, Darton, Longman & Todd, 1975

McCool, G, *Catholic Theology in the Nineteenth Century: The Quest for a Unitary Method*, New York, Seabury Press, 1977

McCool, G, *From Unity to Pluralism*, New York, Fordham University Press, 1992

McCutcheon, R, *Critics Not Caretakers*, Albany, State University of New York Press, 2001

McDermott, E, *Distinctive Qualities of the Catholic School*, Washington, DC, National Catholic Educational Association, 1997

McFayden, A, *The Call to Personhood*, Cambridge, Cambridge University Press, 1990

McGettrick, B, 'Management and values', in *The Management of educational policy: Scottish perspectives*, edited by W, Humes & M. MacKenzie, London, Longman, 1994

McGhee, M, (ed), *Philosophy, Religion and the Spiritual Life*, Cambridge, Cambridge University Press, 1992

McGrady, A, & Williams, K, 'Religious Education and State Policy in Ireland', *Panorama*, vol. 7, no. 1, 1995, pp.116-132

McGrath, J, *Baron Friedrich von Hügel and the Debate on Historical Christianity*, San Francisco, Mellen Research University Press, 1993

McGrath, M, *The Price of Faith: The Catholic Church and Catholic Schools in Northern Ireland*, Dublin, Irish Academic Press, 1999

McInerny, D, (ed) *The Common Things*, Washington, American Maritain Association, published by The Catholic University of America, 1999

McKeown, M, 'The Paradoxes of Catholic Education', *The Furrow*, vol. 23, no. 11, 1982, pp.680-685

McLaughlin, D, *The Catholic School: Paradoxes and Challenges*, Strathfield, NSW, St Paul's Publications, 2000

McLaughlin, T.H, '"Education for All" and Religious Schools', *Education for a plural society: philosophical perspectives on the Swann Report*, ed by Haydon, G, University of London Institute of Education, Bedford Way Paper, no.30, 1987

McLaughlin, T.H., *Parental rights in religious upbringing & religious education within a liberal perspective*, PhD thesis, University of London Institute of Education, 1991

McLaughlin, T.H, 'Fairness, controversiality and the common school', *Spectrum*, vol.24, no.2, 1992, pp.105-118

McLaughlin, T.H, 'Citizenship, Diversity and Education: a philosophical perspective', *Journal of Moral Education*, vol.21, no.3, 1992, pp.235-250

McLaughlin, T.H, 'The Ethics of Separate Schools', in *Ethics, Ethnicity and Education*, edited by Leicester, M and Taylor, M, London, Kogan Page, 1992

McLaughlin, T.H, 'Mentoring and the Demands of Reflection,' *Collaboration and Transition in Initial Teacher Training*, ed by Wilkin, M, and Sankey, D, London, Kogan Page, 1994

McLaughlin, T.H, 'The Scope of Parents' Educational Rights', *Parental Choice in Education*, ed by Halstead, J.M, London, Kogan Page, 1994

McLaughlin, T.H., 'Values, Coherence & the School,' *Cambridge Journal of Education*, vol. 24, no. 3, 1994, pp.453-470

McLaughlin, T.H, Carr, D, Haldane, J, Pring, R, 'Return to the Crossroads', *British Journal of Educational Studies*, vol. XXXXIII, No. 2, June 1995, pp.162-178

McLaughlin, T.H., 'Liberalism, Education & the Common School', *Journal of Philosophy of Education*, vol. 29, no. 2, 1995, pp.239-255

McLaughlin, T.H. O'Keefe, J & O'Keeffe, B, (eds), *The Contemporary Catholic School*, London Falmer Press, 1996

McLaughlin, T.H., 'Education of the whole child', in *Education, Spirituality & the Whole Child*, edited by Ron Best, London, Cassell, 1996

McLaughlin, T.H., 'Education, Multiculturalism & the Demands of Recognition', in *Education, the State & the Multicultural Challenge*, edited by Maria Amilburu, Pamplona, Ediciones Universidad de Navarra, 1996

McLean, G, (ed) *Philosophy and the Integration of Contemporary Catholic Education*, Washington, The Catholic University of America, 1962

McMahon, J, Neidhart, H, and Chapman, J, (eds) *Leading the Catholic School*, Richmond, Victoria, Spectrum Publications, 1997

Mendus, S, 'Tolerance and recognition: education in a multicultural society', *Journal of Philosophy of Education*, vol. 29, no. 2, 1995, pp.191-201

Mernissi, F, *Islam and Democracy*, London, Virago Press, 1993

Miedema, S and de Ruyter, D, 'On determining the limits of denominational schools', *Panorama*, 1996

Milroy, D, 'What makes a Catholic School Catholic?', *Priests and People*, August-September, 1996, pp.336-339

Milton, J, *Areopagitica & other tracts*, London, Dent, 1907

Mitchell, B, *Faith and Criticism*, Oxford, Clarendon Press, 1994

Möhler, J.A., *Unity in the church or the principle of Catholicism*, edited and translated by Peter Erb, Washington, DC, The Catholic University of America Press, 1996

Moore, M.E.M, *Teaching from the Heart*, Minneapolis, Fortress Press, 1991

Moore, M.E.M, 'Teaching Christian particularity in a pluralistic world', *British Journal of Religious Education*, vol. 17, no. 2, 1995, pp.70-83

Moran, G, *A Grammar of Responsibility*, New York, Crossroad, 1996

Moran, G, *Showing How: The Act of Teaching*, Valley Forge, Pennsylvania, Trinity Press International, 1997

Morgan, J, 'A Defence of Autonomy as an Educational Ideal', *Journal of Philosophy of Education*, vol. 30, no. 2, 1996, pp.239-252

Morris, A, 'The Academic Performance of Catholic schools', *School Organization*, vol. 14, 1994, pp.81-89

Morris, A, 'The Catholic School Ethos: its effect on post-16 student academic achievement, *Educational*

Studies, vol. 21, no. 1, 1995, pp.67-83

Morris, A, 'Same mission, same methods, same results? Academic & religious outcomes from different models of the Catholic school', *British Journal of Educational Studies*, December 1997, pp.378-391

Morris, A, 'So Far, So Good: levels of academic achievement in Catholic schools', *Educational Studies*, Vol. 24, no. 1, 1998, pp.83-94

Morris, A, 'Catholic and other secondary schools: an analysis', *Educational Research*, vol. 40, no. 2, 1998, pp.181-190

Mouw, R, and Griffioen, S, *Pluralisms & Horizons*, Grand Rapids, Eerdmans, 1993

Murgatroyd, S, and Morgan, C, *Total Quality Management and the School*, Buckingham , Open University Press, 1993

Murphy, A, *The Implication of Roman Catholic Doctrine for Curriculum in Roman Catholic Schools*, MPhil thesis, University of Wales at Aberystwyth, 1994

Murray, D, *A Special Concern The Philosophy of Education: A Christian Perspective*, Dublin, Veritas, 1991

Murray, J.C., *The Problem of Religious Freedom*, London, Geoffrey Chapman, 1965

Newman, J.H., *The Idea of a University*, London, Longmans and Green, 1912

Newman, J.H., *Sermons Preached on Various Occasions*, London, Longmans, Green & Co, 1921, (originally published 1857)

Newman, J.H., *The Development of Christian Doctrine*, London, Sheed and Ward, 1960

Newman, J.H., *University Sermons*, introduced by D.M. McKinnon and J.D Holmes, London, SPCK, 1970

Newman, J.H., *An Essay in Aid of a Grammar of Assent*, introduced by Nicholas Lash, Notre Dame, Indiana, University of Notre Dame Press, 1979

Nichols, A, *From Newman to Congar*, Edinburgh, T & T Clark, 1990

Nichols, A, *Byzantine Gospel: Maximus the Confessor in Modern Scholarship*, Edinburgh, T&T Clark, 1993

Nichols, A, *Epiphany. A Theological Introduction to Catholicism*, Collegeville, Minnesota, The Liturgical Press, 1996

Nichols, K, *Voice of the Hidden Waterfall*, Slough, St Paul Publications, 1980

Nichols, K, 'Theology and the Dual System', unpublished paper at International Symposium on Church Schools, Durham University, 1996

Nichols, K, *Refracting the Light: Learning the Languages of Faith*, Dublin, Lindisfarne/Veritas, 1997

Nichols, T, *That All May Be One: Hierarchy and Participation in the Church*, Collegeville, Minnesota, The Liturgical Press, 1997

Nordberg, R 'Curricular Integration in Catholic Education' *Religious Education*, vol. 82, no. 1, 1987, pp.127-142

Norton, D, *Imagination, Understanding, and the Virtue of Liberality*, Lanham, Maryland, Rowman and Littlefield Publishers, 1996

Nouwen, H, *Reaching Out*, London, Collins, Fount, 1980

O'Brien, D, 'A Catholic Future for Catholic Higher Education?', *Catholic Education: A Journal of Inquiry and Practice*, vol. 1, no. 1, September 1997, pp.37-50

O'Connell, M, *Critics on Trial*, Washington, DC, Catholic University of America Press, 1994

O'Hear, A, 'Values, Education and Culture', in *Education, Values and Culture*, The Victor Cook Memorial Lectures, Centre for Philosophy and Public Affairs, University of St Andrews, 1992

O'Keefe, J, and Haney, R, (eds) *Conversations in Excellence*, Boston and New York, Boston College/National Catholic Educational Association, 1998

O'Keeffe, B, *Schools for Tomorrow*, London, Falmer Press, 1988

O'Keeffe, B, 'Catholic Education in an Open Society: the English Challenge', in *The Catholic School and the European Context, edited* by V.A. McClelland, Hull University, Aspects of Education, Number 46

O'Keeffe, B, 'Fairness - A Missing Theme in Education', *Law & Justice*, no 124/125, 1995, pp.3-16

O'Keeffe, B, 'Beacons of Hope', *The Tablet*, 24/4/97, pp.667-8

O'Keeffe, B, 'The Changing Role of Catholic Schools in England and Wales: From Exclusiveness to Engagement', in *Leading the Catholic School*, edited by John McMahon, Helga Neidhart & Judith

Chapman, Richmond Virginia, Australia, Spectrum Publications, 1997

Oldenski, T, *Liberation Theology and Critical Pedagogy in Today's Catholic Schools*, New York, Garland Publishing, 1997

O'Leary, D, (ed) *Religious Education and Young Adults*, Slough, St Paul Publications, 1983

O'Leary, J, *Religious Pluralism and Christian Truth*, Edinburgh, Edinburgh University Press, 1996

O'Neill, M, 'Toward a Modern Concept of Permeation', *Momentum*, vol.10, May, 1979, pp.48-50

O'Sullivan, O, *The Silent Schism*, Dublin, Gill & Macmillan, 1997

Ozga, J, 'Deskilling and Professions: Professionalism, Deprofessionalisation and the new managerialism', in *Managing Teachers as Professionals*, edited by Hugh Busher and Rene Saran, London, Kogan Page, 1995

Pailin, D, *A Gentle Touch*, London, SPCK, 1992

Palmer, P *To Know As We Are Known*, San Francisco, Harper & Row, 1983

Pattison, S, 'The Shadow Side of Jesus', *Studies in Christian Ethics*, vol. 8, no. 2, 1995, pp.54-67

Pattison, S, *The Faith of the Managers*, London, Cassell, 1997

Paul, E.F, *et al* (eds), *Cultural Pluralism and Moral Knowledge*, Cambridge, Cambridge University Press, 1994

Paul, E.F. *et al* (eds), *The Communitarian Challenge to Liberalism*, Cambridge, Cambridge University Press, 1997

Pavlischek, K, *John Courtney Murray & the dilemma of religious toleration*, Thomas Jefferson University Press, 1994

Pelikan, J, *The Vindication of Tradition*, New Haven, Yale University Press, 1984

Pena-Ruiz, H, *Dieu et Marianne: Philosophie de la laïcité*, Paris, Presses Universitarires de France, 1999

Penzenstadler, J, 'Meeting Religious Diversity in a Catholic College', *Religious Education*, vol. 91, no. 3, 1996, pp.382-395

Perks, S, *The Christian Philosophy of Education Explained*, Whitby, Avant Books, 1992

Peters, R.S., *Ethics and Education*, London, Allen and Unwin, 1966

Peterson, M *Philosophy of Education*, Leicester, Intervarsity Press, 1986

Pius X (Pope), *On the Doctrines of the Modernists (Pascendi Dominici Gregis)* and *Syllabus Condemning the Errors of the Modernists (Lamentabili Sane)*, Boston, St Paul Editions, nd (originally 1907)

Pius XI (Pope), *Divini Illius Magistri/On Christian Education of Youth*, in *Selected Papal Encyclicals and Letters*, vol. 1, 1896-1931, London, Catholic Truth Society, 1939

Pollard, J, 'Why We Do What We Do : A Reflection on Catholic Education & Catholic Schools', *Living Light*, vol. 25, no. 2, 1989, pp.103-111

Porcher, L, & Abdallah-Pretceille, M, *Ethique de la diversité et éducation*, Paris, PUF, 1998

Postman, N *Teaching as a conserving activity*, New York, Dell Publishing, 1979

Postman, N, *The End of Education*, New York, Vintage, 1996

Power, F. C, and Lapsley (eds) *The Challenge of Pluralism, Education, Politics and Values*, University of Notre Dame Press, 1992

Prangley. J, 'Examination factories', *The Tablet*, 15/2/97, pp.207-208

Pring, R, 'Liberal & Vocational Education: A Conflict of Value,' in *Education, Values and the State*, edited by John Haldane, Centre for Philosophy and Public Affairs, University of St Andrews, 1994

Pring, R, *Closing the Gap: Liberal education & vocational preparation*, London, Hodder & Stoughton, 1995

Pring, R, 'Values and Education Policy', in *Values in Education and Education in Values*, edited by Mark Halstead and Monica Taylor, London, Falmer Press, 1996

Pring, R, 'Markets, Education and Catholic Schools', in *The Contemporary Catholic School*, edited by Terence McLaughlin, Joseph O'Keefe and Bernadette O'Keeffe, London, Falmer Press, 1996

Pybus, E, and McLaughlin, T.H., *Values, Education & Responsibility*, University of St Andrews, 1995

Pyke, N, 'The Churches recover their voice', *The Tablet*, 24/5/97, pp.662-4

Pyke, N, 'Young minds in trouble' *The Tablet*, 15/2/97, pp.210-211

Quicke, J, 'Differentiation: a contested concept', *Cambridge Journal of Education*, vol. 25, no. 2, 1995, pp.213-224

Quinton, A, 'Culture, Education and Values' in *Education, Values and Culture*, The Victor Cook Memorial Lectures, edited by John Haldane, Centre for Philosophy and Public Affairs, University of

St Andrews, 1992

Ranson, S, *Towards the Learning Society*, London, Cassell, 1994

Ranson, S & Stewart, J, *Management for the Public Domain: Enabling the Learning Society*, London, Macmillan, 1994

Raphael, T, *The Role of the Church School in a Multi-faith City*, London, London Diocesan Board for Schools, 1991

Redden, J, and Ryan, F, *A Catholic Philosophy of Education*, Milwaukee, The Bruce Publishing Company, 1956

Rescher, N, *Ethical Idealism*, Berkeley, University of California Press, 1987

Riordan, P, *A Politics of the Common Good*, Dublin, Institute of Public Administration, 1996

Roberts, R, 'Our Graduate Factories' *The Tablet*, 11/10/97, pp.1295-1297

Roebben, B, 'Do we still have faith in young people?', *Religious Education*, vol. 90, 3/4, 1995, pp.327-345

Rohr, R, and Martos, J, *Why Be Catholic?*, Cincinnati, St Anthony Messenger Press, 1989

Rosenak, M, *Roads to the Palace*, Oxford, Berghahn, 1999

Rosenblum, N, (ed) *Liberalism and the Moral Life*, Cambridge, Massachusetts, Harvard University Press, 1989

Rouner, L, (ed) *Selves, People and Persons: what does it mean to be a self?*, Notre Dame, Indiana, University of Notre Dame Press,1992

Rudd, D and Sullivan, E, *Working for Unity*, Diocese of Arundel and Brighton, 1993   ,

Ruddle, P.J., 'The Ecumenical Dimension in the Work of Baron Friedrich von Hügel' *Ephemerides Theologicae Lovanienses*, vol. 50, Part 4, 1974, pp.231-254

Rudduck, J., Harris, S., Wallace, G., 'Coherence and Students' Experience of Learning in the Secondary School', *Cambridge Journal of Education*, vol.24, no.2, 1994, pp.197-211

Rummery, R, *Catechesis and Religious Education in a Pluralist Society*, Sydney, Dwyer, 1975

Ruyter, D de, 'Christian Education in a pluralistic society', paper given at St Edmund's College, Cambridge University 14/12/95

Ruyter, D de and Miedema, S, 'School, identity & the conception of the good. The denominational tradition as an example', *Studies in philosophy and education*, 1996

Ryan, D, *The Catholic Parish*, London, Sheed & Ward, 1996

Sachs, J, *The Christian Vision of Humanity*, Collegeville, Minnesota, Michael Glazier Book, 1991

Sacks, J, *The Persistence of Faith*, London, Weidenfeld & Nicholson, 1991

Sacred Congregation for Catholic Education, *The Catholic School*, London, Catholic Truth Society, 1977

Sacred Congregation for Catholic Education, *Lay Catholics in Schools: Witnesses to faith*, London, Catholic Truth Society, 1982

Sacred Congregation for Catholic Education, *Educational Guidance in Human Love*, London, Catholic Truth Society, 1983

Sacred Congregation for Catholic Education, *The Religious Dimension of Education in a Catholic School*, London, Catholic Truth Society, 1988

Saint-Jean, R, *L'Apologétique philosophique*: Blondel 1893-1913, Paris, 1966

Sandel, M, *Liberalism and the Limits of Justice*, Cambridge, Cambridge University Press, 1982

Sandel, M, *Democracy's Discontent*, Cambridge, Massachusetts, Harvard University Press, 1996

Sandsmark, S, 'Religion - Icing on the Educational Cake', *Religious Education*, vol. 90, nos3/4, 1995, pp.427-432

Sandsmark, S, *Is World View Neutral Education Possible and Desirable?*, Carlisle, Paternoster Press, 2000

Scheffler, I, *In Praise of the Cognitive Emotions*, London, Routledge, 1991

Schindler, D, *Heart of the World, Center of the Church*, Edinburgh, T & T Clark, 1996

Schmitz, K, *At the Center of the Human Drama: The Philosophical Anthropology of Karol Wojtyla*, Washington, DC, The Catholic University of America Press, 1993

School Curriculum and Assessment Authority, *Consultation on values in education and the community*, London, 1996

Schreiter, R, *The New Catholicity*, New York, Orbis, 1997

Schwobel, C & Gunton, C, (eds) *Persons, Divine and Human*, Edinburgh, T. &T. Clark, 1992

Selbourne, D, *The Principle of Duty*, London, Sinclair Stevenson, 1994

Sergiovanni, T, *Moral Leadership*, San Francisco, Jossey-Bass, 1992

Sertillanges, A, *The Intellectual Life: Its Spirit, Conditions, Methods*, translated by Mary Ryan, Cork, The Mercier Press, 1946

Shea, W, *Trying Times*, Atlanta, Scholars Press, 1999

Shorter, A, *Toward a Theology of Inculturation*, London, Geoffrey Chapman, 1988

Shortt, J and Cooling, T, (eds) *Agenda for Educational Change*, Leicester, Apollos, 1997

Siegel, H, 'What Price Inclusion?', *Teachers College Record*, vol. 97, no. 1, 1995, pp.6-31

Singh, B, 'Shared Values, Particular Values, and Education for a Multicultural Society,' *Educational Review*, vol. 47, no.1, 1995, pp.11-24

Skolimowski, H, *Living Philosophy*, London, Arkana, 1992

Smeyers, P, 'Education and the educational Project I: the atmosphere of post-modernism', *The Journal of Philosophy of Education*, vol. 29, no. 1, 1995, pp.109-119

Snik, G & Jong, J de, 'Liberalism and Denominational Schools', *The Journal of Moral Education*, vol. 24, no. 4, 1995, pp.395-407

Sokolowsi, R, *Eucharistic Presence*, Washington, DC, The Catholic University of America Press, 1994

Spiecker, B, 'Commitment to Liberal Education', *Studies in Philosophy and Education*, vol. 15, 1996, pp.281-291

Stagaman, D, *Authority in the Church*, Collegeville, Minnesota, Liturgical Press, 1999

Standish, P, 'Postmodernism and the Education of the Whole Person', *Journal of Philosophy of Education*, vol. 29, no. 1, 1995, pp.121-135

Stiltner, B, *Religion and the Common Good*, Lanham, Maryland, Rowman & Littlefield, 1999

Stradling, R and Saunders, L *Differentiation: A Practical Handbook of Classroom Strategies*, Coventry, NCET, 1993

Sturzo, L, *The True Life*, London, Geoffrey Bles, 1947

Sullivan, F, *Creative Fidelity: Weighing and Interpreting Documents of the Magisterium*, Dublin, Gill & Macmillan, 1996

Sullivan, J, 'Subjectivity and Religious Understanding', *Theology*, November 1982, pp.410-417

Sullivan, J, 'Lonergan, Conversion and Objectivity', *Theology*, September 1983, pp.345-353

Sullivan, J, 'Living Tradition', *The Tablet*, 23/1/82, pp.80-81

Sullivan, J, 'Living Tradition', *The Downside Review*, vol. 105, January 1988, pp.59- 66

Sullivan, J, 'Blondel and a Living Tradition for Catholic Education', *Catholic Education: A Journal of Inquiry and Practice*, vol. 1, No. 1, September 1997, pp.67-76

Sullivan, J, 'Leading Values and Casting Shadows', *Pastoral Care in Education*, vol. 15, no. 3, September 1997, pp.8-12

Sullivan, J, 'Leading Values and Casting Shadows in Church Schools', *Journal of Religious Education*, 2001, forthcoming

Sullivan, J, 'Compliance or Complaint: Some Difficulties Regarding Teachers in Catholic Schools', *Irish Educational Studies*, vol. 17, 1998

Sullivan, J, *Catholic Schools in Contention*, Dublin, Veritas, 2000

Sundermeier, M & Churchill, R, (eds) *The Literary & Educational Effects of the Thought of John Henry Newman*, Lewiston, New York (and Lampeter, Wales,) The Edwin Mellen Press, 1995

Suttle, B, 'The Need for and Inevitability of Educational Intolerance', *Philosophy of Education*, University of Illinois, 1995, pp.448-455

Tanner, K, *Theories of Culture*, Minneapolis, Fortress Press, 1997

Tarrant, J, 'Education and Conceptions of Democracy: a Reply to Bonna Haberman', *Journal of Philosophy of Education*, vol. 30 no. 2, 1996, pp.289-293

Taylor, C, *Multiculturalism*, edited by Amy Gutman, Princeton, New Jersey, Princeton University Press, 1994

Teilhard de Chardin, P, *Lettres Intimes à Auguste Valensin, Bruno de Solage, Henri de Lubac, André Ravier, 1919 –1955*, ed by Henri de Lubac, Paris, 1974

Thatcher, A, 'Making the Difference - Theology of Education and Church Schools', unpublished paper at International Symposium on Church Schools, Durham University, 1996

Thévenot, X, and Joncheray, J, *Pour un éthique de la pratique éducative*, Paris, Desclée, 1991

Thiel, J, *Senses of Tradition*, New York, Oxford University Press, 2000

Thiessen, E.J., 'A Defense of a Distinctively Christian Curriculum', *Religious Education*, vol. 80, no. 1, 1985, pp.37-50

Thiessen, E.J., *Teaching for Commitment*, Montreal, McGill-Queen's University Press, 1993

Thiessen, E.J., 'Liberal Education, Public Schools, & the Embarrassment of Teaching for Commitment', *Philosophy of Education*, University of Illinois, 1995, pp.473-481

Thiessen, E.J., 'Fanaticism and Christian Liberal Education: A Response to Ben Spiecker's "Commitment to Liberal Education"', *Studies in Philosophy and Education*, vol. 15, 1996, pp.293-300

Tilley, T, *Inventing Catholic Tradition*, New York, Orbis, 2000

Treston, K, *Transforming Catholic Schools*, Brisbane, Creation Enterprises, 1992

Ungoed-Thomas, J, 'Vision, Values and Virtues', in *Values in Education and Education in Values*, edited by Mark Halstead and Monica Taylor, London, Falmer Press, 1996

Van der Ven, J, *Education for Reflective Ministry*, Louvain, Peeters, 1998

Van Manen, M *The Tact of Teaching*, London, Ontario, The Althouse Press, 1993

Vargish, T, *Newman: The Contemplation of Mind*, Oxford, Clarendon Press, 1970

Veling, T, *Living in the Margins,* New York, Crossroad, 1996

Vergioux, A, 'Education, Time and Liberty', Papers of Philosophy of Education Society of Great Britain Conference, Oxford, 1995, pp.162-165

Vermes, P, *Buber on God and the Perfect Man*, Scholars Press, 1980

Veverka, F, 'The Ambiguity of Catholic Educational Separatism', *Religious Education*, vol.80, no. 1, 1985, pp.64-100

Volf, M, *Exclusion and Embrace*, Nashville, Abingdon, 1996

Walker, A, *Telling the Story*, London, SPCK, 1996

Walsh, M, 'The Battle for St Philip's', *The Tablet*, 10/10/92, pp.1261-2

Walsh, M and Davies, B (eds) *Proclaiming Justice and Peace: Documents from John XXIII to John Paul II*, London, Collins Liturgical Publications, 1984

Walsh, P, *Education and Meaning*, London, Cassell, 1993

Walsh, P, 'Education and Celebration', *Spectrum*, vol. 26, no. 2, 1994, pp.105-114

Walsh, P, 'A Jesuit School', paper delivered at International Symposium on Church Schools, Durham University, 1996.

Walzer, M, *Thick and Thin*, Notre Dame, Indiana, University of Notre Dame Press, 1994

Walzer, M, 'Education, democratic citizenship and multiculturalism', *Journal of Philosophy of Education*, vol. 29, no. 2, 1995, pp.181-189

Warnet, M and Klein, J, 'The levels of Religious Schooling and Practices of Teachers and their perception of school leadership', *British Journal of Religious Education*, vol. 19, No. 3, 1997, pp.157-163

Watson, B (ed) *Priorities in Religious Education*, London, Falmer Press, 1992

Webb, S, *Taking Religion to School*, Grand Rapids, Brazos Press, 2000

Wells, D *The Supply of Catholic Teachers*, London, Catholic Education Service, 1994

Whelan, J *The Spirituality of Friedrich von Hügel*, London, Collins, 1971

White, J, *Education and the End of Work*, London Cassell, 1997

Whitehead, M, 'The Changing Face of the Catholic Independent Schools', in *Private and Independent Education*, edited by V. A, McClelland, The University of Hull, Aspects of Education series, no 35, 1986

Whyte, G, 'Religion, Education & an Indeterminate Constitution', *Doctrine & Life*, vol. 47, May/June, 1997, pp.274-283

Wiame, B, *Pour un inculturation de l'enseignement religieux*, Brussels, Lumen Vitae, 1997

Wilcox, B, 'Schooling, School Improvement & the Relevance of Alasdair MacIntyre', *Cambridge Journal of Education*, vol. 27, no. 2, 1997, pp.249-260

Wilcox, J, and King, I, (eds) *Enhancing Religious Identity*, Washington DC, Georgetown University Press, 2000

Williams, B *Ethics and the Limits of Philosophy*, London, Fontana, 1985

Williams, K, 'The Case for Democratic Management in Schools', *Irish Educational Studies*, vol. 8, no. 2, 1989, pp.73-86

Williams, K, 'State Support for Church Schools: Is it justifiable?', *Studies in Education*, vol. 11, no. 1,

1995

Williams, K, 'The Religious Dimension of Secular Learning: an Irish dilemma', *Panorama*, 1996

Williams, K, 'Parents' Rights and the Integrated Curriculum', *Doctrine & Life*, vol. 47 March, 1997, pp.142-150

Williams, K, 'Education & human diversity: The ethics of separate schooling revisited', *British Journal of Educational Studies*, vol. 46, No. 1, March 1998, pp.26-39.

Wilson, K, 'Unnatural Selection', *Education*, 23/2/96, p.12.

Wolf, S, 'Two Levels of Pluralism', *Ethics*, no 102, 1992, pp.785-798

Wolff, A. de, 'The Identity of Christian Schools', unpublished paper presented at the Philosophy of Education Society of Great Britain Conference, Oxford, 1997

Young, R, 'Decolonising Education: The Scope of Educational Thought', *Studies in Philosophy and Education*, vol. 15, no. 4, 1996, pp.309-322.

Youniss, J, and Convey, J, (eds) *Catholic Schools at the Crossroads*, New York, Teachers College Press, 2000

Youniss, J, Convey, J, and McLellan, J, (eds) *The Catholic Character of Catholic Schools*, University of Notre Dame Press, 2000

INDEX

UNIVERSITY OF WALES COLLEGE NEWPORT
LIBRARY
AND
INFORMATION
SERVICES
CAERLEON